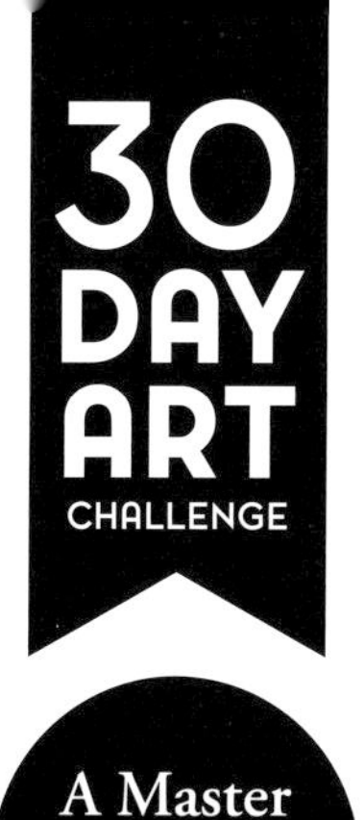

A Master Class for Beginners

BOLD AND BEAUTIFUL WATERCOLOR SKIES

Learn to Paint Stunning Clouds, Sunsets, Galaxies, and More

Zaneena Nabeel **AURORA BY Z**

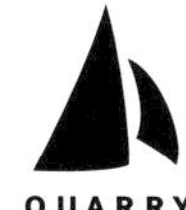

Quarto.com

First Published in 2023 by Quarry Books, an imprint of The Quarto Group,
100 Cummings Center, Suite 265-D, Beverly, MA 01915, USA.
T (978) 282-9590 F (978) 283-2742

Quarry Books titles are also available at discount for retail, wholesale, promotional, and bulk purchase. For details, contact the Special Sales Manager by email at specialsales@quarto.com or by mail at The Quarto Group, Attn: Special Sales Manager, 100 Cummings Center, Suite 265-D, Beverly, MA 01915, USA.

10 9 8 7 6 5 4 3 2

ISBN: 978-0-7603-8294-3

Digital edition published in 2023
eISBN: 978-0-7603-8295-0

Library of Congress Cataloging-in-Publication Data is available.

Design and Layout: Cindy Samargia Laun
Cover Image: Nabeel Mohammed

Printed in China

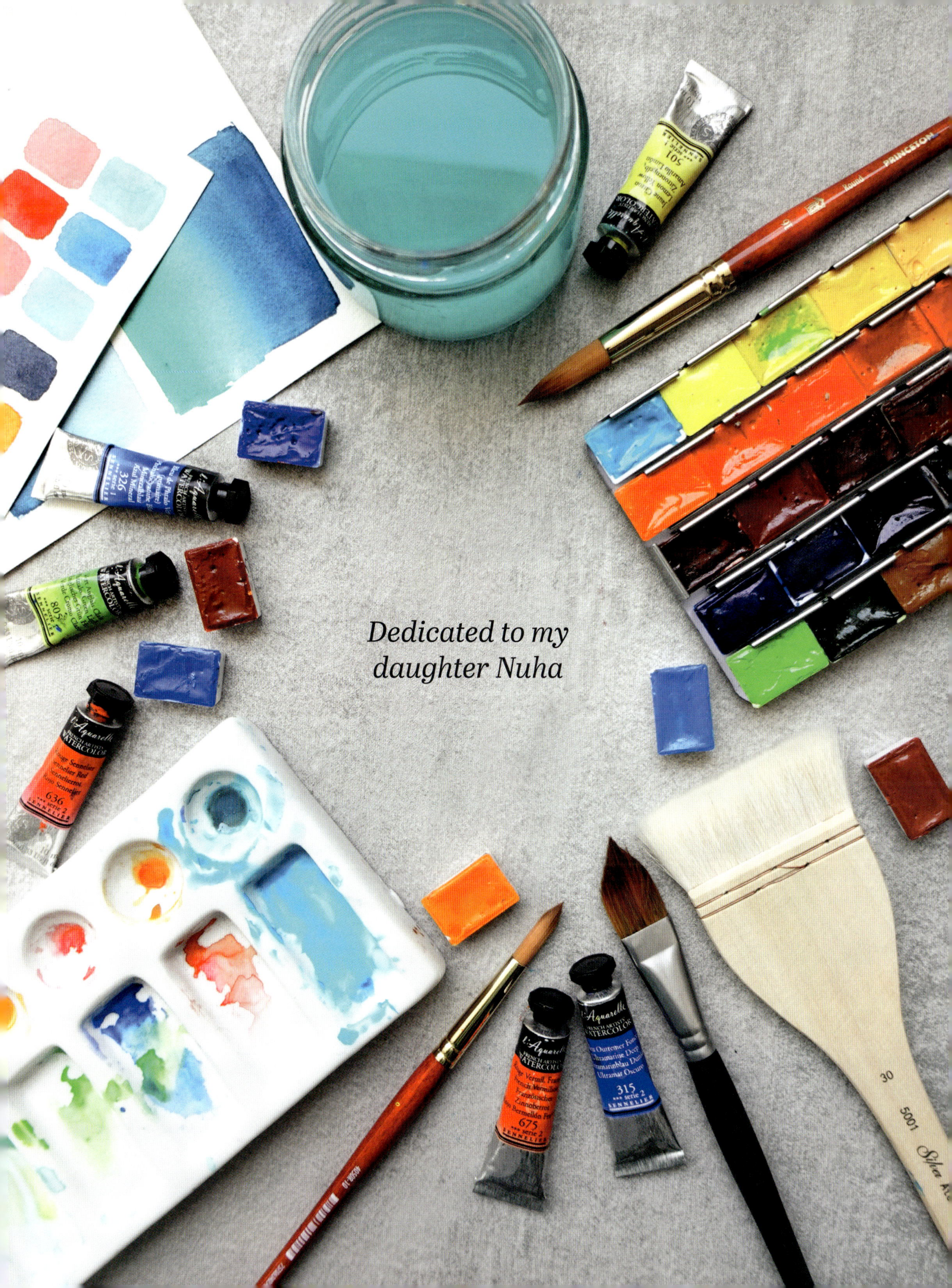

Dedicated to my daughter Nuha

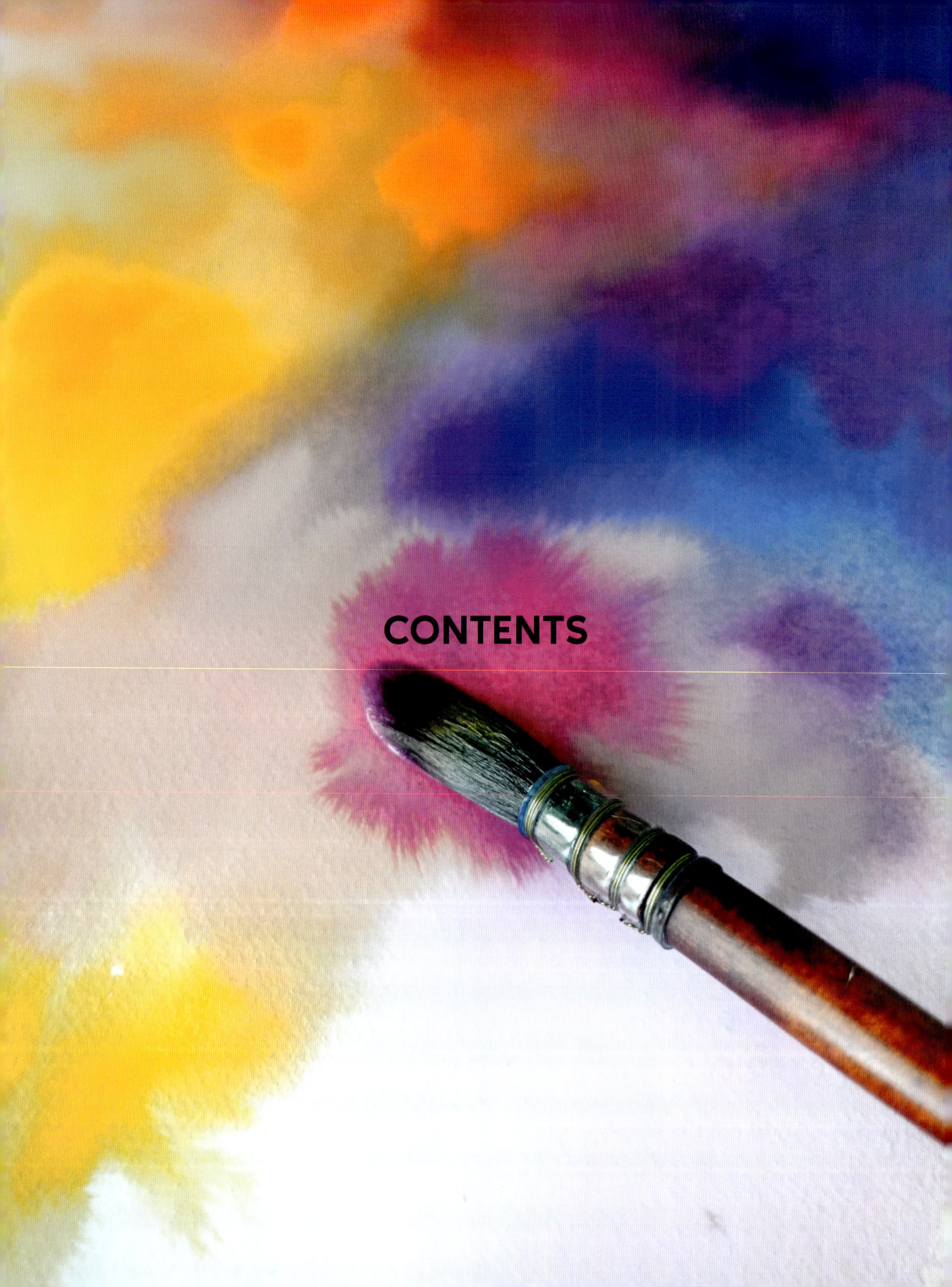

CONTENTS

GETTING TO KNOW WATERCOLOR

BOLD AND BEAUTIFUL SKIES: 30 DAYS, 30 PROJECTS

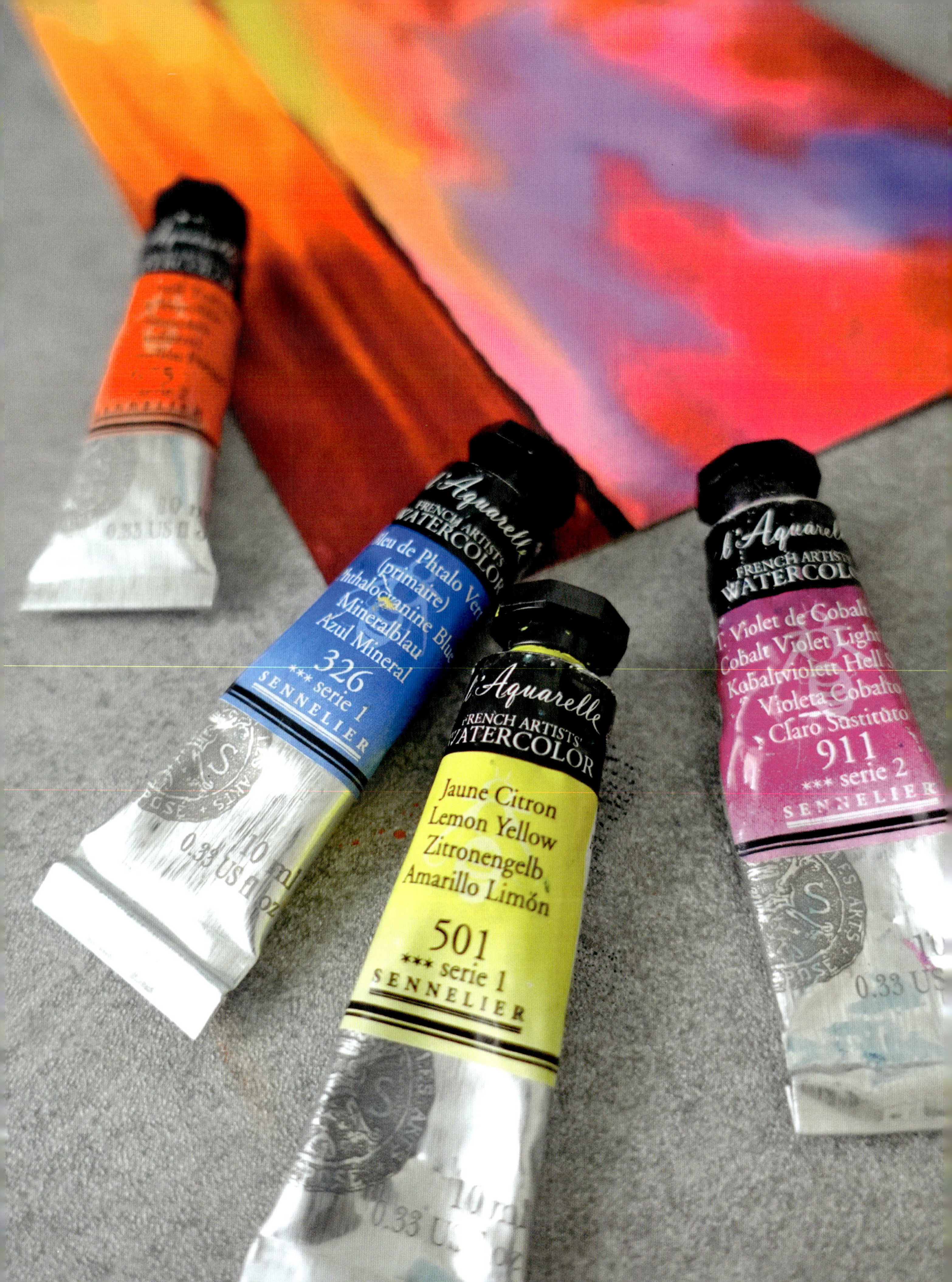
l'Aquarelle
FRENCH ARTISTS'
WATERCOLOR
(primaire)
Mineralblau
Azul Mineral
326
serie 1
SENNELIER
l'Aquarelle
FRENCH ARTISTS'
WATERCOLOR
Jaune Citron
Lemon Yellow
Zitronengelb
Amarillo Limón
501
serie 1
SENNELIER
911
serie 2
SENNELIER

INTRODUCTION

From a very young age I was interested in arts and crafts. My mom used to paint with us, and we used to do lots of crafts together. I still remember the day at school when we were asked to talk about our ambition. I was so excited and told the class I wanted to be an artist, and my teacher corrected me, saying, "That's your hobby. We are talking about ambition." The other kids started laughing, and I instantly changed it to doctor.

Throughout my school days, I was an average student. The only subjects I was good at were art subjects. My notebooks were full of random sketches and doodles. But I cut myself off from art because it could never be a career choice, or so I thought, or so I was taught. Little did I know I could have a career out of my hobby. After I broke away from art, I devoted all my attention to my studies and eventually became an architect. I got married and had a full-time job. But, to distract myself from the hustle and bustle of everyday life, I decided to get back into my hobby after eleven years. It was like reuniting with a long-lost friend. It was one of the most beautiful reunions.

For almost a year, I painted for myself. I explored different mediums, watched YouTube tutorials, and improved my skills. But my life changed when I started posting my artwork on Instagram and when I finally decided to show my work to the world. I did not realize that all these wonderful opportunities would come my way and that every year I would get closer to a career I never thought existed.

I painted on the weekends and late at night and slowly became recognized as an artist. My Instagram account started to grow, and I got the chance to work with big brands in the art world. I also led online and offline art workshops and gradually decided to give up my architecture career to try a career in art. It was more like turning my escape project into a career. Looking back, I feel that this was one of the best decisions I've ever made in my life. You may have heard the quote, "Do what you love and you will never work another day in your life." I used to think that was terrible advice. But when I made a career shift to something I'm deeply passionate about, I felt there was some truth to that quote.

Although I work in many mediums, I have a strong affection for watercolor, perhaps because it's the first medium I ever tried. I was three years old when my mother introduced me to watercolor painting. I enjoyed playing with the colors, and I still do. My fascination with this medium has grown greatly over the years.

Unlike sculpture or other more complex art practices, watercolor is accessible for everyone. There's no reason to feel intimidated by creating art because it's the process of creating that brings the benefit, not the quality of the results. Indeed, everyone *can* make art, and everyone *should* make art.

This book is designed especially for beginners who want to relax and have fun painting. Even if you're a first-time watercolorist, you'll enjoy exploring this book. We'll begin by talking about the materials and basic techniques and try thirty bold and beautiful skies, from day and night to the cosmos. I would recommend you take it as a daily challenge for thirty consecutive days to see your progress, especially if you're just starting out with watercolor. These projects are just perfect for any beginner to get some colors out and play along. It's important that you get comfortable with the techniques as a complete beginner so that you feel more confident throughout the process and feel a sense of satisfaction that motivates you to keep going.

The main goal I want to teach you is to get creative, relax, and develop the confidence to explore new themes and new color combinations with watercolor. You do not have to follow the book in the exact order. Just flip through the pages and start anywhere. You can always stop and start again where you left off. Remind yourself to enjoy the process, go with the flow, and accept mistakes when you make some.

I believe it's very important for everyone to invest a little time in a creative task every day if possible. If it is not possible to make time for art every day, find a rhythm that suits you. The most important things are commitment and consistency. If you take this book as a daily challenge, you can build an artistic routine and continue to paint daily, implementing what you learn in the exercises. Remember that everyone needs different amounts of time to learn something new. Enjoy the process without worrying about the outcome. You may need a few more tries to get the result you want. If you're ever frustrated or upset because you did not get the result you wanted, take a break. Accept failure as part of the process and learn from it without giving up.

With a little practice and patience, ANYONE can paint.

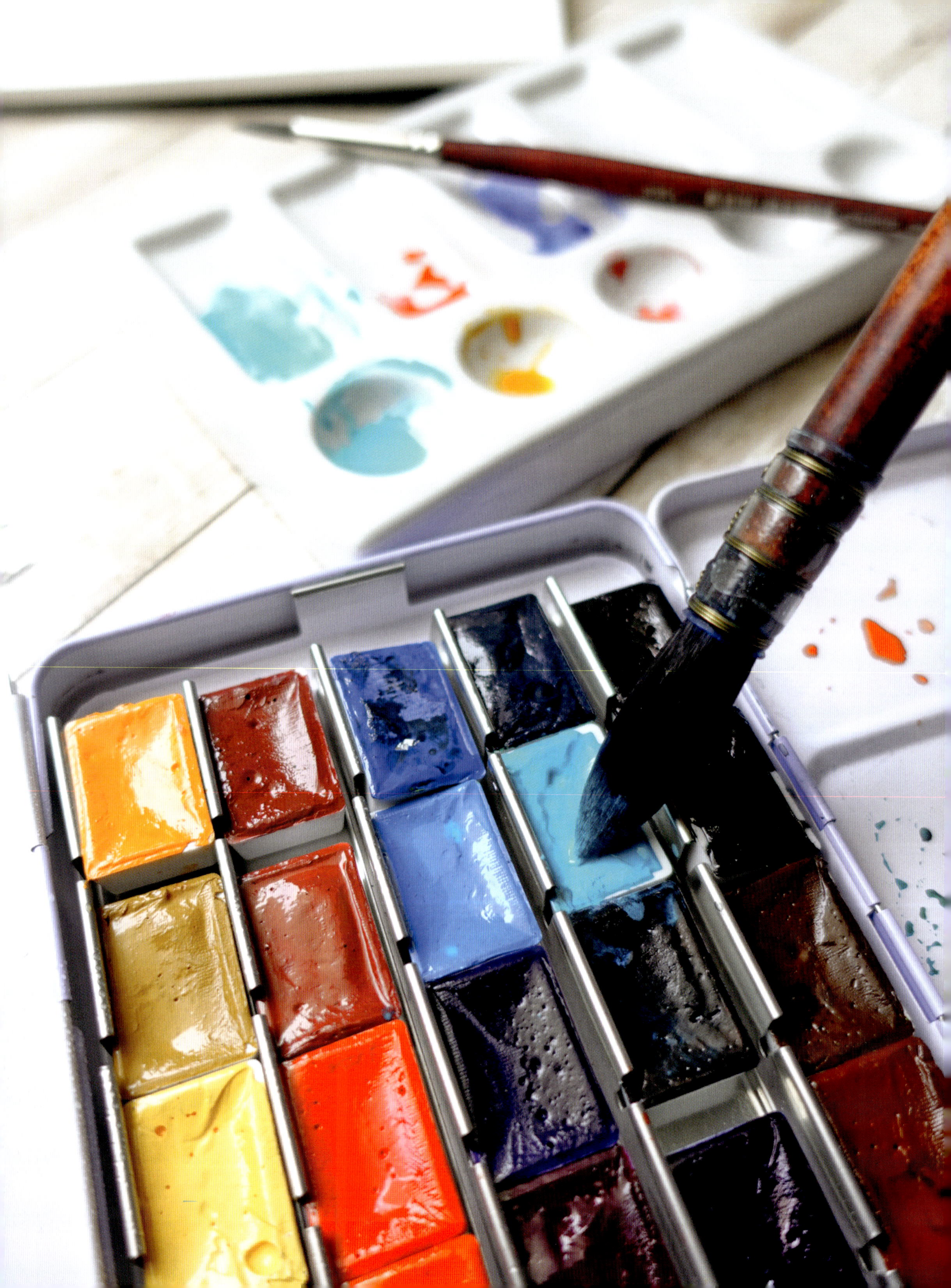

GETTING TO KNOW WATERCOLOR

Watercolor is one of the most unique mediums for creating art.

Its unpredictability and unique properties make it a favorite medium of many artists, and the possibilities offered by this beautiful medium are endless.

Working with watercolor is so much fun. Wetting the paper with clear water, pouring the colors, and watching them blend and bleed into each other is a joy to watch. It can be extremely challenging to paint with watercolor at times, but it can also be incredibly rewarding if you just take the time to understand the medium.

In this chapter, we'll talk about the essential materials and the basic techniques you need to know to get started.

MATERIALS

To get started with watercolor painting, you'll need five essential art materials: watercolor paint, brushes, watercolor paper, a mixing palette, and a container of water. You don't need to buy the most expensive art supplies when you're starting out. Start with what you have on hand and expand as you become more familiar with the medium.

WATERCOLOR PAINTS

Watercolor is made up of finely ground pigment suspended in a binder made of gum arabic and other additives to preserve and stabilize the paint. You might have seen expensive watercolor brands as well as very cheap ones. Some brands are so expensive that a single 5 milliliter tube costs the same as a whole set of paints from another brand. Brands charge for their watercolors based on the amount of pigments they use. Some of them use high-quality pigments without fillers or impurities. This is what makes them so expensive.

There are several types of watercolor paints on the market. The most common form is in a metal tube. You can squeeze the amount of paint you want fresh out of the tube. If you work with tubes, you'll need a palette to mix your colors.

Then there's paint that comes as dry cakes in small plastic containers that are travel friendly and best for plein air painting. You need to pick up the pigments from the containers with a wet brush. You can also spray the containers with a little water a few minutes before painting to soften them.

Watercolor is also available in liquid form, which is made out of concentrated dye or pigment solution. It can be used at full strength to produce a very vivid result, or it can be diluted by adding water to produce a softer look.

In addition to the tubes, pans, and liquids, you can buy watercolor paints in the form of pencils, sticks, markers, and sheets.

BRUSHES

There are a few things to consider when choosing a watercolor brush. It should be able to hold a good amount of water, have a fine tip, and spread the paint evenly on the paper.

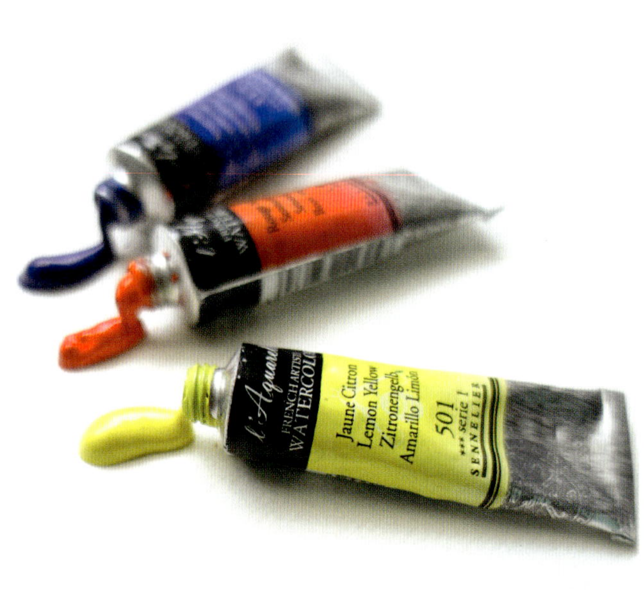

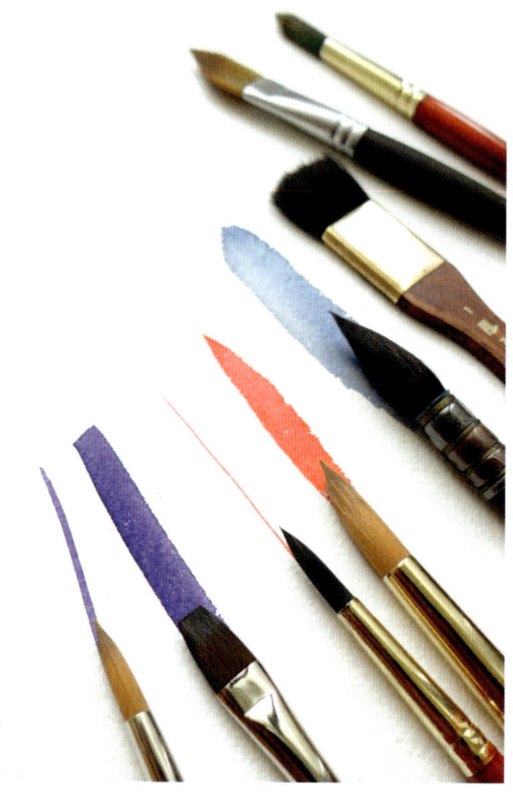

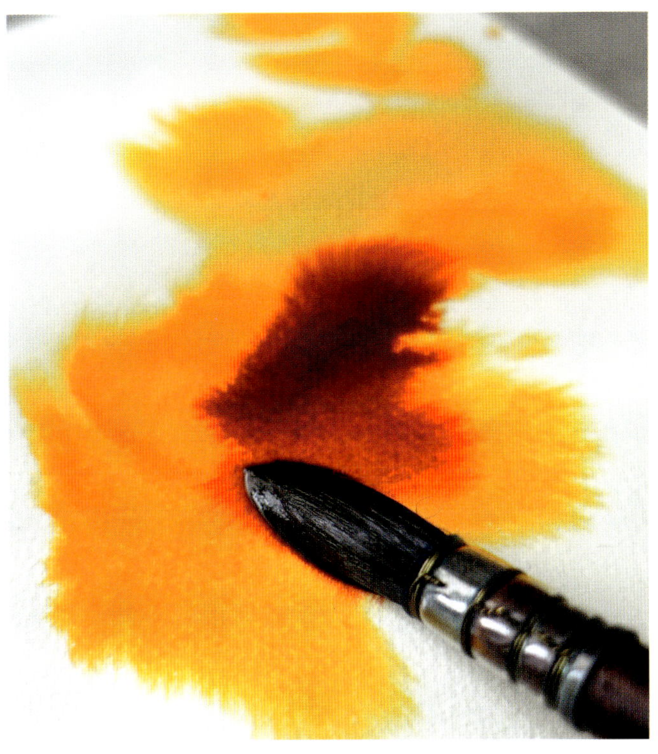

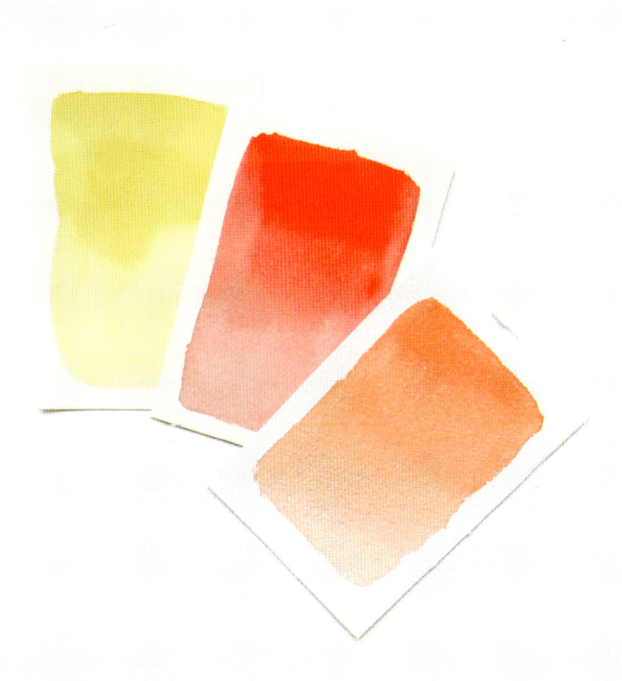

Brushes come in all different shapes and sizes. There are round, flat, wash, hake, filbert, fan, angle, mop, and rigger brushes. The most common brush sizes range from 000 (small) to 24 (large). However, you do not need all of these sizes. You can achieve wonderful results with as few as three or four brushes. If you choose a good-quality brush and take good care of it, it can last a lifetime or longer. Start with the most commonly used brushes: round and flat.

The round brush is the most versatile form of brush for painting. It gives you more control over the flow of paint on the paper. The pointed tip allows you to draw thin lines, which you can easily thicken by pressing the brush onto the paper.

The second most common brush is the flat brush. It's good for applying washes and for linear brushstrokes. There's also a wash brush—a wide flat brush used for applying large washes.

I paint mostly small format paintings, and my preferred brushes are round brushes of sizes 2, 6, and 12 and flat brushes of size ¾ inch (2 cm). You can also start with a similar assortment and expand your collection as you become more advanced with watercolors.

PAPER

A high-quality watercolor paper is as important as the paints and brushes you use. Just like paints and brushes, watercolor paper comes in student and artist grade. Student paper is made primarily from cellulose, while artist paper is made from 100% cotton.

Other factors to consider when buying watercolor paper are the texture and weight of the paper. Watercolor paper comes in three different surface finishes: rough, hot pressed (HP), and cold pressed (CP). Rough watercolor paper has a textured surface, hot-pressed watercolor paper has a fine-grained, smooth surface, and cold-pressed watercolor paper has a slightly textured surface that falls somewhere between rough and hot-pressed paper.

Watercolor paper also comes in different weights. This actually indicates the thickness of the paper. Lighter weight paper works well for light washes and illustrations. If you're working with multiple layers of washes, choose a paper that is at least 140 lb or 300 gsm.

Because watercolor painting is mostly about water control and how the paint behaves on the paper, the type of paper you use will have a big impact on the result. When you work on artist paper, the quality of your work will improve significantly. No matter what brand I use, I always opt for 100% cotton watercolor paper that is cold pressed and at least 140 lb (300 gsm) thick.

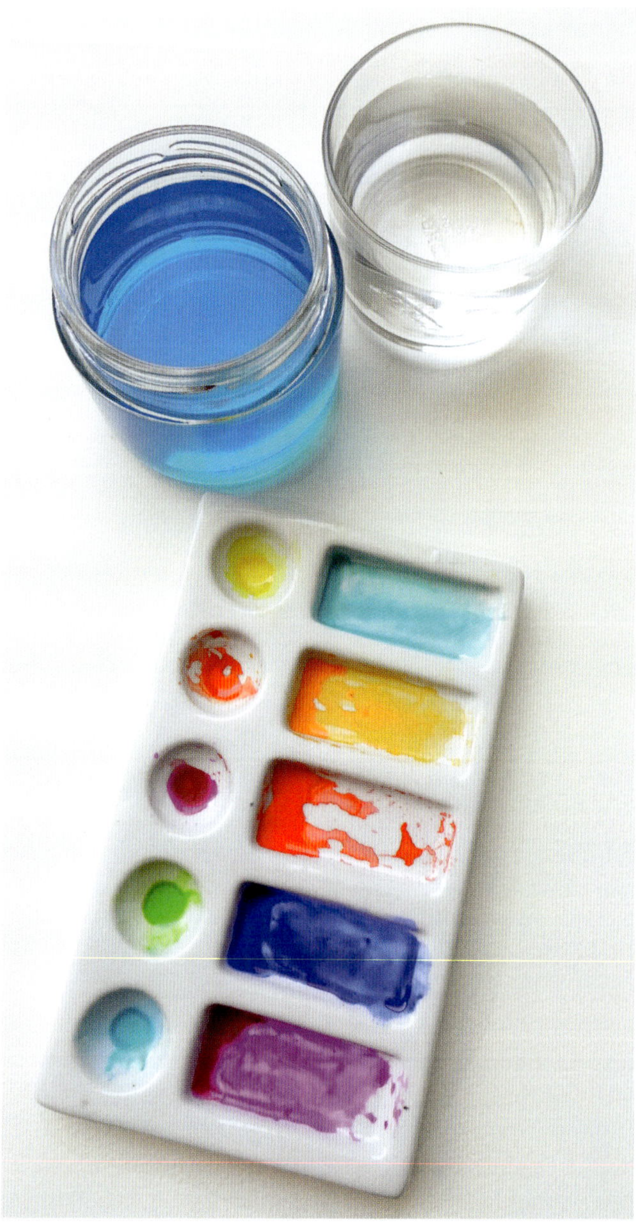

MIXING PALETTE

As the name suggests, a mixing palette is used to mix colors. They come in different designs and are made of plastic or ceramic. Choose a palette where you have room to mix the colors. You can leave the excess paint on the palette and activate it by spraying it with water if needed.

A WATER CONTAINER

When working with watercolors, you need to thoroughly rinse your brushes frequently so they are clean before you load the next color. It's advisable to have two containers of water ready.

OTHER MATERIALS

In addition to the essential materials you need for watercolor painting, here are some other helpful tools.

Masking Tape and Drawing Board

Masking tape is mainly used to secure the paper on the drawing board so that it's fixed on a surface when painting. This will give you a clean edge for the painting and prevent the paper from curling too much. It can also be used for masking (creating a protective barrier on the paper) and for creating a straight horizon line.

Pencil, Sharpener, and Eraser

A 2B pencil is best for sketching, and you should always keep it sharp using a pencil sharpener. You'll also need an eraser to fix your mistakes.

Paper Towel or a Cotton Cloth

These are ideal for cleaning purposes and can also be used for lifting paint from the paper and employing the dry brush technique.

Hair Dryer or Heat Tool

This can be used to speed up the drying process so that you don't need to wait for the layers to dry.

tips

- *Color names are not always reliable. So when you buy a new tube of watercolor paint, always pay attention to the pigment number.*
- *At the end of your painting session, clean your brush with a mild soap or shampoo and leave it upright. If you care for it properly, you'll never have to buy the same brush again.*
- *When painting, always keep some paper scraps next to you to test the colors.*
- *When using watercolor in pans, always spray some water on it before you start painting. Let it soak for 5 to 10 minutes to activate the pigments.*

ESSENTIAL TECHNIQUES

While there are many watercolor techniques, there are four basic techniques you should know to get started with the medium. These include *wet-on-dry*, *wet-on-wet*, *dry-on-dry*, and *watercolor washes*. These are simple techniques that will give you more confidence when you pick up the brush, and just by practicing them, you can create wonderful works of art. Now, let's take a look at each of them.

WET-ON-WET

Wet-on-wet is the most popular watercolor technique. It simply means you apply wet paint to a wet paper or add details with wet paint on a freshly painted background. Wet your paper evenly by applying a layer of clean water.

Drop some wet paint onto the wet paper and watch the paint spread and bloom. This means you have less control over how the paint behaves on the paper, and it also means you can create dramatic effects with this technique.

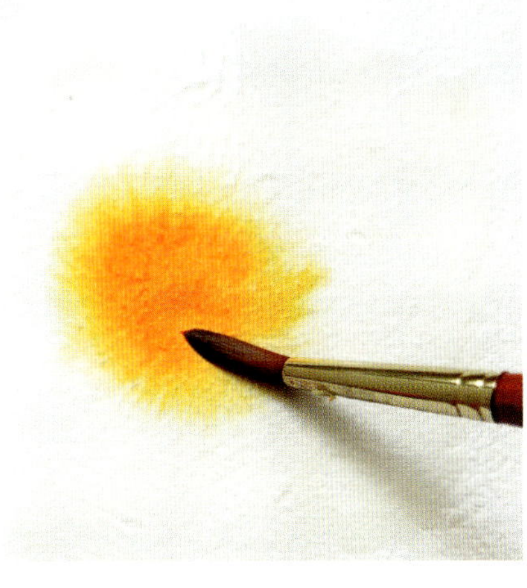

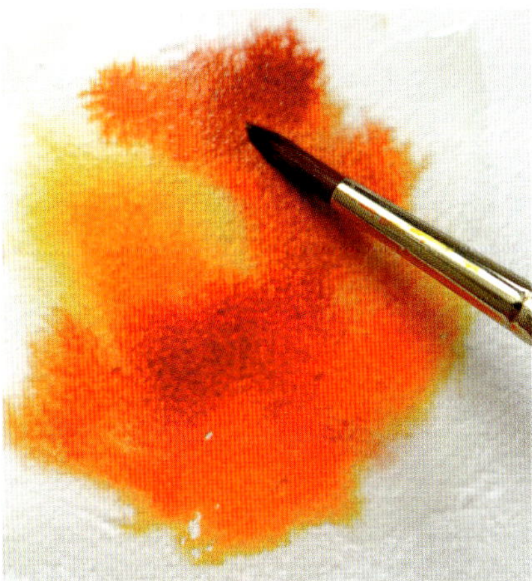

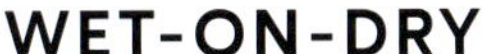

WET-ON-DRY

As the name suggests, the paint is applied wet (diluted with water) to the dry paper with a brush. Wet-on-dry simply means that you apply wet paint to dry paper or add detail with wet paint on a dry background.

With this technique, you have more control over where your paint goes because the paper is not wet. It doesn't fade or bleed as much as with the wet-on-wet technique. This technique is great for adding detail and giving your painting sharp, clean edges.

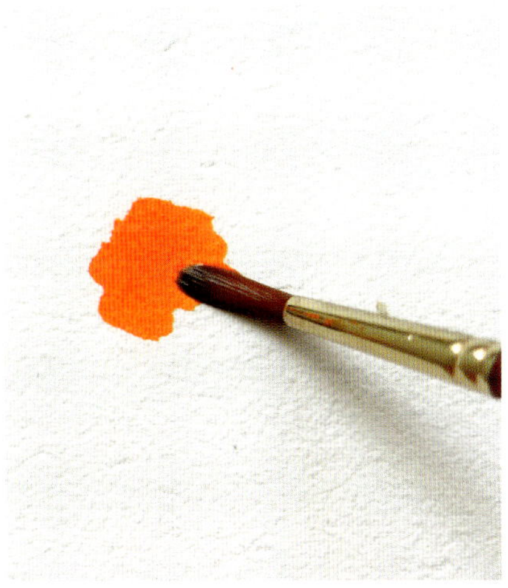

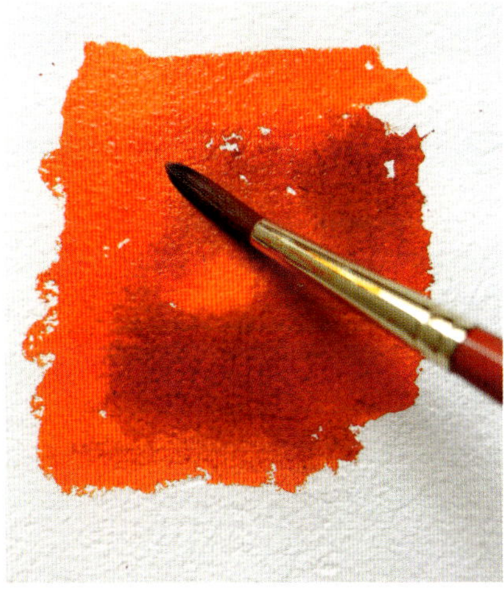

DRY-ON-DRY

Dry on-dry technique is also known as the dry brush technique. For this method, you should use as little water as possible. You can also dab your brush on a paper towel to remove the excess water. This technique is ideal for creating a rough texture or for creating a glistening water surface. Depending on the shape and size of the brush you use, you can achieve a variety of effects. Because the paint is dry, the color remains as it was applied. It doesn't fade or bleed.

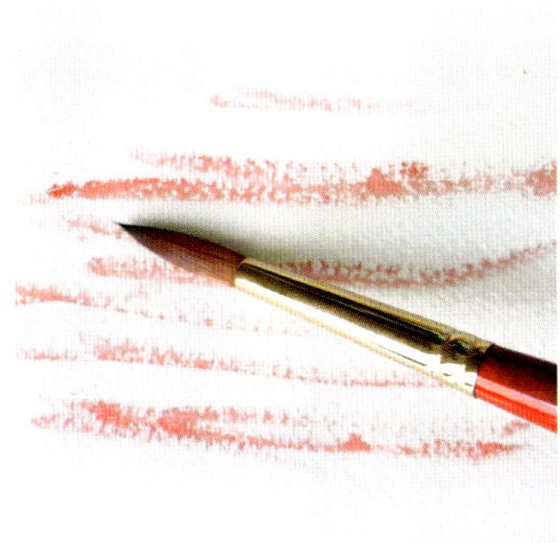

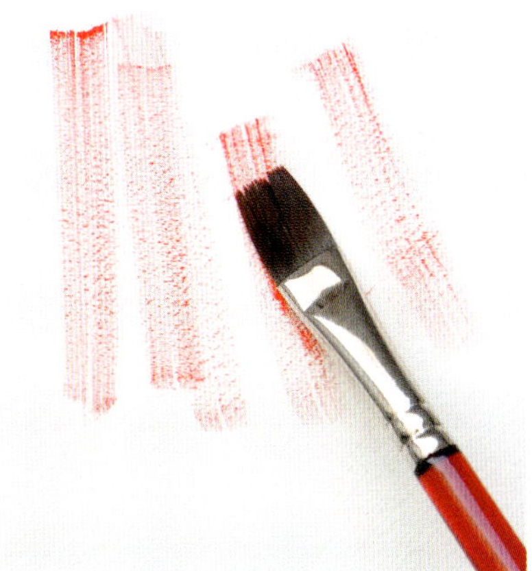

WATERCOLOR WASHES

The wash is the foundation of a sky painting. It can be a flat wash of a single color or a dramatic splash of multiple colors. Once you become familiar with the different type of watercolor washes, you can paint beautiful skies and backgrounds.

There are four basic washes:

- Flat wash
- Gradient or graded wash
- Variegated wash
- Wet-on-wet wash

All of these watercolor washes can be done using either the wet-on-wet or wet-on-dry method. Your choice of technique will depend on how big the area is. Wet-on-dry is suitable for small areas. If the area to be filled is very large, you'll need to use the wet-on-wet approach and apply a layer of clean water on the paper before applying the paint.

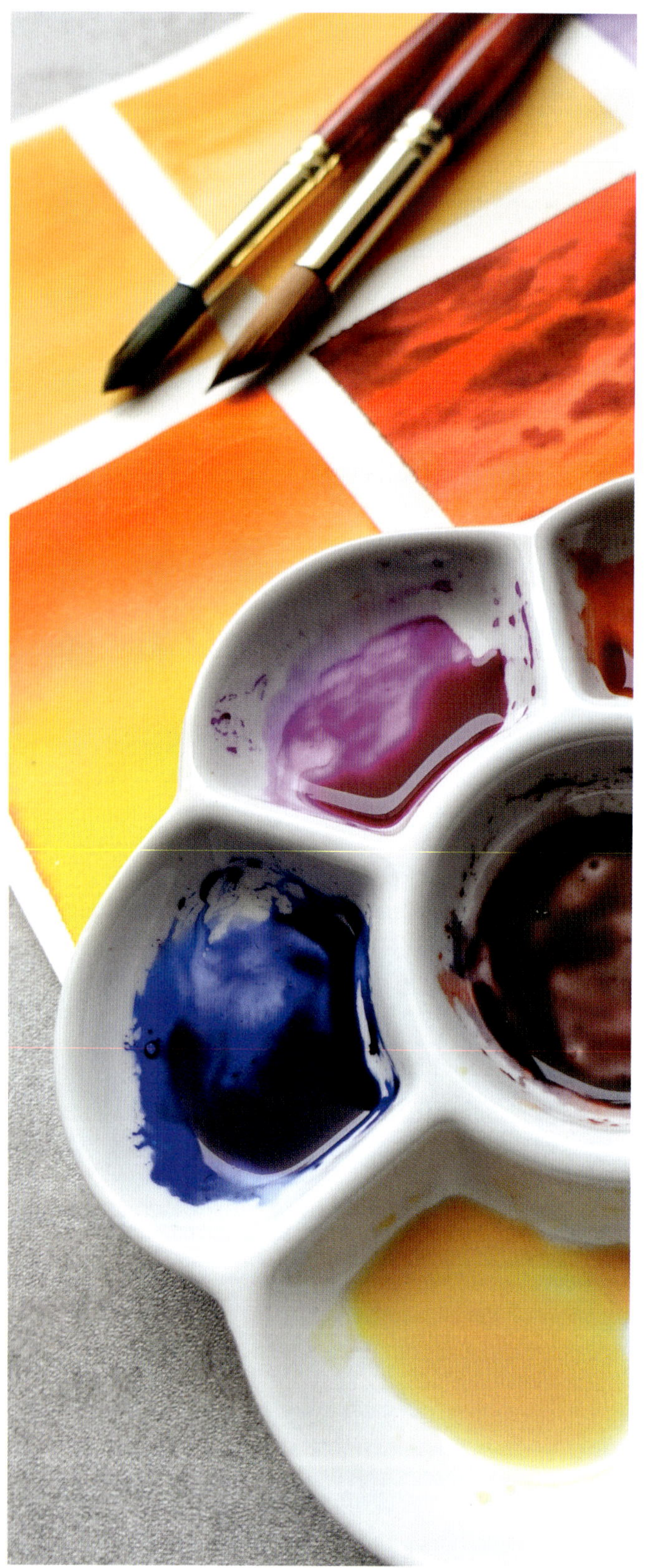

tips

- *If possible, keep a separate brush—preferably a wide wash brush—just for applying water to the paper.*
- *Mix enough of your colors before you start painting so you don't run out while you're working.*
- *Gravity helps pull the color down along the surface, which creates a smooth, consistent, and even application. Try mounting your paper on a drawing board and place it in an inclined position, especially if you're working on a large-scale painting.*
- *Try the various washes in both wet-on-wet and wet-on-dry versions so you can understand the differences and find out which wash type is right for you.*

FLAT WASH

With the flat wash technique, we want to create a smooth, even layer of a single color without visible brushstrokes. Use a flat brush and apply paint in one direction for the best result. Always work from the top to the bottom. If necessary, you can tilt your paper so gravity will help the paint flow downward.

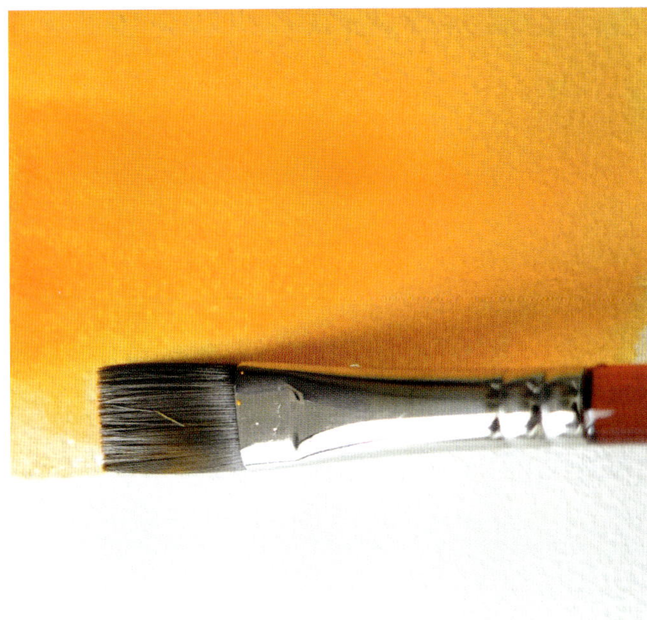

Flat wash: wet-on-dry.

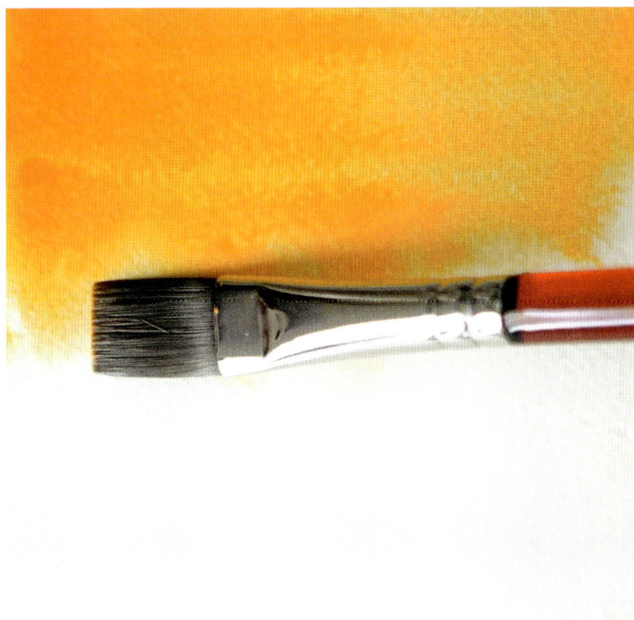

Flat wash: wet-on-wet.

GRADIENT OR GRADED WASH

This technique can be used to create beautiful gradient skies. Again, you can use either the wet-on-wet technique or the wet-on-dry technique.

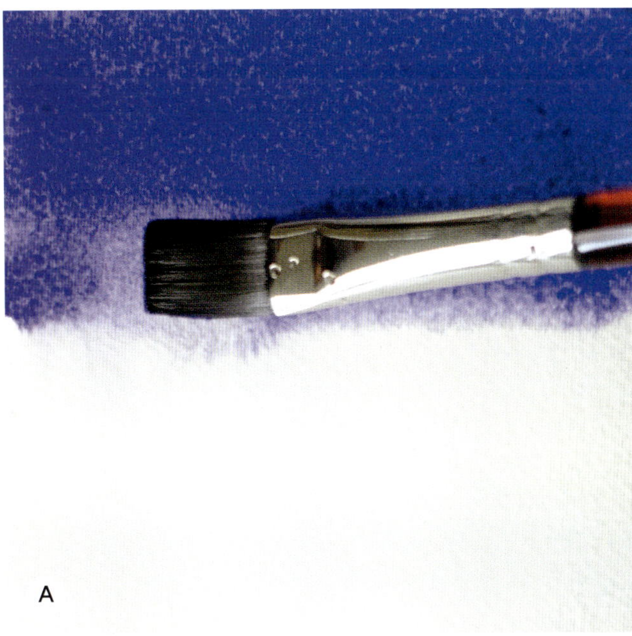

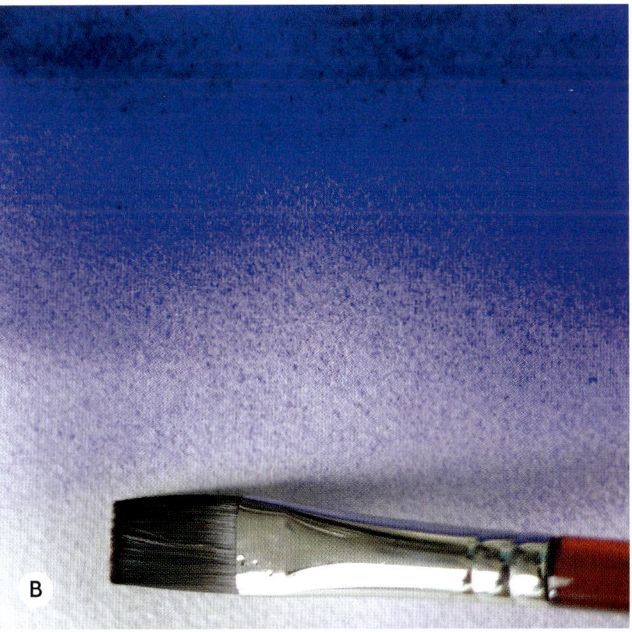

Start with a dark value of your color (A) and gradually lighten it as you paint. (B) Flat brushes are better for this technique. Work your way down with single, even strokes, from left to right, starting from the upper-left corner.

VARIEGATED WASH

A variegated wash is when you begin painting using one color and then transition into another color while seamlessly blending the two. This look can be created either using the wet-on-wet or wet-on-dry approach.

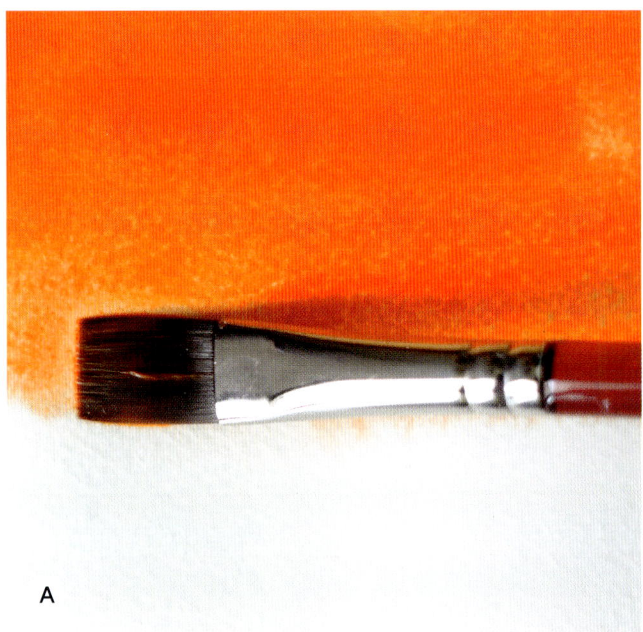

1. Dip your flat brush in your first color and begin painting even brushstrokes across your paper. Continue until you reach the center of your paper. (A)

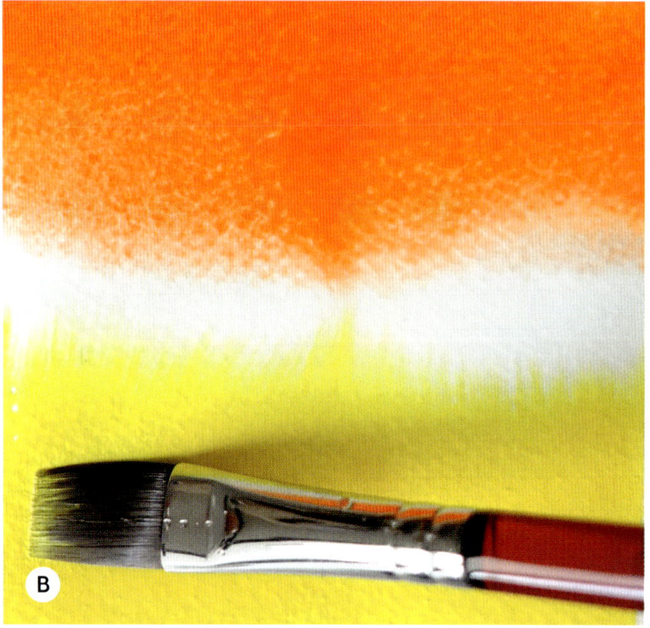

2. While your painting is still wet, quickly clean your brush and start painting with your second color. Apply that from the bottom, working upward toward the first color. (B)

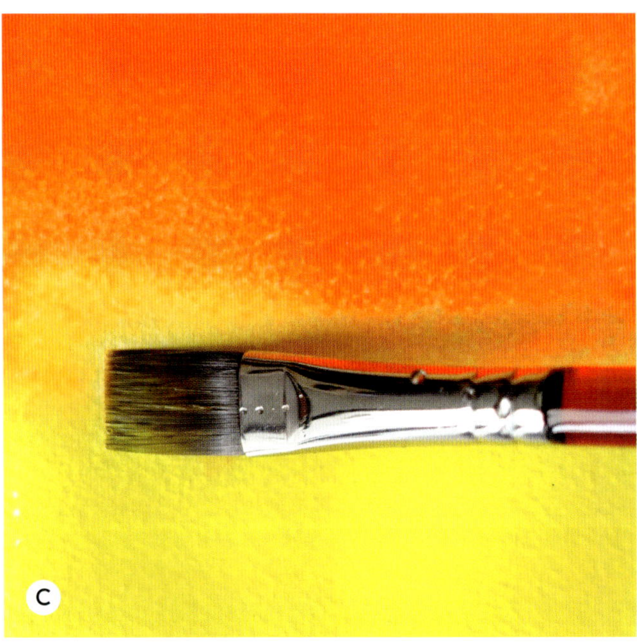

3. Keep running your brush from left to right in a horizontal direction until you get a clean blend. (C)

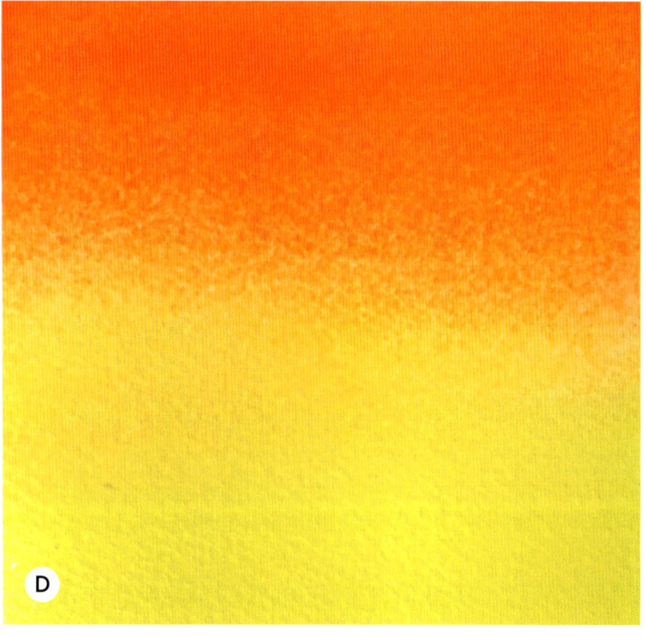

4. Notice how beautifully the two pigments join in the center of your paper? It's gorgeous, isn't it? (D)

WET-ON-WET WASH

A wet-on-wet wash is a technique that many artists choose when they want to play with multiple colors and create unique and interesting results. Choose two or more colors and simply drop them onto a wet background. You can enjoy how the colors blend and bleed into each other, creating a very dramatic mix. Using this technique, you can create different types of fun and playful backgrounds and dramatic skies.

Note that you must add paint while the paper is still wet, which means you must work quickly and consistently.

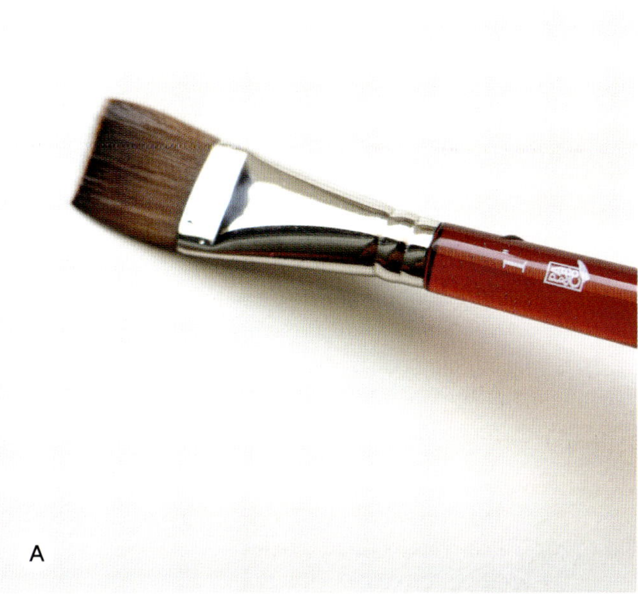

A

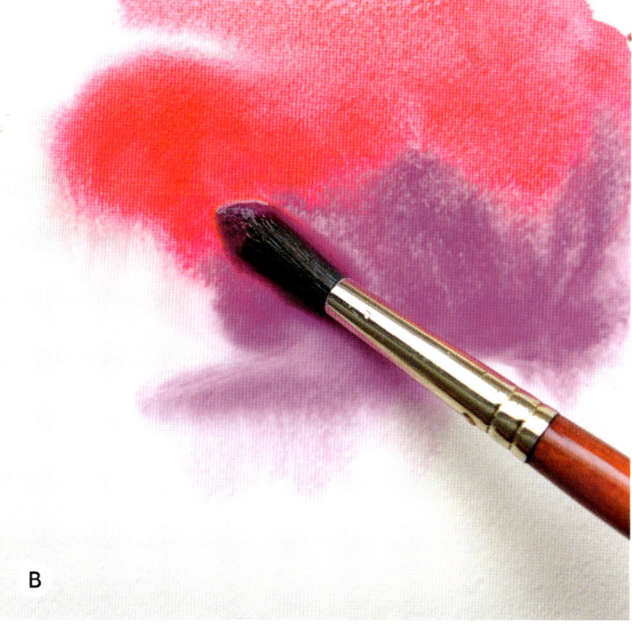

B

1. Use a wash brush to apply a layer of clean water to the paper. Run the brush over it a few times to make sure the paper is evenly wet. (A)

2. Select your colors and apply them to the wet paper. (B)

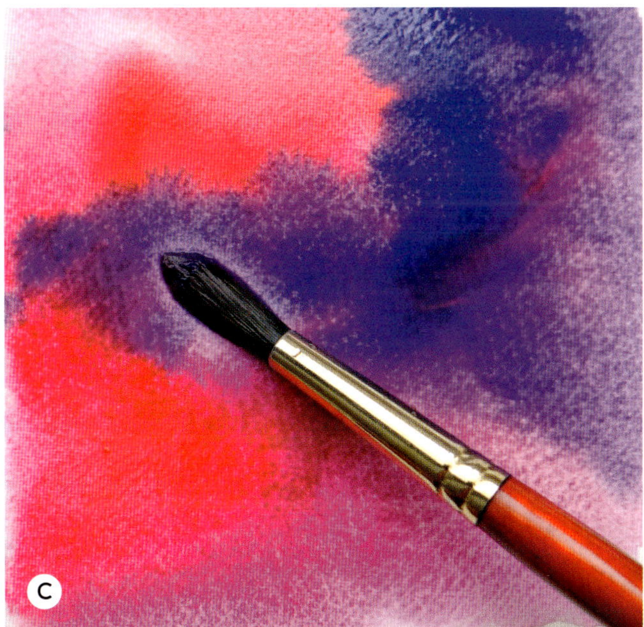

C

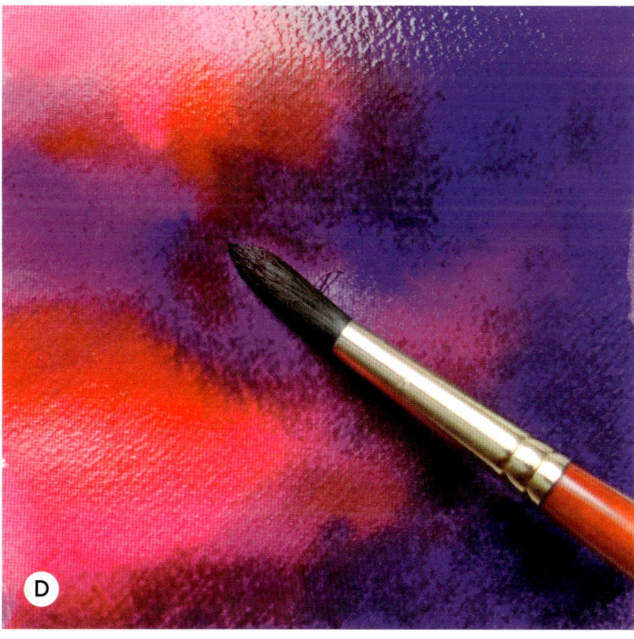

D

3. Use two or more colors to create a dramatic result. Use different tonal values to make the blend even more interesting. (C)

4. The possibilities are endless and limited only by your imagination. (D)

COLOR AND VALUE

Color theory is both the science and the art of using colors. It explains how colors are perceived and how they mix, match, and contrast. It's much more fun to make art when you understand colors and how they interact.

Before we get started with the 30-Day Watercolor Challenge, you'll want to familiarize yourself with some basics so you'll feel comfortable mixing colors. In my early days as an artist, I blindly selected colors from my palette without knowing how they would interact with each other. It took me a while to realize that I could create my own color palette for my paintings to get better results.

A color wheel is probably one of the most useful things you can paint for yourself and keep close at hand as you work. You can easily understand the mixing ratios of colors by looking at the color wheel, and you can also create unique colors by changing the mixing ratios.

In this book, we explore a wide range of color combinations that will help you better understand your colors and learn how to make bold and beautiful color choices.

THE COLOR WHEEL

The circular arrangement of colors that shows the various relationships among them is referred to as a color wheel. The color relationships on a basic twelve-color color wheel are divided into three categories: primary colors, secondary colors, and tertiary colors.

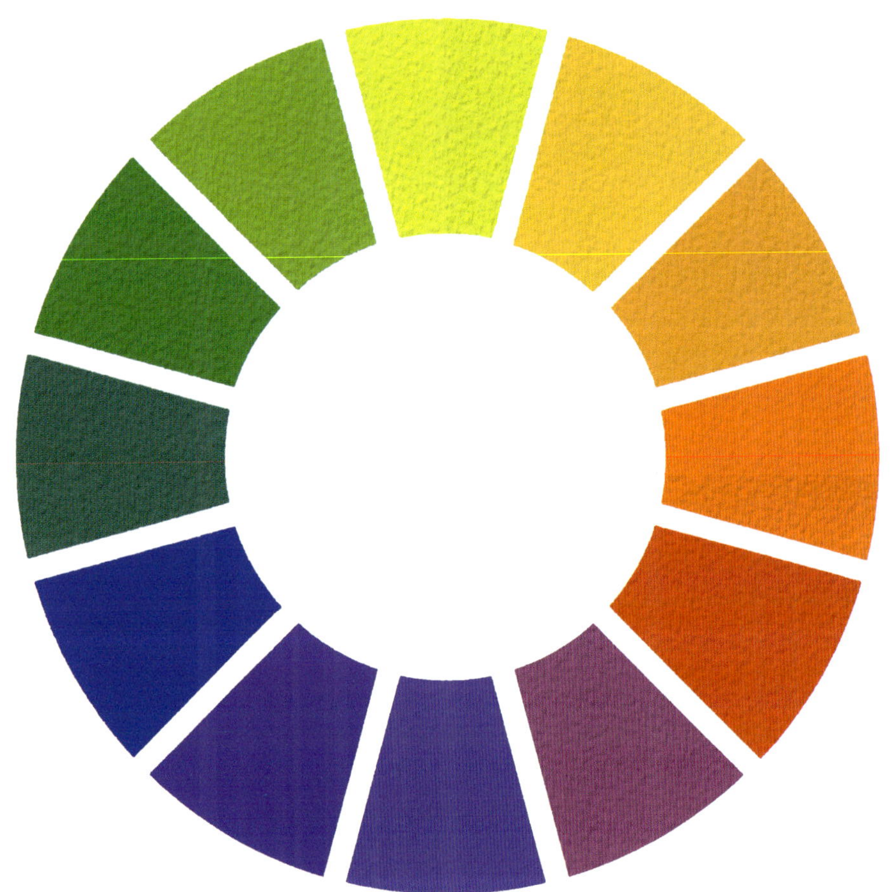

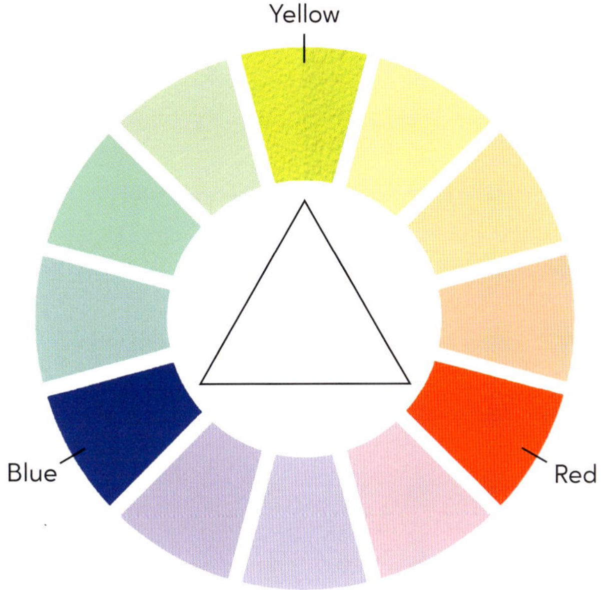

Primary Colors

The three primary colors are **red, yellow, and blue.** You can mix any color by mixing the primary colors, which is why they're referred to as primary.

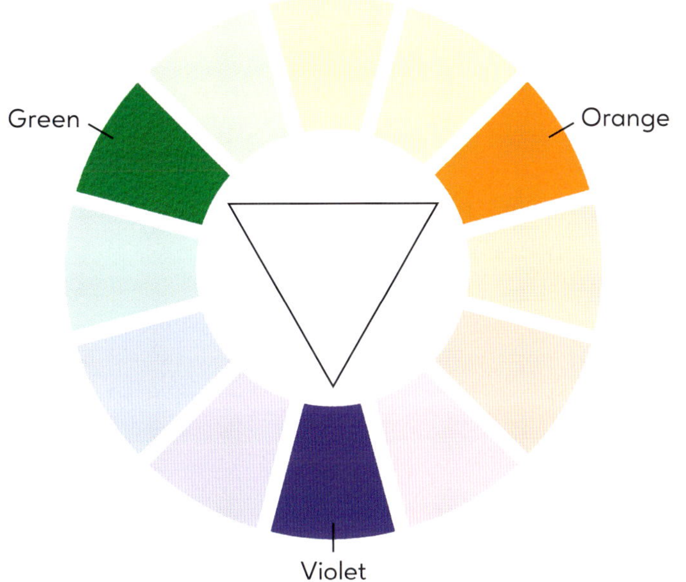

Secondary Colors

The three secondary colors—**orange, green, and violet**—are created by mixing equal amounts of two primary colors. On the color wheel, the secondary colors are located between the primary colors.

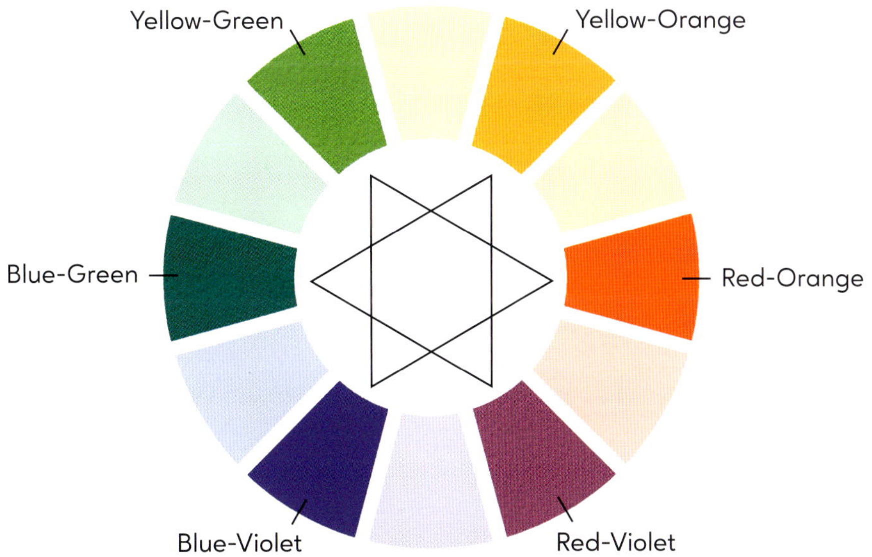

Tertiary Colors

The six tertiary colors—**blue-green and yellow-green; yellow-orange and red-orange; and blue-violet and red-violet**—are each a mixture of one primary and one secondary color. On a color wheel, tertiary colors sit between the primary and the secondary colors that are used to mix them.

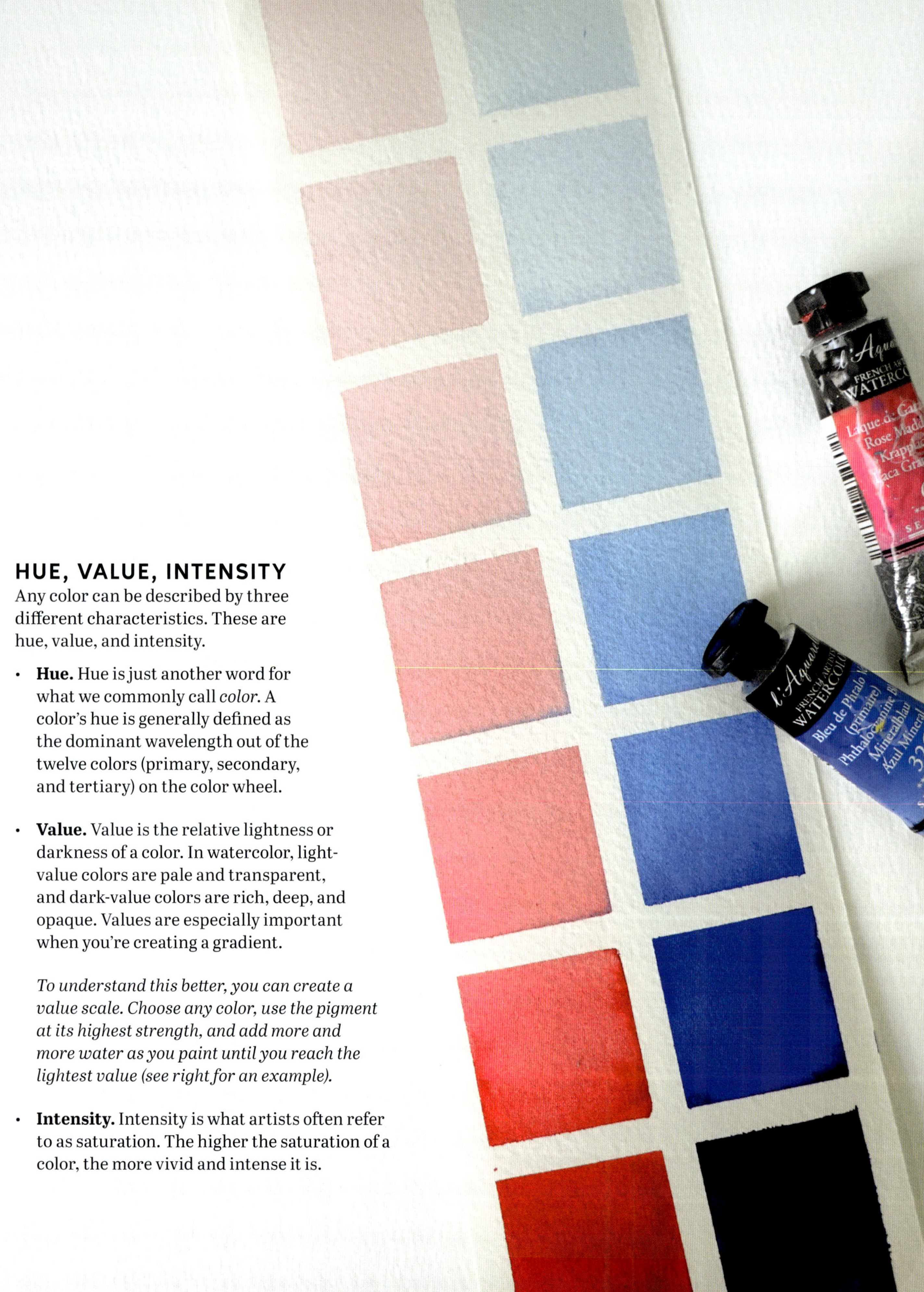

HUE, VALUE, INTENSITY

Any color can be described by three different characteristics. These are hue, value, and intensity.

- **Hue.** Hue is just another word for what we commonly call *color*. A color's hue is generally defined as the dominant wavelength out of the twelve colors (primary, secondary, and tertiary) on the color wheel.

- **Value.** Value is the relative lightness or darkness of a color. In watercolor, light-value colors are pale and transparent, and dark-value colors are rich, deep, and opaque. Values are especially important when you're creating a gradient.

  To understand this better, you can create a value scale. Choose any color, use the pigment at its highest strength, and add more and more water as you paint until you reach the lightest value (see right for an example).

- **Intensity.** Intensity is what artists often refer to as saturation. The higher the saturation of a color, the more vivid and intense it is.

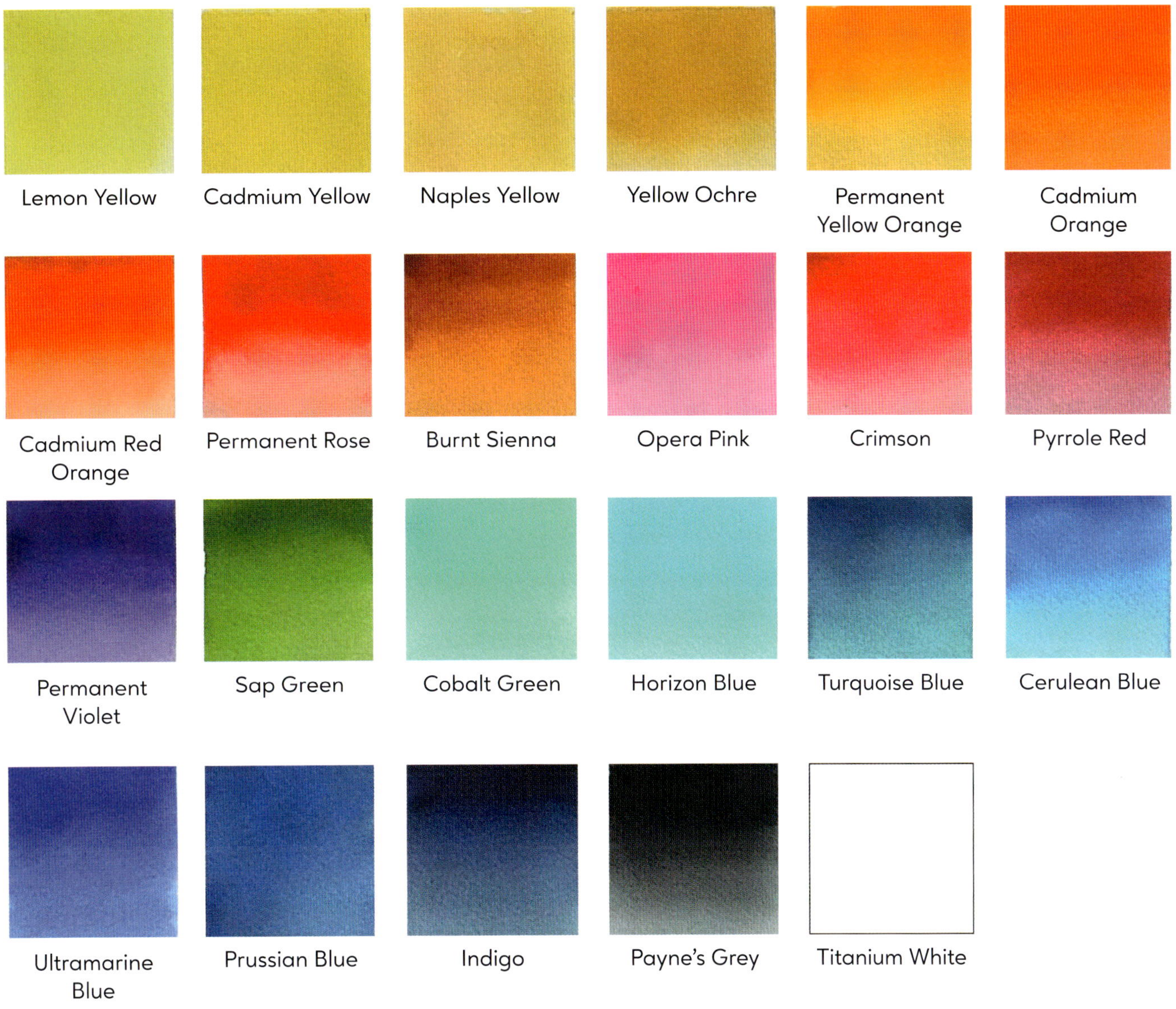

Lemon Yellow	Cadmium Yellow	Naples Yellow	Yellow Ochre	Permanent Yellow Orange	Cadmium Orange
Cadmium Red Orange	Permanent Rose	Burnt Sienna	Opera Pink	Crimson	Pyrrole Red
Permanent Violet	Sap Green	Cobalt Green	Horizon Blue	Turquoise Blue	Cerulean Blue
Ultramarine Blue	Prussian Blue	Indigo	Payne's Grey	Titanium White	

COLORS IN MY PALETTE

If you are just starting out with watercolor painting, you may not have a wide selection of colors with you. But the best part is that you do not have to have a large selection of colors, because you can easily mix and create most colors. Above is a list of all the colors I will use in the projects described in the book. You certainly do not need that many colors or the exact same colors to recreate the projects. You can choose the colors you prefer for the sky or use colors that are very similar to the ones I use.

I recommend using artist-quality watercolor paints for the best results. Some of the artist paints I like are from the following brands: Daniel Smith, Schmincke, Winsor & Newton, White Nights Watercolor, and Sennelier.

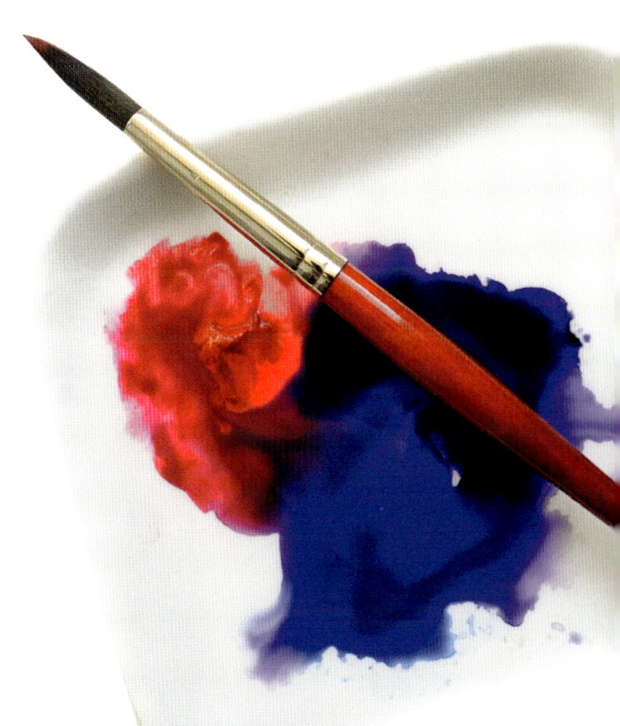

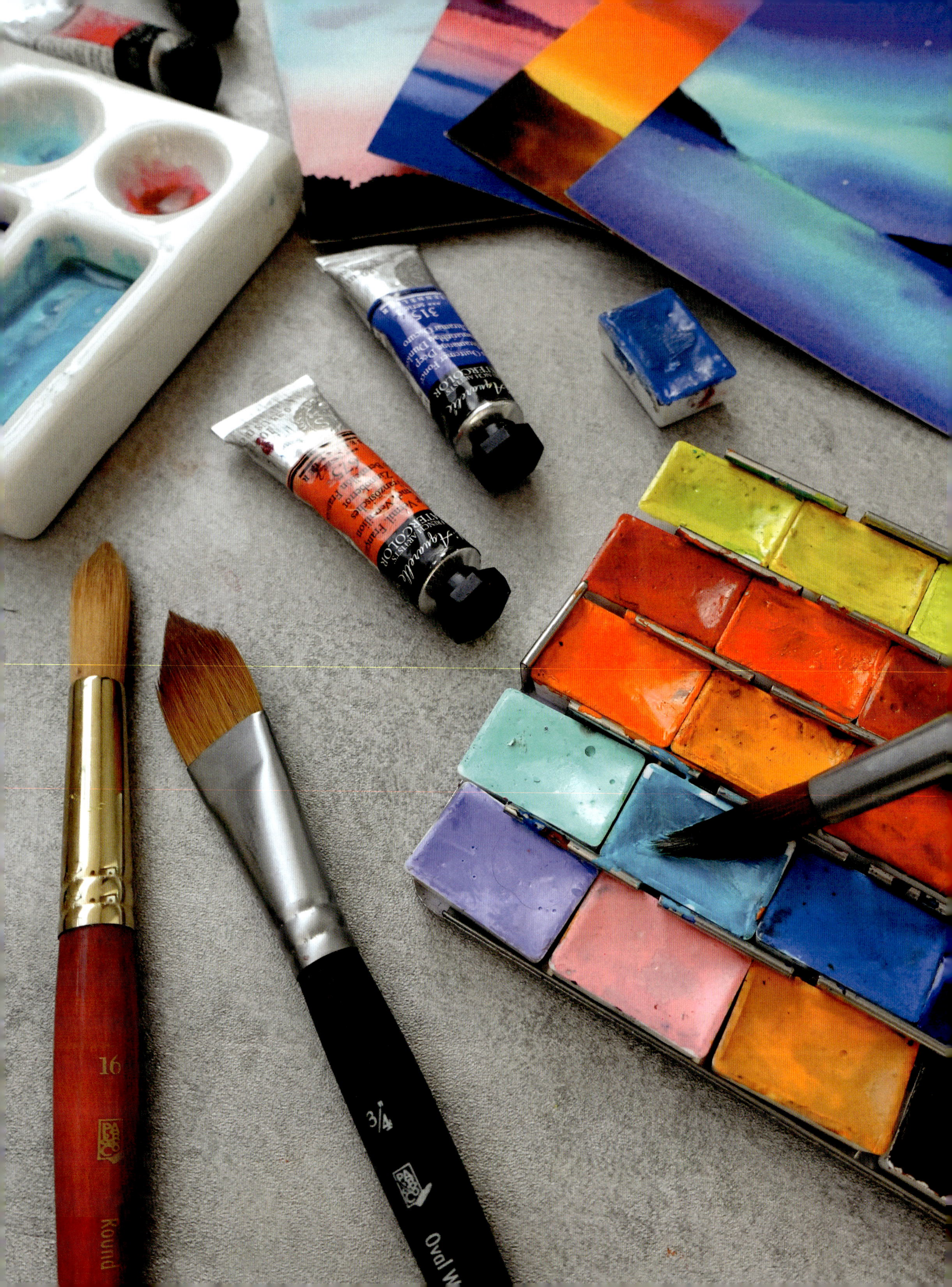
16
Round
3/4

BOLD AND BEAUTIFUL SKIES: 30 DAYS, 30 PROJECTS

Develop a consistent art routine and make art a part of your day.

Art is a great stress reliever. Whether you are simply splashing colors on a paper or creating an incredibly complex piece, it's a great way to unwind from the hustle and bustle of everyday life. I am someone who paints something absolutely every day—some days it's just a few minutes, and some days it's hours. No matter how long the time is at the end of the day, I make time for myself to play with colors. That's how I started creating thirty-day watercolor challenges, and I encourage everyone to try it as well. Each day's project offers you a new color palette, a new subject to explore, new techniques, and a new approach. It will forever change the way you look at a blank page. Once you have completed an art challenge, a blank page will never be a deterrent again. You'll be bursting with ideas and ready to take your skills to a whole new level.

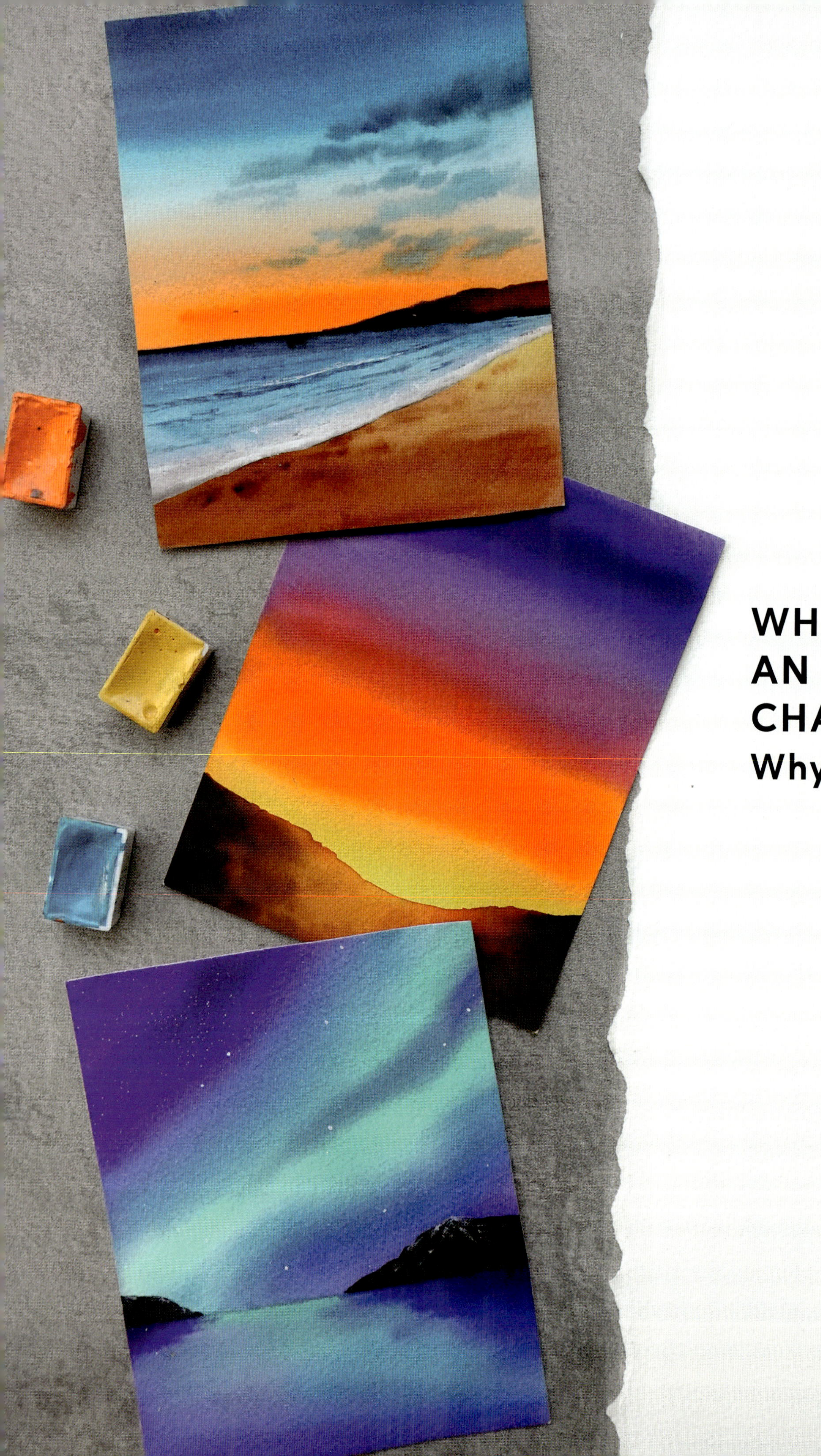

WHAT'S AN ART CHALLENGE?

Why Do One?

A daily art practice can help you develop your skills; build your confidence in trying new colors, techniques, or subjects; and most importantly, take away the fear of starting with a blank sheet. You may be surprised at what you come up with, even if you participate in an art challenge simply for fun.

When I began my art journey, I started with a thirty-day project. I stayed consistent and created a watercolor landscape each day. I was surprised at how much my skills improved and I had an extensive knowledge of color mixing and essential techniques. That's when I realized that I could improve my skills and find a career in art if I kept practicing.

This art challenge is not about creating a masterpiece every day; I just want you to take out the paints and paint something from the book every day.

You can either follow the sequence or flip to one of the pages, follow the instructions, and create a bold and beautiful painting. You can make it as big or as small as you like. I love to paint artwork on a smaller scale. That way, I can finish the painting in one go and not be overwhelmed with the process.

Through simple yet bold and beautiful step-by-step projects for each day of the month, this book will help you discover the master artist in you. Start with the first few days and get into the flow of watercolor painting. At the end of thirty days, you'll see how far you've come.

Ready to take your creative skills to the next level? Let's start with one painting a day!

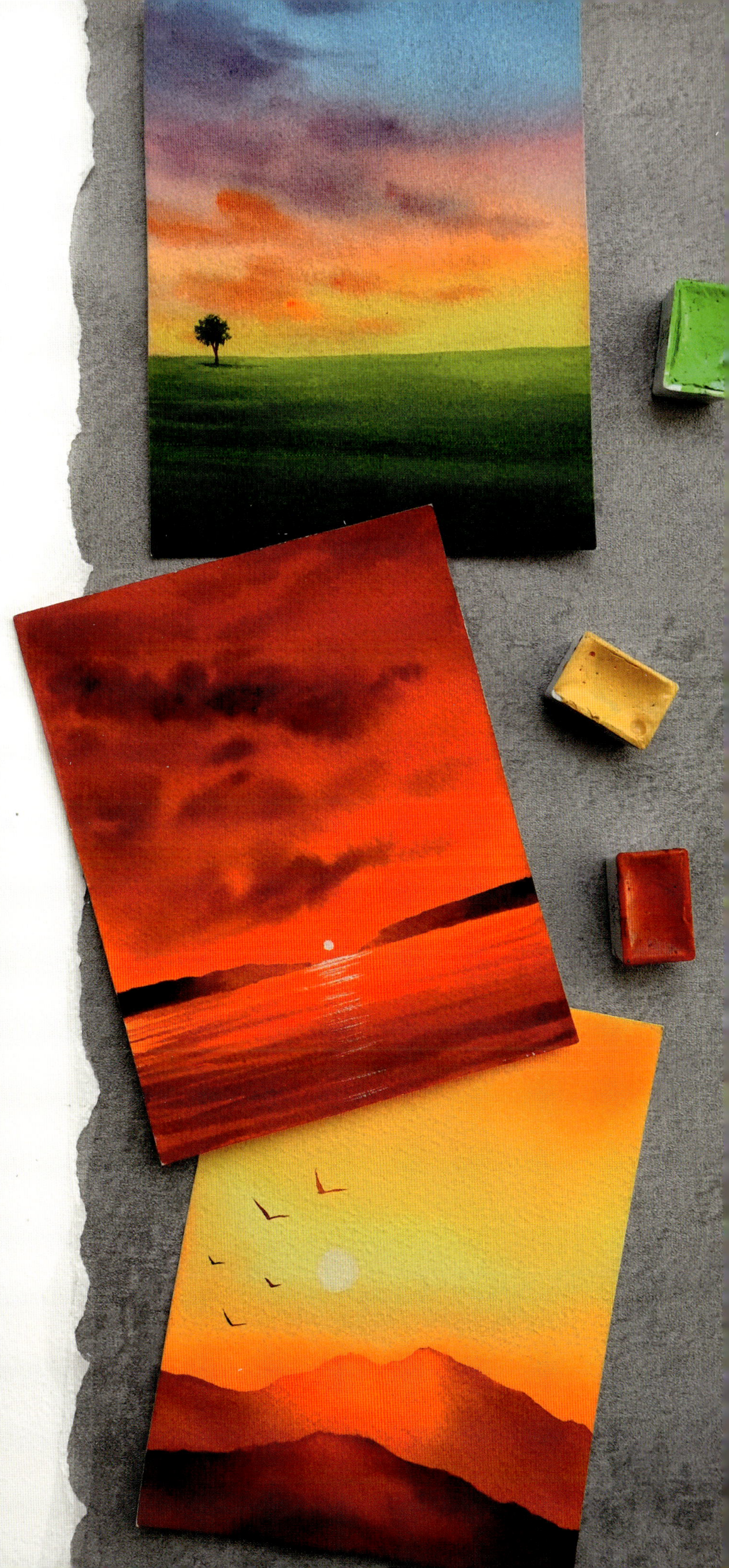

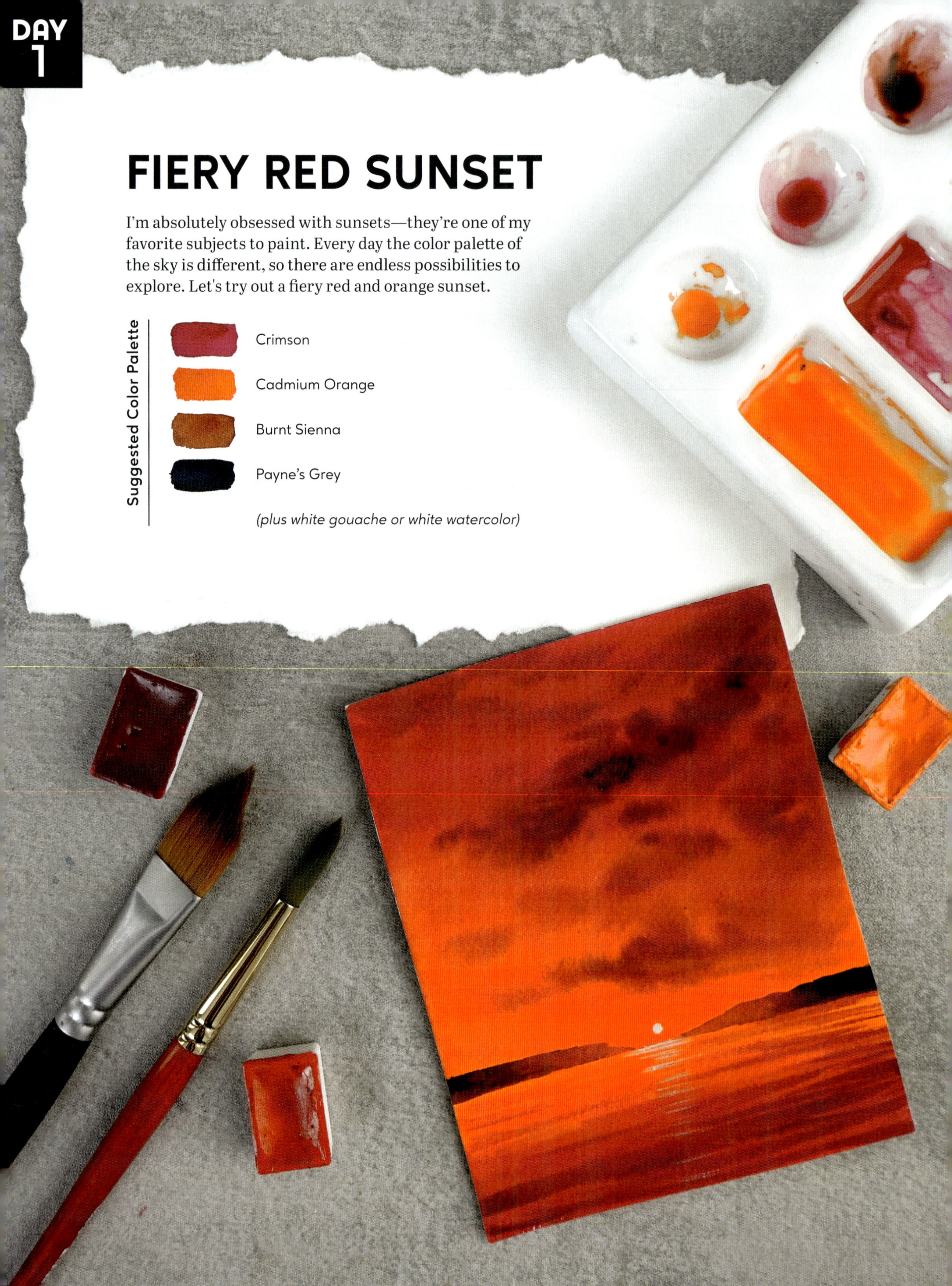
DAY 1

FIERY RED SUNSET

I'm absolutely obsessed with sunsets—they're one of my favorite subjects to paint. Every day the color palette of the sky is different, so there are endless possibilities to explore. Let's try out a fiery red and orange sunset.

Suggested Color Palette

- Crimson
- Cadmium Orange
- Burnt Sienna
- Payne's Grey

(plus white gouache or white watercolor)

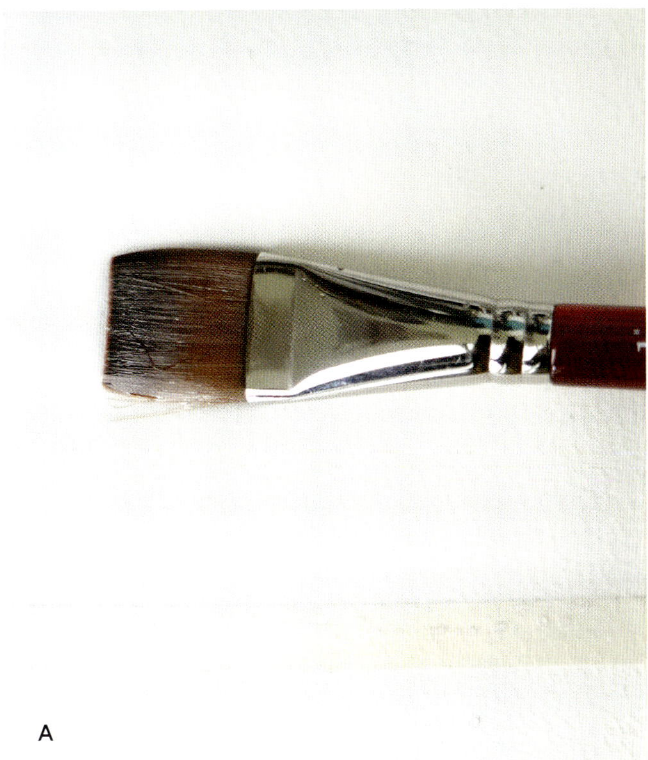

A

Step 1: Securing and Wetting the Paper. Secure your paper to a drawing board. Place a piece of masking tape slightly below the center of the paper to separate the sky and the lake. Apply an even layer of clean water to the entire sky. (A)

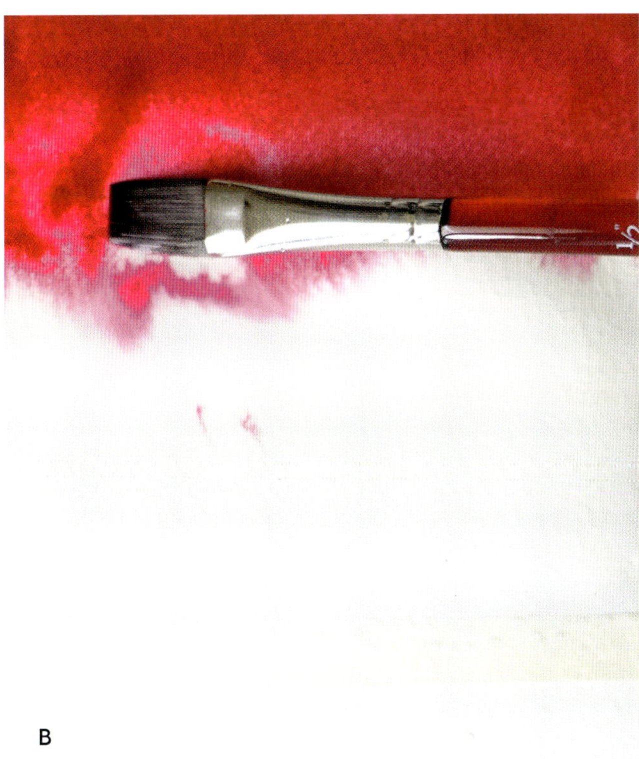

B

Step 2: Sky—Base Layer. Our first painting step is to create a variegated wash of Crimson and Cadmium Orange. Use a flat brush to paint Crimson along the top half of the sky. (B)

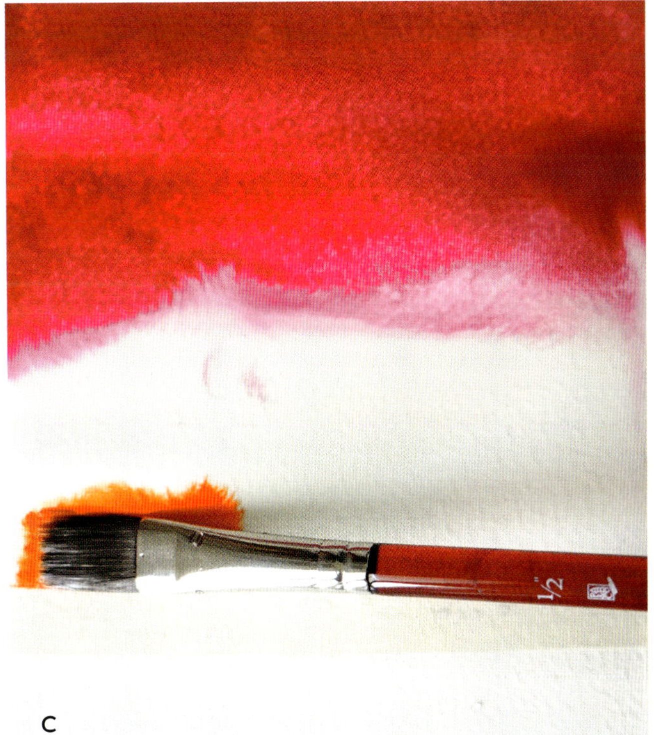

C

Once you reach halfway, clean your brush and switch to Cadmium Orange. Start at the bottom and work your way up to the Crimson. (C)

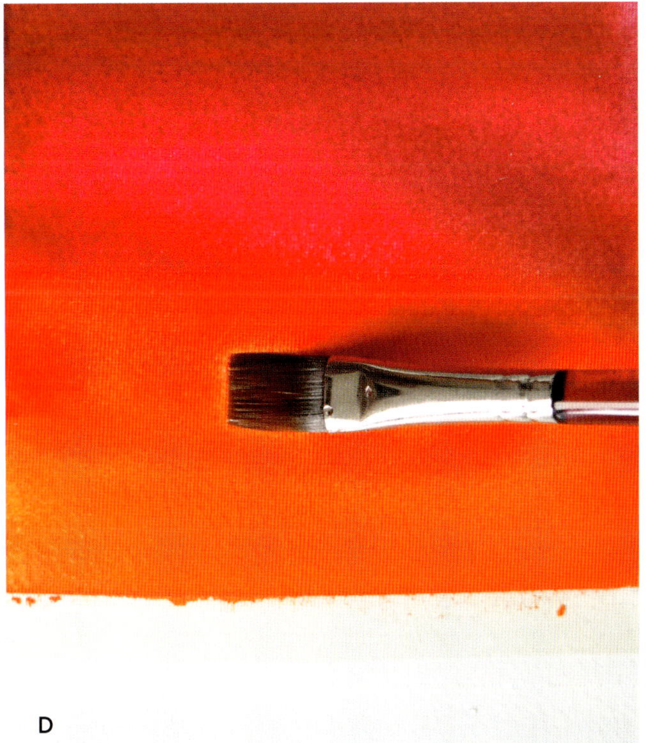

D

Carefully move the brush horizontally from left to right, making sure the blending is even. (D)

(continued)

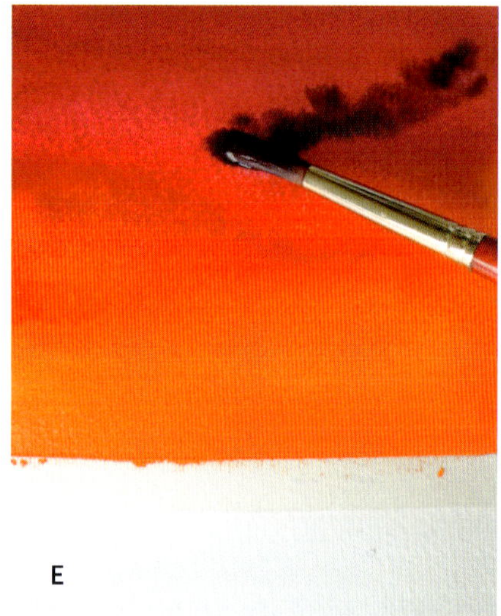

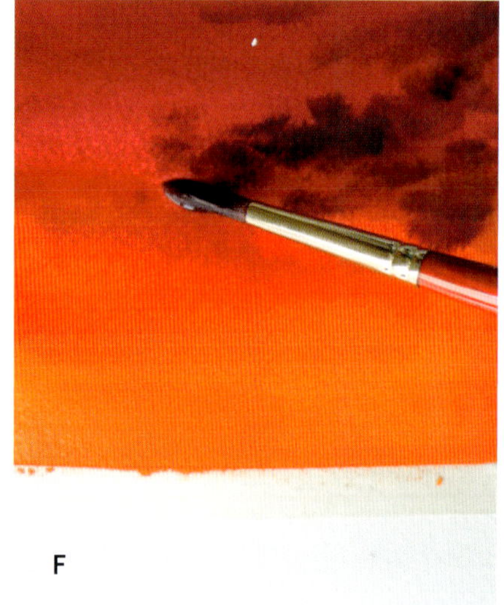

Step 3: Clouds. We need to add the clouds while the background is still wet, so quickly mix a little Crimson and Payne's Grey to get a dark red. Add the dark red in random shapes on the wet background. (E)

Add more clouds to make the sky look dramatic. (F, G) Stop once you're satisfied with the result. Let dry completely.

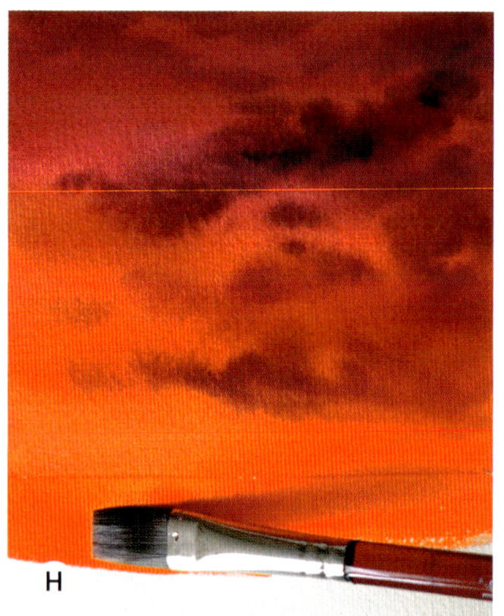

Step 4: Lake and Waves. Carefully peel off the masking tape. Begin at the horizon with a variegated wash of Cadmium Orange and Crimson. Apply the color directly to the dry paper. There's no need to wet the paper first. Start with Cadmium Orange (H) and then clean your brush and switch to Crimson halfway through. (I)

To add the waves, apply thick and thin lines in dark red to the wet background: thicker and darker lines at the bottom of the painting and lighter and thinner lines closer to the horizon line. (J)

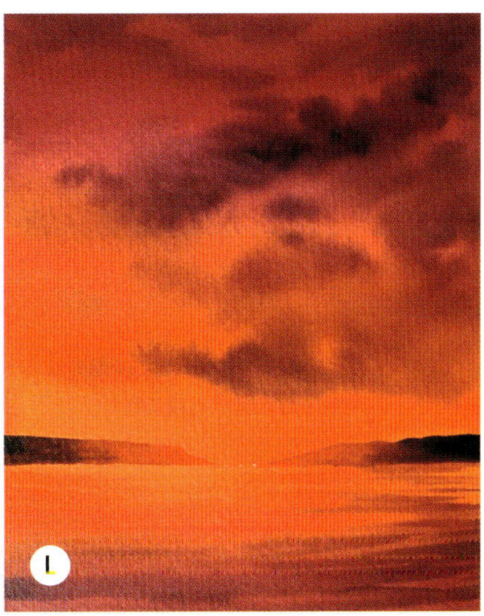

Step 5: Final Details. To add mountains on opposite sides of the lake along the horizon line, start with Burnt Sienna (K) and then clean your brush and switch to Payne's Grey to complete them. (L)

Add the sun and its reflection in the water. Use a small, clean brush with a pointed tip to apply a small circle of white gouache or white watercolor in the center. The paint needs to be slightly dry, so before applying it, dab the loaded brush several times on a paper towel. For the reflection, add small horizontal lines to the water, leaving some space between them. Add reflection lines until you reach the bottom to finish the painting. (M, N)

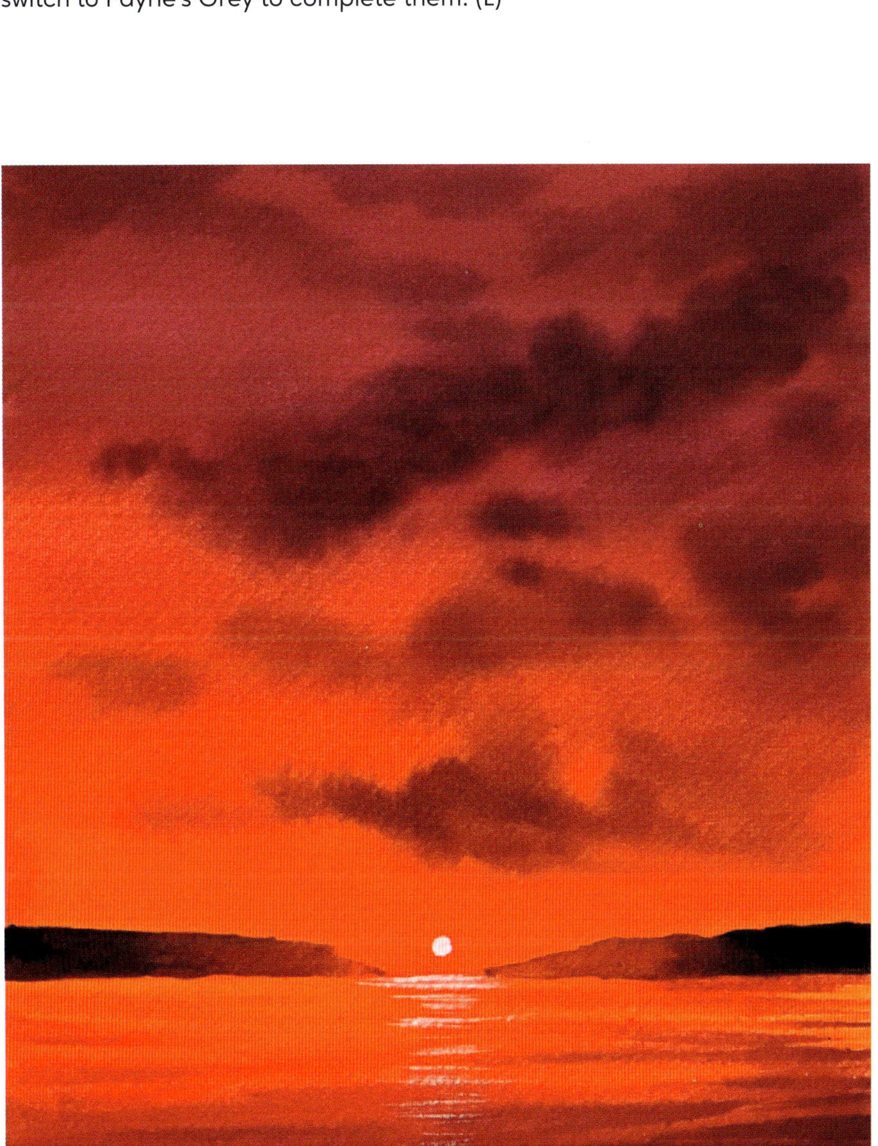

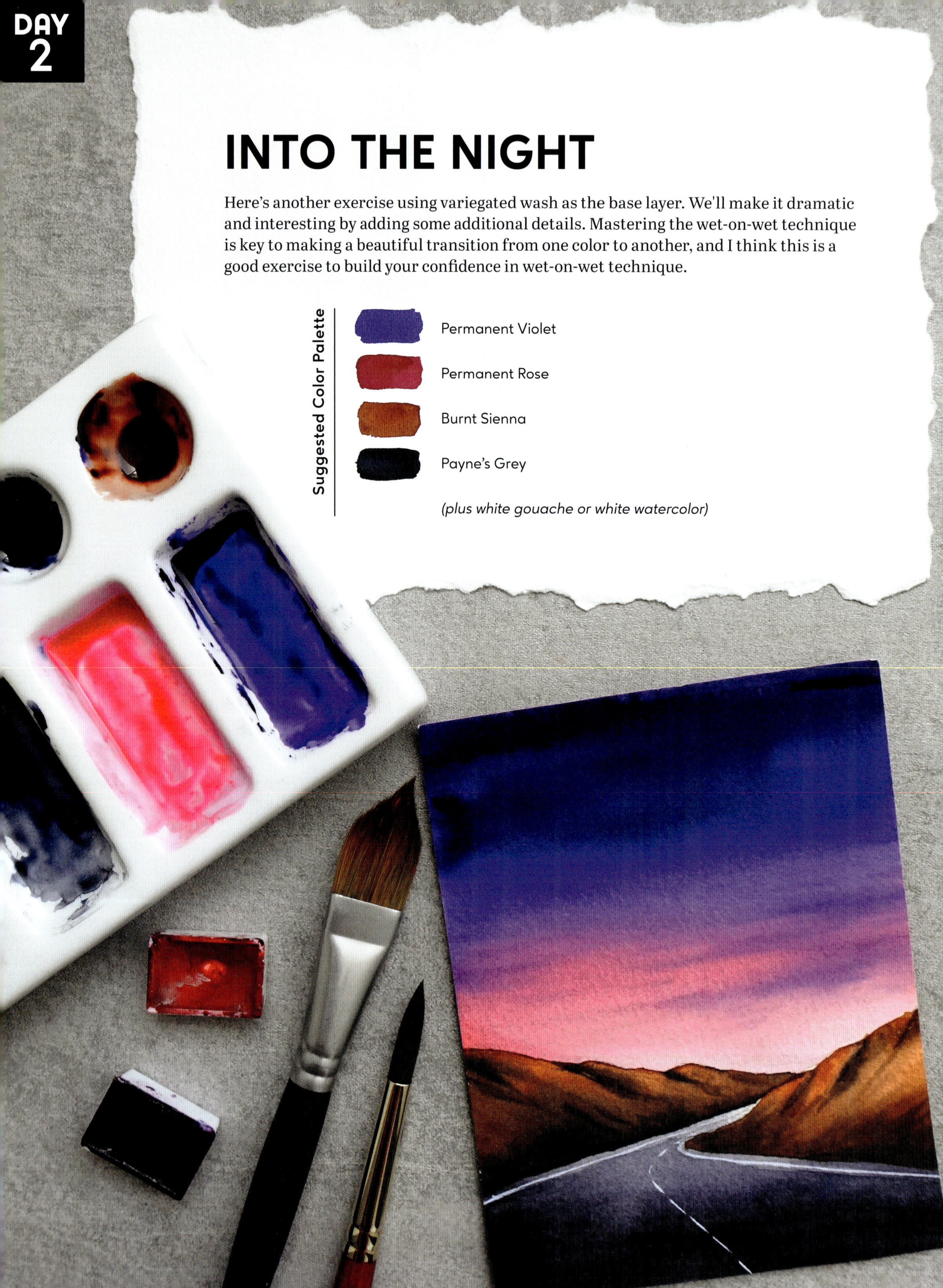

DAY 2

INTO THE NIGHT

Here's another exercise using variegated wash as the base layer. We'll make it dramatic and interesting by adding some additional details. Mastering the wet-on-wet technique is key to making a beautiful transition from one color to another, and I think this is a good exercise to build your confidence in wet-on-wet technique.

Suggested Color Palette

- Permanent Violet
- Permanent Rose
- Burnt Sienna
- Payne's Grey

(plus white gouache or white watercolor)

Step 1: Adding the Sketch. Add a light pencil sketch of the mountains and the road. (A)

Step 2: Securing and Wetting the Paper; Painting the Sky. Secure your paper to a drawing board. Apply an even layer of clean water to the sky. Use a medium-size flat brush to paint the sky. Start with Permanent Violet (B) and paint along the top half of the sky. (C)

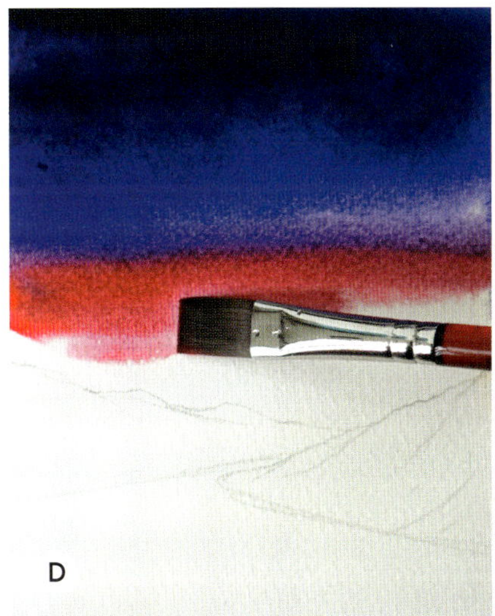

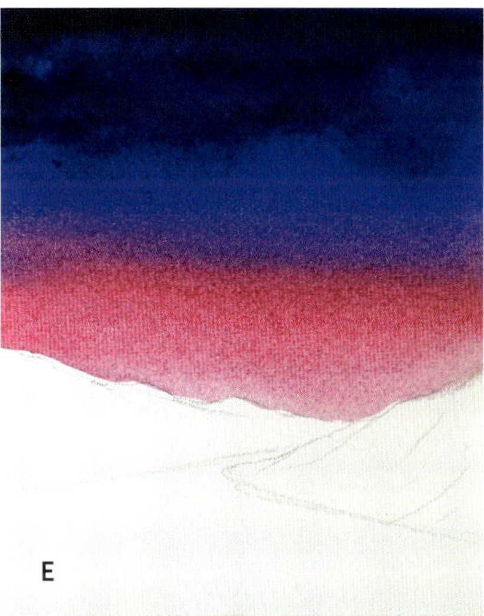

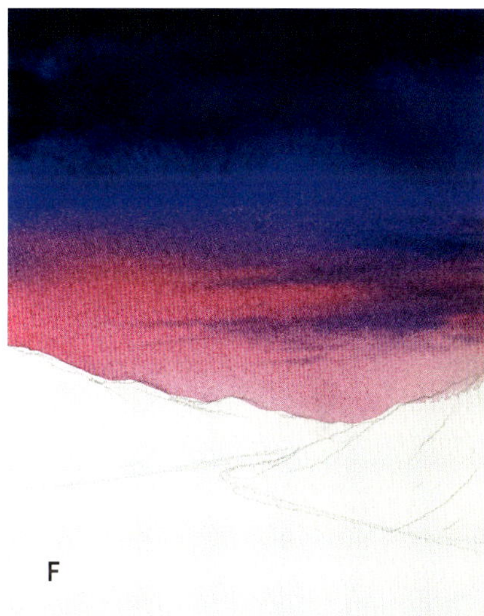

Clean your brush and switch to Permanent Rose. Add it right where you left off with the Permanent Violet and blend well. (D)

Quickly rinse your brush and continue with even horizontal brushstrokes until you reach the mountains, adding clean water as necessary to lighten the color. (E)

Use a medium-size round brush to paint a few thick stripes on the sky with the Permanent Violet to make the sky more interesting. This step is optional. If you don't want to add extra details, you can skip this step. (F)

(continued)

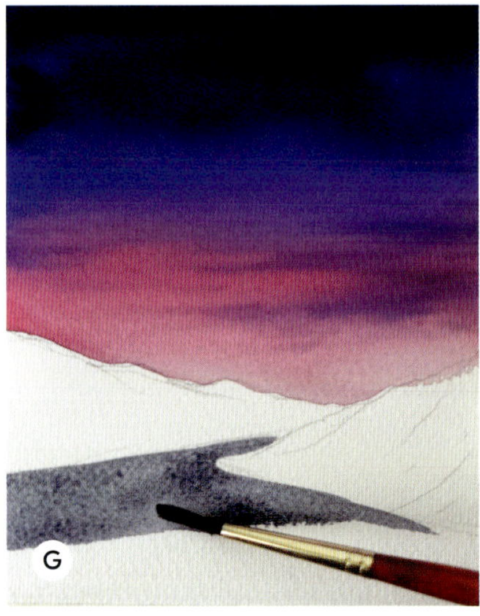

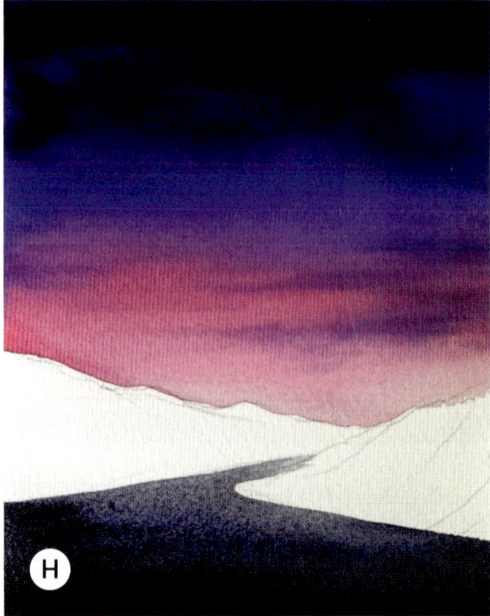

Step 3: Road—Base Layer. Use Payne's Grey to paint the road. Start with a light tone of Payne's Grey (G) and gradually make it darker. (H) Let dry completely.

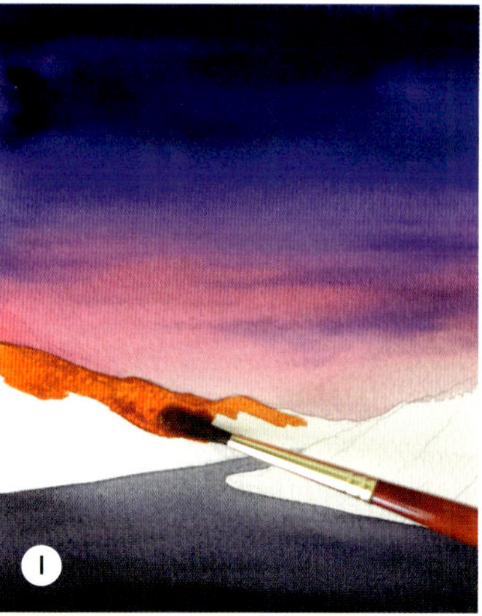

Step 4: Mountains. Paint the mountain in the background first. Start with a medium tone of Burnt Sienna and apply it carefully, following the sketch of the mountain. (I)

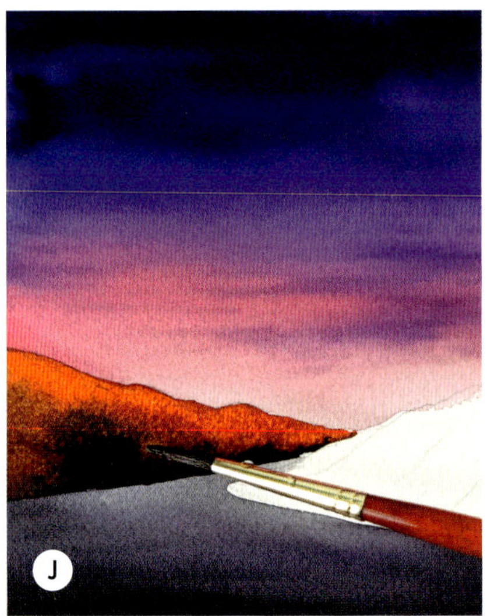

As you get closer to the road, switch to a darker tone of Burnt Sienna (Payne's Grey + Burnt Sienna). (J) This is the base layer of the mountain.

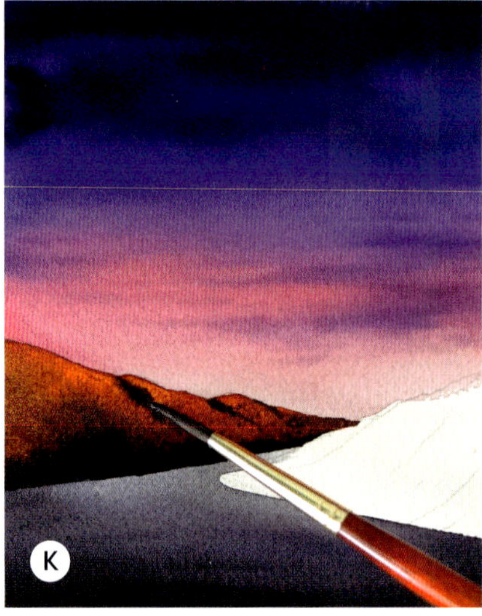

Before this layer dries, add some detail to give the mountain texture. If you look at the ridge line of the mountain, you can see the saddles (dips). Use the darker tone of Burnt Sienna and add it along the slopes of the mountain. (K)

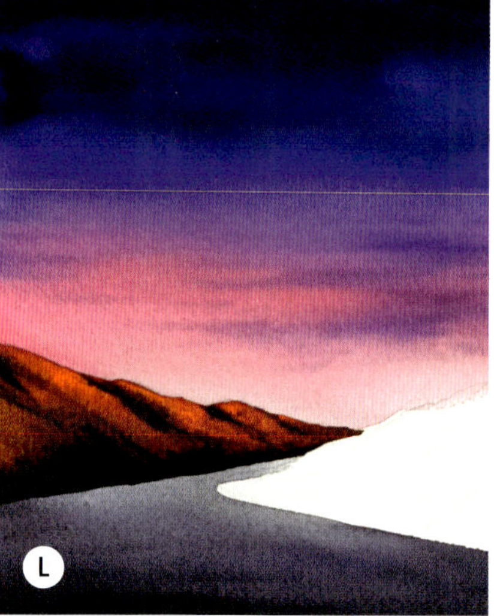

Vary the thickness by applying more or less pressure to the brush for a combination of thick and thin lines. (L)

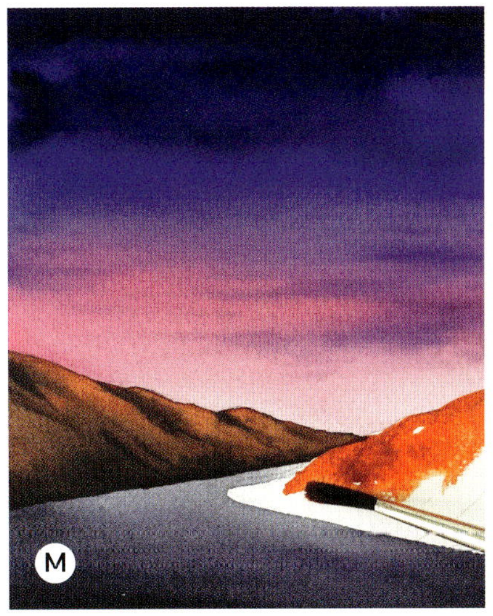

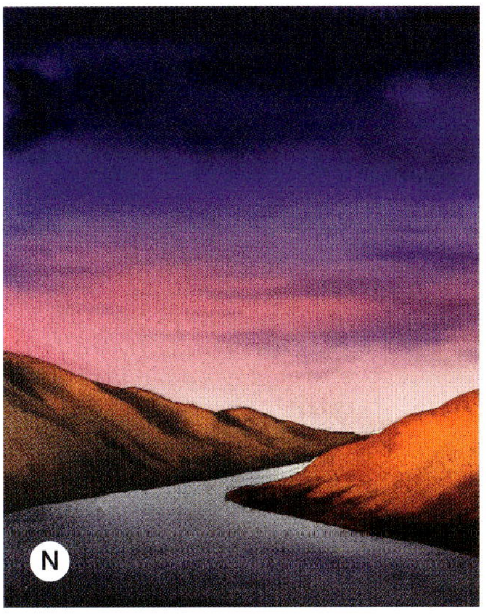

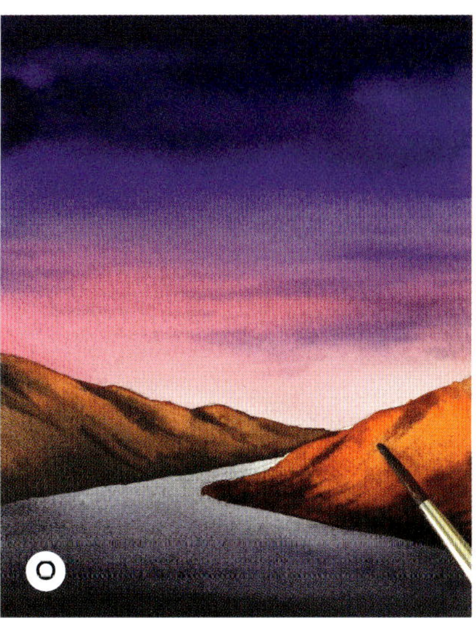

Once this is dry, paint the second mountain in the foreground using the same method. (M, N, O)

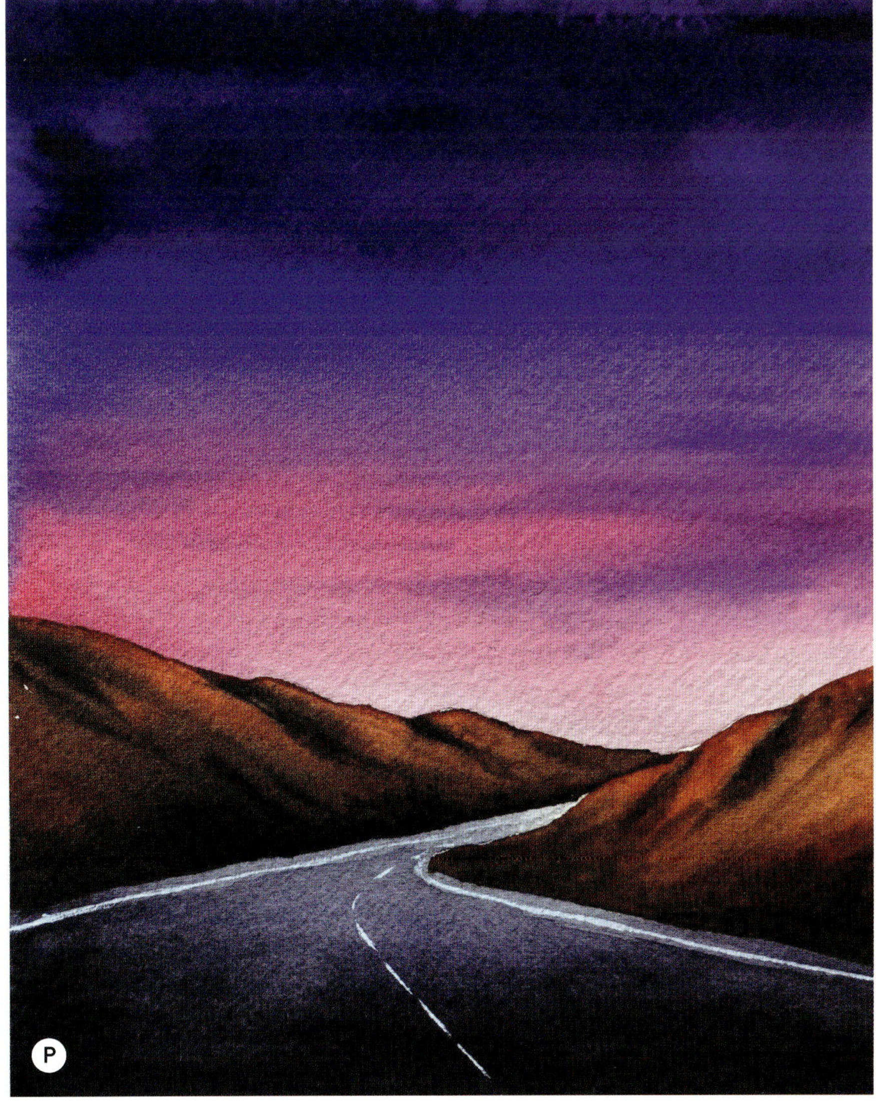

Step 5: Final Details. Use white gouache or white watercolor and a pointed brush and add the road markings by following the curve of the road. Add a dashed line in the middle and continuous lines on either side. (P)

DREAMY EVENING

We're using four colors to paint this dreamy evening sky. With this exercise, you'll become more confident blending colors. To make the painting extra impressive, we'll add a mountain that glows in the evening sun.

Suggested Color Palette

- Permanent Violet
- Permanent Rose
- Cadmium Orange
- Cadmium Yellow
- Burnt Sienna
- Payne's Grey

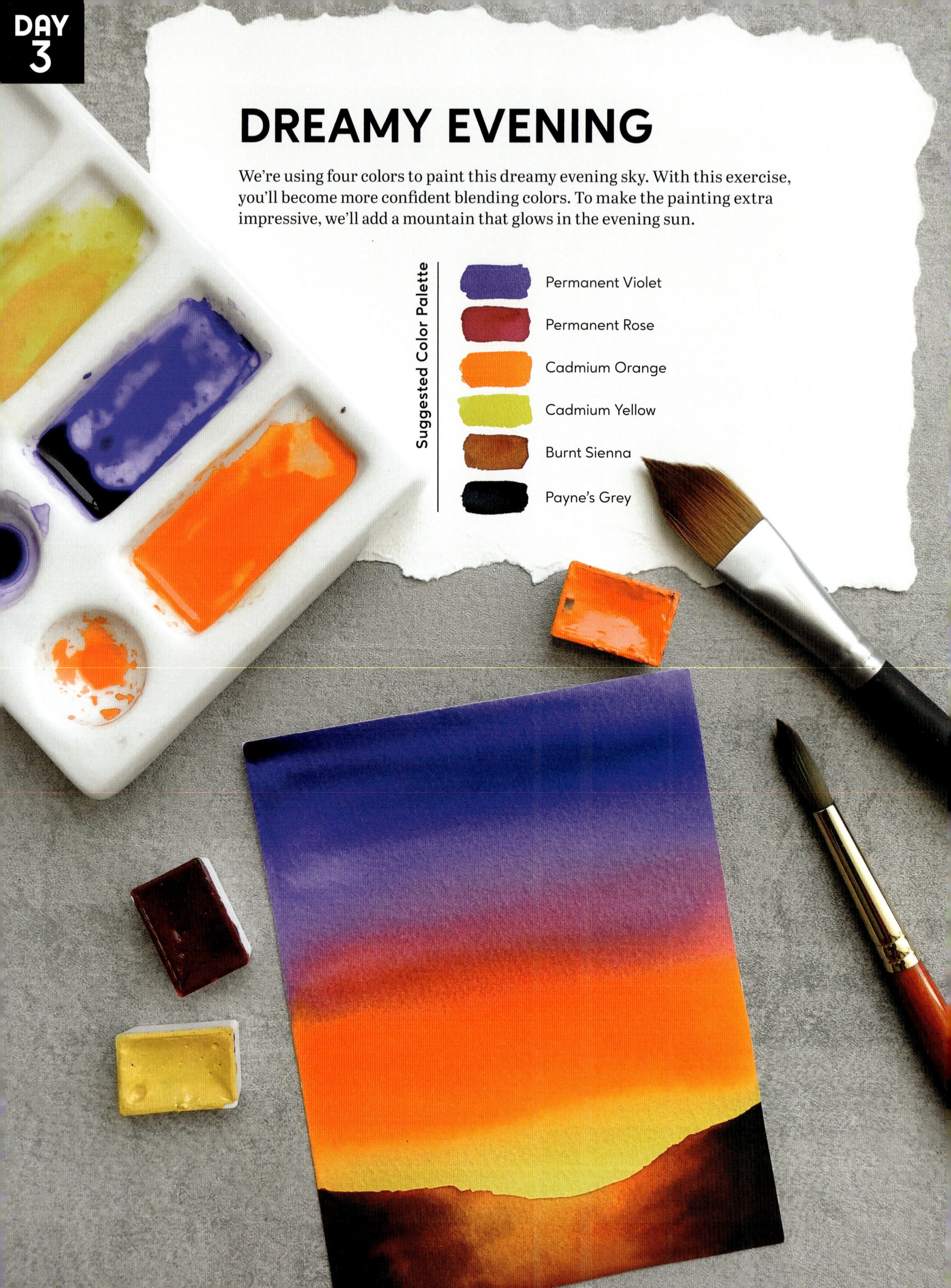

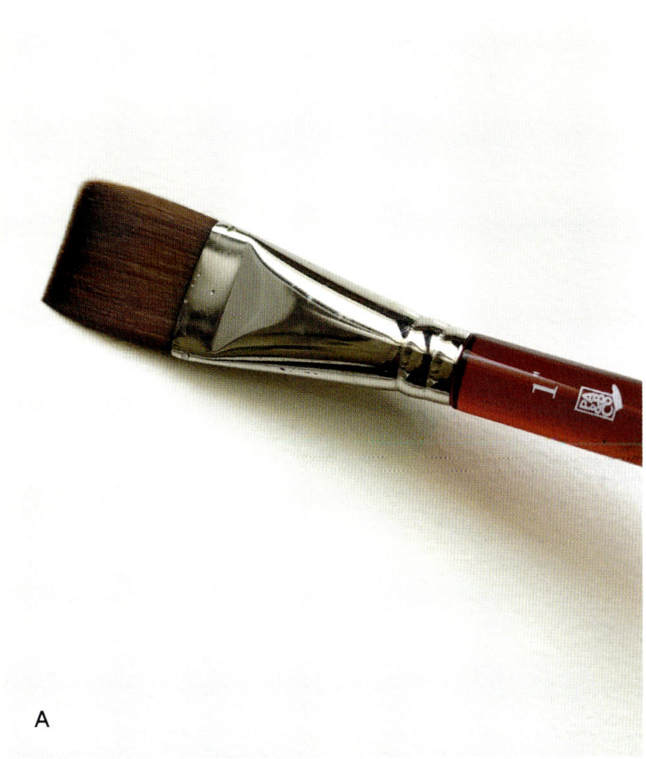
A

B

Step 1: Securing and Wetting the Paper. Secure your paper to a drawing board. Apply an even layer of clean water to the entire paper. (A)

Step 2: Sky. Load up a flat brush with an intense tone of Permanent Violet and apply it to the top. (B)

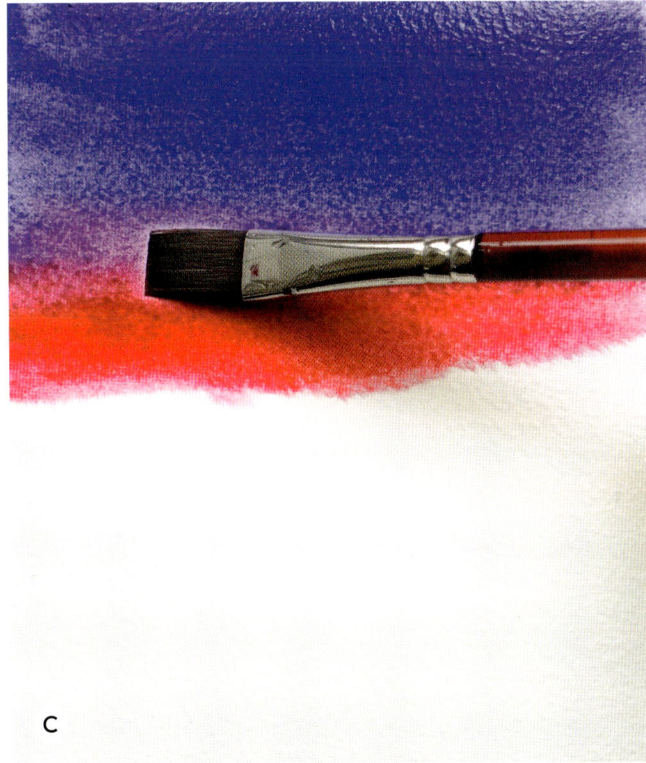
C

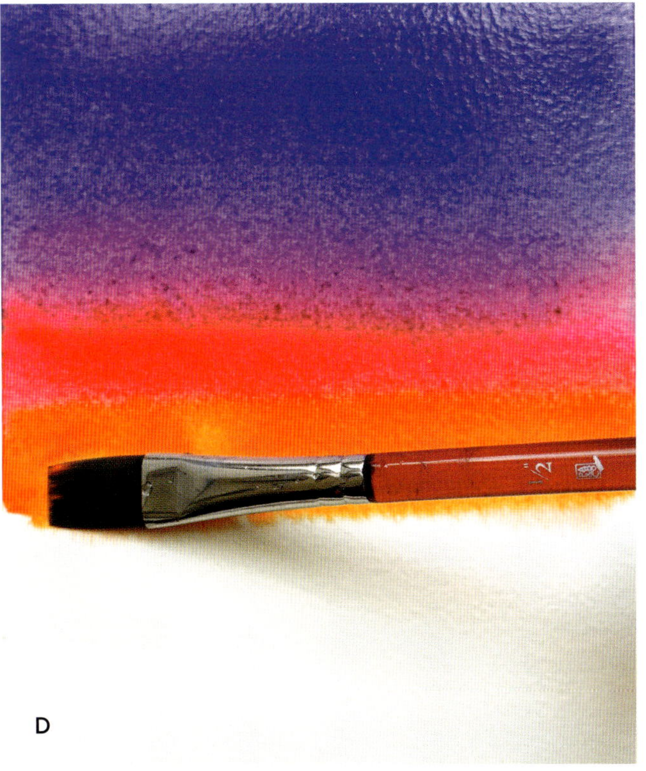
D

Once you reach one-quarter of the way down, clean your brush and switch to Permanent Rose. Apply it evenly, moving the brush horizontally from left to right. (C)

Clean your brush again and switch to Cadmium Orange and blend it with the Permanent Rose. (D)

(continued)

E

F

Repeat the same step with the Cadmium Yellow to complete the sky. (E, F)

tips

- *When blending four different colors for the sky, you have to work fast. Prepare the colors in advance so that you don't waste any precious time.*
- *Tailor the color ratios to your own taste. If you want more Permanent Violet in your sky, add more of that color and reduce the other colors. The same applies to all four colors.*

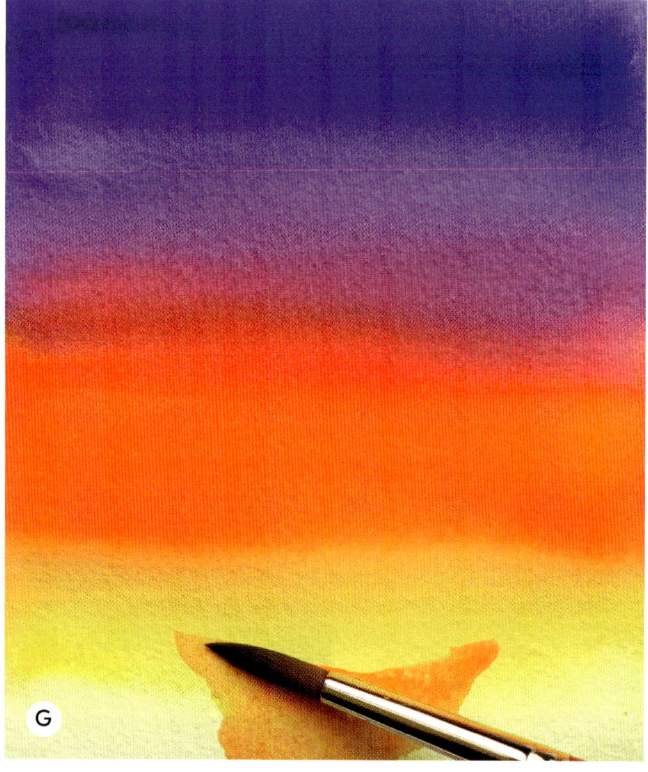

G

Step 3: Mountain. Start with a medium shade of Cadmium Orange and add it in the middle. I'm adding a saddle in the mountain ridge. Use a medium-size round brush to paint the mountain. (G)

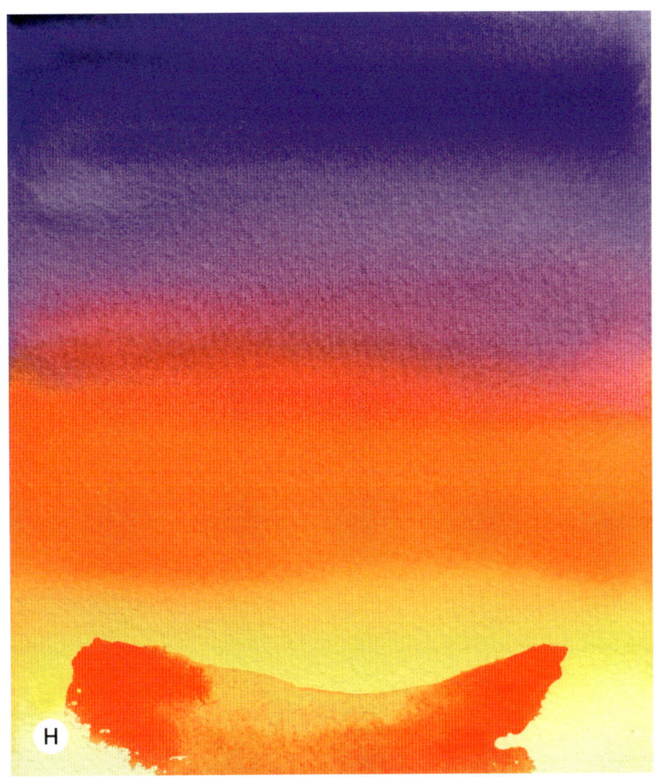

Continue to build up the colors on both sides using a much more intense tone of Cadmium Orange. (H)

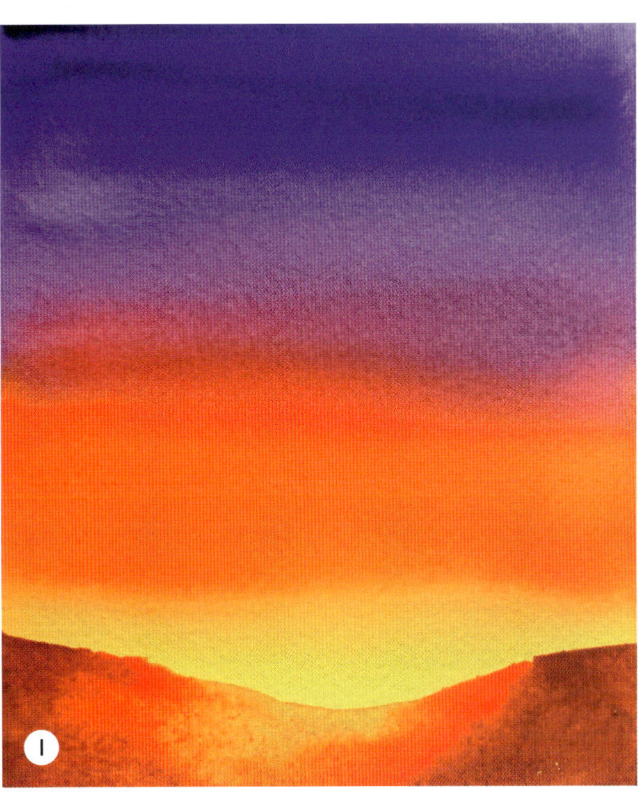

Repeat the same step with Burnt Sienna to complete the shape of the mountain. (I)

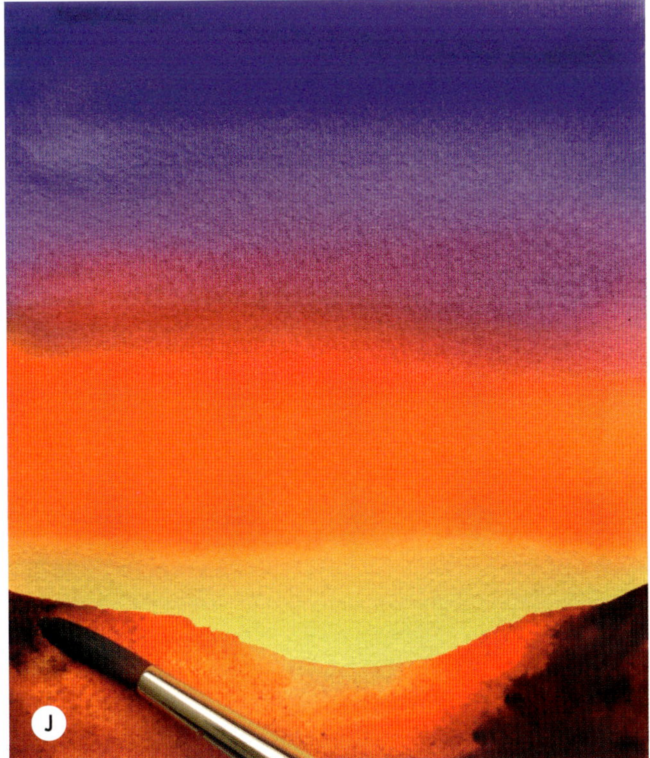

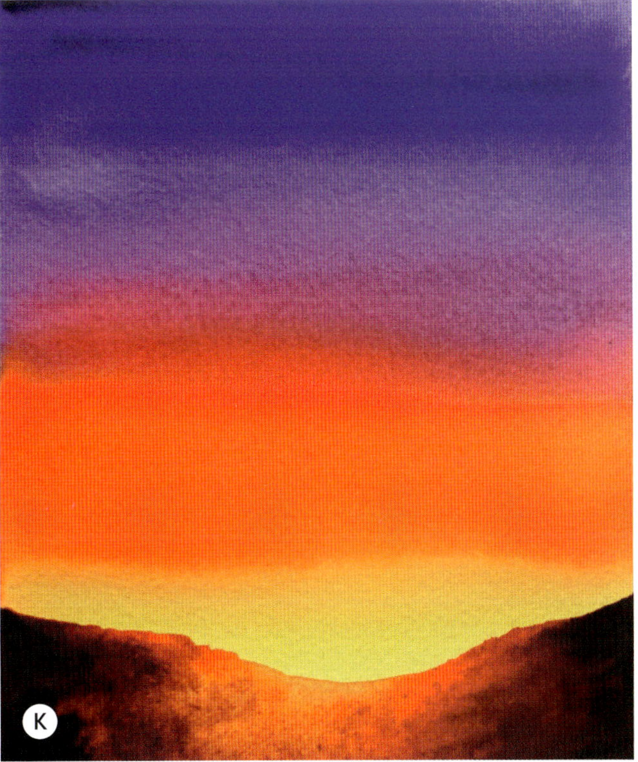

Add a darker shade of Burnt Sienna to both sides. (J) Gently keep smudging the colors into each other to create a smooth transition. (K) You can repeat this step if you want to make the colors even more intense.

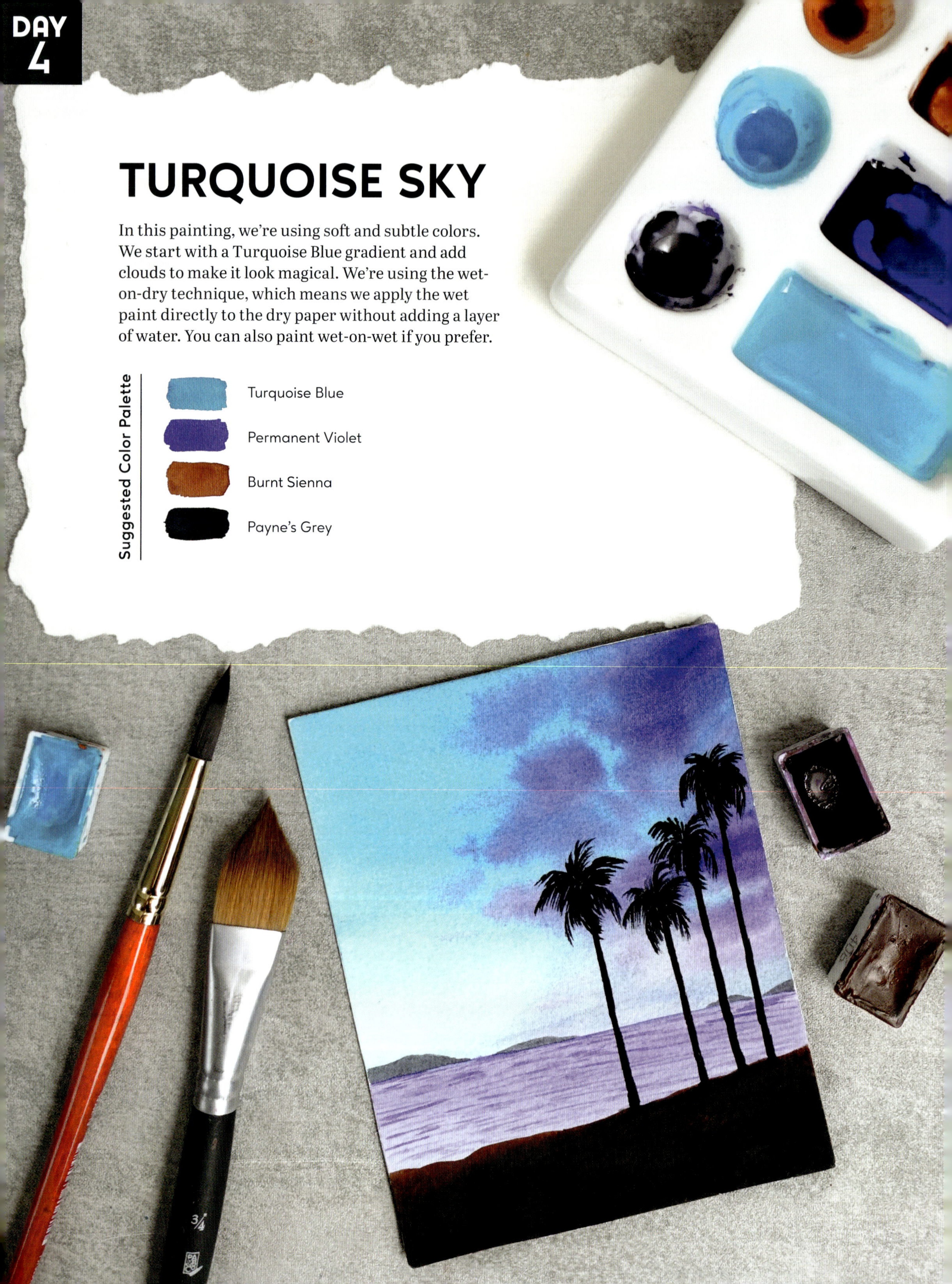

TURQUOISE SKY

In this painting, we're using soft and subtle colors. We start with a Turquoise Blue gradient and add clouds to make it look magical. We're using the wet-on-dry technique, which means we apply the wet paint directly to the dry paper without adding a layer of water. You can also paint wet-on-wet if you prefer.

Suggested Color Palette

- Turquoise Blue
- Permanent Violet
- Burnt Sienna
- Payne's Grey

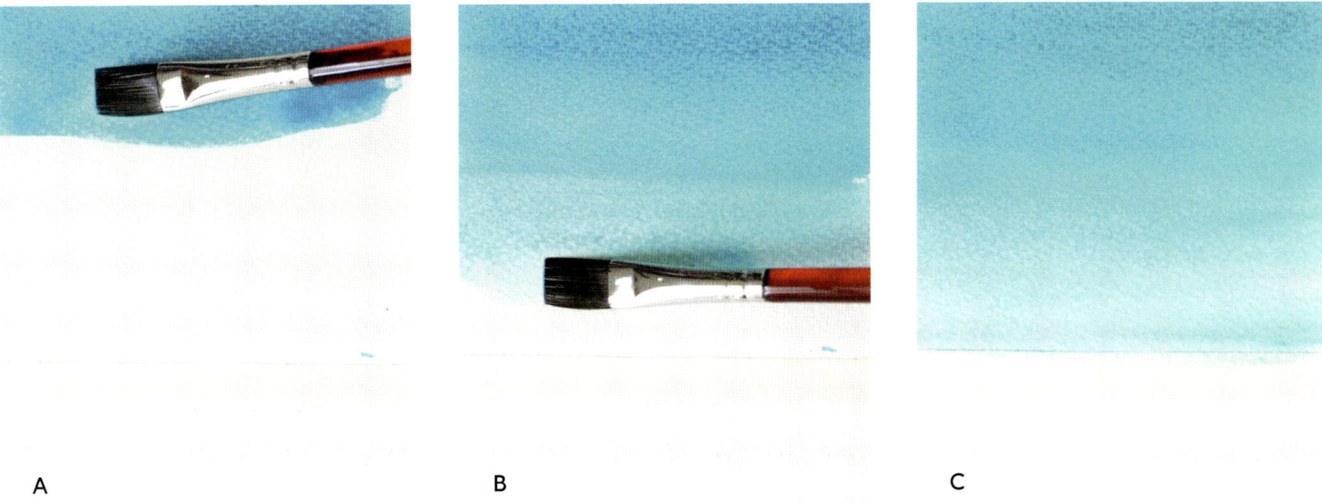

Step 1: Securing and Masking the Paper; Painting the Sky. Secure your paper to a drawing board. Place a piece of masking tape slightly below the center of the paper to separate the sky and the sea. Load your flat brush with a medium value of Turquoise Blue and paint half the sky. (A) Quickly rinse your brush and continue with even horizontal brushstrokes until you reach the horizon line, adding clean water as necessary to lighten the color. (B, C)

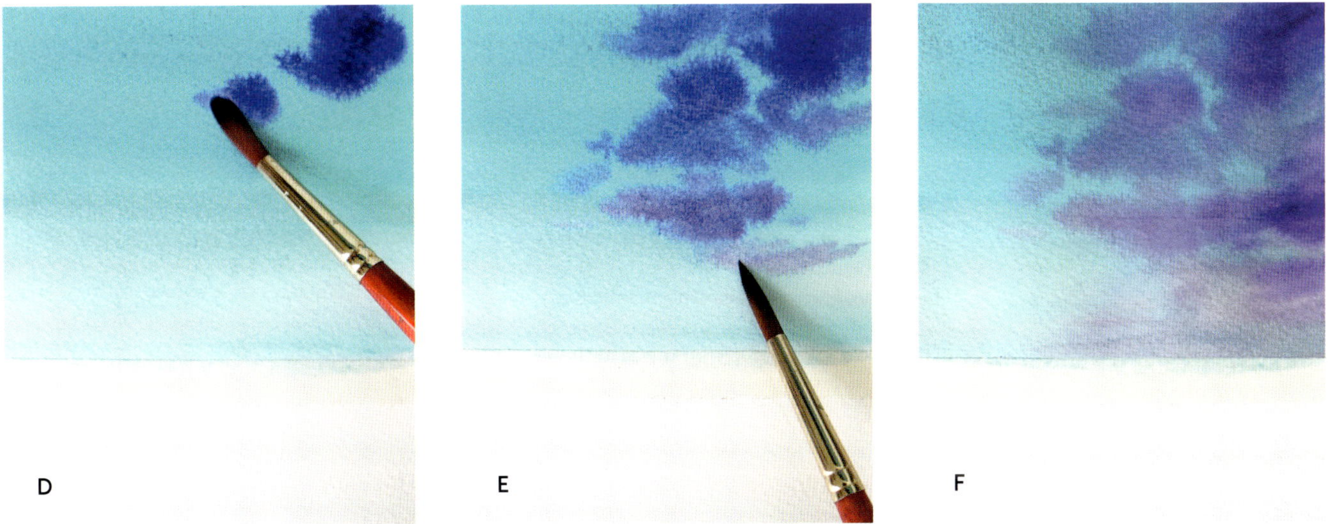

Step 2: Clouds. To add the clouds, we'll work with the wet-on-wet technique, which means we need to act quickly and add the clouds while the background layer is still wet. Choose a medium tone of Permanent Violet and add the clouds with a round brush. (D) Just as we painted the background layer toward the horizon line, use a lighter shade of Permanent Violet when adding the clouds closer to the horizon. (E) Let dry completely. (F)

(continued)

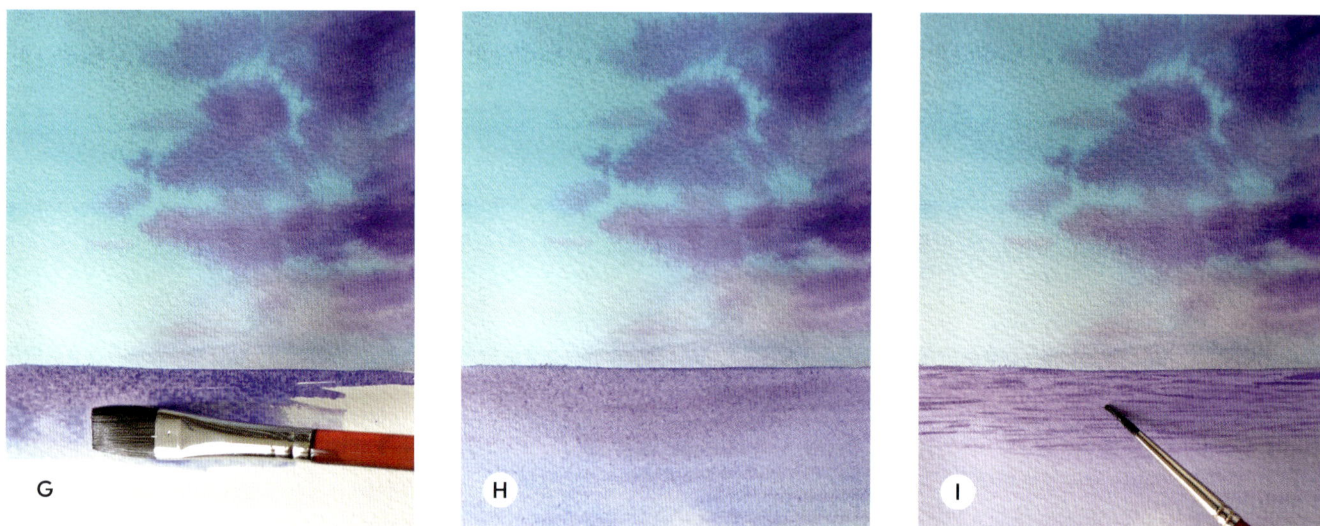

Step 3: Sea. Carefully peel off the masking tape. Use the wet-on-dry technique and paint the entire bottom part in a light value of Permanent Violet. (G) Let dry completely. (H) The sea looks pretty flat, so let's add some details to make it more interesting. Switch to a smaller brush and paint small lines in the top half with a medium purple shade. The lines don't have to be evenly spaced, just fill in the top half as shown. (I)

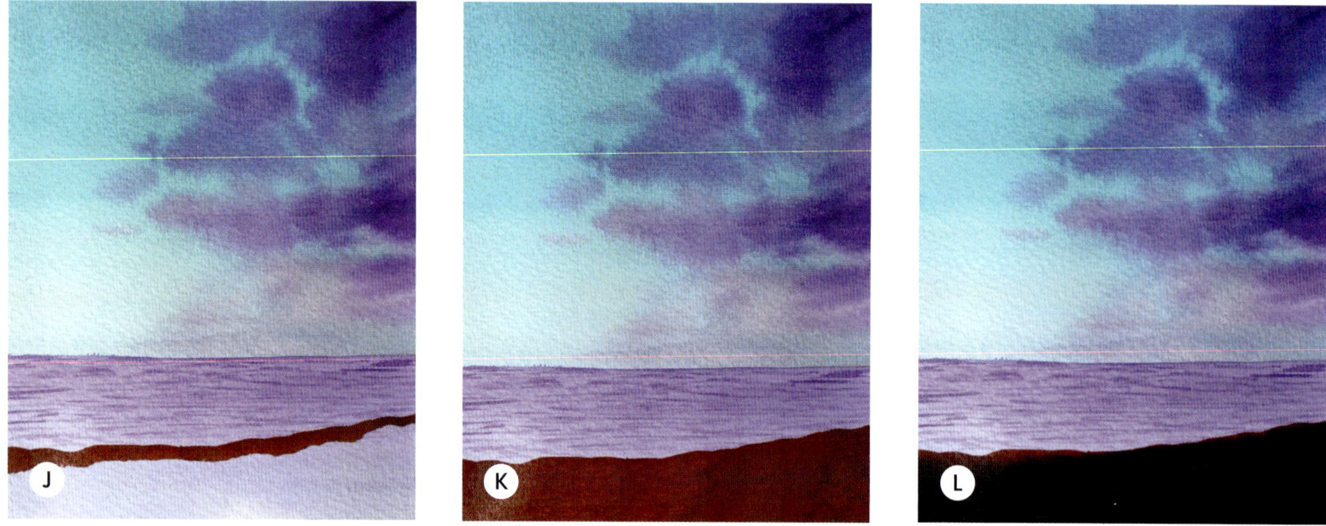

Step 4: Shore. Start by adding an irregular line with a medium value of Burnt Sienna. (J) Now that you've separated the shore and the sea, switch to a darker value of Burnt Sienna (Payne's Grey + Burnt Sienna) and fill in the beach. (K, L)

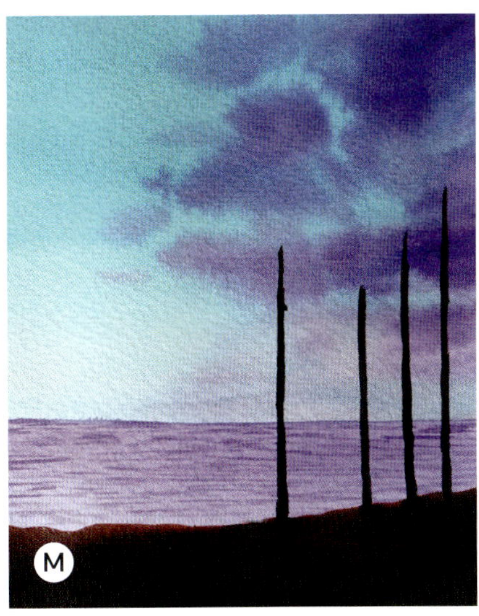

Step 6: Palm Trees. We'll add four palm trees, using Payne's Grey. Start with the tree trunks, making them different heights. (M)

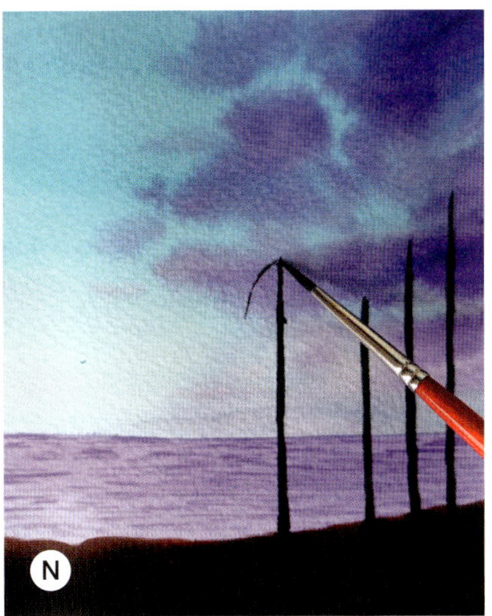

Add the frond stems using a detailing brush or a brush with a pointed tip. (N) Add leaves to the frond stems (O).

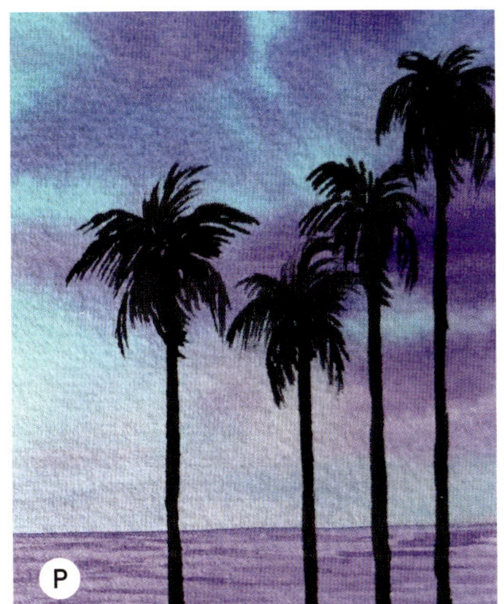

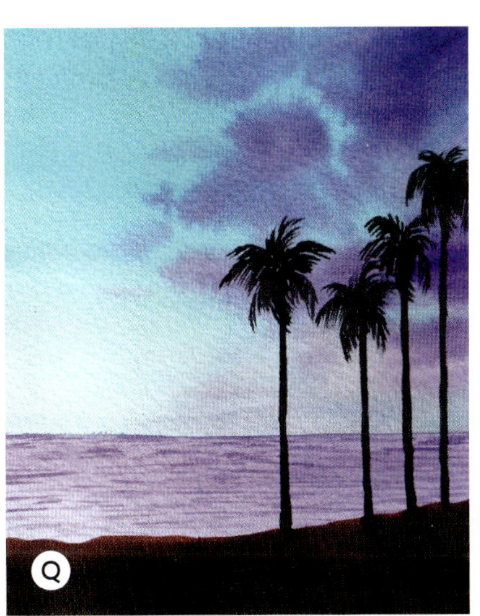

Repeat to fill in the leaves on each tree. (P, Q)

Add a few small mountains along the horizon line to finish the painting. To make it look like the horizon line is far away, use a lighter value of Payne's Grey. (R)

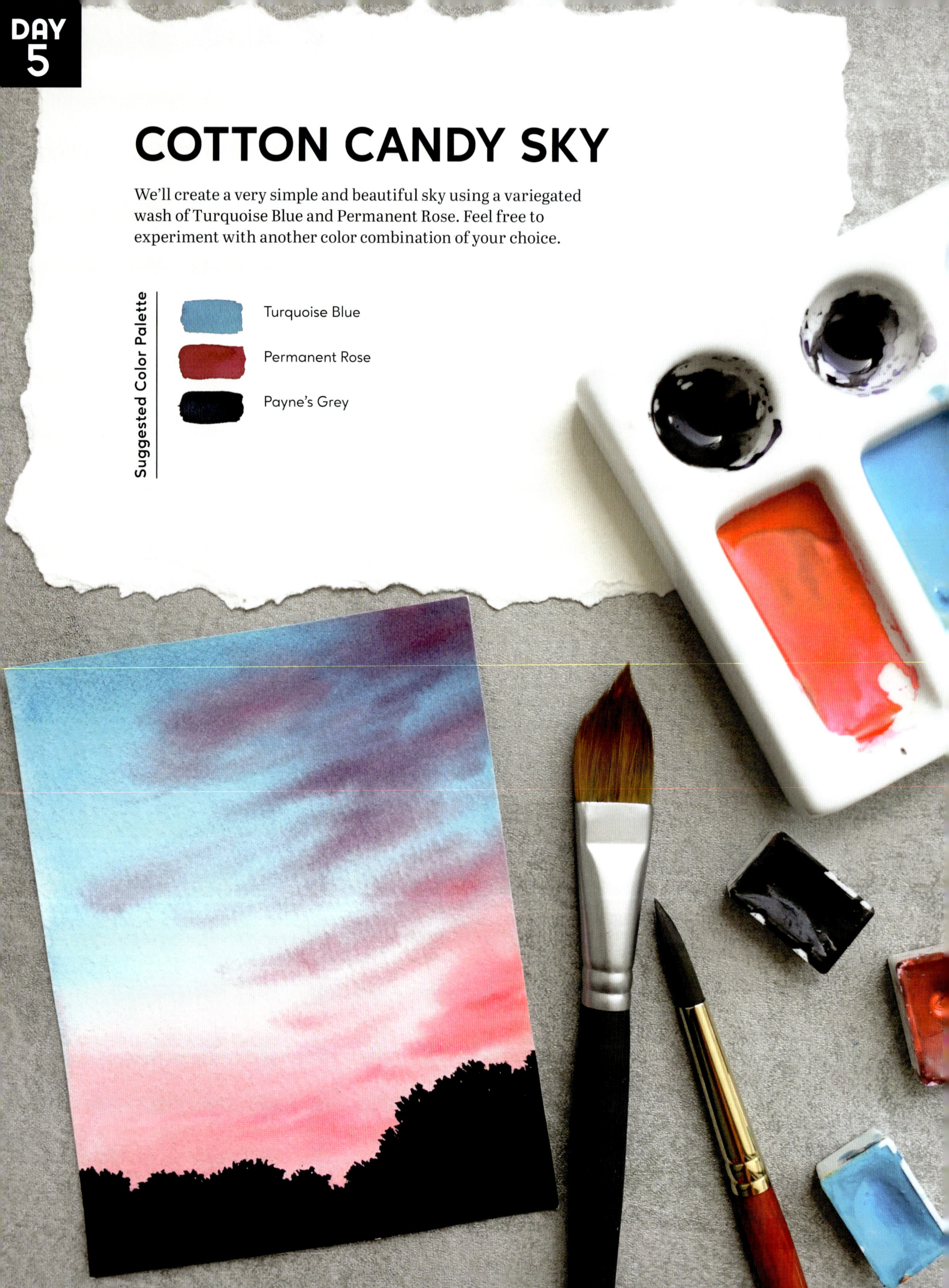

DAY 5

COTTON CANDY SKY

We'll create a very simple and beautiful sky using a variegated wash of Turquoise Blue and Permanent Rose. Feel free to experiment with another color combination of your choice.

Suggested Color Palette

- Turquoise Blue
- Permanent Rose
- Payne's Grey

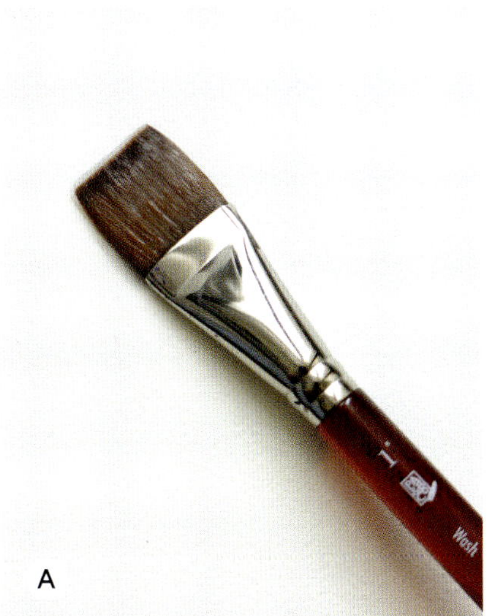

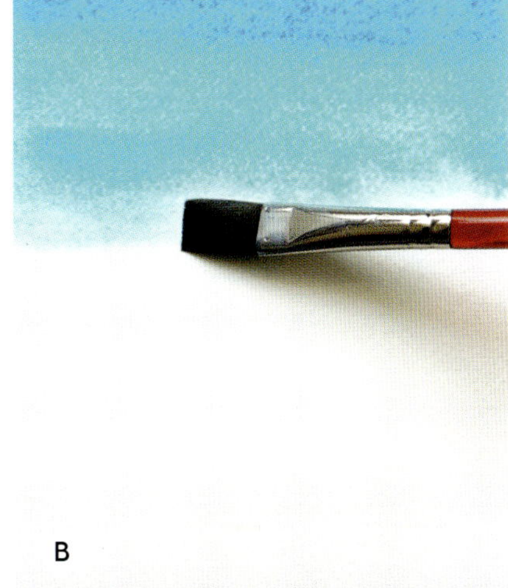

Step 1: Securing and Wetting the Paper. Secure your paper to a drawing board. Apply an even coat of clean water to the entire paper. (A)

Step 2: Sky—Base Layer. Paint the base layer using medium values of Turquoise Blue and Permanent Rose. Start with a medium value of Turquoise Blue and paint downward using a flat or round brush. (B) Quickly rinse your brush and continue with even horizontal brushstrokes until you reach halfway, adding clean water as necessary to lighten the color. (C)

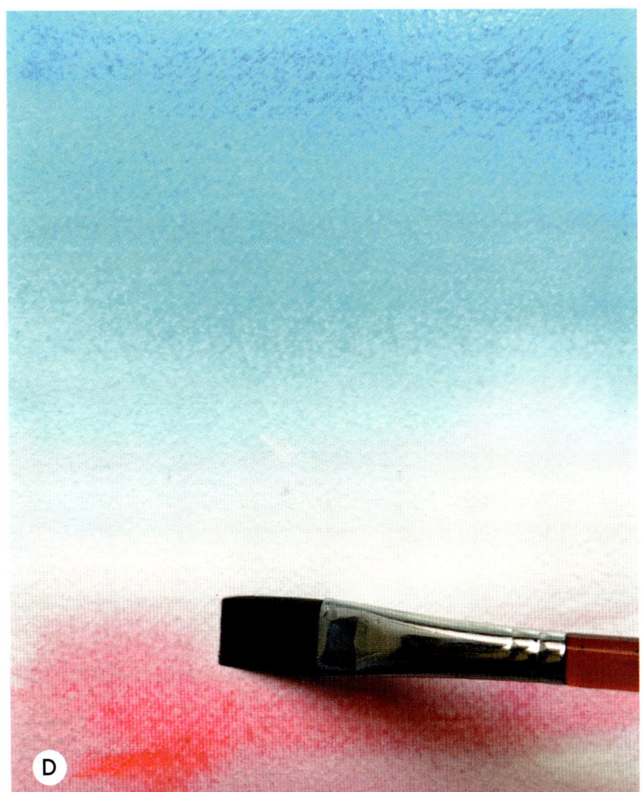

Clean your brush and switch to a medium value of Permanent Rose. Start adding it from the bottom and paint upward. (D) As you're about to reach the Turquoise Blue, quickly rinse your brush and continue with even horizontal strokes until you reach the Turquoise Blue, adding clean water as necessary to lighten the color. (E)

(continued)

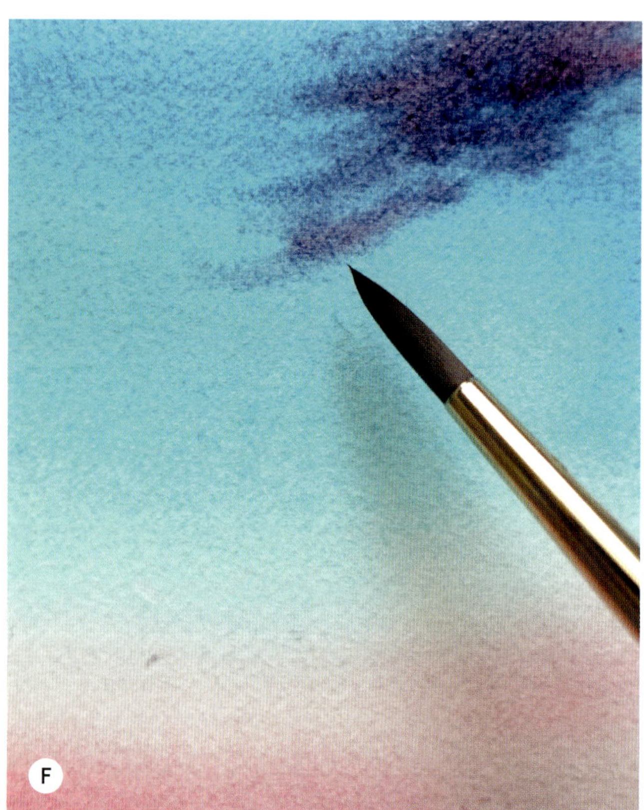

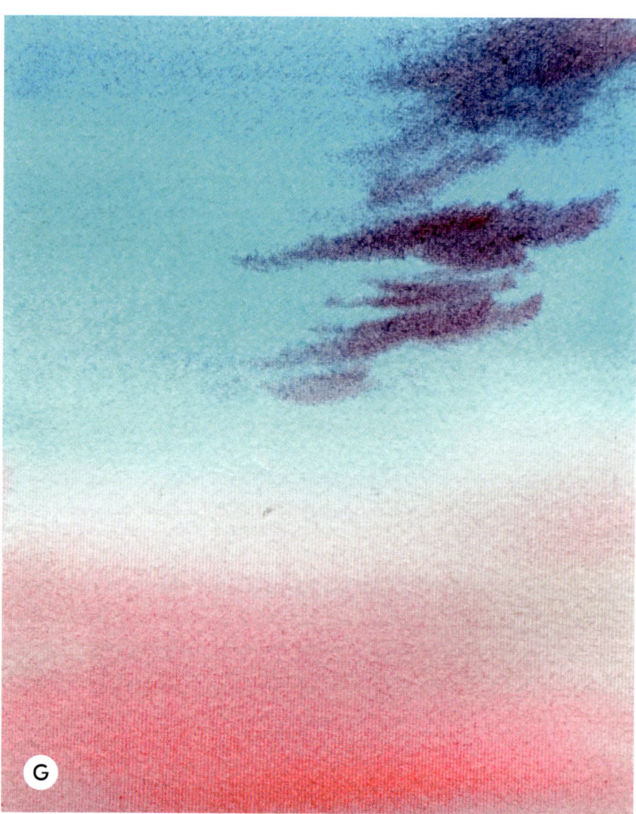

Step 3: Clouds. We'll use wet-on-wet technique to create the clouds. Use a medium-size round brush and load a brighter value of Permanent Rose. (F) While the background is still wet, drop Permanent Rose in a very random way to create some clouds. They can be of different sizes and shapes. (G)

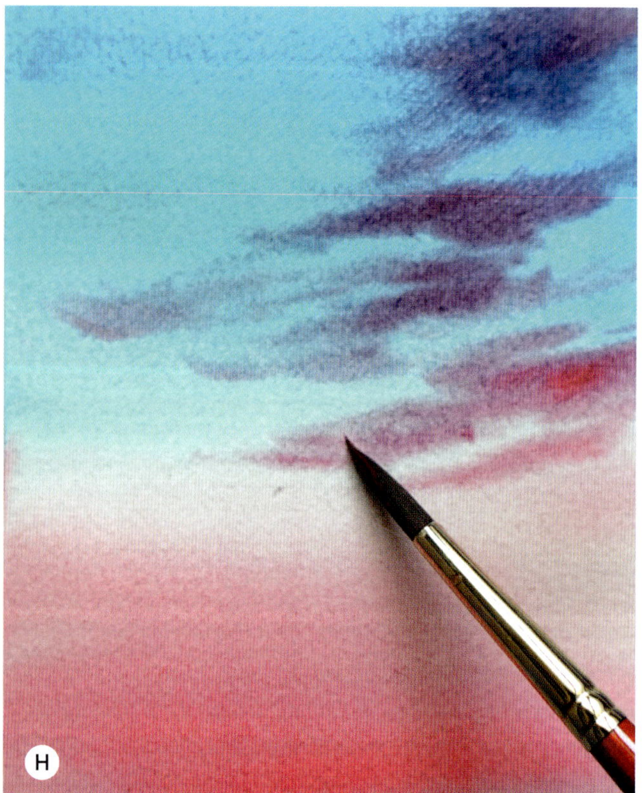

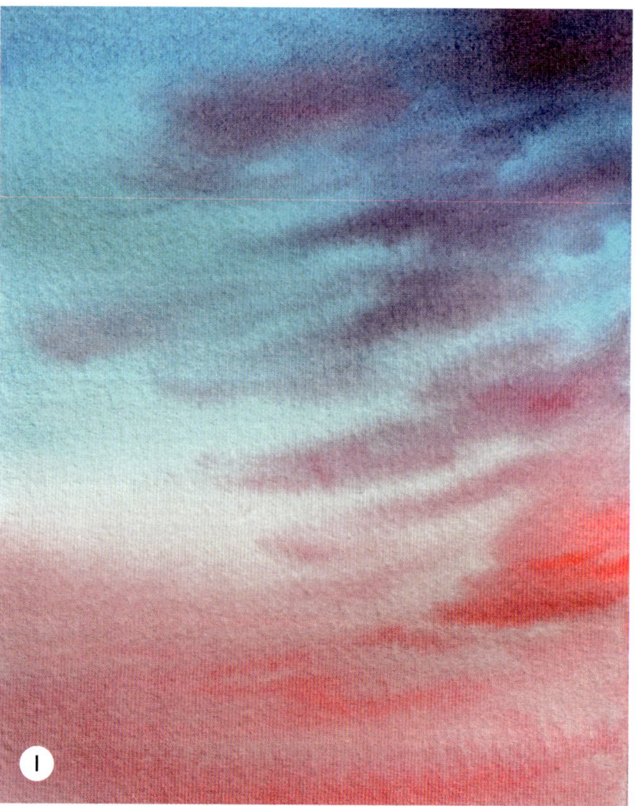

Don't add too many clouds. Our aim is to achieve a soft sky. (H, I) With a lot of clouds the sky will look dramatic and will negate that calm and peaceful feel. Let dry completely.

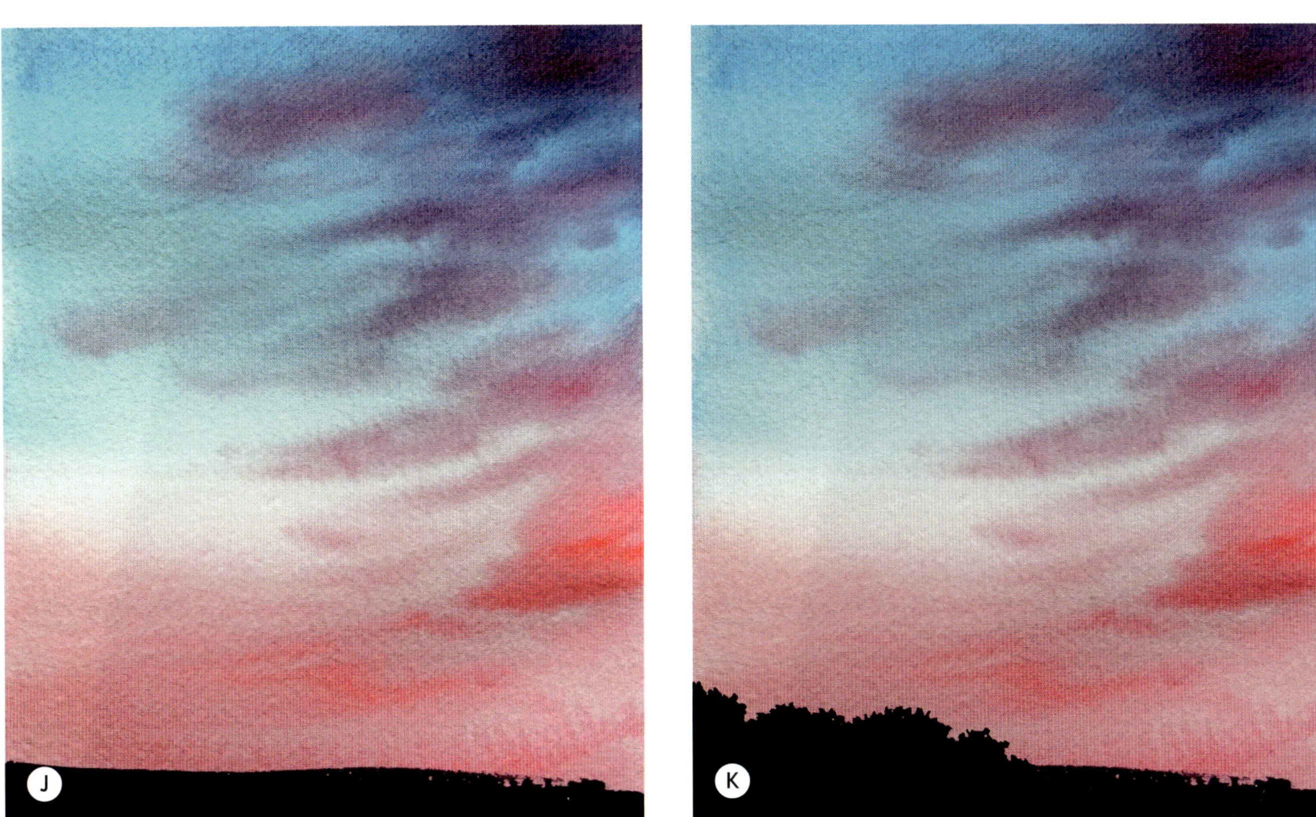

Step 4: Details. For this painting, we're going with a simple silhouette. Start by adding a thick band of trees and plants using Payne's Grey. (J) Add random patterns for the branches and leaves using the tip of your brush. (K)

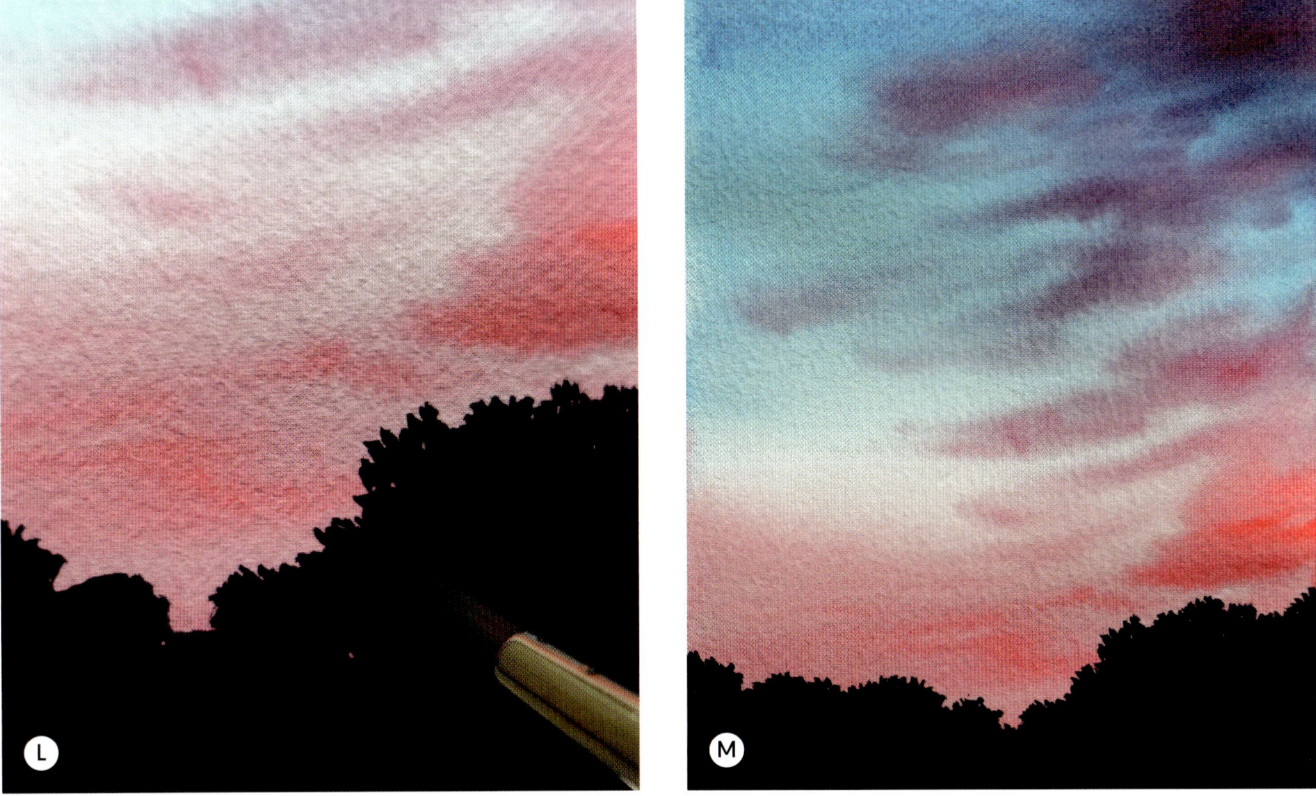

The branches and leaves don't need to be perfect. Keep adding them at various heights until it looks natural. (L, M)

STARRY NIGHT

Our next project is a dramatic starry night. We'll use bold and bright colors to create a night sky effect. For this project, we'll use the wet-on-dry technique so that the colors don't lose their opacity.

Suggested Color Palette

- Cerulean Blue
- Permanent Violet
- Turquoise Blue
- Payne's Grey

(plus white gouache or white watercolor)

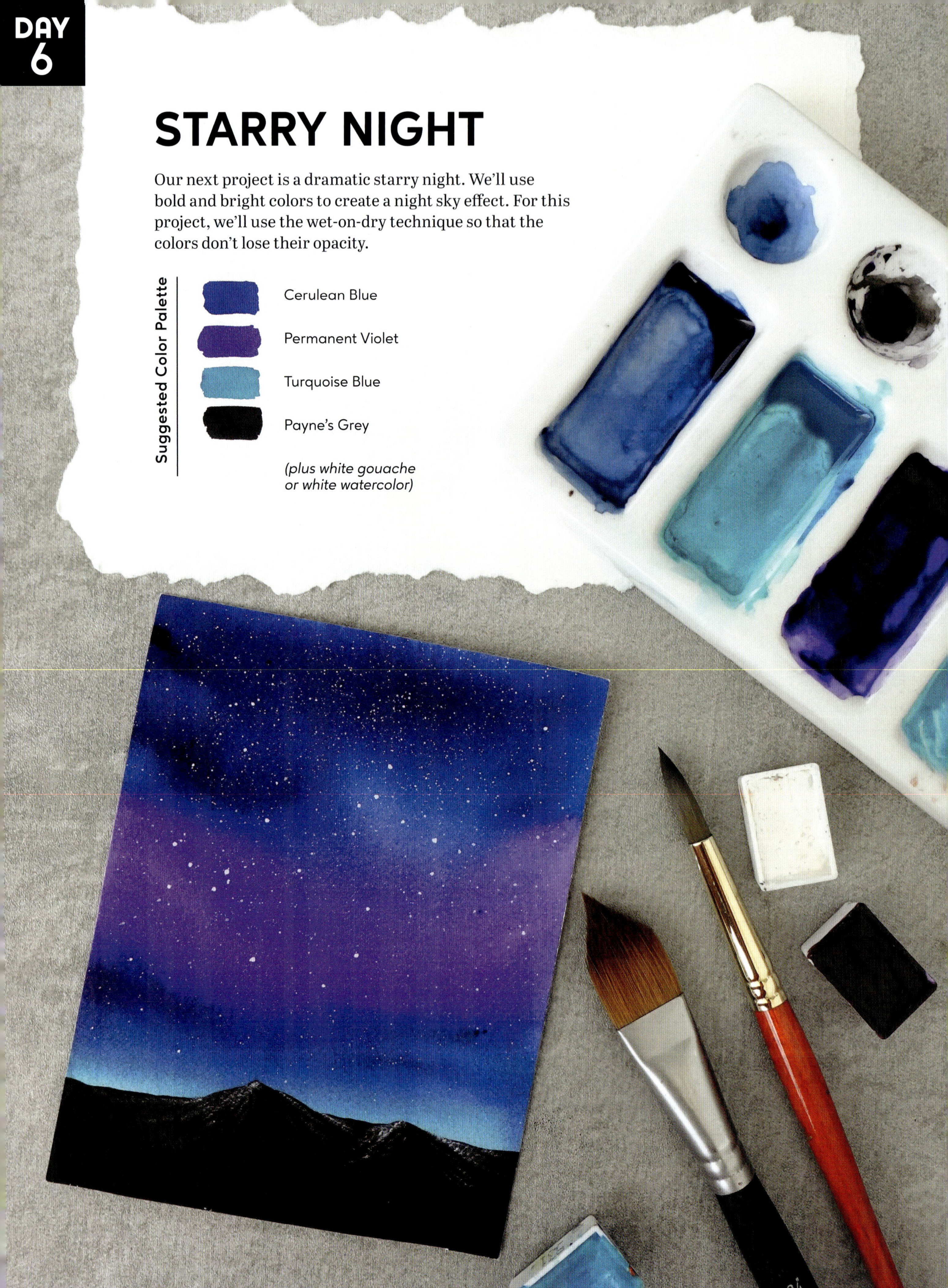

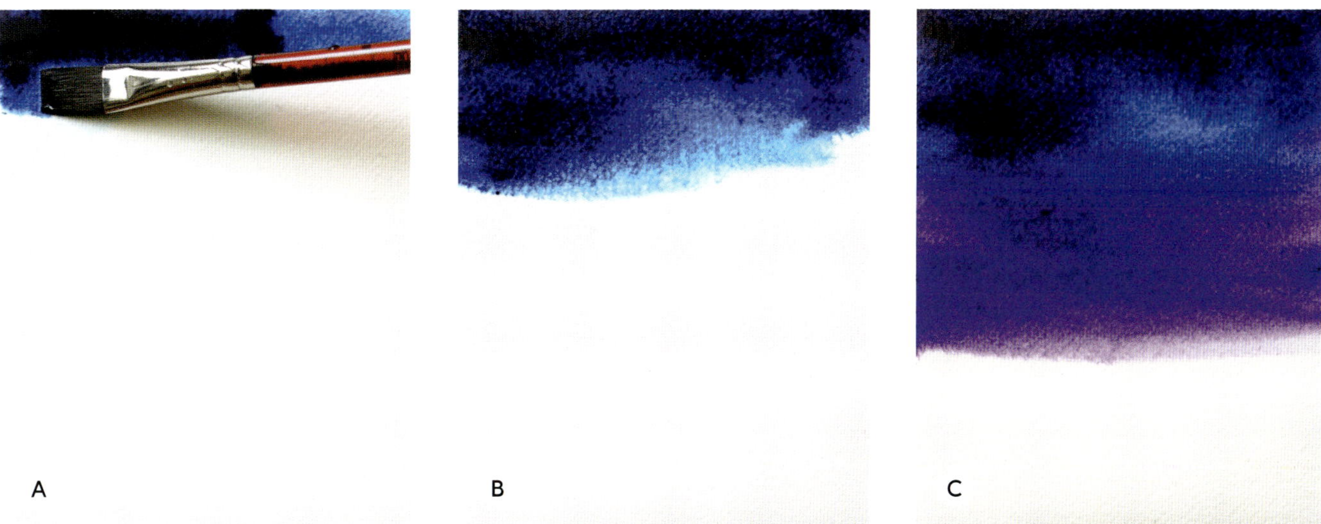

Step 1: Sky. Because we're using the wet-on-dry technique, you don't need to make the background wet, and you can directly lay the first color. You can use a medium-size flat brush or round brush. Start with a lighter value of Cerulean Blue (A) and paint downward until you fill a quarter of the sky. (B) Clean your brush and switch to Permanent Violet. Add it underneath the Cerulean Blue until you almost reach the center of the paper. (C)

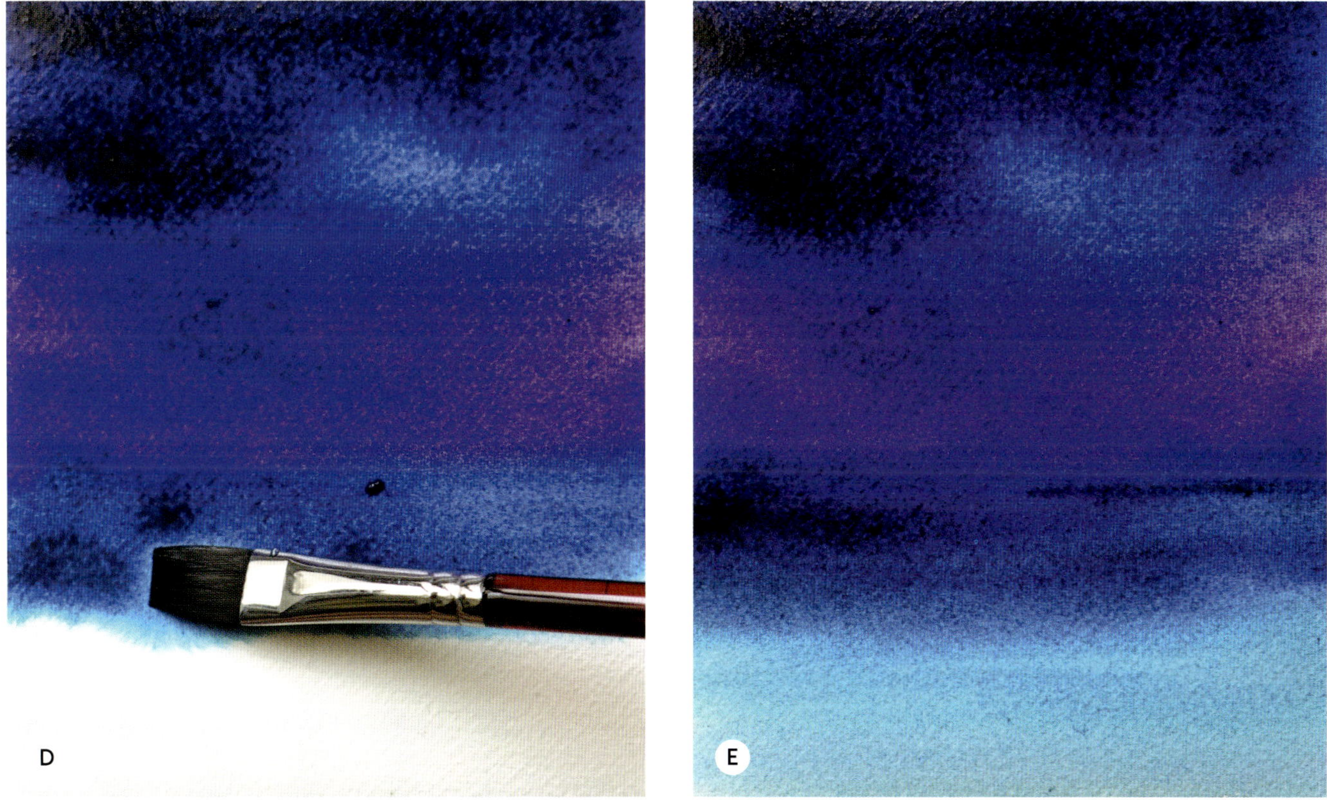

Clean your brush again and switch to Turquoise Blue (D) and paint downward. When you reach almost three-quarters of the paper, quickly rinse your brush and continue with even horizontal brushstrokes until you reach the bottom, adding clean water as necessary to lighten the color. (E) The background layer doesn't have to be even. It can have some lighter values and darker values in between to make the sky look more dramatic. Let dry completely.

(continued)

Step 2: Stars. To add the stars, you can use either white gouache or white watercolor. There are several methods to add the stars. I always prefer splattering them by tapping on my brush. This is a simple method.

Use white gouache or white watercolor. The consistency of the paint should not be too watery or too thick, but somewhere in between. Only add a few drops of water. The color will lose its opacity if you add too much water, and the stars won't be bright enough.

Load any of your smaller size brushes with the white paint. If you feel like your paint is too watery, you can dab the brush several times on a paper towel to remove the excess water. Tap on the brush using another brush and create as many stars as you want. (F)

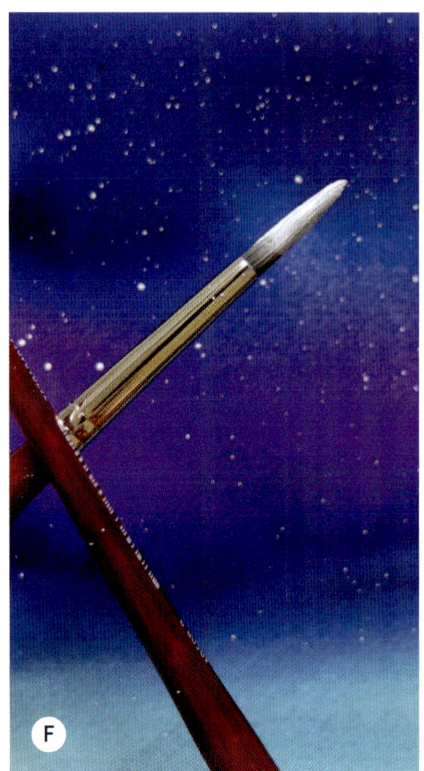
F

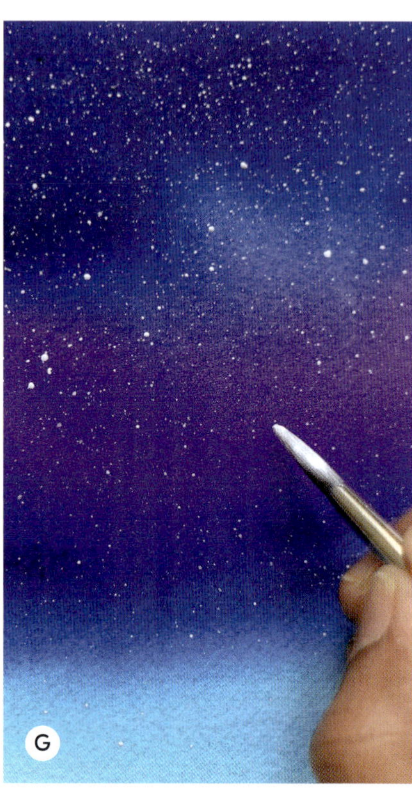
G

If needed, try splattering on a scrap piece of paper first to make sure the consistency is right. Using the same brush, add a few dots in a random way to show the bigger stars. (G)

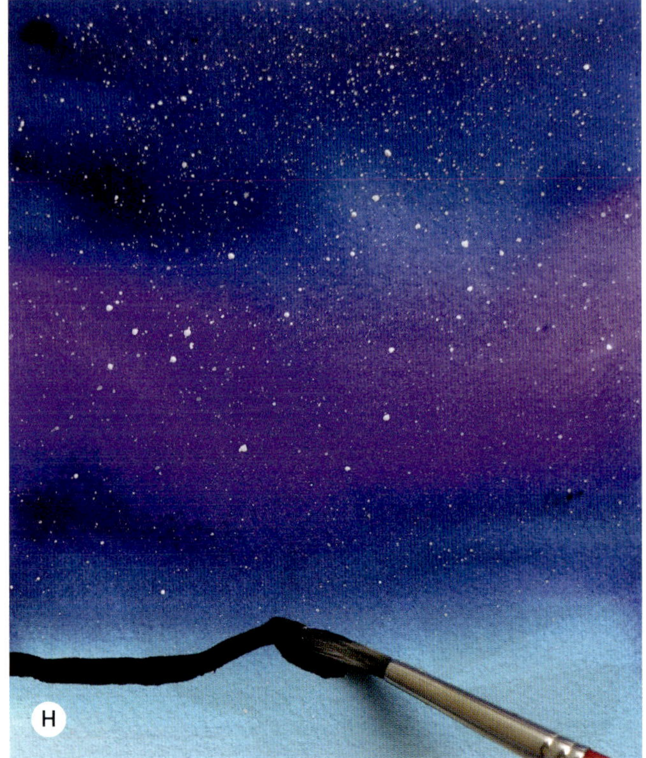
H

I

Step 3: Snowy Mountains. Add the basic shape of the mountain (H) and fill it in with a darker value of Payne's Grey. (I)

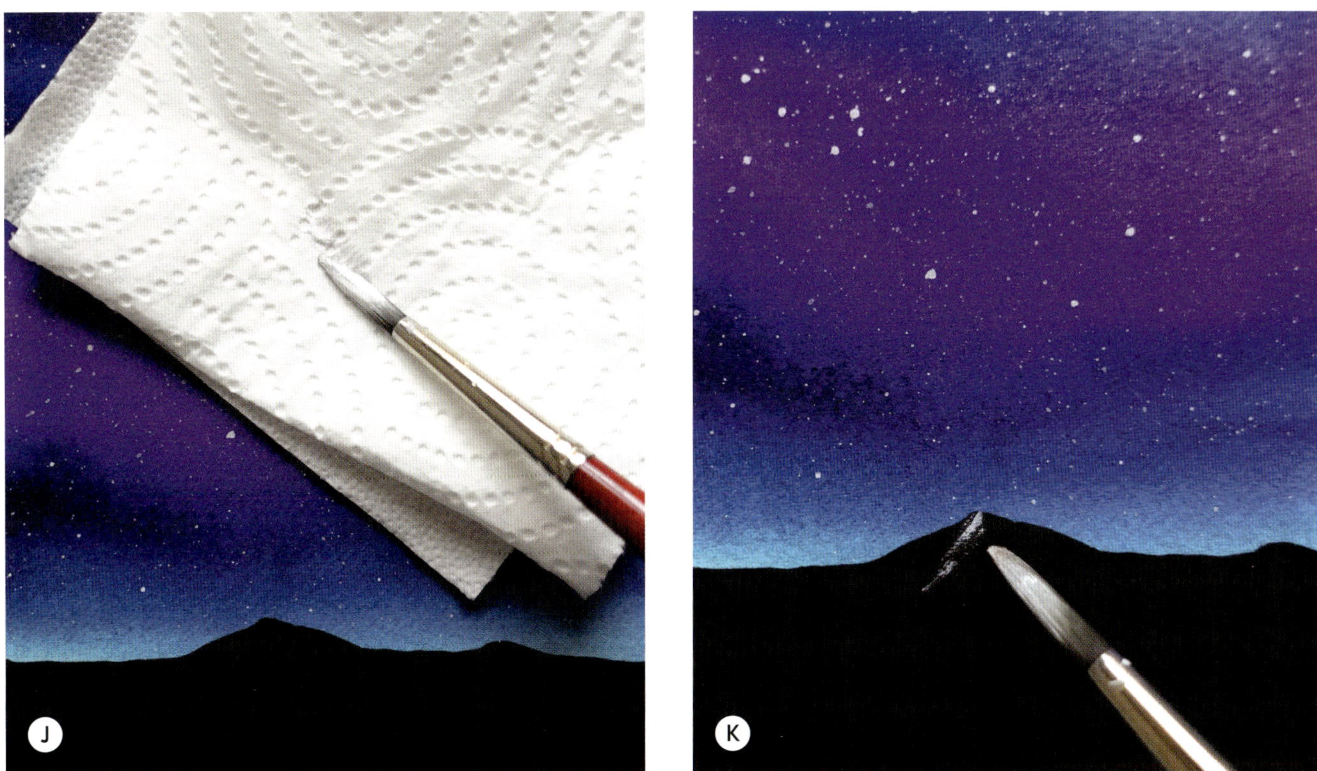

To give it a snowy feel, we need to introduce some white texture on the peaks of the mountains. For this we need dry paint. After loading the brush with white gouache or white watercolor, dab it several times on a paper towel to remove the excess water. (J) Starting at the peak of the mountain, add a few lines downward, making sure not to add too many. (K)

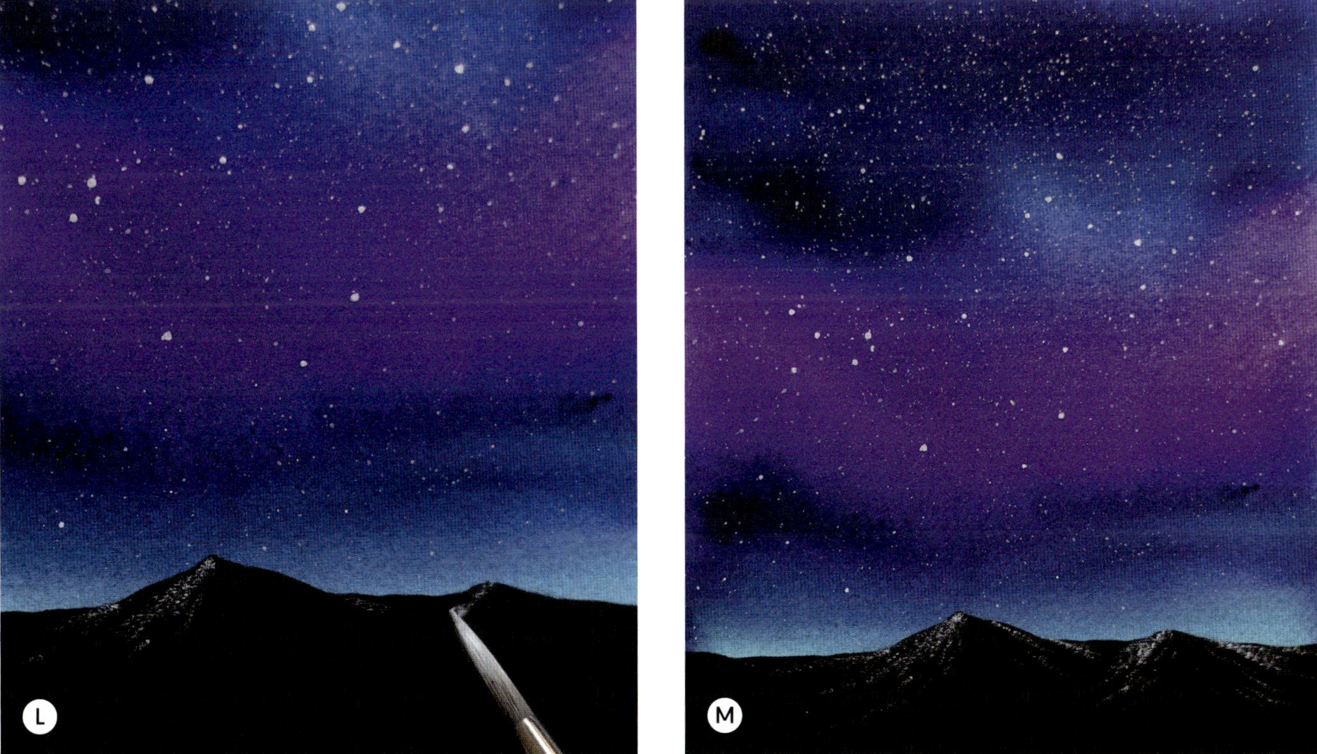

Finish the painting by repeating this step until you feel like you have achieved a snowy feel to your mountains. (L, M)

PURPLE SKY

This is a simple but very interesting painting where we'll mainly use two colors: Permanent Violet and Payne's Grey.

Suggested Color Palette

- Permanent Violet
- Payne's Grey

(plus white gouache or white watercolor)

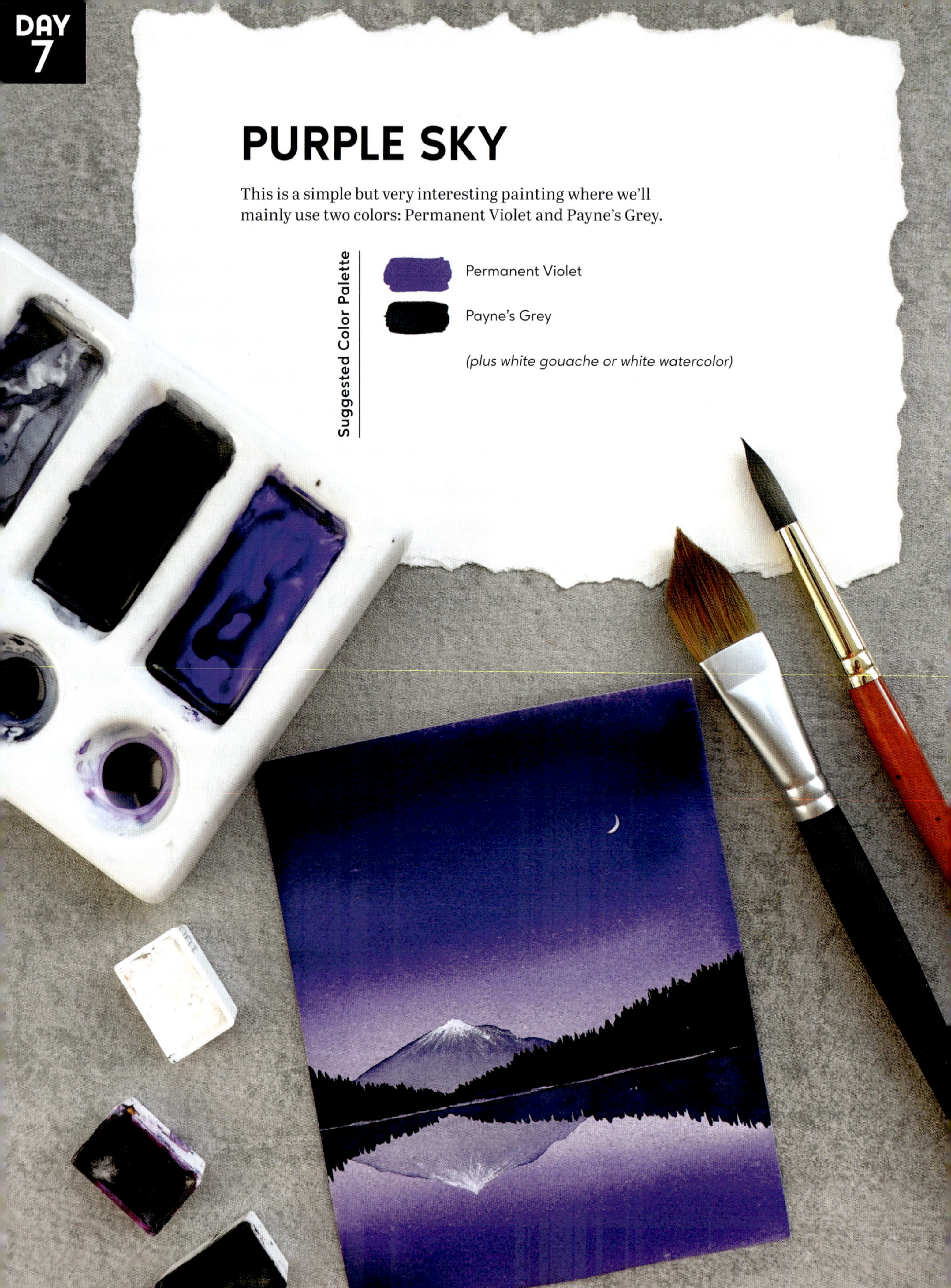

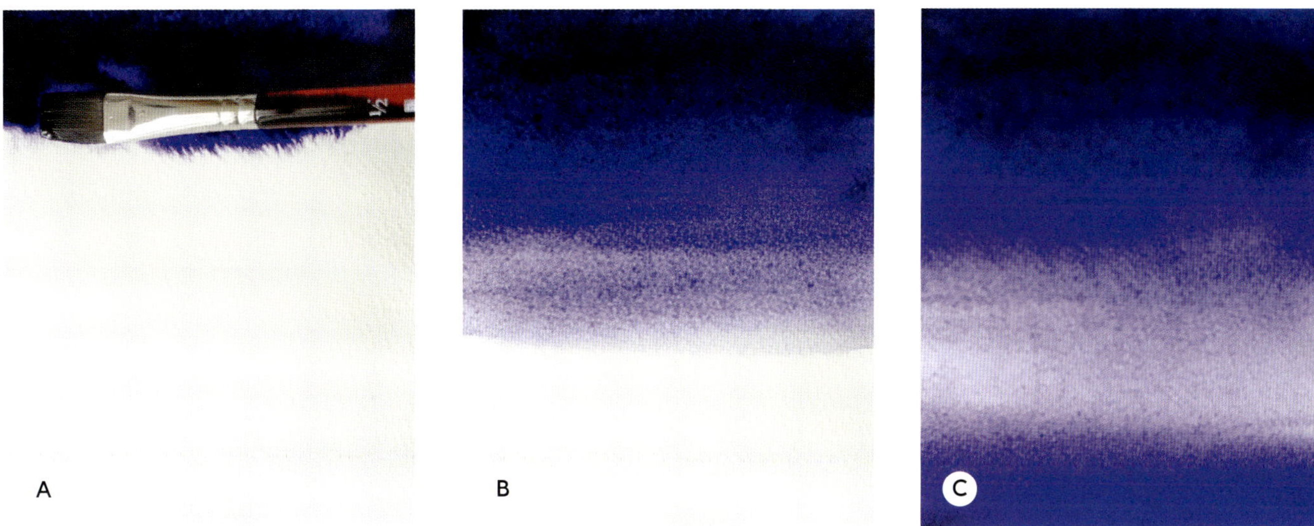

Step 1: Securing and Wetting the Paper; Sky—Base Layer. Secure your paper to a drawing board. Apply an even coat of clean water to the entire paper. Begin by painting the entire background plane. We'll assume that the horizon line is slightly below the center of the paper. Keep this in mind when you apply the colors. Using a flat brush, start with Permanent Violet and paint downward. (A) Once at the horizon line, quickly rinse your brush and continue with even horizontal brushstrokes until you reach three-quarters of the paper, adding clean water as necessary to lighten the color. (B) Add more Permanent Violet starting from the bottom. (C) Let dry completely.

Step 2: Mountains. Draw a horizon line slightly below the center of the paper. (D) The goal is to add the same details above and below the horizon line. We'll use medium values below the horizon line for the reflection and darker values above the horizon line for the details.

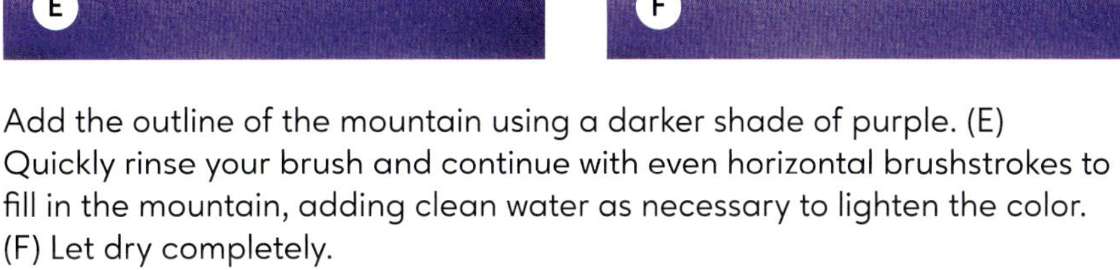

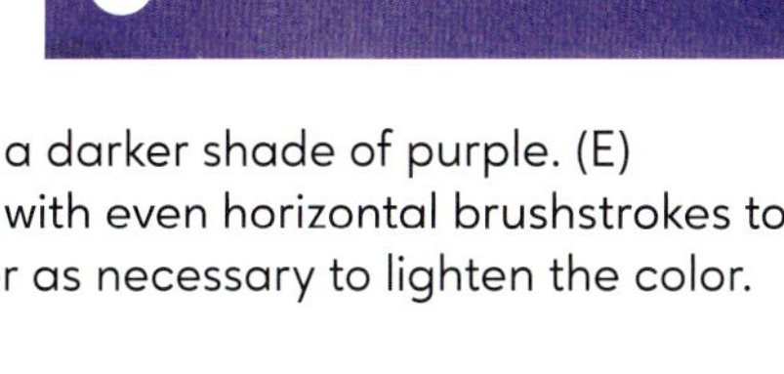

Add the outline of the mountain using a darker shade of purple. (E) Quickly rinse your brush and continue with even horizontal brushstrokes to fill in the mountain, adding clean water as necessary to lighten the color. (F) Let dry completely.

(continued)

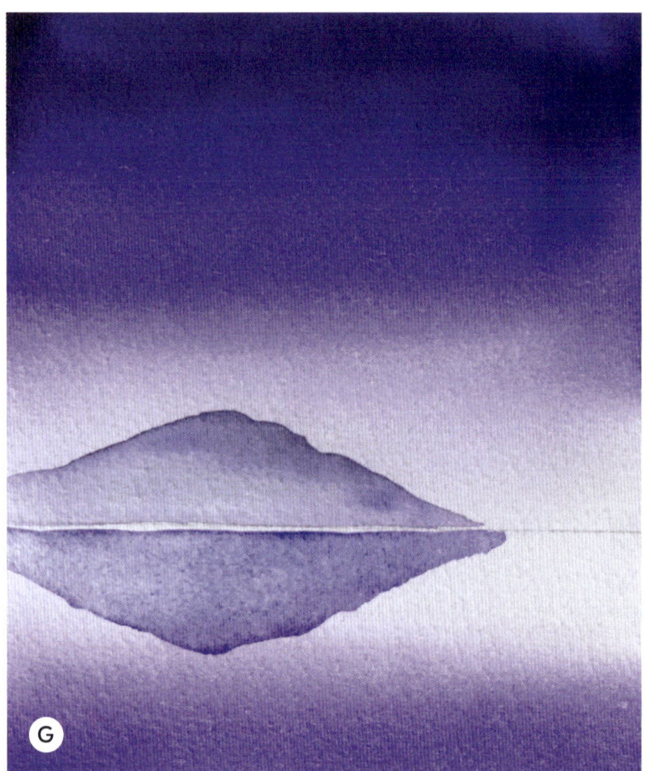

Use a slightly lighter value of the color you used for the mountain and add a similar shape below the horizon line, leaving a small gap. (G) Let it dry. Before proceeding with each step, it's important that the previous layer is completely dry; otherwise, the colors may spread into each other. Add some simple trees along the horizon line using Payne's Grey. Use the tip of the brush to paint in closely spaced lines. (H) Vary the height to make it look more natural, with taller trees on the sides and shorter trees in the middle. (I) Let dry completely.

Just as we added the reflection of the mountain, we need to create a reflection for the trees. (I) Go with a medium tone of Payne's Grey and add a mirror image of the trees under the horizon line. Don't forget to leave a small gap in between. (J)

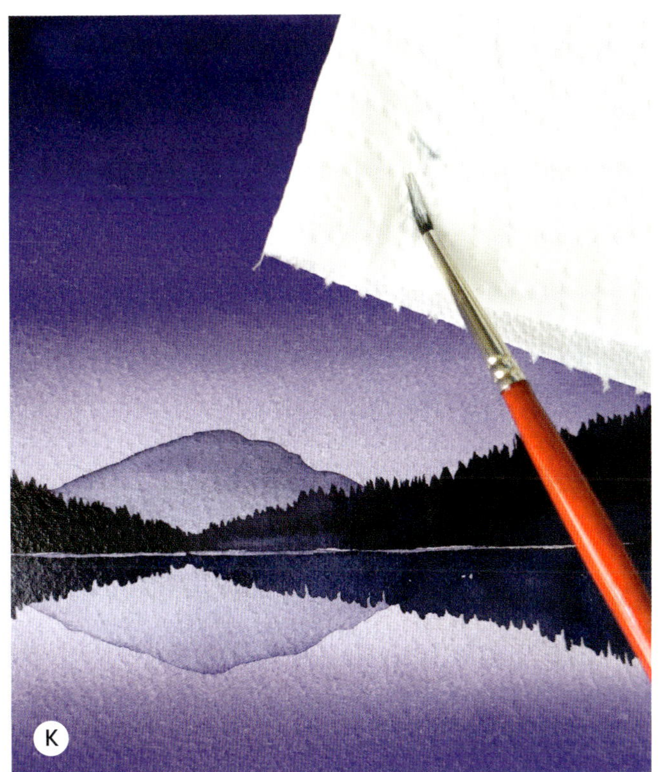

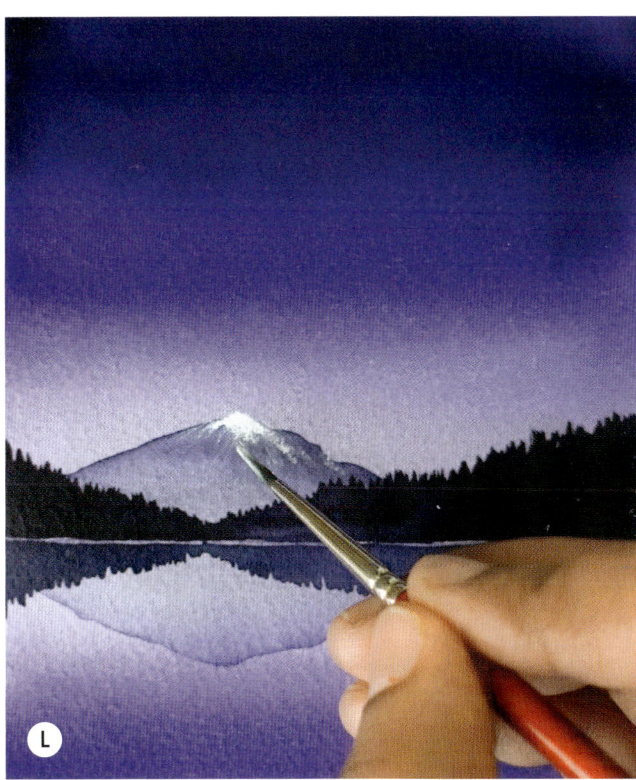

Step 3: Final Details. Use either white gouache or white watercolor for the final details. The first step is to paint snow on the mountain. For this, we need dry paint. Add a small amount of water to the white paint. After loading the brush with paint, dab it several times on a paper towel to remove the excess water. (K) Add some dry brushstrokes from the top of the mountain toward the bottom. (L)

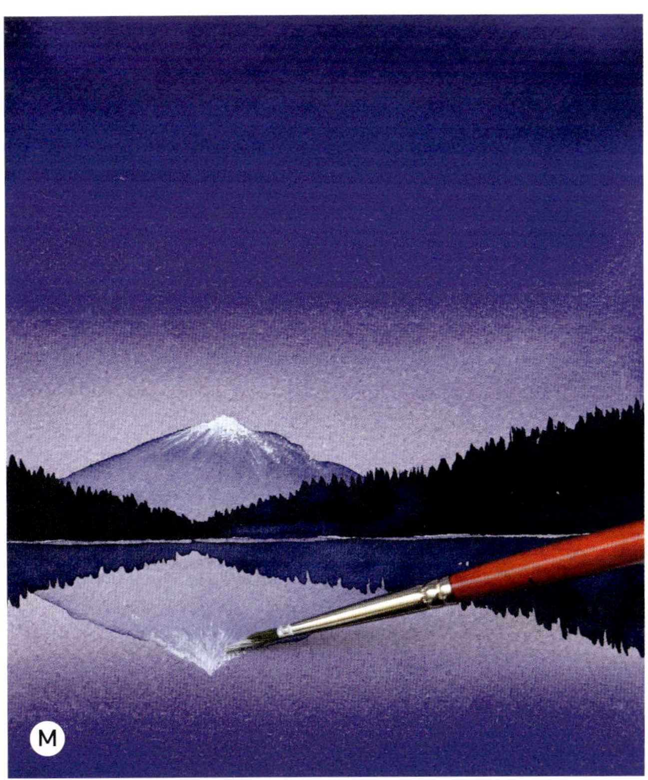

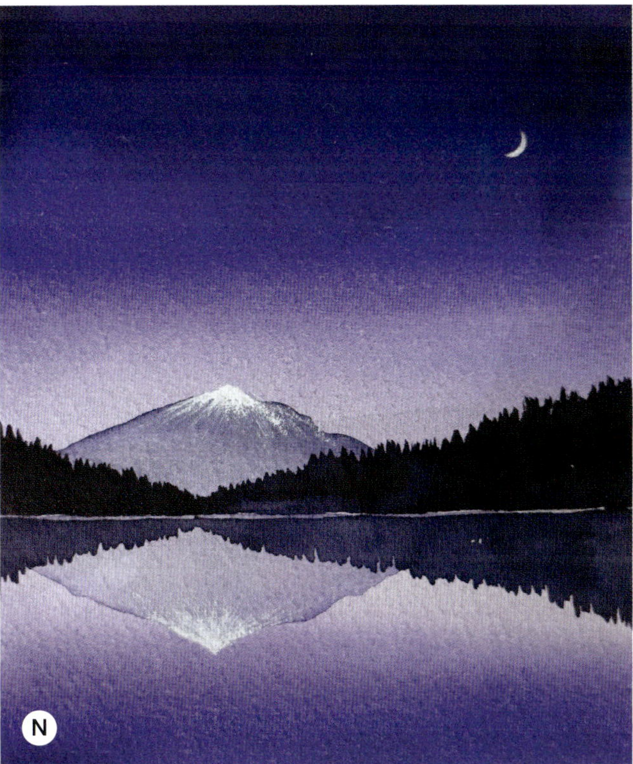

Add snow to the reflection by repeating the same step. It's easier to add it if you turn the paper upside down. (M) Add a small crescent moon in the sky to finish the painting. (N)

DAY 8

GREEN MEADOWS

Our next project is a simple green landscape. Everyone enjoys a walk through a green meadow. The lush foliage is so calming and soothing.

Suggested Color Palette

- Turquoise Blue
- Permanent Rose
- Cadmium Orange
- Cadmium Yellow
- Lemon Yellow
- Sap Green
- Payne's Grey
- Brown

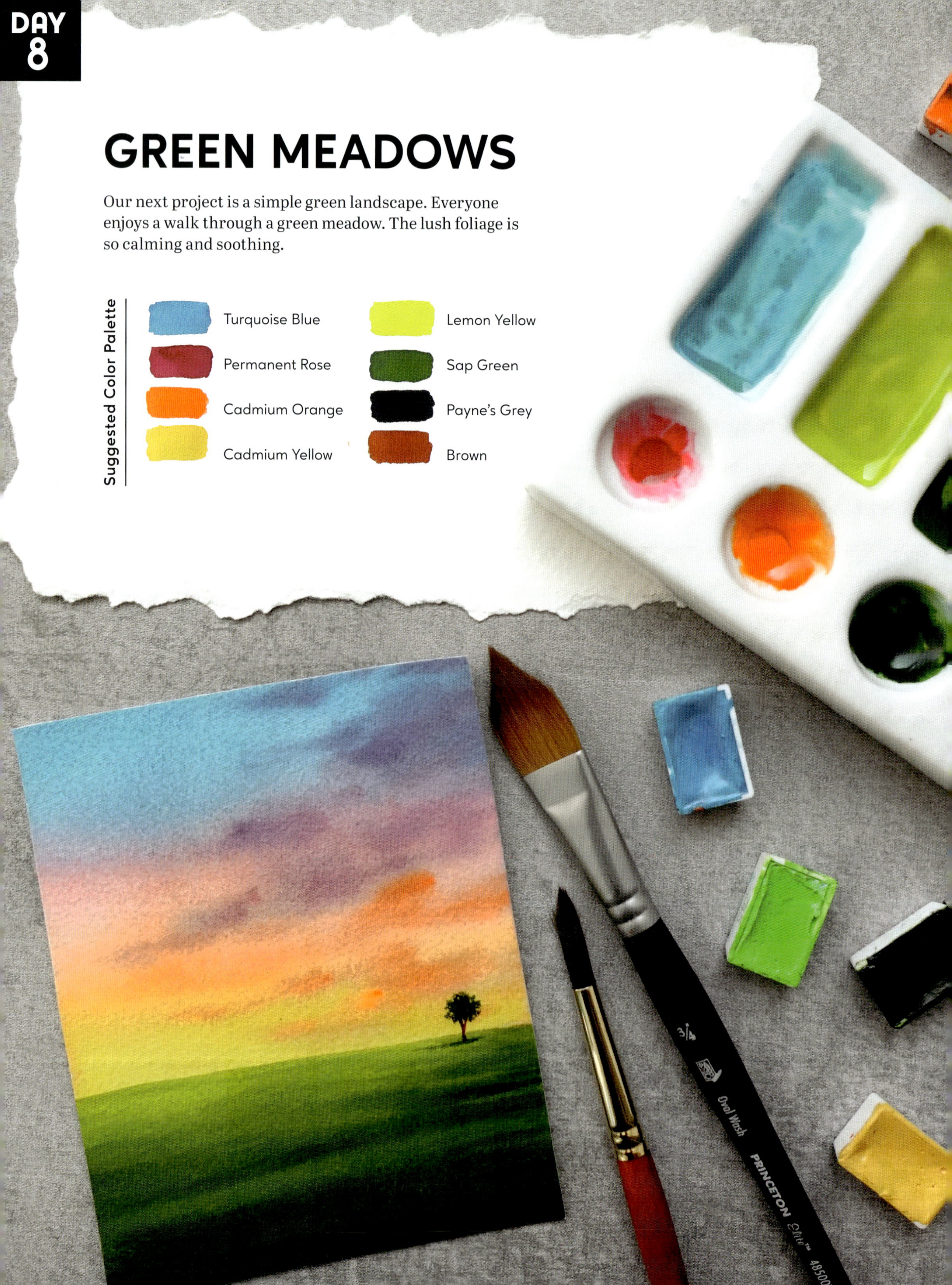

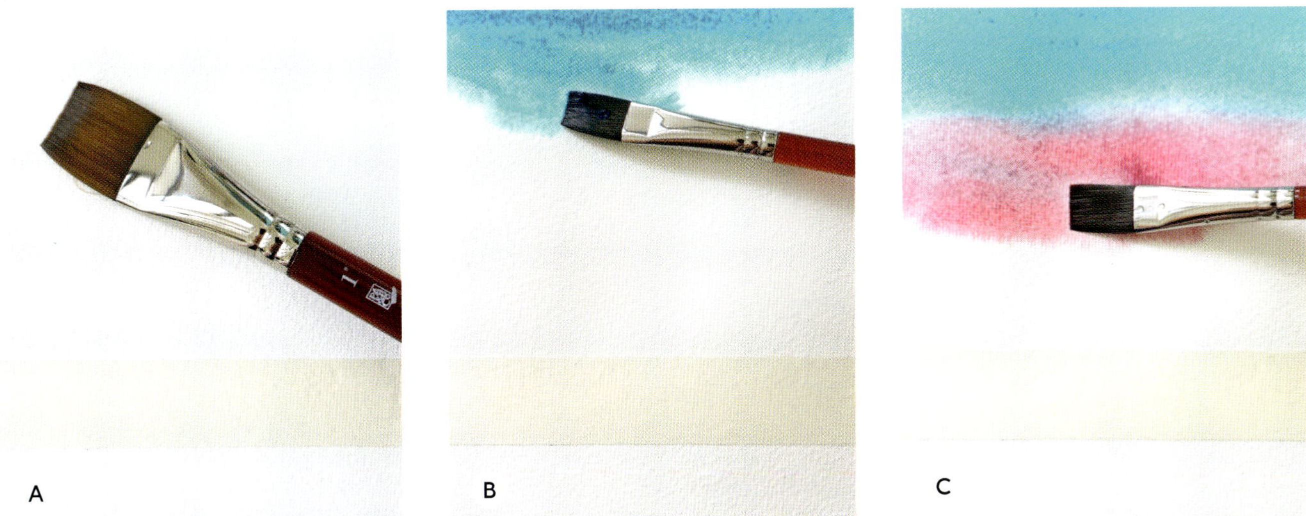

Step 1: Securing, Masking, and Wetting the Paper; Painting the Sky—Base Layer. Secure your paper to a drawing board. Place a piece of masking tape just below the center of the paper to separate the sky and the meadow. Apply an even layer of clean water to the sky. (A) You'll need four colors for the sky. Make sure they are ready before you begin. Start applying the colors to the wet sky. Using a flat brush, begin with a medium value of Turquoise Blue (B) and paint downward. Clean your brush and switch to Permanent Rose, blending the colors together. (C)

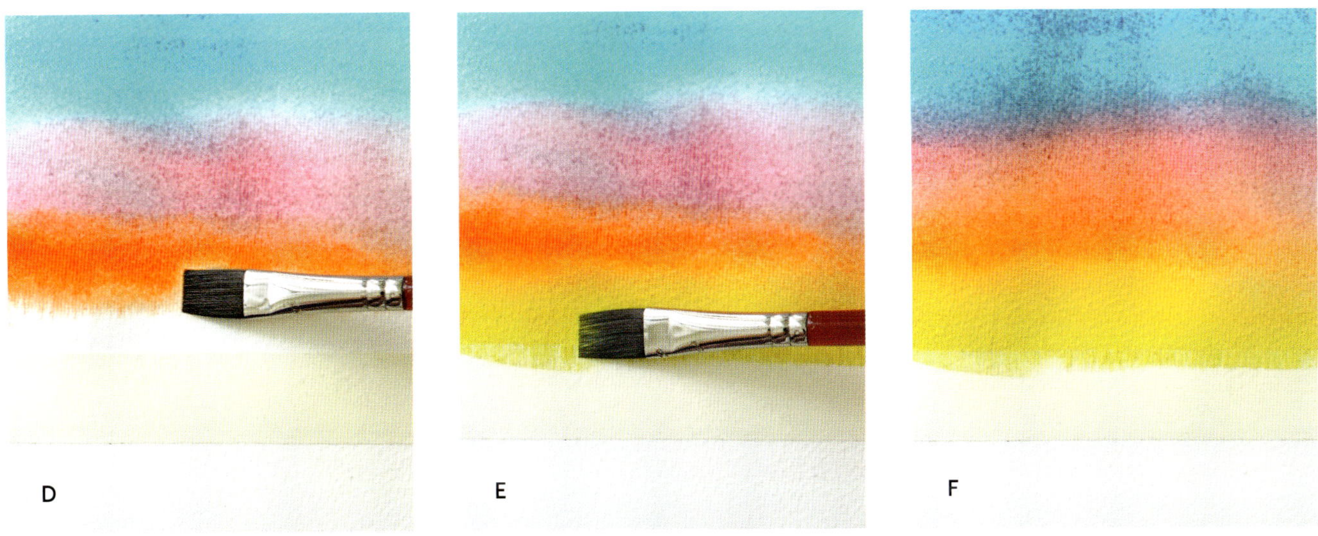

Apply the Cadmium Orange (D) and Cadmium Yellow (E) using the same method and blend all the colors. (F) The base layer is now complete. Before it dries, we need to add the clouds.

(continued)

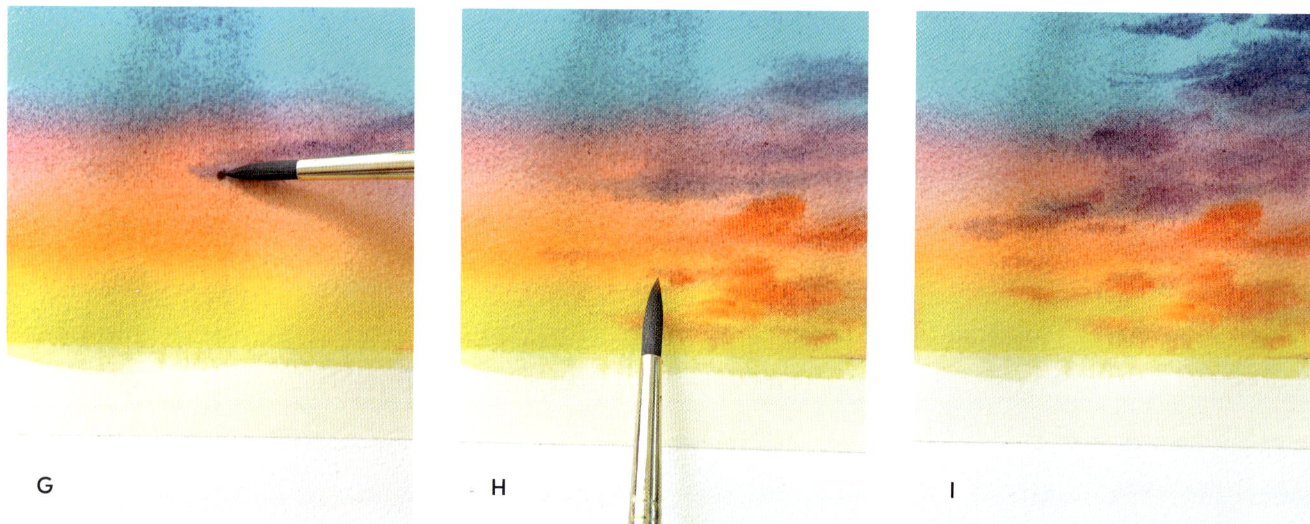

Step 2: Clouds. We'll use two colors for the clouds: purple for the blue and pink areas and a bolder shade of orange for the yellow and orange areas. Start with one shade, either purple or orange, and begin adding the clouds before the background dries. All you need to do is drop the wet color onto the wet background. (G) Add the clouds in different sizes to make your sky look more interesting. You can add more clouds if you want a dramatic sky. (H) Let dry completely. (I)

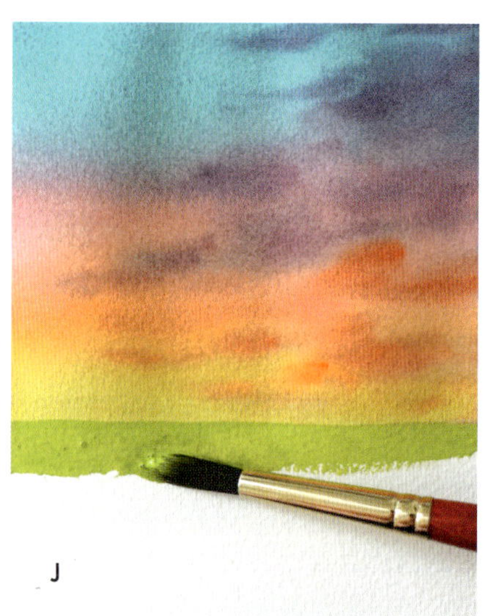

Step 3: Meadow. For the meadow, we'll use three colors: a lighter shade of green, a medium shade, and a darker shade. Carefully peel off the masking tape. Start at the top of the meadow with the lighter green. (J) Create the lighter green by mixing a little Sap Green with Lemon Yellow.

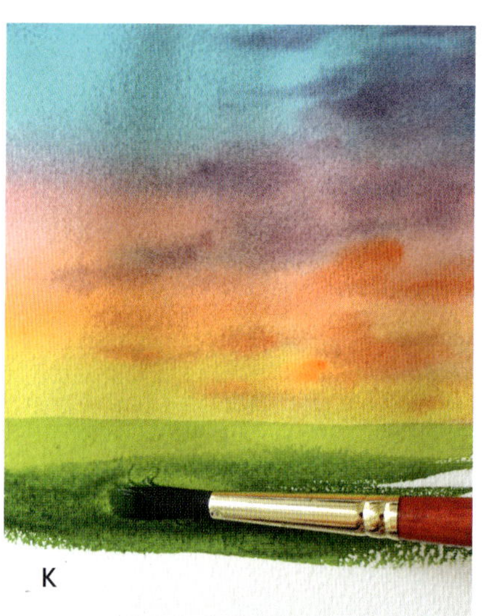

Clean your brush and switch to Sap Green. (K) Add that underneath the lighter green and blend together.

Continue adding Sap Green until you almost reach the bottom. Clean your brush and switch to a darker tone using either Payne's Grey or Indigo. (I'm using Payne's Grey here.) (L)

Add some lines on the wet background with the same color and add some shadows. (M)

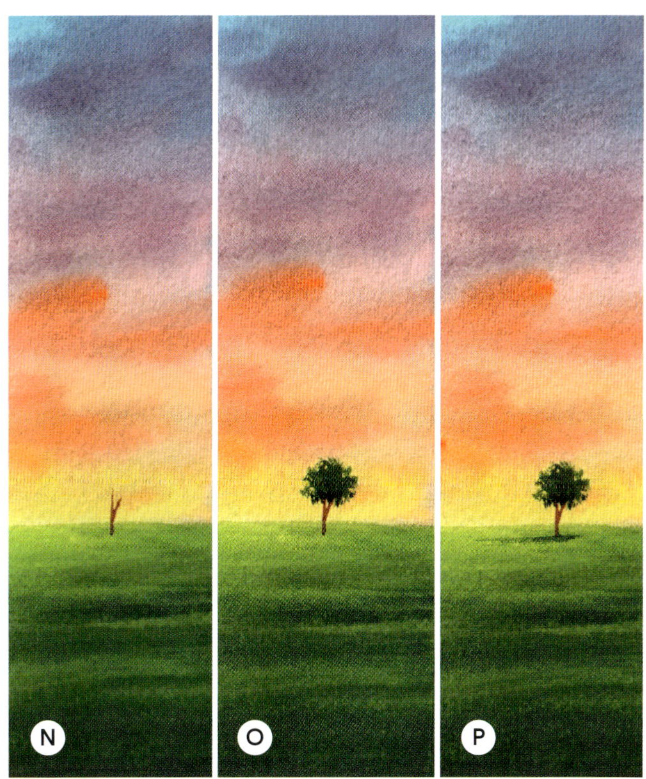

Step 4: Final Details—Tree. To define the horizon line and give a sense of distance, we'll add a small tree close to the horizon line. This tree is very far away, so you don't have to worry about the details.

Use a medium shade of brown to add the tree trunk. (N) Clean your brush and switch to Sap Green to add foliage to the top of the tree. Simply use the tip of your brush and dab it onto the paper over and over to create a rough shape. (O) Clean your brush and switch to Payne's Grey. Add some darker dots or small patterns to the bottom of the foliage to represent the shadows and deeper tones. (P)

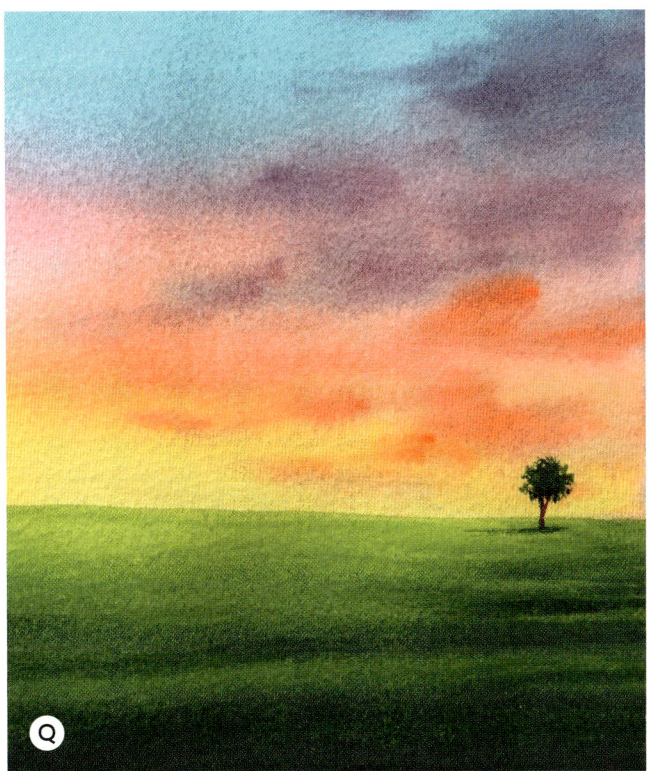

Step 5: Shadows. Choose a medium shade of green and add a line on the meadow on the left side to finish the painting. (Q)

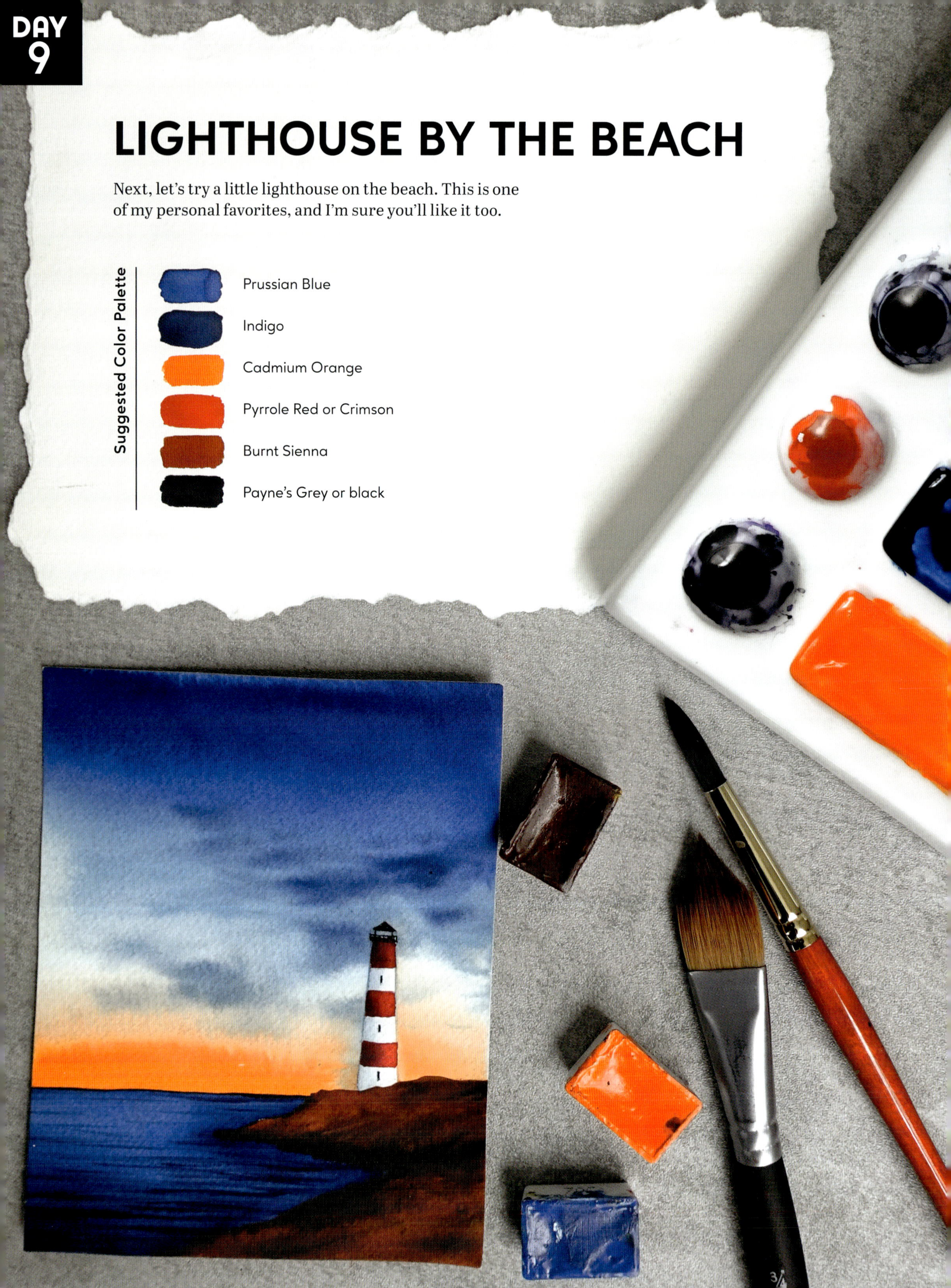

DAY 9

LIGHTHOUSE BY THE BEACH

Next, let's try a little lighthouse on the beach. This is one of my personal favorites, and I'm sure you'll like it too.

Suggested Color Palette

- Prussian Blue
- Indigo
- Cadmium Orange
- Pyrrole Red or Crimson
- Burnt Sienna
- Payne's Grey or black

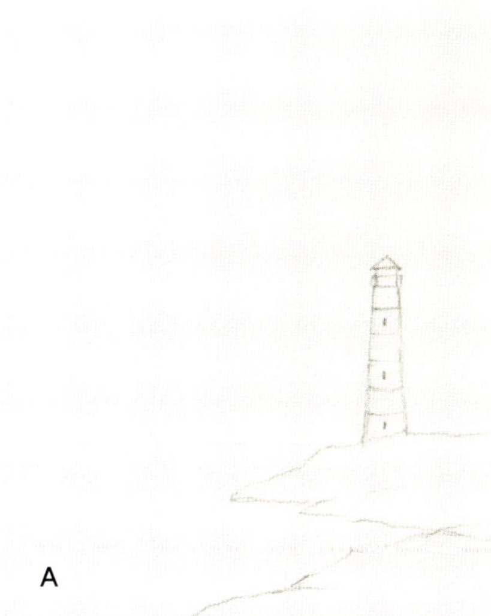

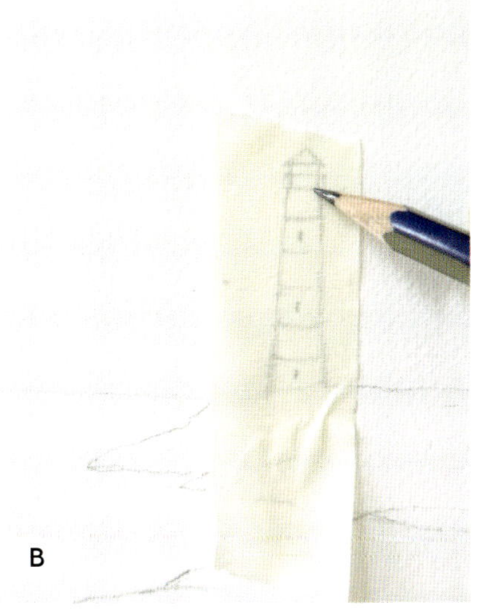

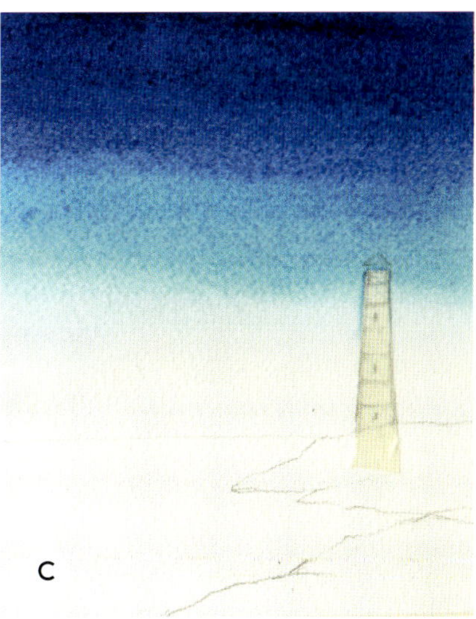

Step 1: Adding the Sketch and Masking the Paper. Add a light pencil sketch of the lighthouse and the rocks. (A)

Mask the lighthouse to keep the paper white using either a piece of masking tape or masking fluid. I'm using masking tape. Trace the lighthouse's outline, remove the masking tape, cut out the shape, and place it back over the lighthouse. (B)

Step 2: Sky—Base Layer. Paint the base layer of the sky using two colors: Prussian Blue and Cadmium Orange. Start with a darker value of Prussian Blue and paint downward, making the tonal value lighter as you go. (C)

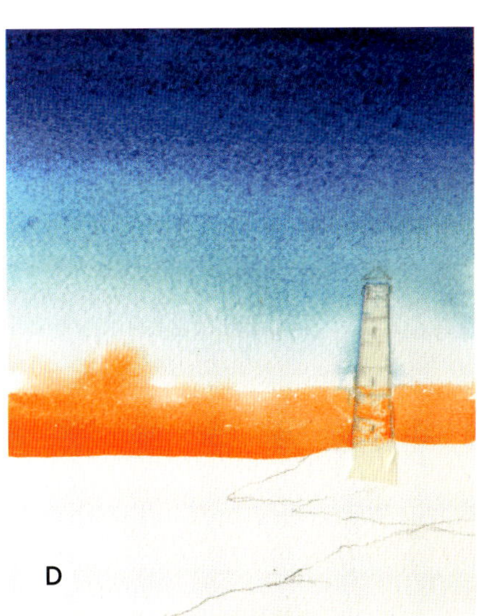

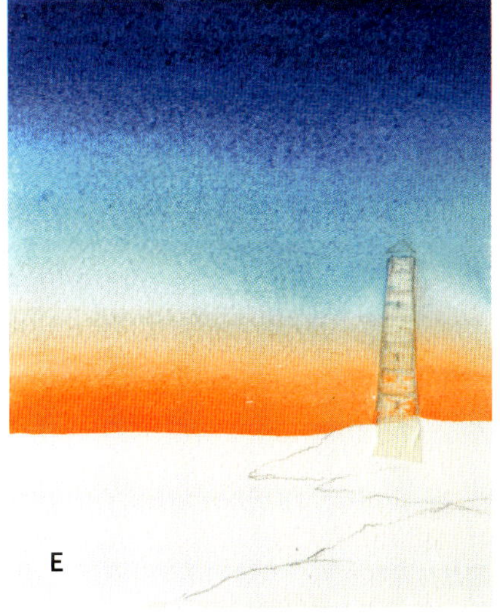

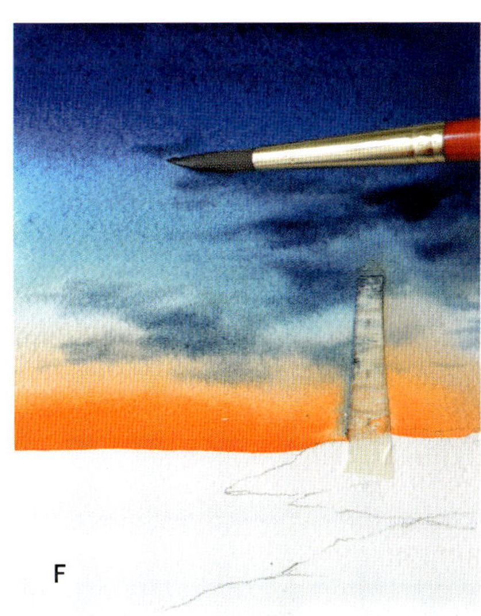

Clean your brush and switch to the Cadmium Orange. Start at the bottom of the horizon and paint upward. Paint with an intense tone and make it lighter as you approach the Prussian Blue, mixing them well. (D, E) Before the background dries, add the clouds.

Use a medium value of Indigo while adding the clouds in the orange areas, and use a darker value of Indigo for the upper areas where you have blue. (F)

(continued)

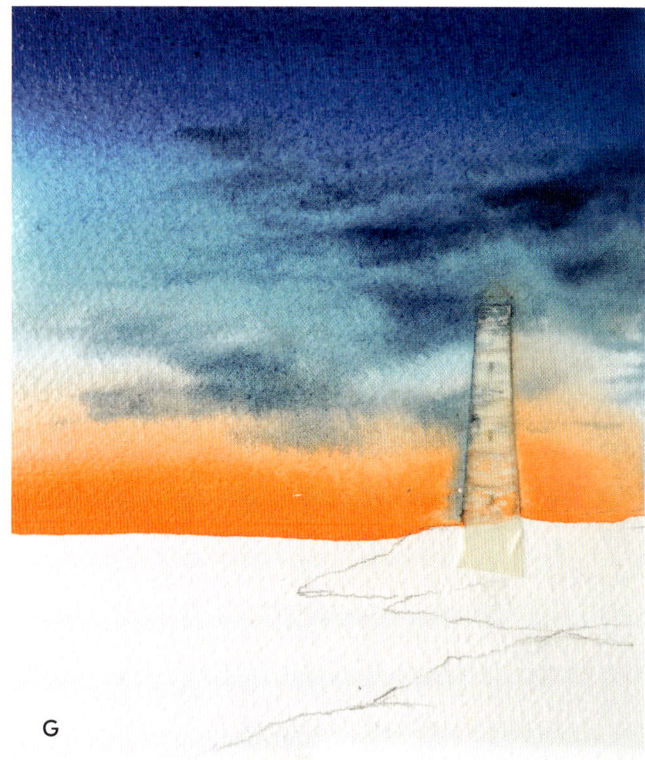

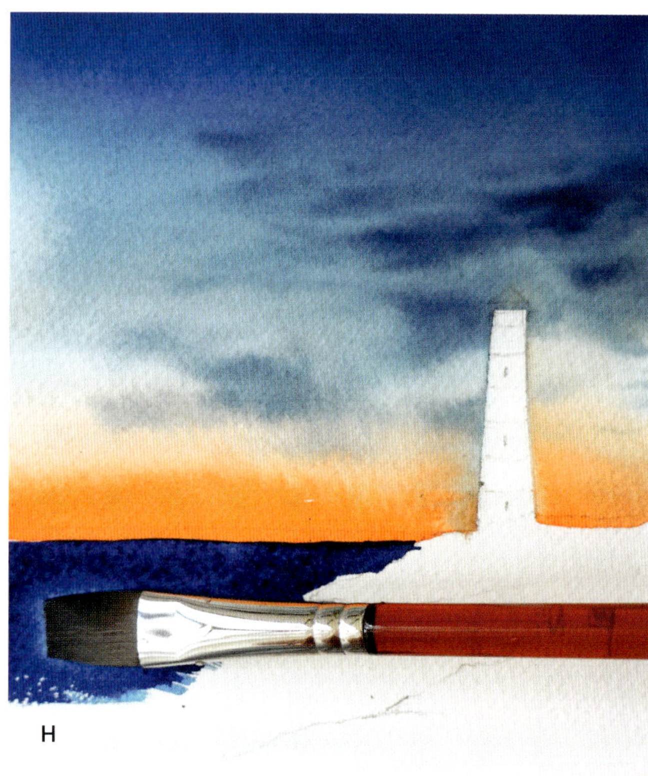

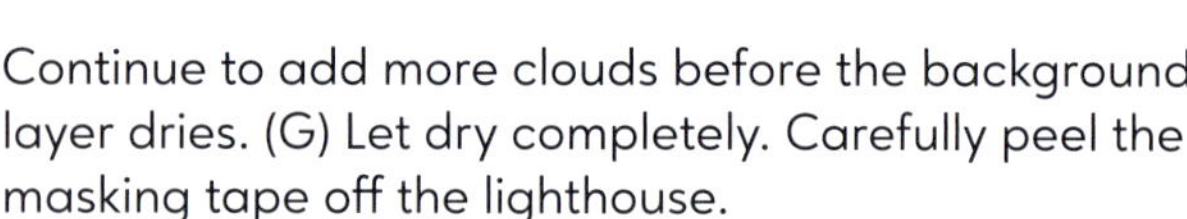

Continue to add more clouds before the background layer dries. (G) Let dry completely. Carefully peel the masking tape off the lighthouse.

Step 3: Sea. Apply a medium tone of Prussian Blue to the entire sea. (H) You can use a flat brush or a round brush for this step. Once you've applied a flat wash of Prussian Blue, clean your brush and switch to a darker value of Indigo. Add it under the rocks to show the shadows and deeper tones. While that dries, start painting the lighthouse.

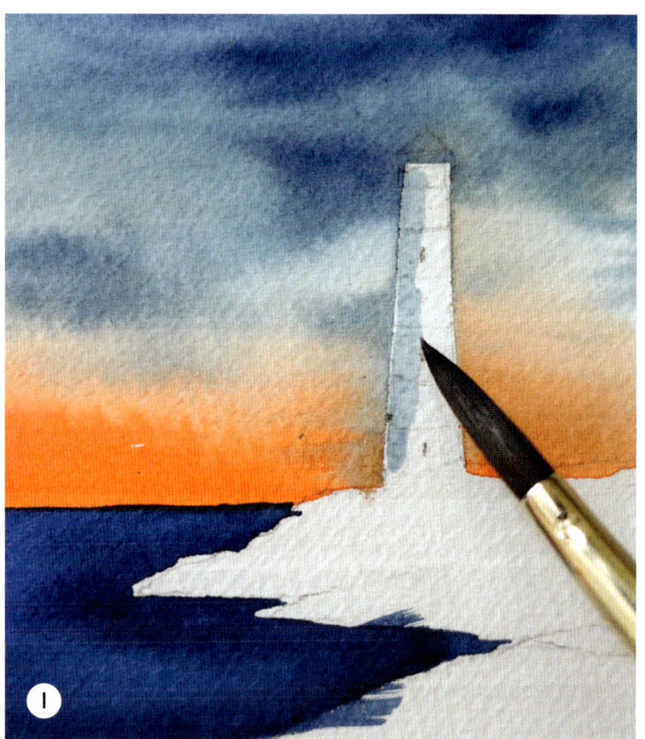

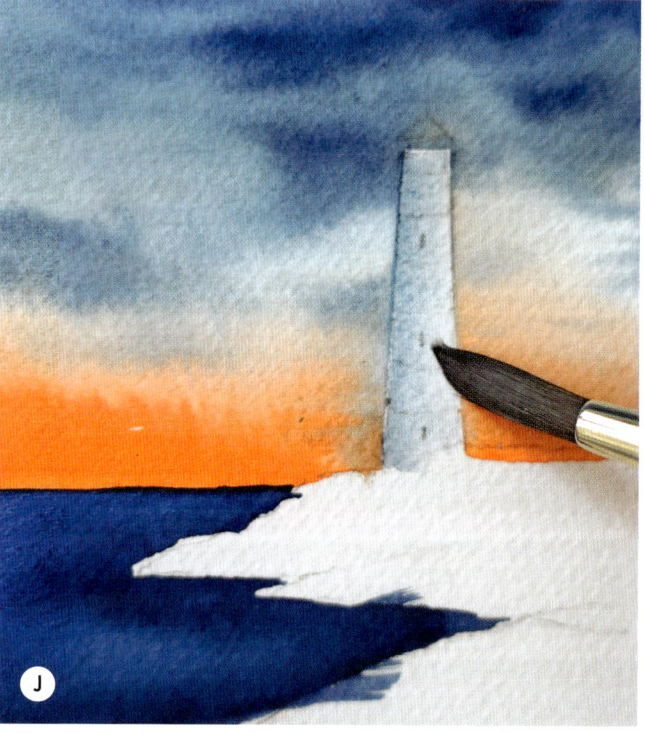

Step 4: Lighthouse—Base Layer. For the lighthouse, we'll paint the base layer first and then add the details once it's completely dry. Use a medium value of Indigo and apply it to the left side of the lighthouse. (I) Quickly rinse your brush and paint the right side, adding clean water as necessary to lighten the color. (J) Let dry completely.

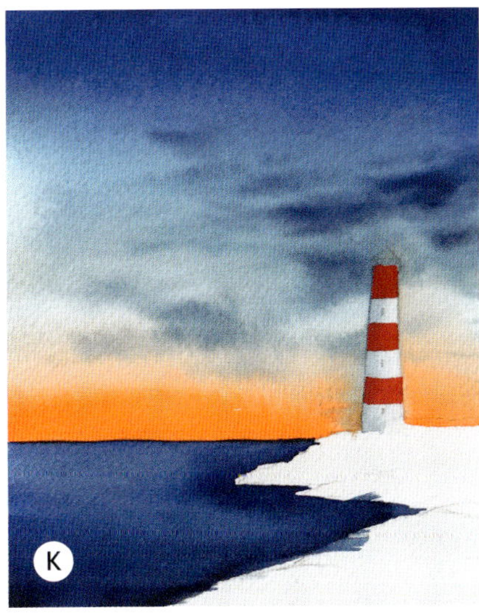

Add Pyrrole Red or Crimson, or any similar shades, on the alternating sections from top to bottom. (K)

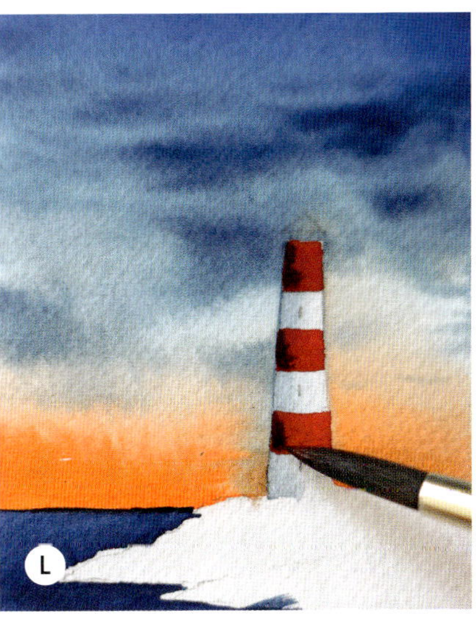

While the paint is still wet, add a darker value on the left side of the red sections (Red + a little Payne's Grey). (L) Let dry completely.

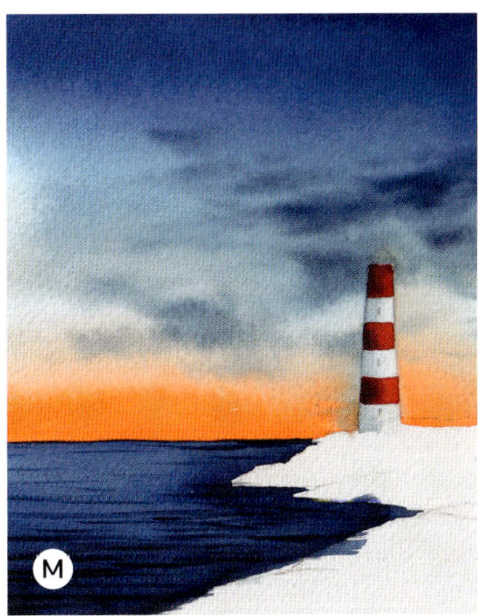

Step 5: Sea Details. While the lighthouse dries, add the final details on the sea. This is a simple step. All you need to do is add a lot of thin, fine lines with a darker shade of Indigo. (M) Use a smaller brush or a brush with a pointed tip for this step.

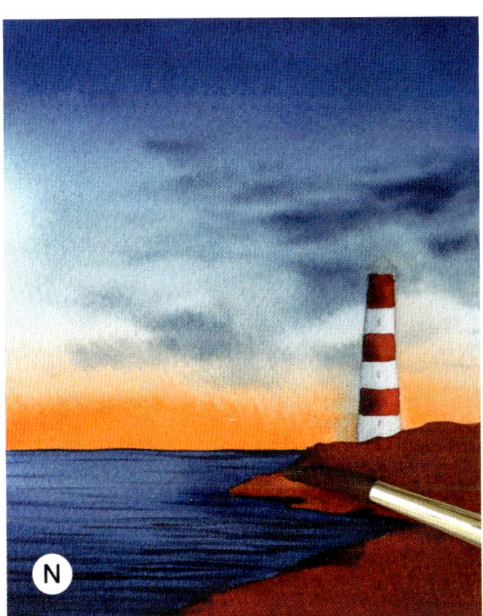

Step 6: Rocks. Fill the entire section of rocks with a medium value of Burnt Sienna. (N)

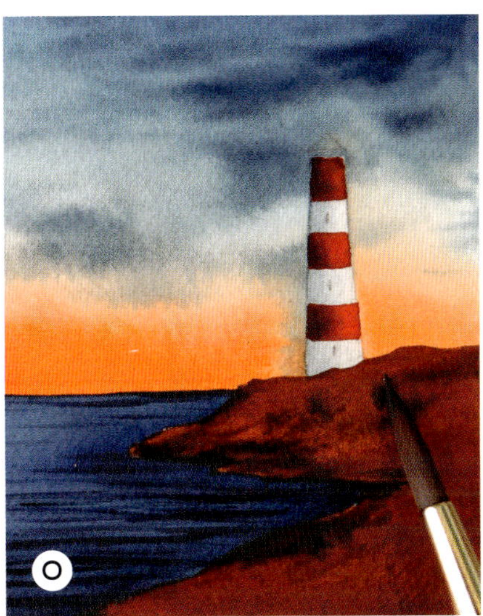

On top of this wet layer, apply some darker tones near the shoreline and on the surface to introduce textures to make it look more realistic. For the darker shade, mix some Payne's Grey or black with the Burnt Sienna. (O)

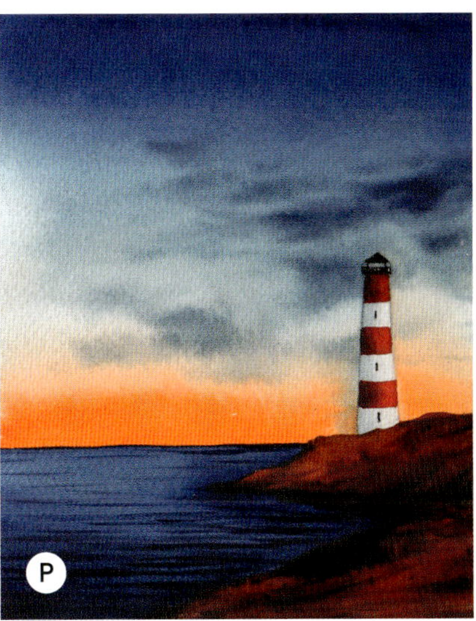

Step 7: Final Details. Add the final details of the lighthouse, including the roof and the window openings, to finish the painting. (P)

DAY 10

GOLDEN HOUR

Our next project is a gorgeous golden evening. The steps are really simple, and you'll learn how to create a stunning luminous evening.

Suggested Color Palette

- Permanent Yellow Orange
- Cadmium Yellow
- Vermillion Hue
- Burnt Sienna
- Payne's Grey or black

(plus white gouache or white watercolor)

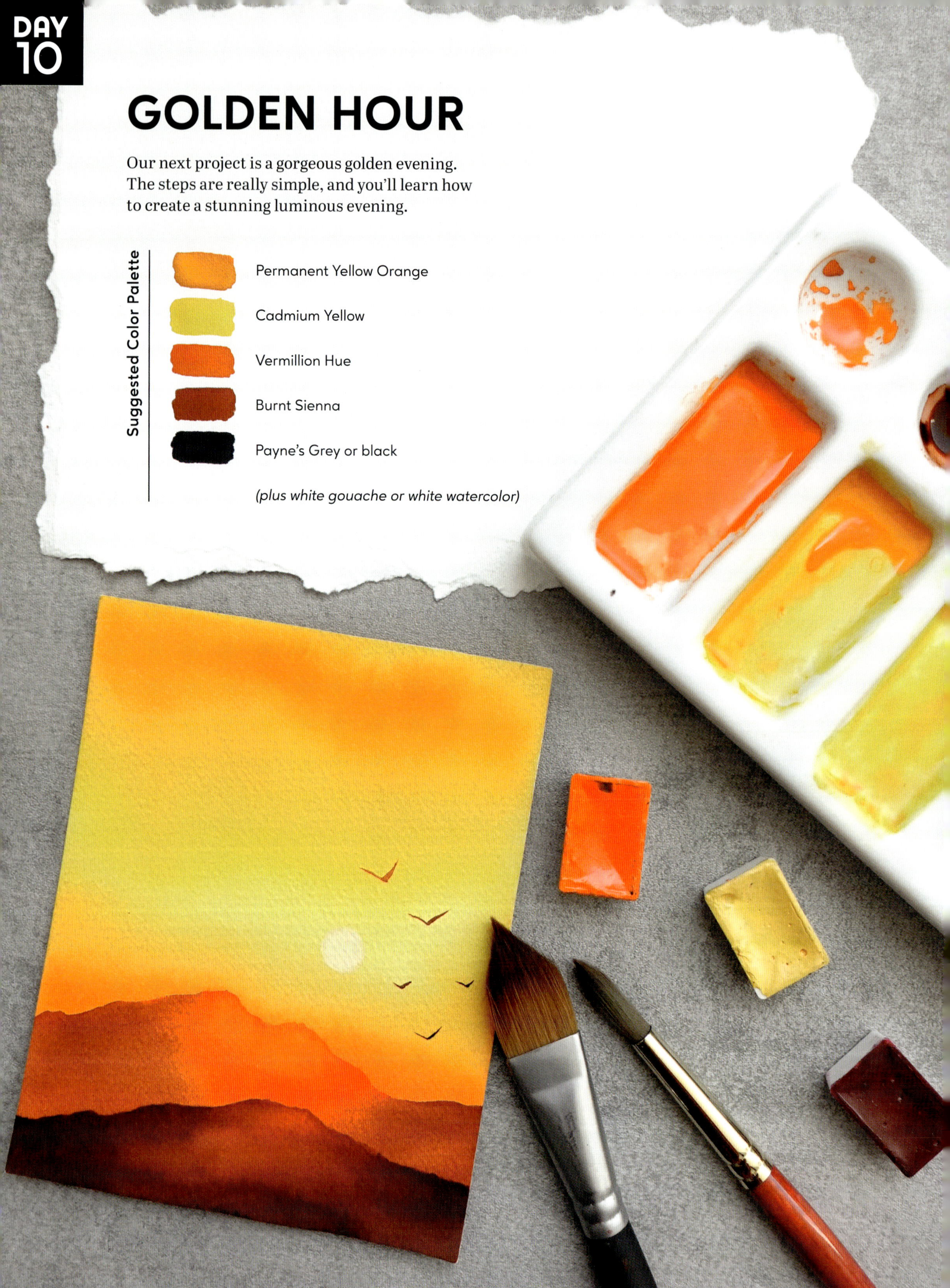

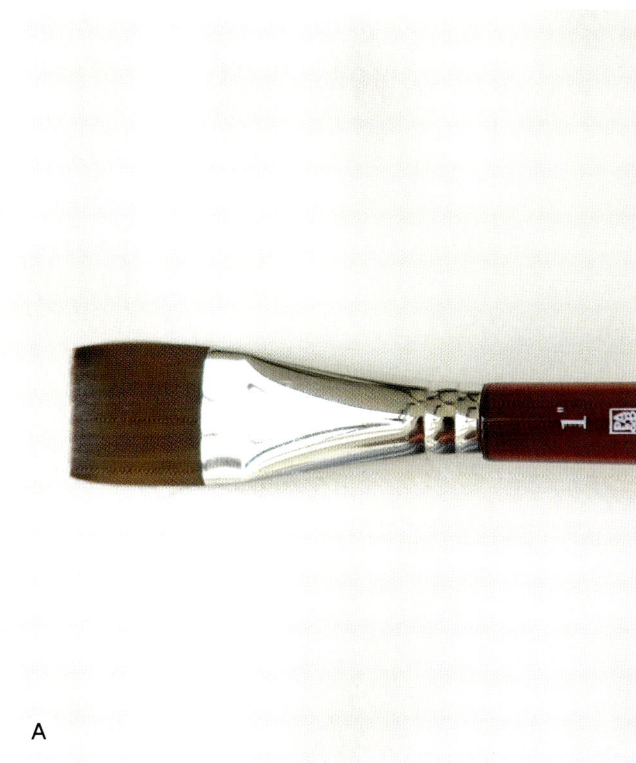
A

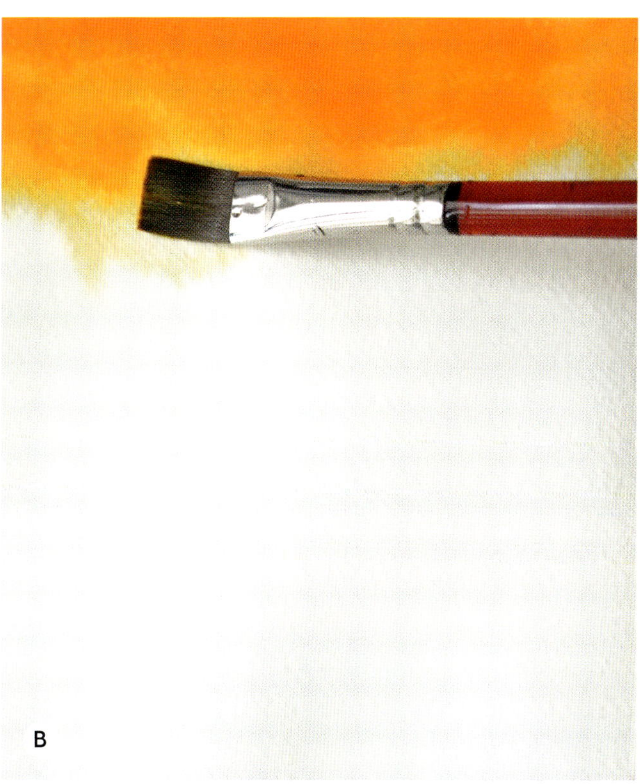
B

Step 1: Securing and Wetting the Paper. Secure your paper to a drawing board. Apply an even layer of clean water to the entire paper. (A)

Step 2: Sky. Start with the first color—Permanent Yellow Orange. Apply a bright and intense value of Permanent Yellow Orange to the top of the paper and paint downward. (B) You can use either a flat brush or a round brush to apply the color.

C

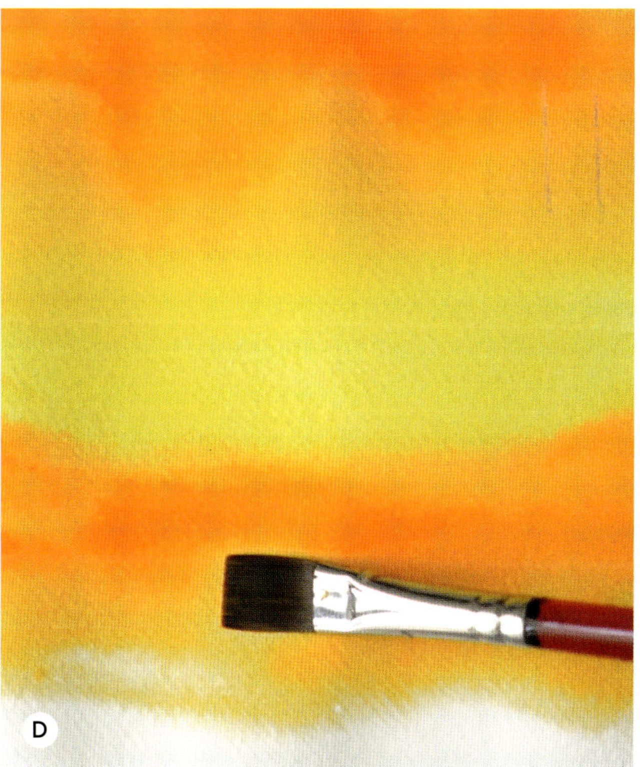
D

Clean your brush and switch to Cadmium Yellow, or another shade of yellow, apply it underneath the Yellow Orange (C), and blend them well.

Clean your brush and then switch back to Permanent Yellow Orange; apply it underneath the Cadmium Yellow (D) and blend again.

(continued)

Clean your brush again and switch to Vermillion Hue or another intense orange. Apply it to the remaining area and try to spread it evenly. (E)

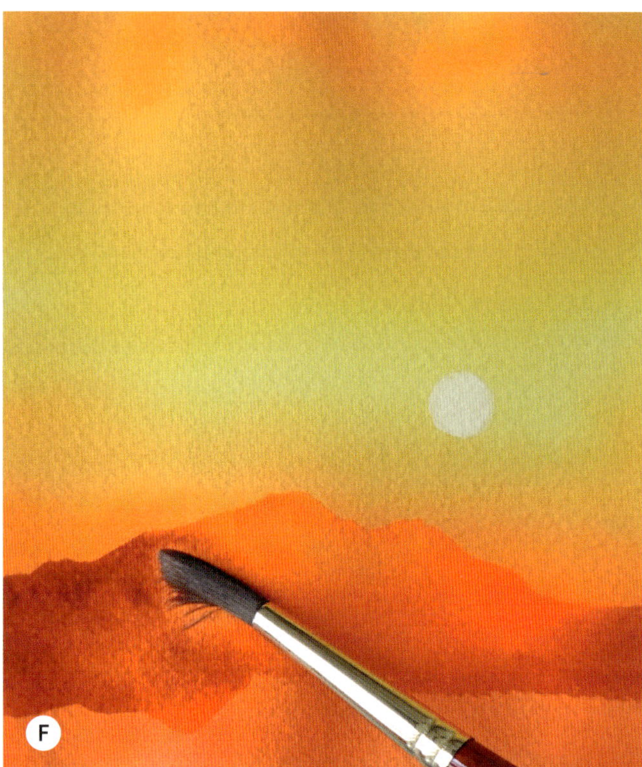

Step 3: Sun; Mountain: Background. Using white gouache or white watercolor, add a small circle in the sky for the sun. Add two layers of mountains: one in the background and one in the foreground. Use medium tones for the background and darker tones for the foreground. This creates a luminous effect. For the background mountain, you can start by adding a light pencil sketch as a guide. Add the basic shape of the mountain using Vermillion Hue. (F)

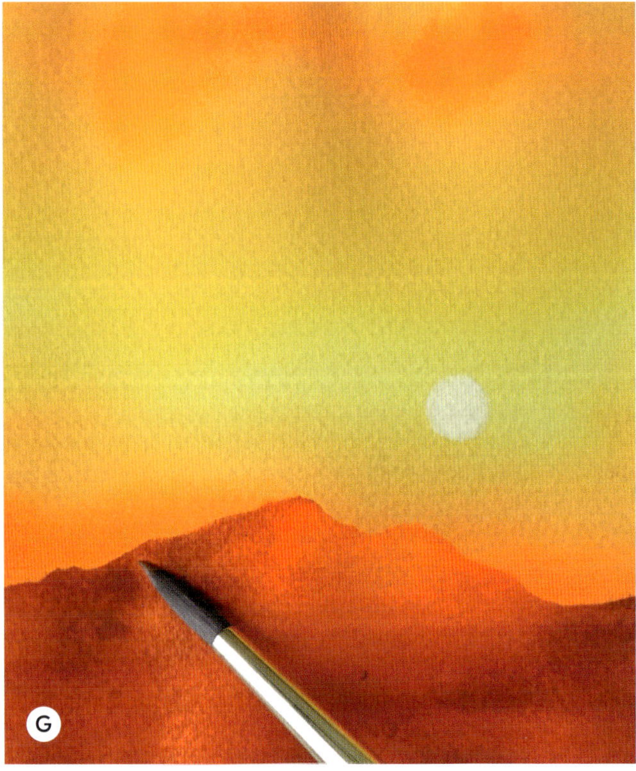

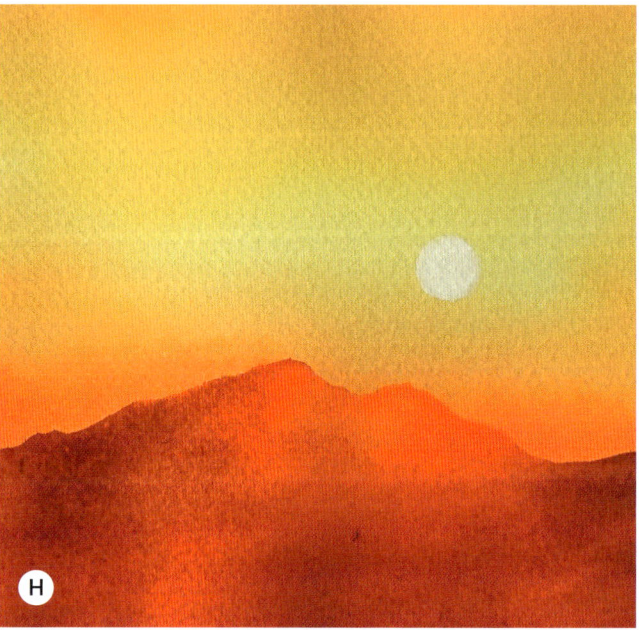

Introduce a medium tone of Burnt Sienna toward either side and the bottom, retaining the orange tones at the center. (G, H) Let dry completely.

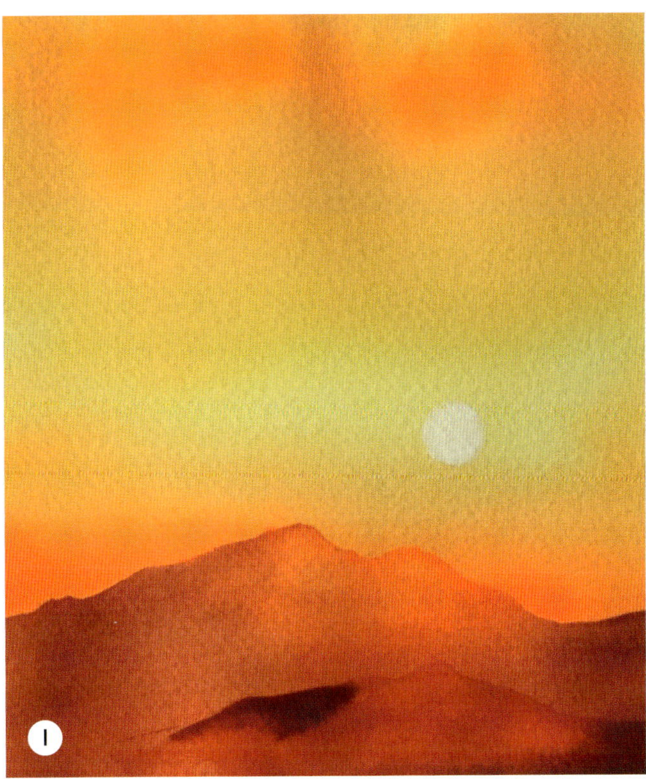

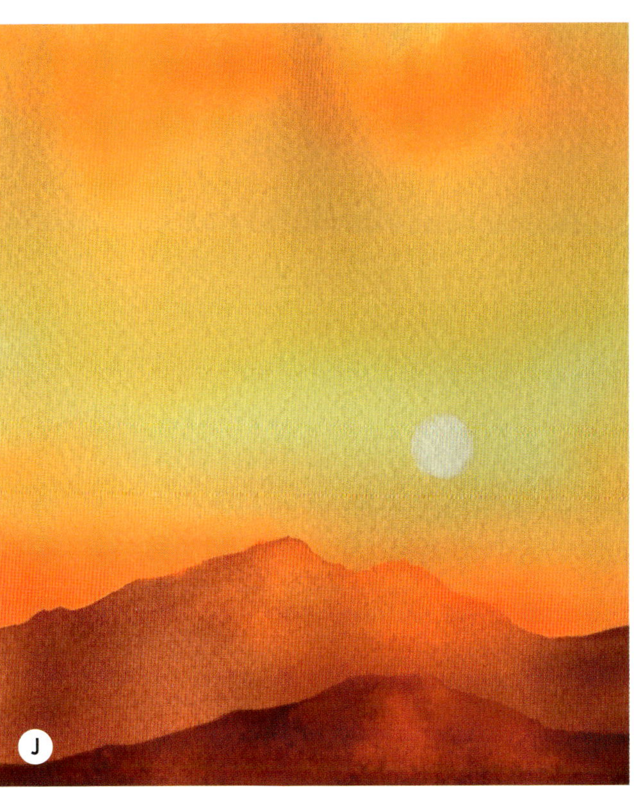

Step 4: Mountain: Foreground. For the second mountain, start with a medium shade of brown and then add a darker shade of brown (Burnt Sienna + Payne's Grey) to both sides and downward. (I)

The second layer of mountain needs to be added a little lower than the first so you don't completely cover the first mountain. (J)

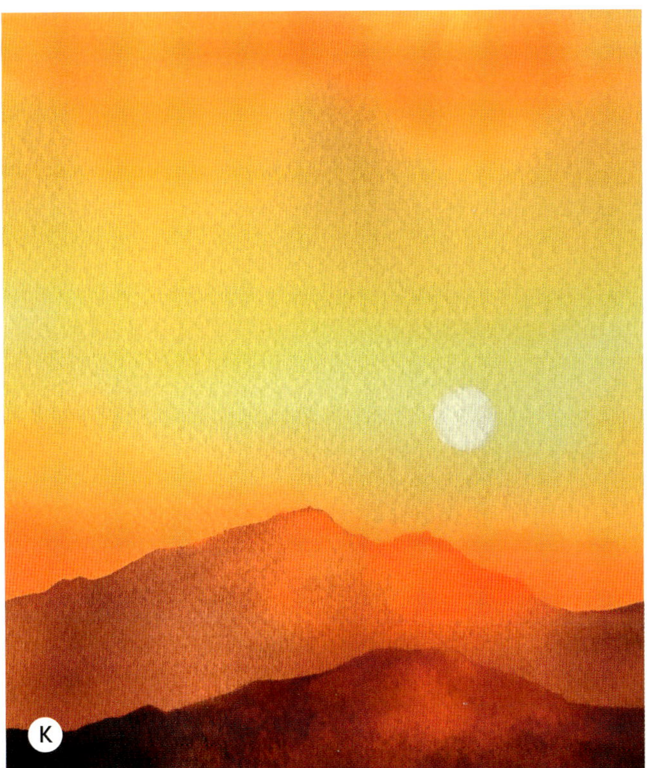

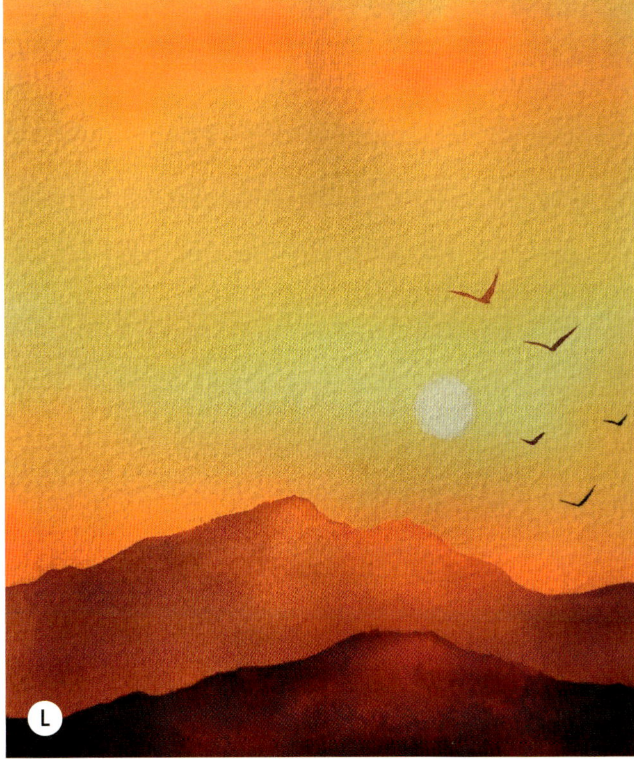

You can add more dark tones to the sides and bottom if needed, but try to keep the medium shade of brown in the center of the mountain, which is necessary to create the light effect. (K)

Add some birds in the sky to finish your painting. If you're painting the birds closer to the sun, use Burnt Sienna, and if you're painting them further away from the sun, you can use Payne's Grey or black. (L)

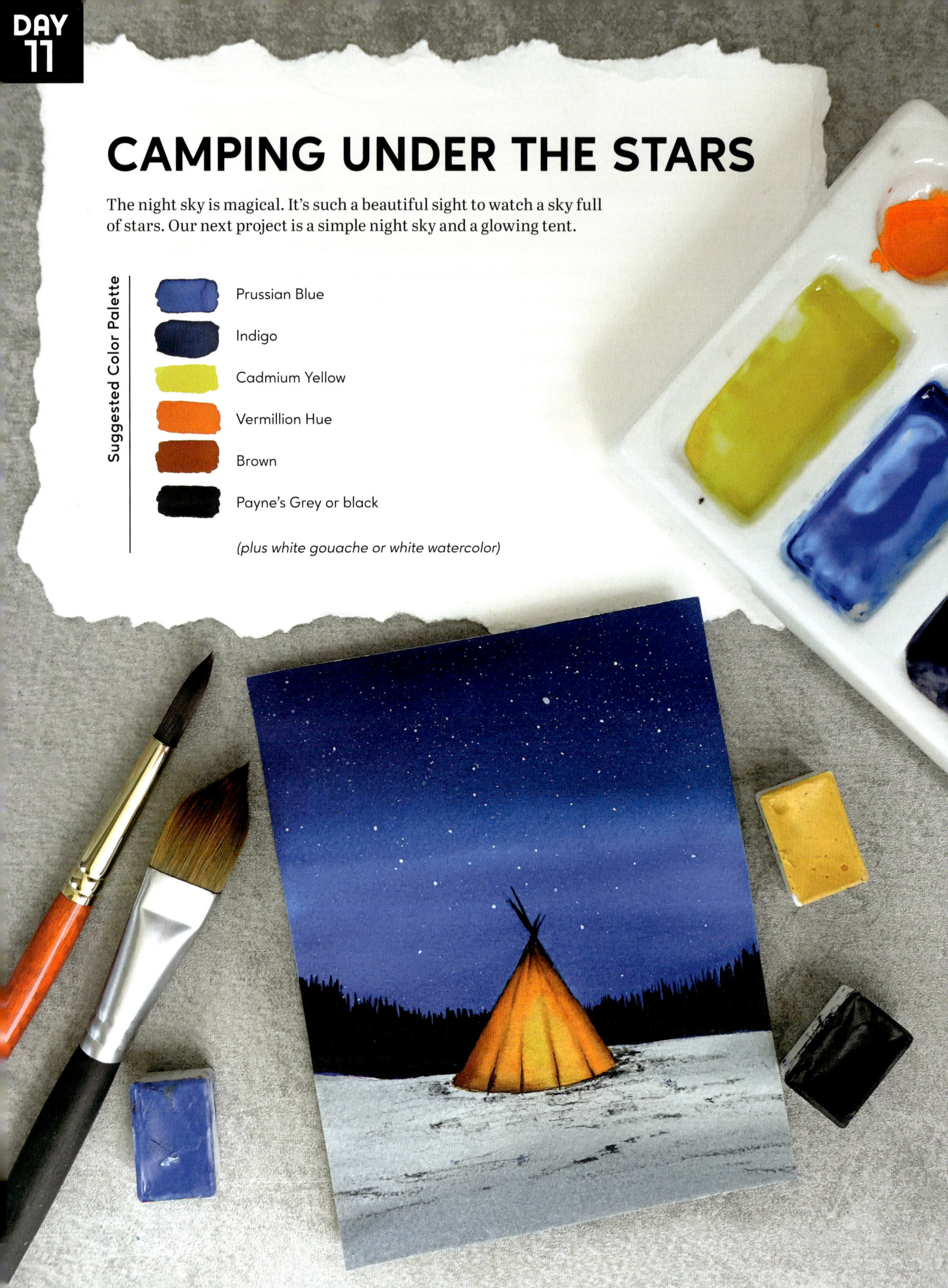

DAY 11

CAMPING UNDER THE STARS

The night sky is magical. It's such a beautiful sight to watch a sky full of stars. Our next project is a simple night sky and a glowing tent.

Suggested Color Palette

- Prussian Blue
- Indigo
- Cadmium Yellow
- Vermillion Hue
- Brown
- Payne's Grey or black

(plus white gouache or white watercolor)

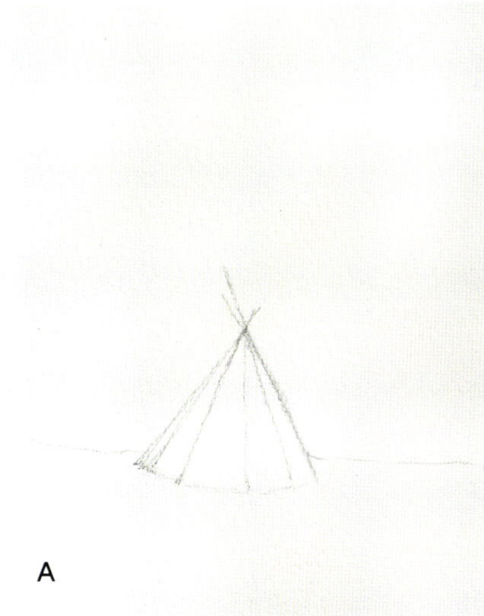

A

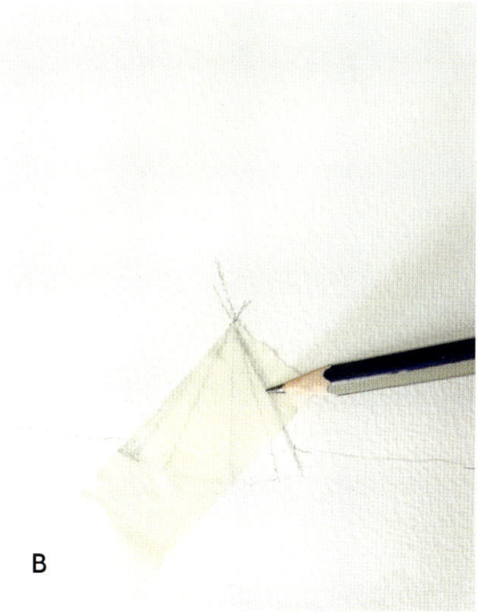

B

C

Step 1: Adding the Sketch and Masking the Paper. First, add a light pencil sketch of a simple triangular tent. Add a line for the ground. (A)

To preserve the white paper, place a piece of masking tape over the tent, trace the shape of the outline, then remove the excess. (B, C) You can also use masking fluid if you prefer.

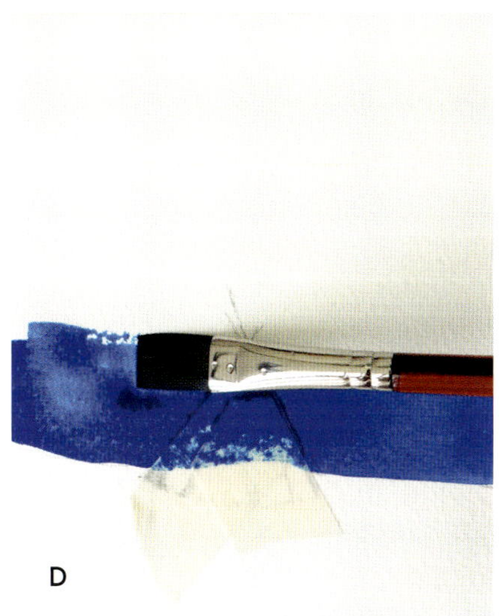

D

E

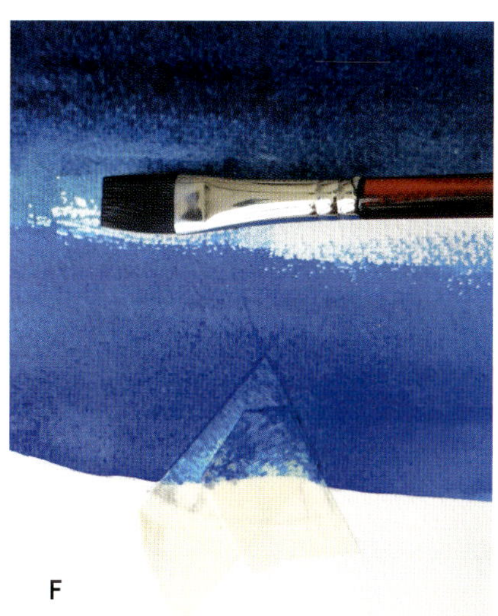

F

Step 2: Sky. Once you've masked the tent, go with an intense tone of Prussian Blue, or any blue of your choice, and start adding that from the bottom and paint upward. (D)

We're using the wet-on-dry technique here, which means applying the paint directly to the dry paper without applying a layer of water. You can use either the wet-on-wet or wet-on-dry technique. (E)

When you reach the halfway point of the sky, clean your brush and switch to Indigo. (F) Apply the paint from top to bottom and blend it with the Prussian Blue. Let dry completely.

(continued)

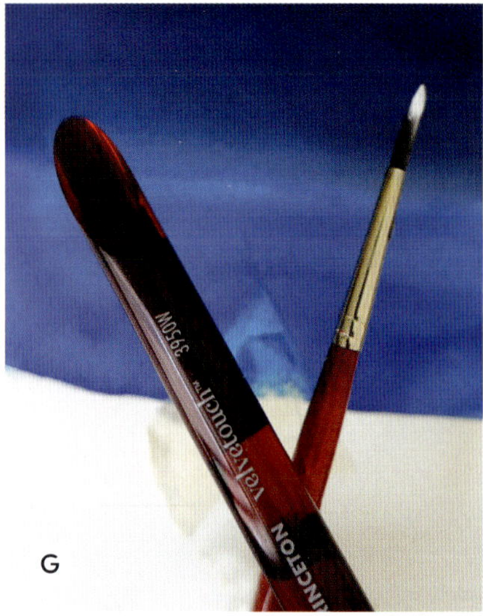

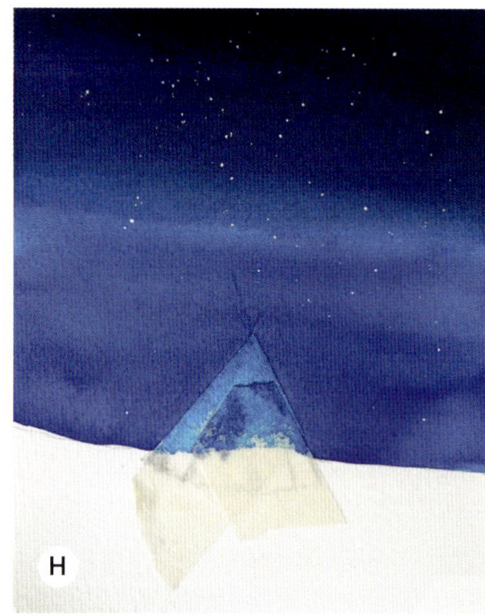

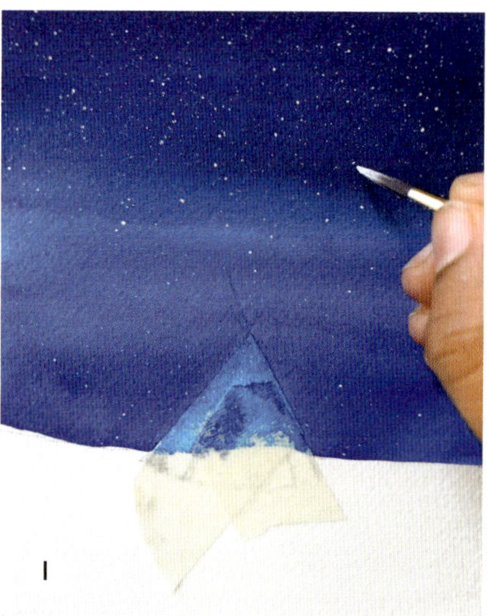

Step 3: Stars. Splatter some stars on the sky to turn it into a starry night. Load some white gouache or white watercolor on one of your smaller brushes and tap on it with another brush to splatter white paint on to your sky. (G)

Repeat the same step to create as many stars as you want. (H)

Add some larger dots with the same brush to show the prominent stars. (I) Let dry completely, then carefully peel the masking tape off the tent.

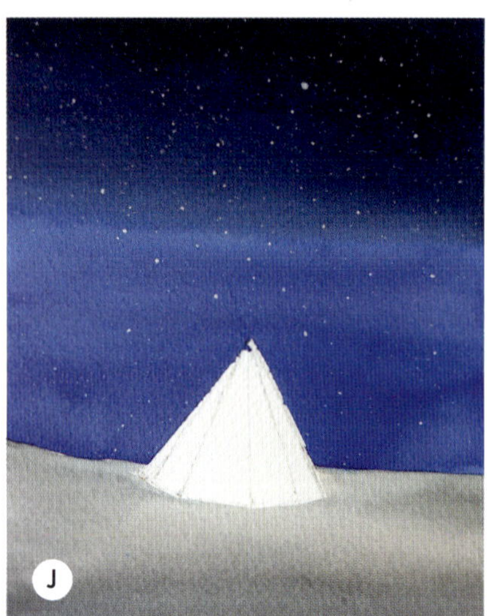

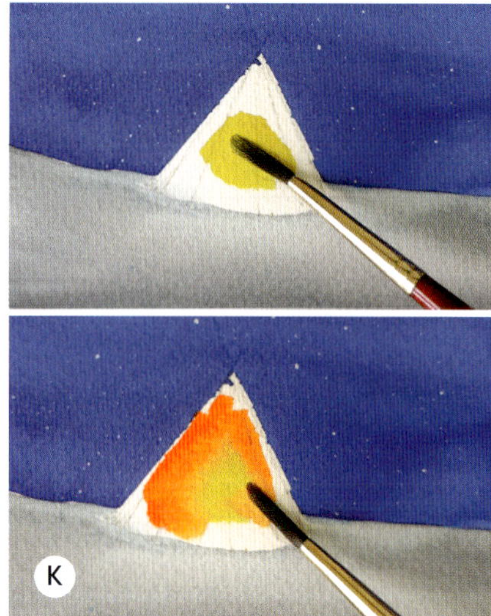

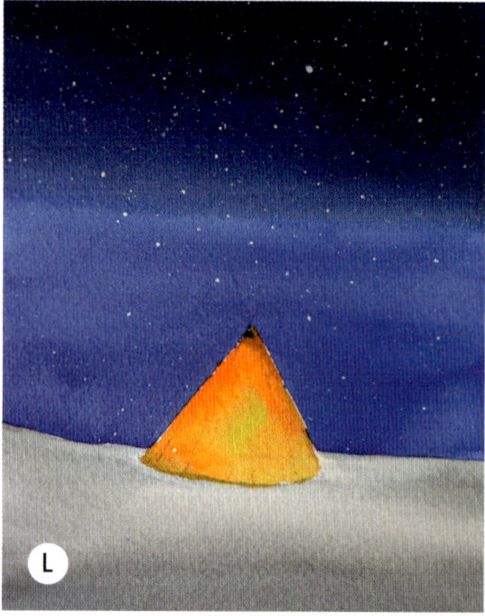

Step 4: Snowy Ground. Create a medium tone of Payne's Grey and start adding that from the bottom, making it lighter as you paint upward. (J) Let dry completely.

Step 5: Tent. To add the deeper tones, use any kind of yellow, orange, brown, and Payne's Grey or black. Have your colors ready before you begin. Start with yellow. Apply an intense shade of yellow in the center. (K)

Clean your brush and quickly switch to Vermillion Hue, or any orange, and add it around the yellow. (L)

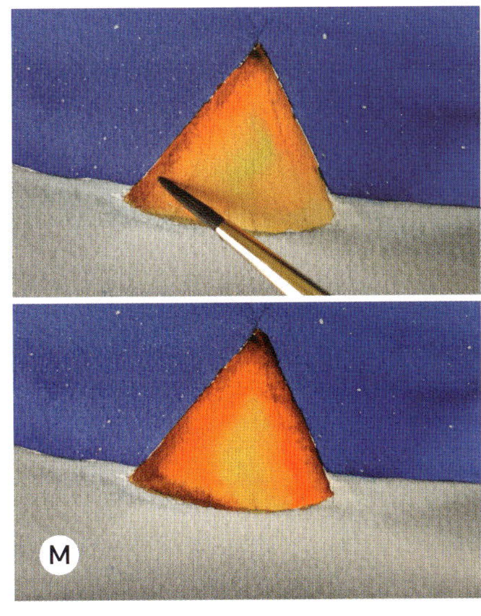

Clean your brush again and switch to brown and add it around the orange to finish the shape. (M)

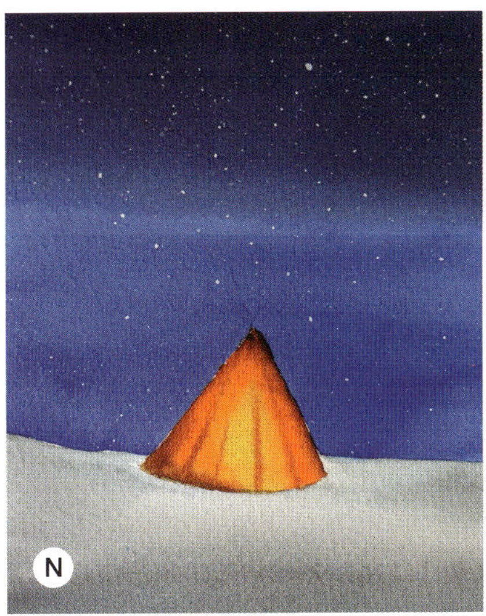

Add the divisions in the tent with a medium value of brown. (N) Let dry completely.

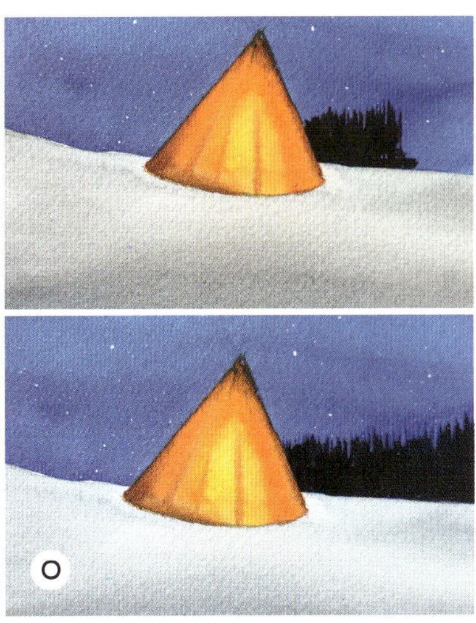

Step 6: Final Details. Add a few simple trees to define the horizon line. (O)

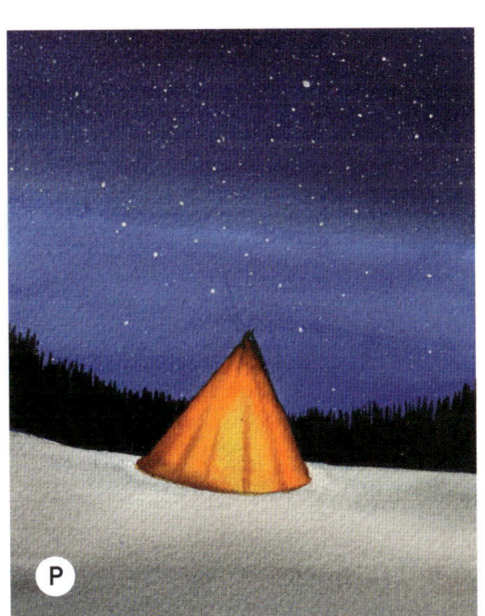

Fill it in with closely spaced lines of different heights. (P)

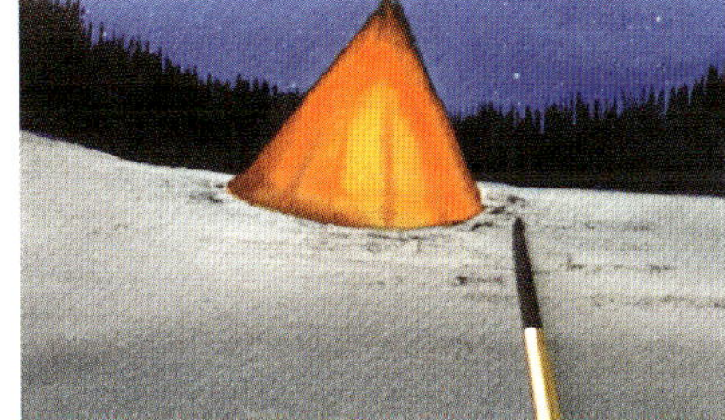

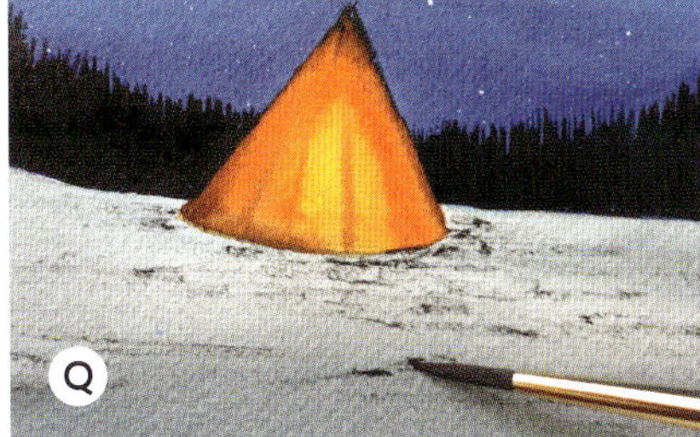

To add some dry textures to the ground, you'll need dry paint. Load a darker value of Payne's Grey on the brush and then dab it several times on a paper towel to remove the excess water. Add some textures on the ground and around the tent. (Q)

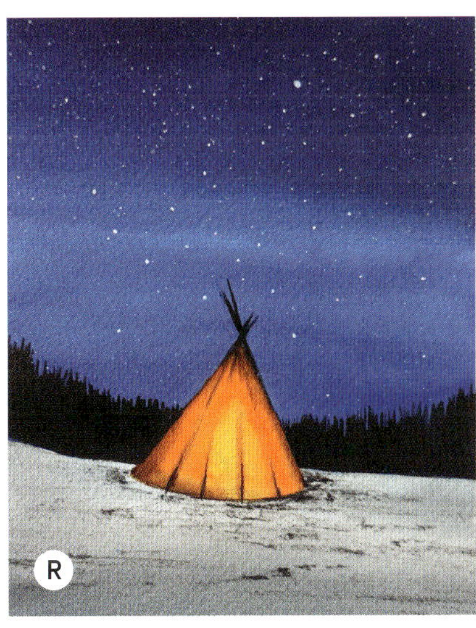

Using a darker value of Payne's Grey, add the tent poles to the top of the tent. (R) Use a medium shade of brown to highlight the divisions of the tent at the bottom to finish the painting.

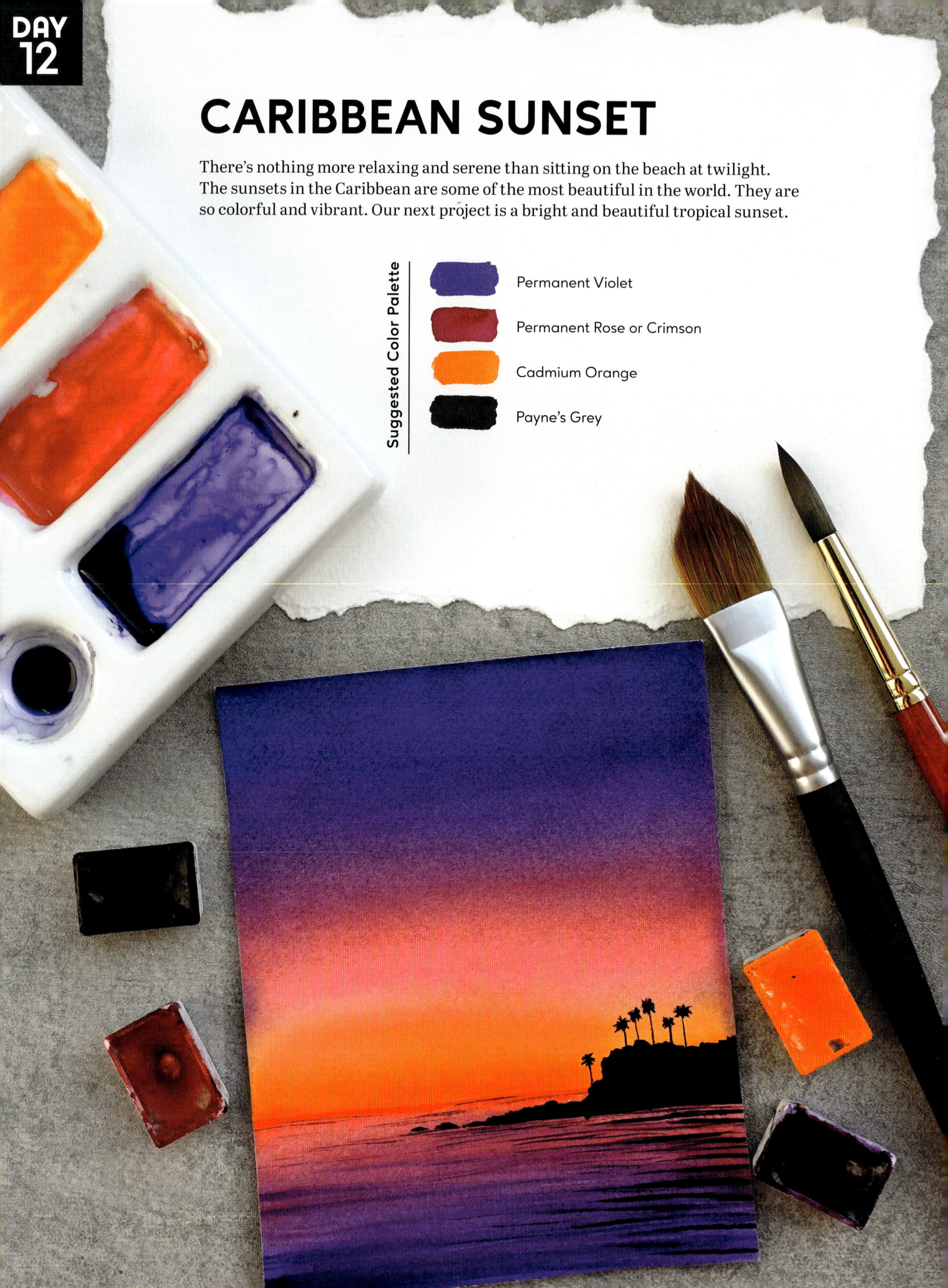

DAY 12

CARIBBEAN SUNSET

There's nothing more relaxing and serene than sitting on the beach at twilight. The sunsets in the Caribbean are some of the most beautiful in the world. They are so colorful and vibrant. Our next project is a bright and beautiful tropical sunset.

Suggested Color Palette

- Permanent Violet
- Permanent Rose or Crimson
- Cadmium Orange
- Payne's Grey

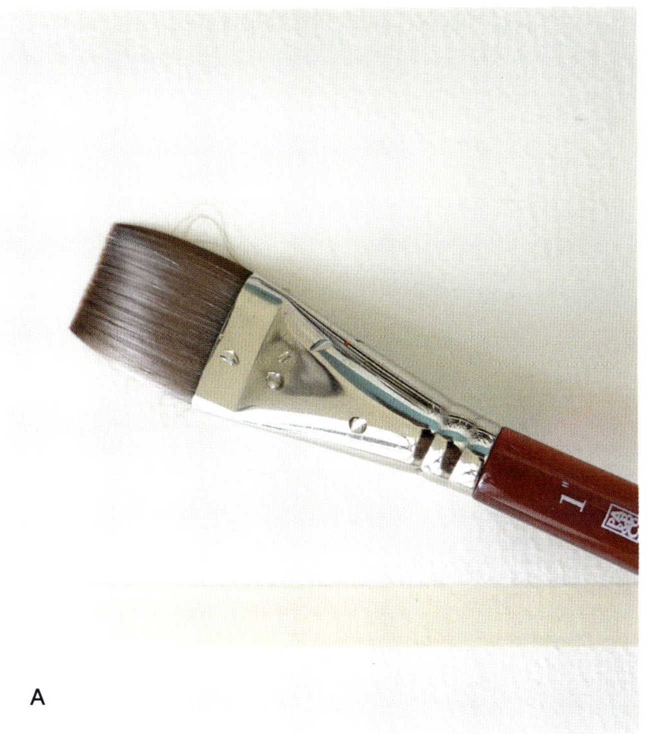

A

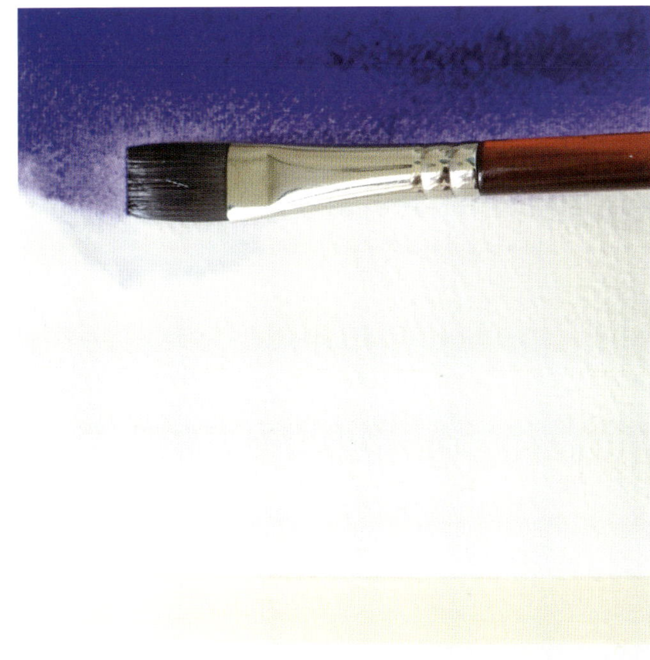

B

Step 1: Securing, Masking, and Wetting the Paper. Secure your paper to a drawing board. Place a piece of masking tape slightly below the center of the paper to separate the sky and the sea. Apply an even layer of clean water to the sky. (A)

Step 2: Sky. For the sky, we'll use a variegated gradient of three colors: Permanent Violet, Permanent Rose, and Cadmium Orange. Apply the Permanent Violet to the top of the sky and paint down one-third of the way. (B)

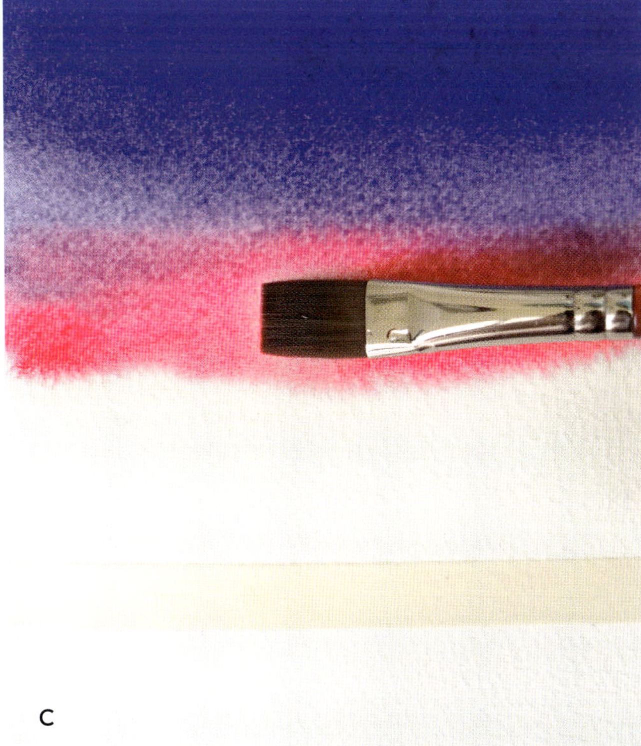

C

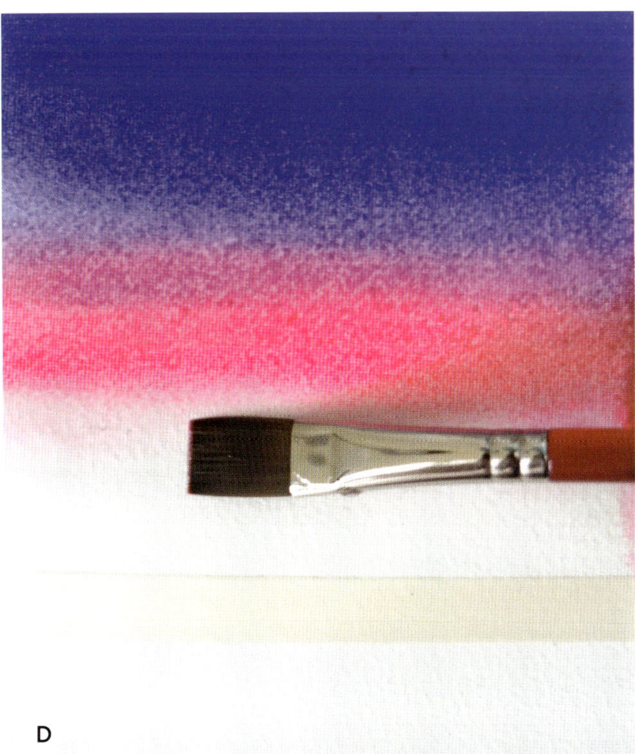

D

Clean your brush and switch to Permanent Rose or Crimson (or a similar shade) and apply it underneath the Permanent Violet (C) until two-thirds of the way down. As you sweep downward, quickly rinse your brush and continue with even horizontal brushstrokes, adding clean water as necessary to lighten the color. (D)

(continued)

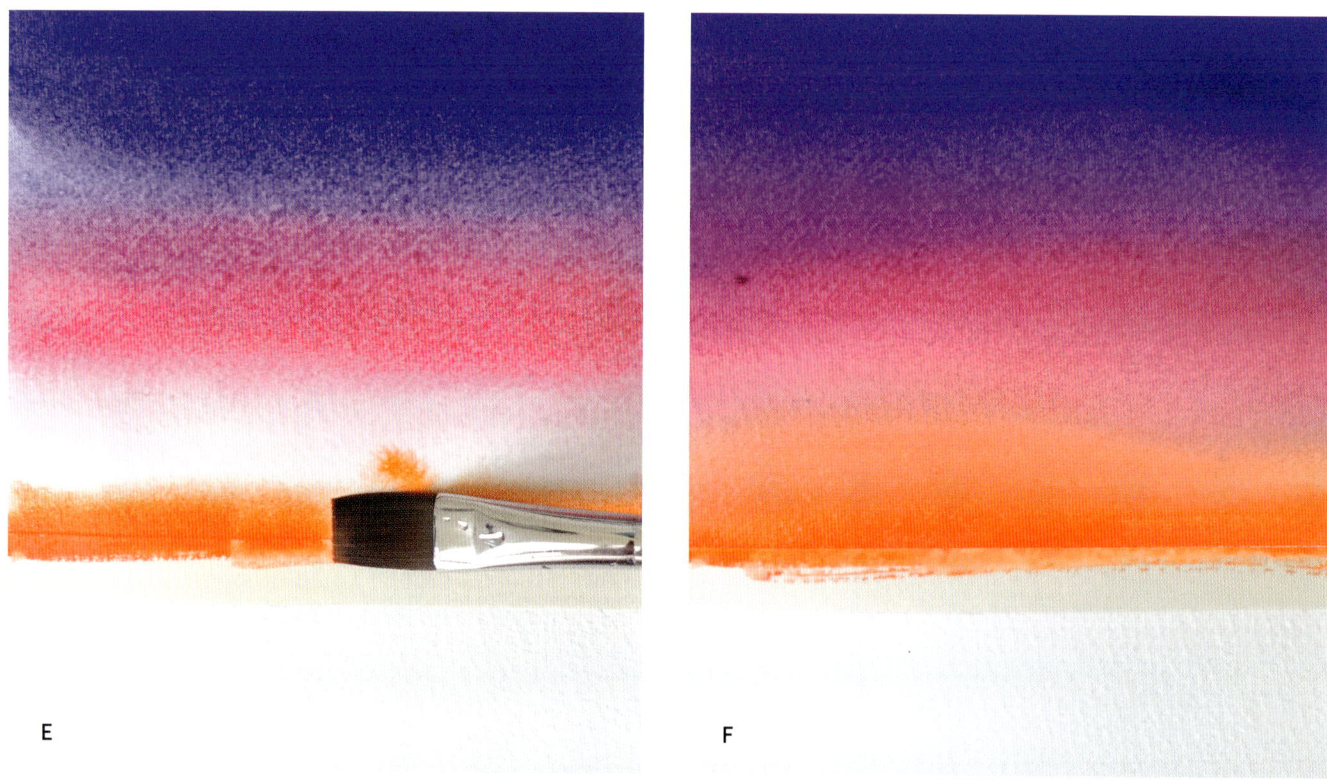

Clean your brush again and switch to Cadmium Orange, (E) applying it along the horizon line. Quickly rinse your brush and continue upward with even horizontal brushstrokes, adding clean water as necessary to lighten the color. Once you've applied all the colors, sweep the brush back and forth horizontally to get an even blend. (F) Let dry completely.

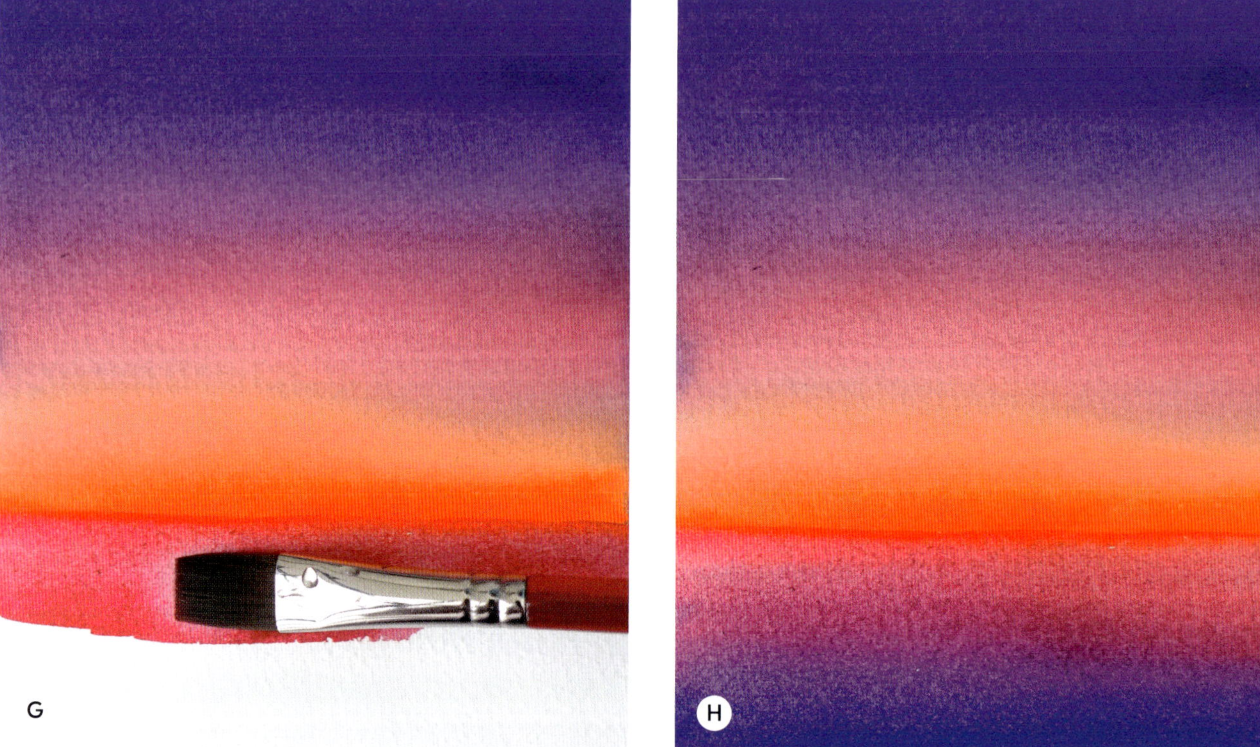

Step 3: Sea—Base Layer. Carefully peel off the masking tape. Start at the horizon line with an intense shade of Permanent Rose and paint downward. (G) Once you reach halfway, clean your brush and switch to Permanent Violet. Fill in the remaining area, blending the two colors together. (H)

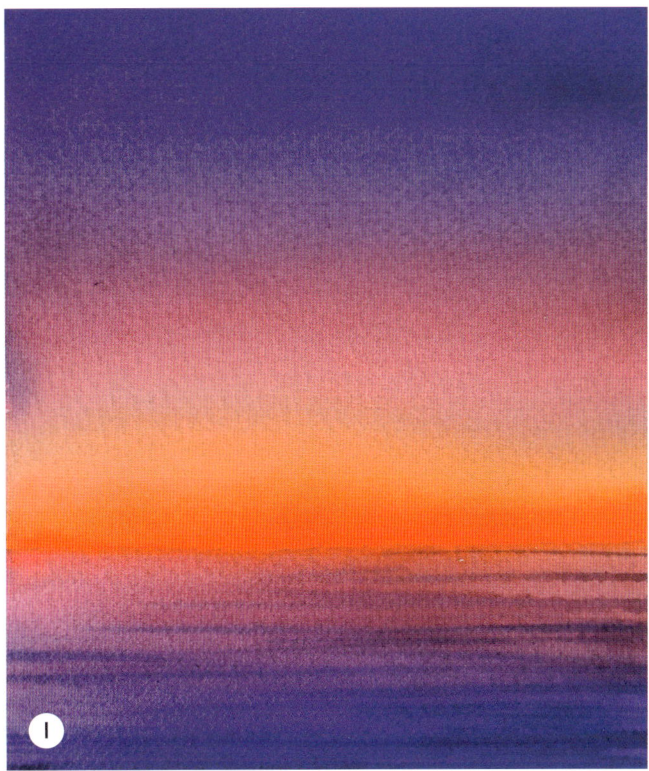

While the base layer is wet, add a few lines to create movement in the water. Use a smaller round brush for this step. (I) Let dry completely.

Step 4: Final Details. Add a small island near the horizon line to add depth to the painting. (J)

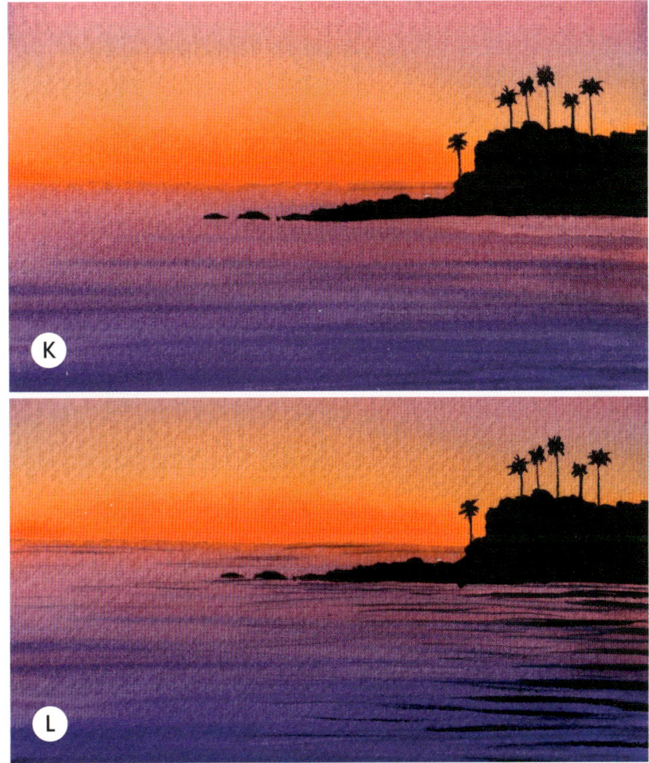

Add some small coconut palm trees on the island. (K, L) You want it to look like they are really far away, so you don't need to add a lot of details; just a small rough shape is enough. Vary the heights of the trees to make them look realistic.

Add the reflection of the island to finish the painting. Use a darker tone of Payne's Grey to add some lines in the water. (M) Leave ample space between them and make them thicker toward the bottom and thinner near the horizon line.

NORTHERN LIGHTS

The Northern Lights or Aurora Borealis are beautiful dancing waves of light that have captivated people for thousands of years. The stunning play of colors is definitely a wonderful subject to paint.

Suggested Color Palette

- Permanent Violet
- Turquoise Blue
- Cobalt Green
- Payne's Grey or black

(plus white gouache or white watercolor)

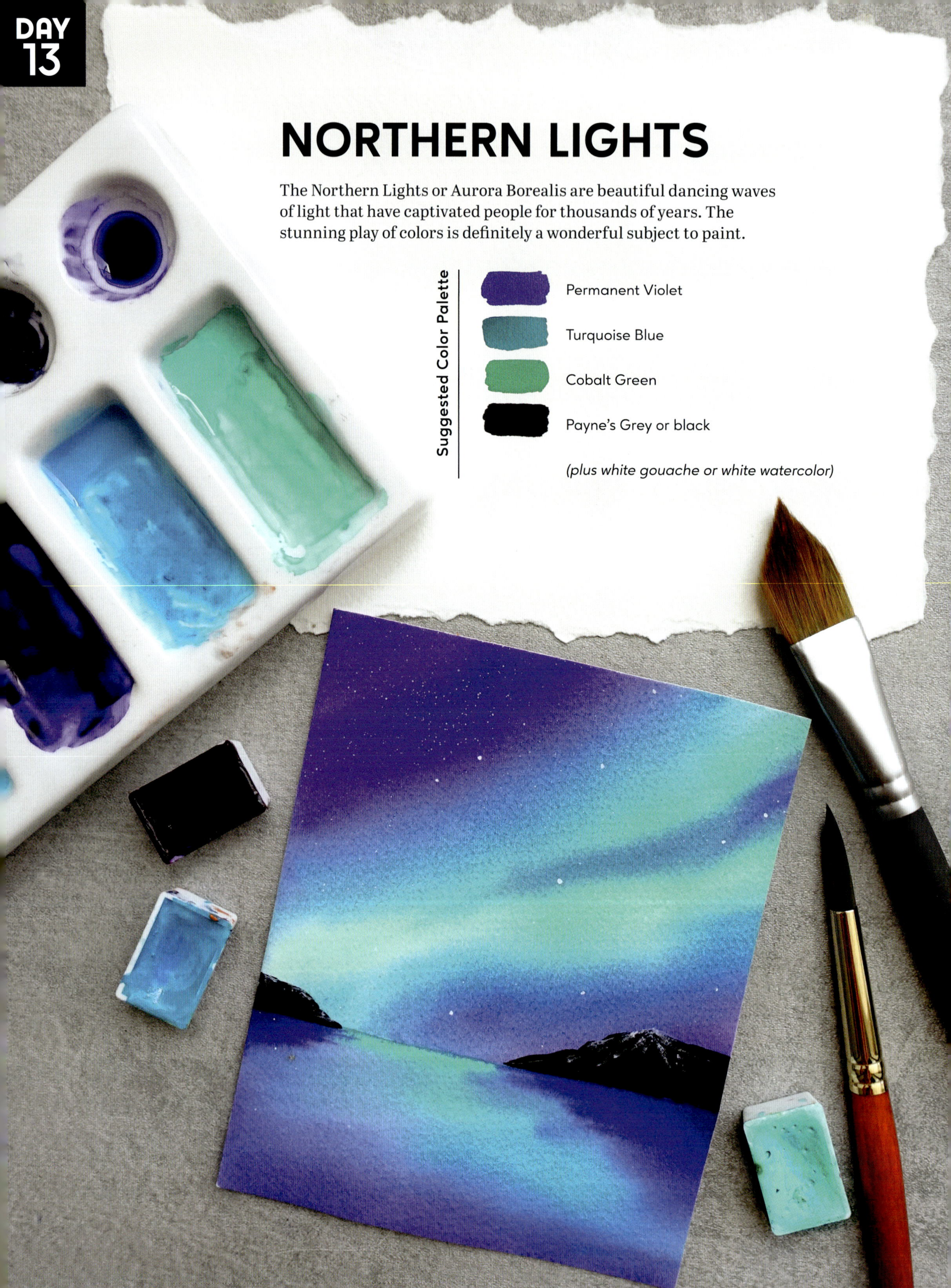

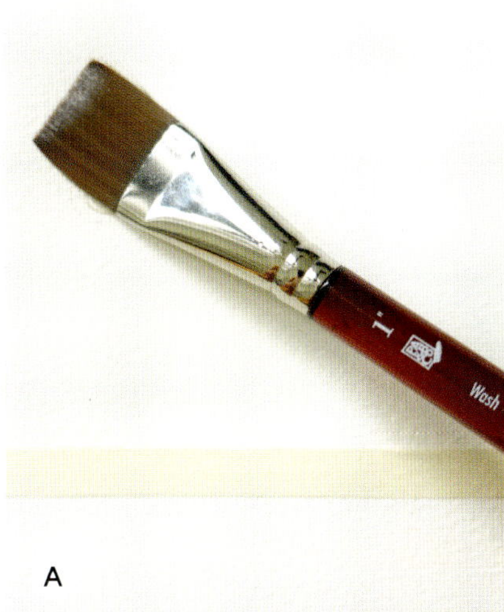

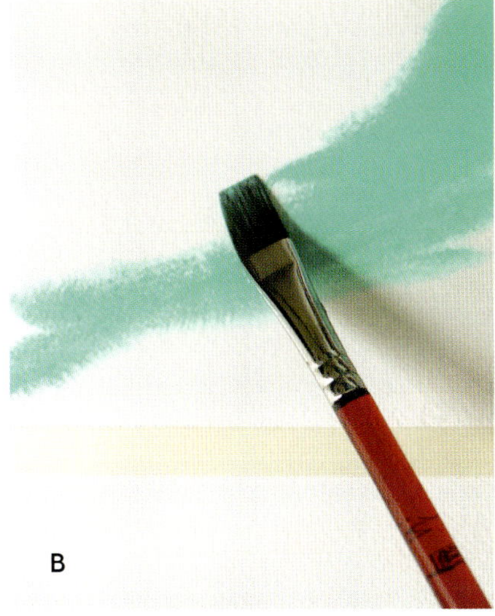

C

Step 1: Securing, Masking, and Wetting the Paper. Secure your paper to a drawing board. Place a piece of masking tape slightly below the center of your paper to separate the sky from the sea. Apply an even layer of clean water to the sky. (A)

Step 2: Sky. I'm going to use three colors. You can leave out one color and use two colors. Try to use a light shade and a dark shade to create contrast. I'm using a ½-inch (13 mm) flat brush to apply the paint. Flat brushes blend colors much better than round brushes. Use Cobalt Green to add a line in the middle of the sky. (B) You can choose any shape for the line—swirled, wavy, or curved. Clean your brush and switch to Turquoise Blue. Add it in a curved shape on either side of the Cobalt Green line. (C)

These lines don't have to be perfect. Just add the color and let it spread. (D)

Clean your brush again and switch to Permanent Violet, adding it to the remaining areas at the top and bottom. (E)

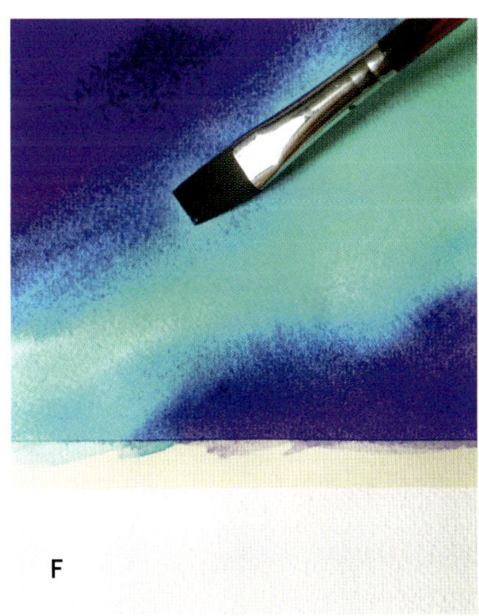

If needed, gently stroke a clean brush over the areas where the colors meet to create a softer and smoother blend. (F)

(continued)

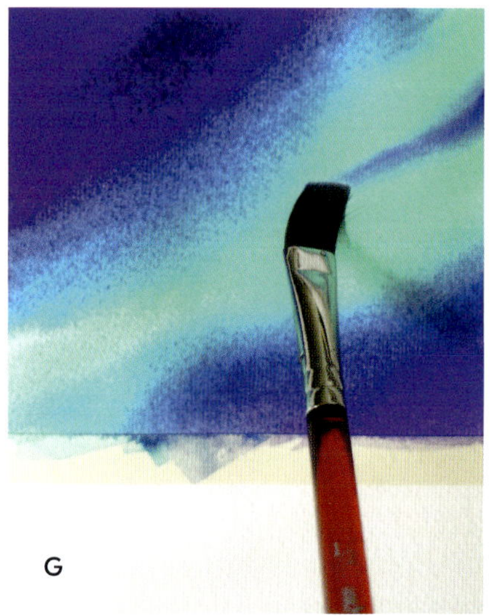

To add contrast, add a curved line of purple in the center. Just drag the brush from the upper-right corner and leave it halfway. (G) Let dry completely.

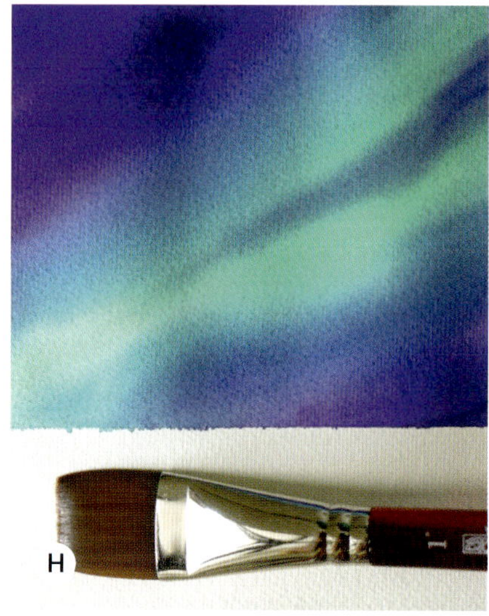

Step 3: Lake. Carefully peel off the masking tape (H) and apply an even layer of clean water to the lower part of the paper.

Start with Cobalt Green and apply it in the middle. (I)

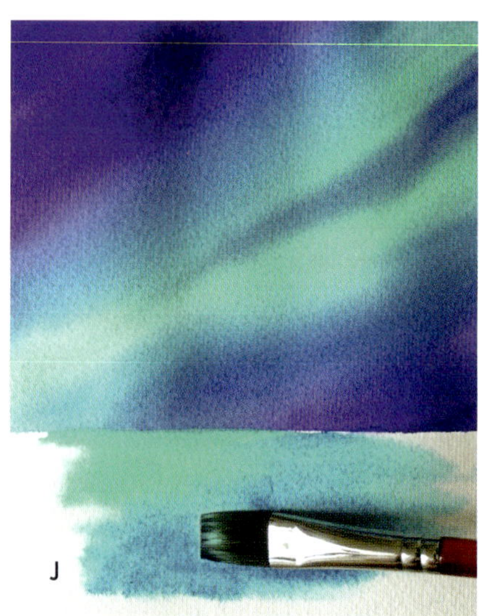

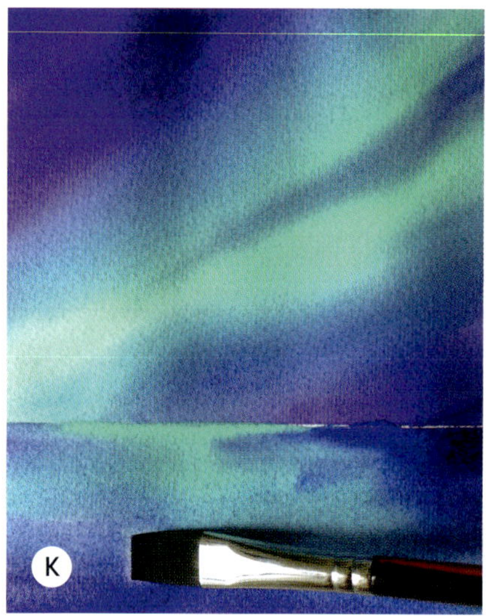

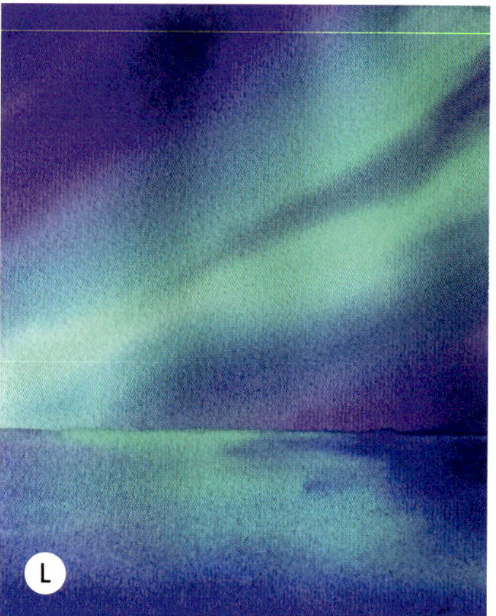

Clean your brush and switch to Turquoise Blue. Apply it underneath the Cobalt Green. (J) Clean your brush again and switch to Permanent Violet, applying it to both sides and the bottom. (K, L)

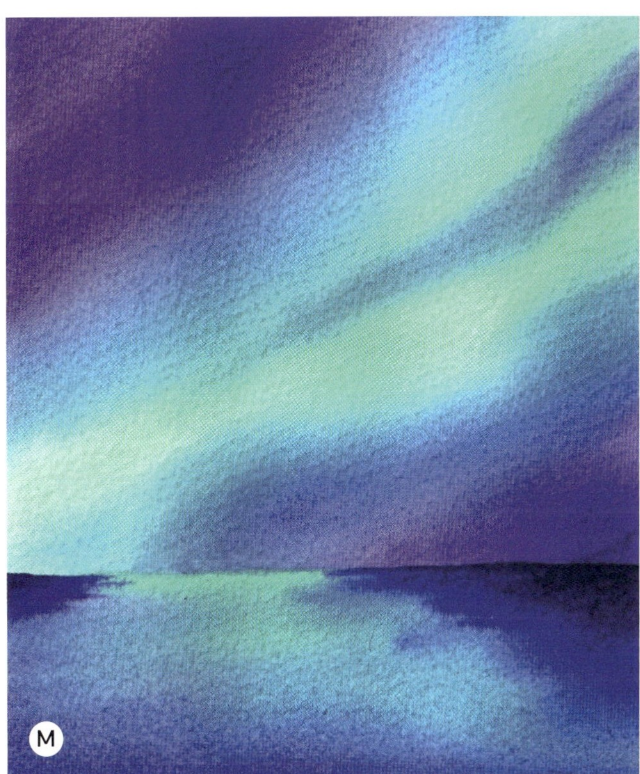

The base layer is ready. Before it dries, use Permanent Violet to add the reflection for the mountains below the horizon line on both sides. (M) Let dry completely.

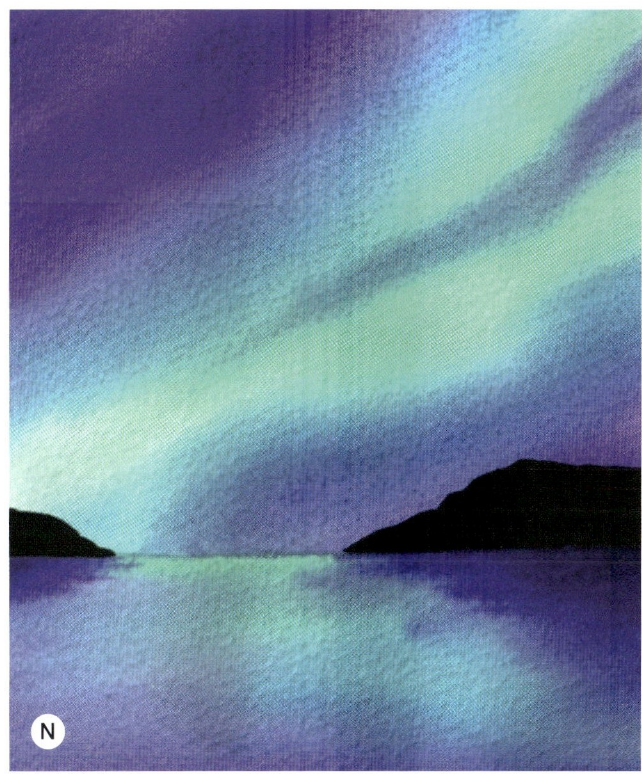

Step 4: Mountains. Use Payne's Grey or black and add mountains along the horizon line directly above their reflections. (N) Let dry completely.

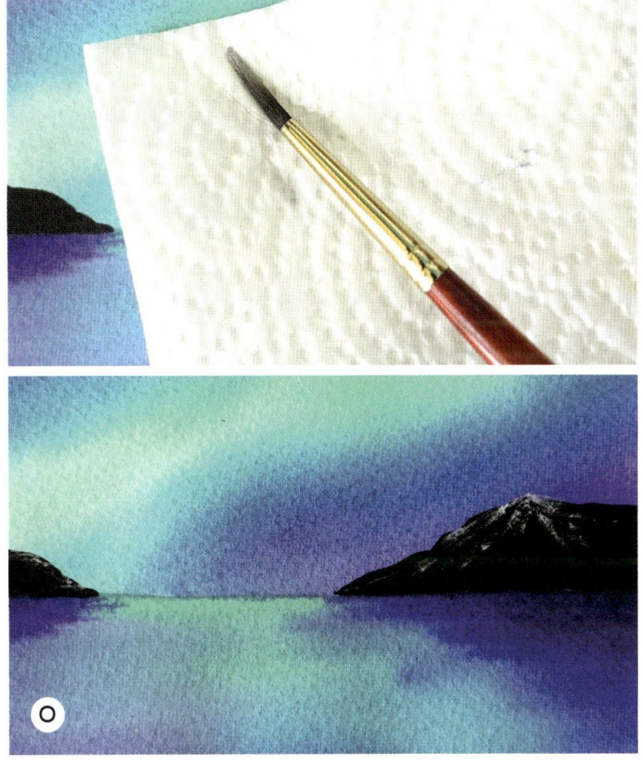

To add some realistic features, add texture with white gouache or white watercolor. After loading a small round brush with paint, dab it several times on a paper towel to remove the excess water. Add some dry brush patterns on the upper part of the mountain. (O)

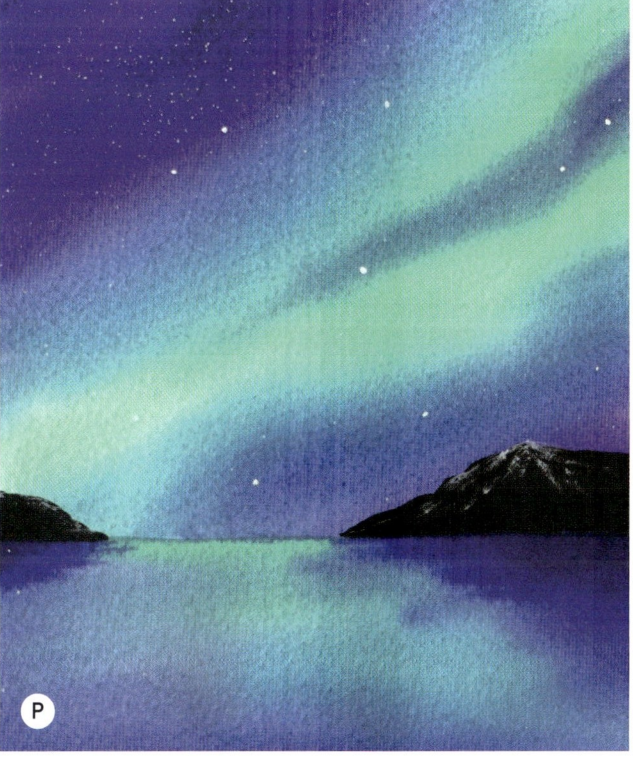

Add some stars to finish the painting. (P)

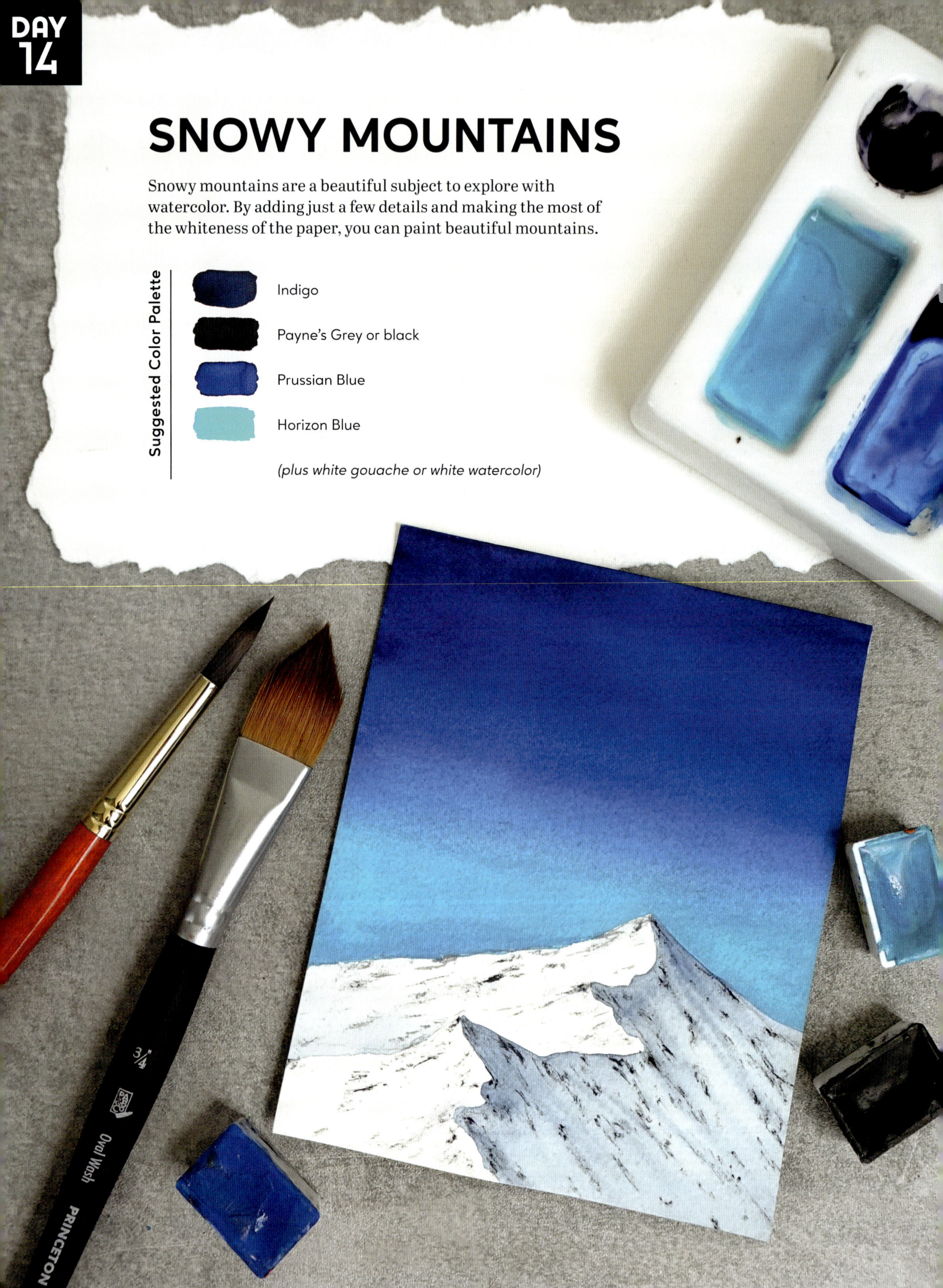

DAY 14

SNOWY MOUNTAINS

Snowy mountains are a beautiful subject to explore with watercolor. By adding just a few details and making the most of the whiteness of the paper, you can paint beautiful mountains.

Suggested Color Palette

- Indigo
- Payne's Grey or black
- Prussian Blue
- Horizon Blue

(plus white gouache or white watercolor)

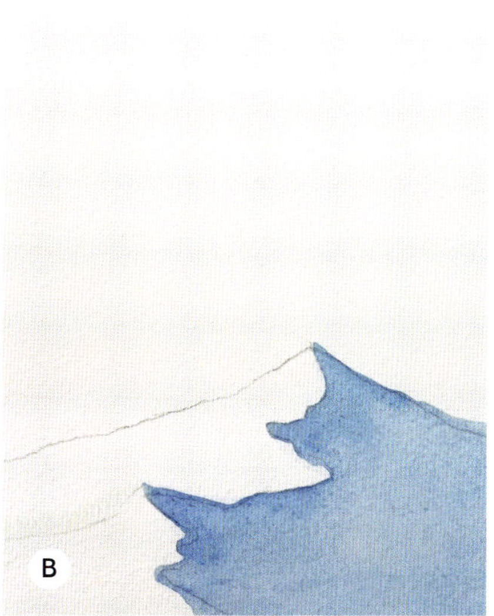

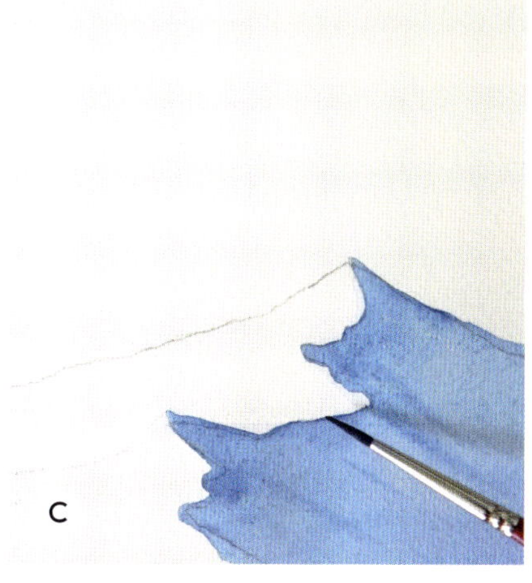

Step 1: Adding the Sketch. Add a light pencil sketch of the mountains. (A)

Step 2: Medium Tones and Shadows. We'll paint the mountain in two steps: first is the base layer where we add the medium tones and then we'll add the details. Leaving the left side of the sketch as it is, begin applying a medium tone of Indigo to the right side, following the line you added in the center. (B) While the background is still wet, add a few lines diagonally to the right with a medium Indigo tone. Make sure you use medium or lighter tones for the base layer so it doesn't get too dark. (C)

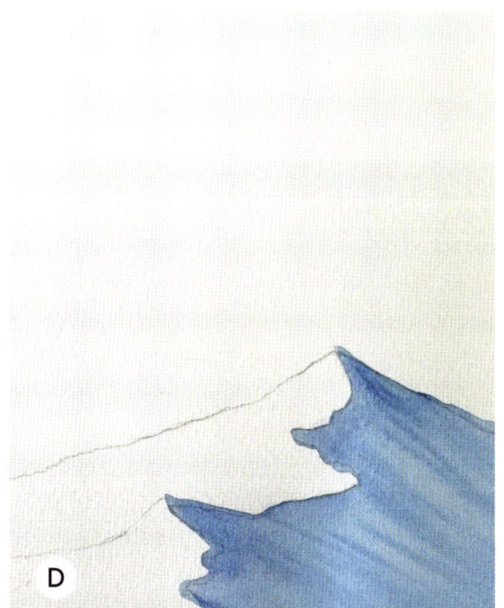

Let dry completely. (D)

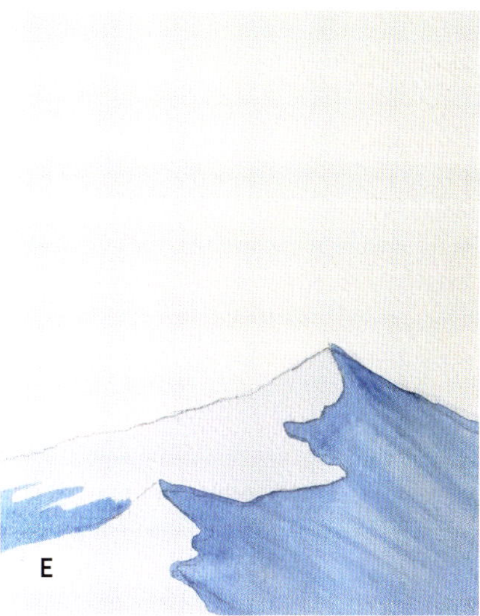

Add the shadows on the left side, trying to keep the tones light. (E)

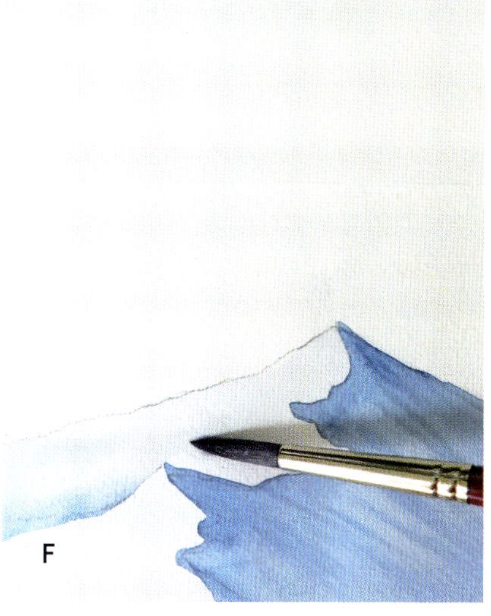

Start with a medium tone and add it along the contour of the upper part of the mountain as shown. (F)

(continued)

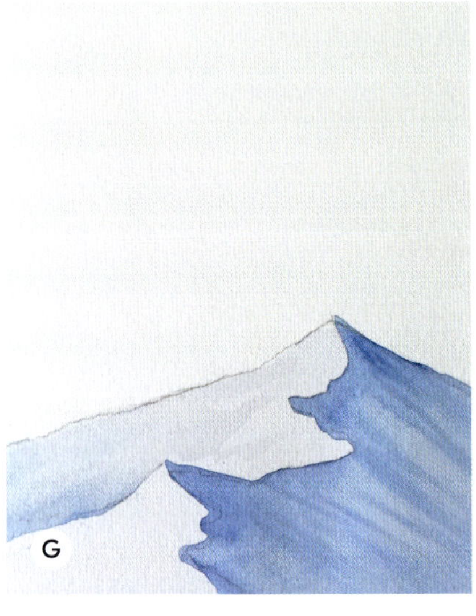

Quickly rinse your brush and continue with even brushstrokes until you fill it in, adding clean water as necessary to lighten the color. (G)

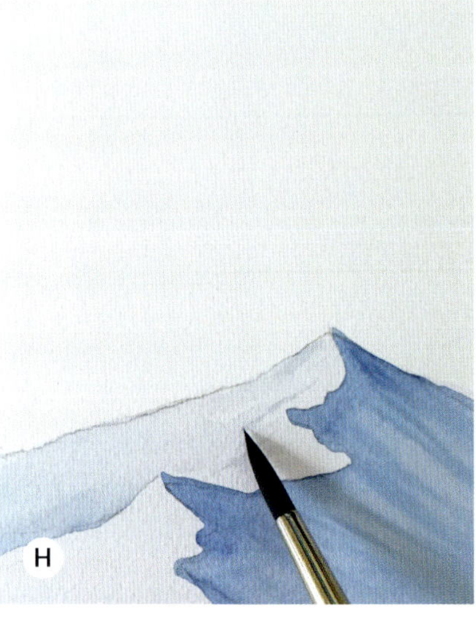

Toward the top, add a few lines using a lighter tone of Indigo. (H) They don't need to be prominent.

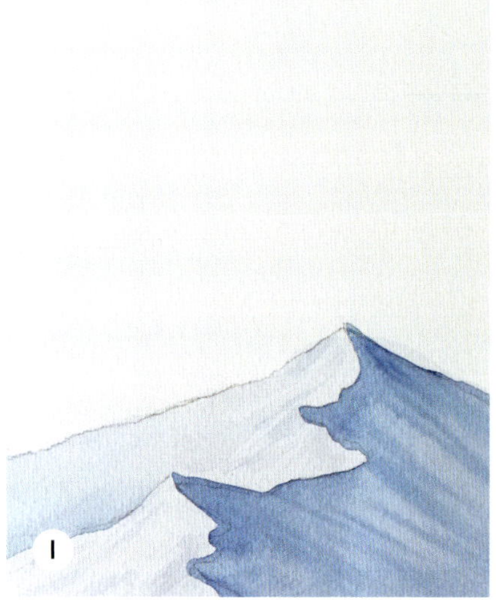

Add a few lines using a lighter tone on the bottom section as well. (I) Let dry completely.

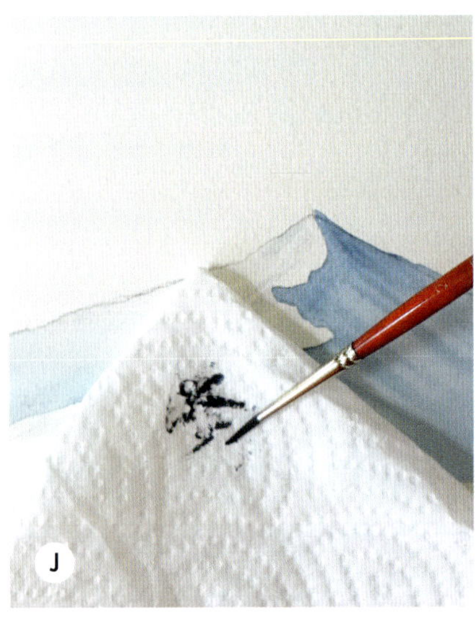

Step 3: Details. Use dry paint to add the details. Load a darker shade of Payne's Grey or black on the brush and dab it several times on a paper towel to remove the excess water. (J)

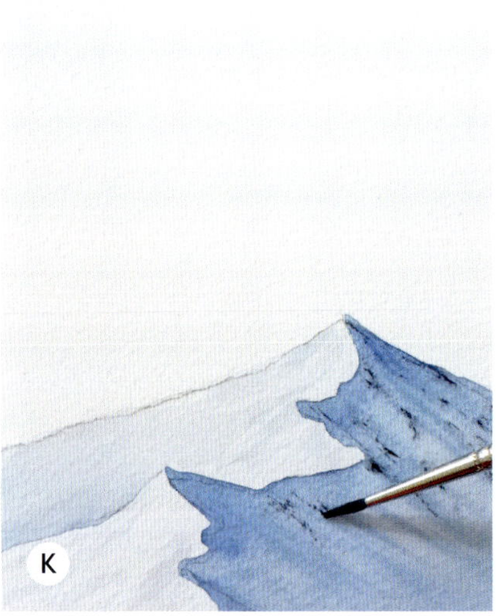

Add some dry brush patterns on both sides of the mountain. (K) These patterns don't have to be any particular size or shape, just add them randomly.

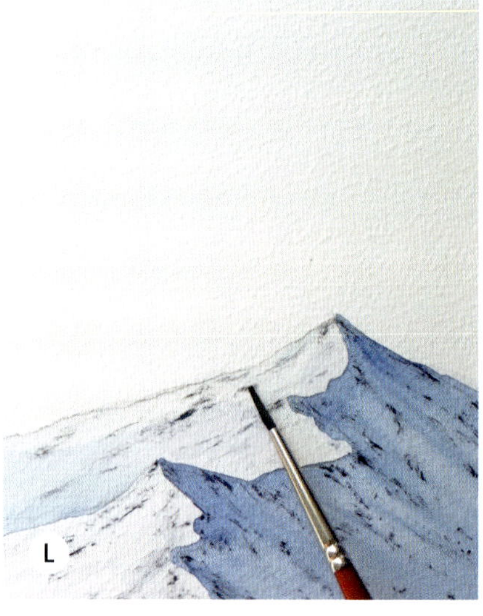

Add more patterns on the right side with the shadows and less patterns on the left side. (L)

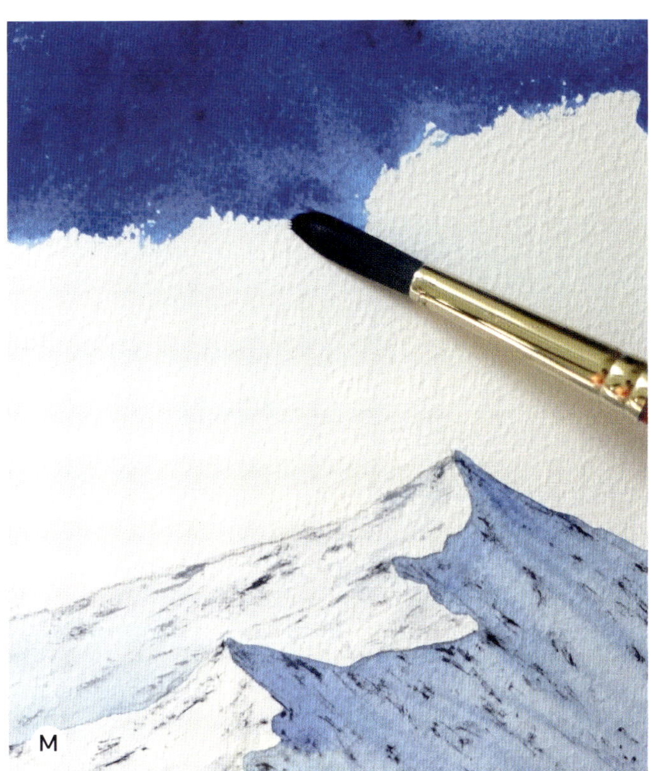

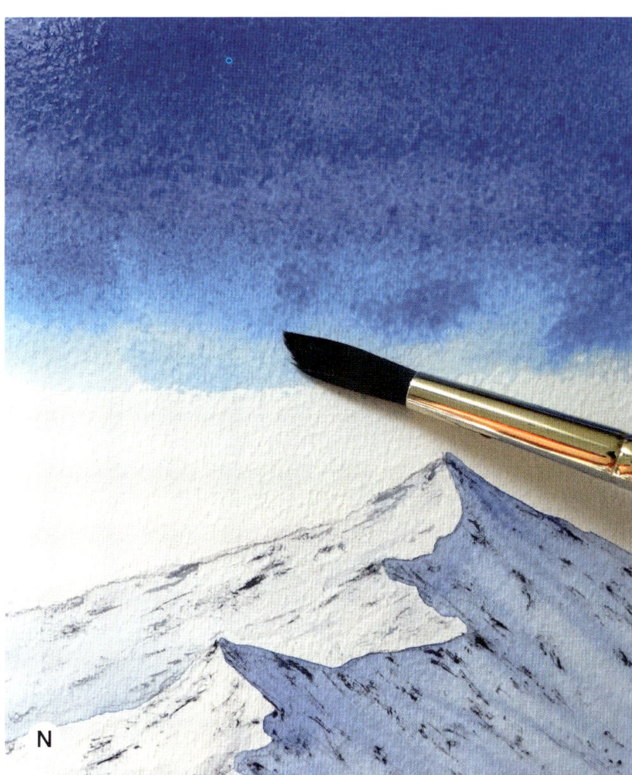

Step 4: Sky. For the sky, use a variegated wash of two colors. I'm using a dark and a light blue (Prussian Blue and Horizon Blue). You can choose any colors you like. Horizon Blue is a pastel blue. If you want to create a similar color, add some white gouache or white watercolor to Turquoise Blue. Apply Prussian Blue to the upper part of the sky. (M) When you reach the middle, clean your brush and switch to Horizon Blue or another pastel blue of your choice. Fill in the remaining area to finish the painting. (N)

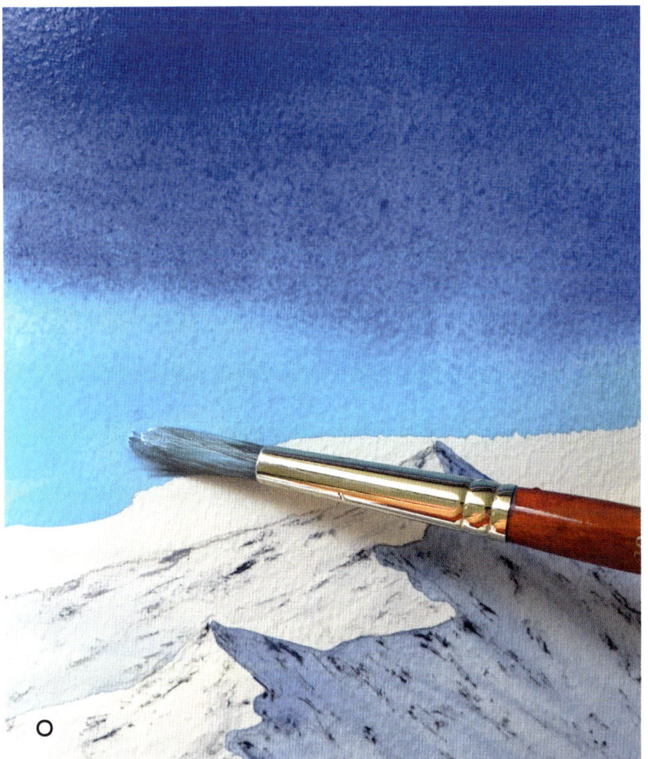

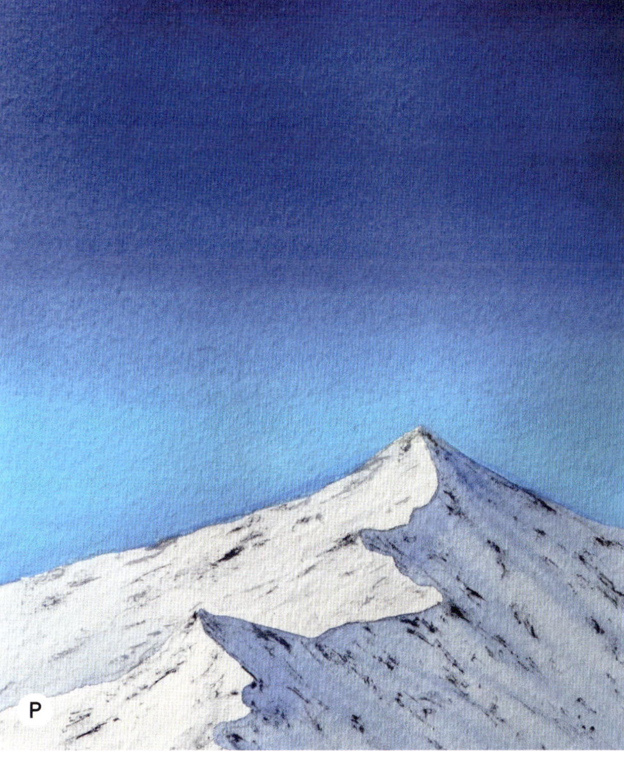

Be careful along the shape of the mountain when applying the paint for the sky. (O, P)

TROPICAL PALMS

Sunsets and palm trees are a theme most of us painted in childhood, and I think it's an evergreen theme that artists explore. I still love painting a bold sky and adding some palm silhouettes. We'll be using the wet-on-wet technique for the sky.

Suggested Color Palette

- Prussian Blue
- Permanent Rose
- Cadmium Orange or Vermillion Hue
- Pyrrole Red
- Payne's Grey or black

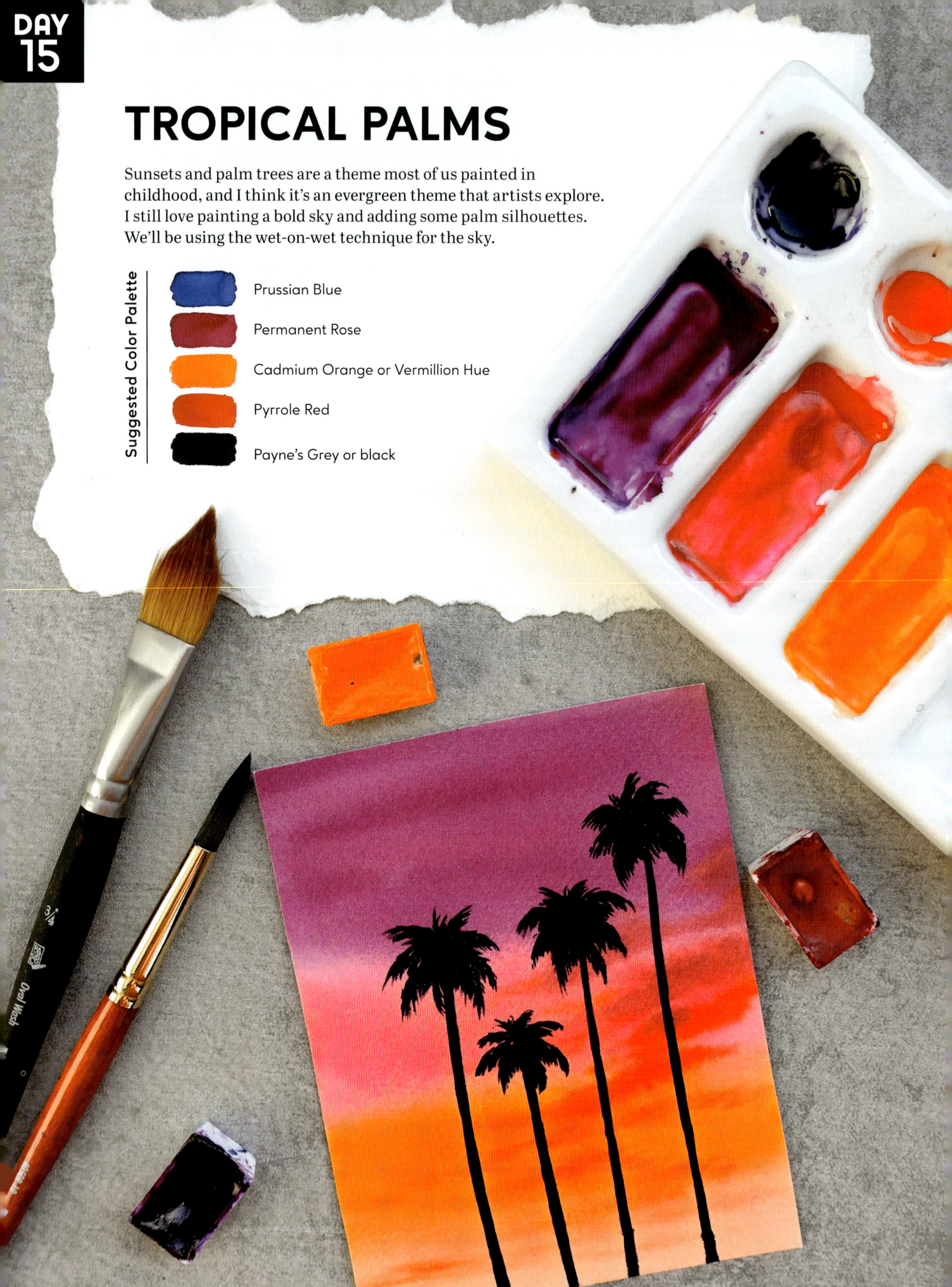

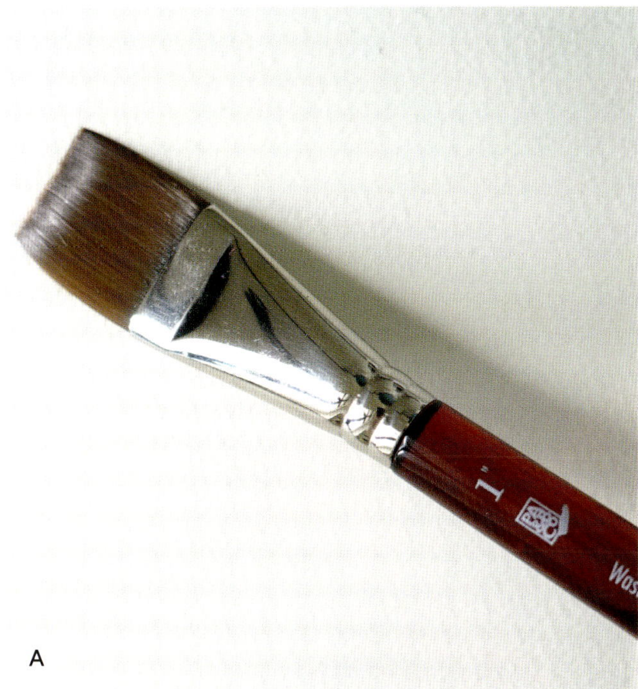
A

Step 1: Securing and Wetting the Paper. Secure your paper to a drawing board. Apply an even layer of clean water to the entire paper. (A)

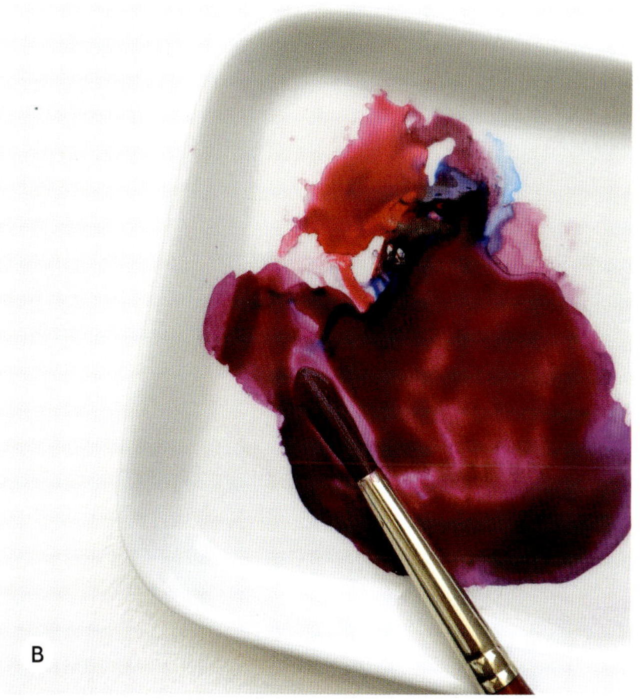
B

Step 2: Sky. For the sky, I'm using three colors: purple, Permanent Rose, and Cadmium Orange. To create the purple, add some Prussian Blue to the Permanent Rose. (B) By varying the ratio of the colors in the mix, your purple will look different.

C

D

If you already have a similar color, use that directly, or just use Permanent Violet. Apply the purple with a flat brush to one-third of the sky. (C) Clean your brush and switch to Permanent Rose. Add it underneath the purple, (D) blending both colors.

(continued)

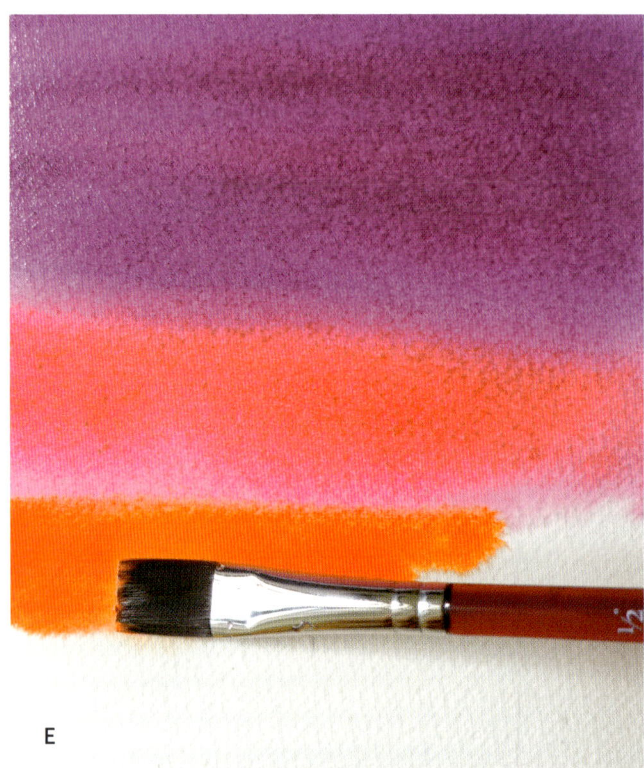

Clean your brush again and switch to Cadmium Orange, or any orange. Add it underneath the Permanent Rose, (E) blending the colors well. Quickly rinse your brush and continue with even horizontal brushstrokes until you reach the bottom, adding clean water as necessary to lighten the color. Add clouds to the wet sky using Pyrrole Red, or any red. (F)

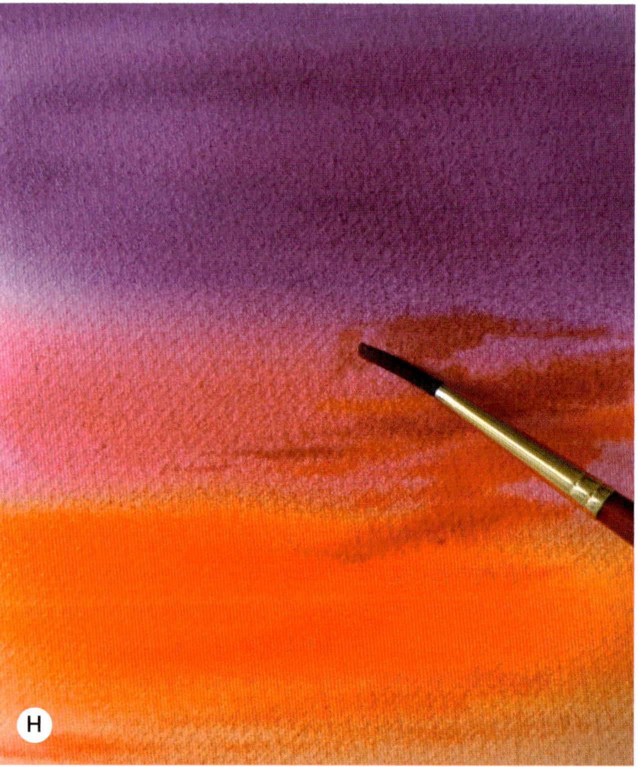

If you want to make the sky even more dramatic, add more clouds before the background dries. (G, H)
Let dry completely.

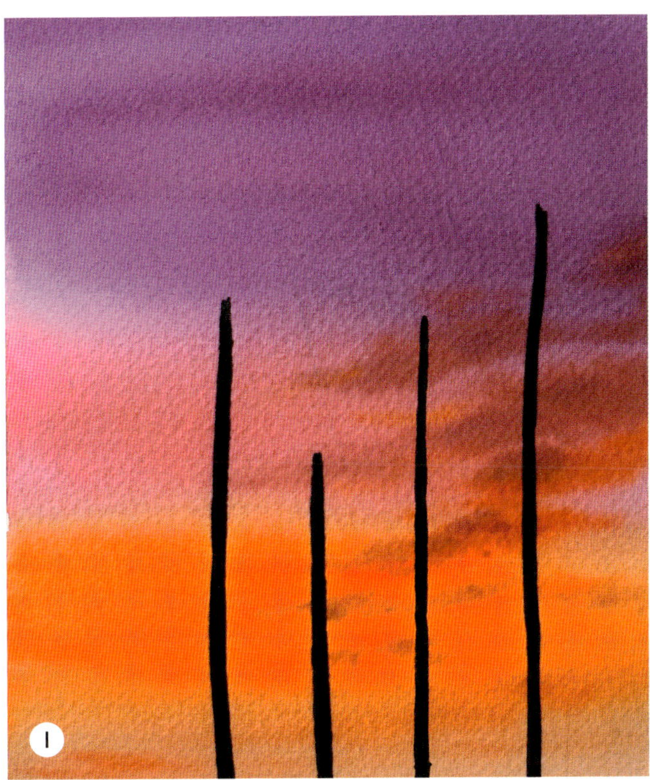

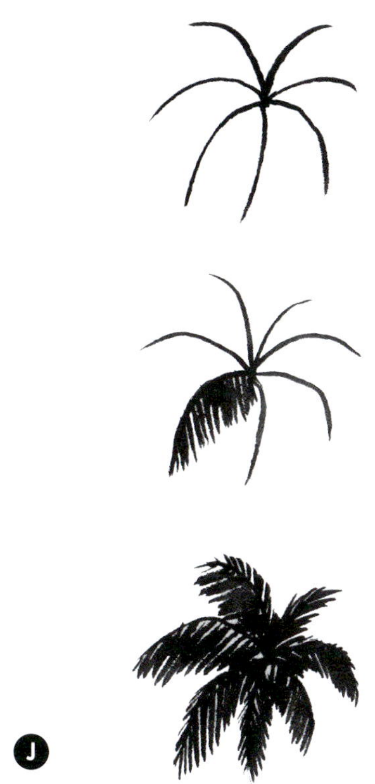

Step 3: Palm Trees. Add the palm trees, starting with the tree trunks. (I) I'm adding four palm trees. You can choose any number: three, four, or five. Make sure you add the palm trees at different heights to make your image look realistic.

When you've finished the trunk, add six or seven curved lines for the frond stems using Payne's Grey or black. (J)

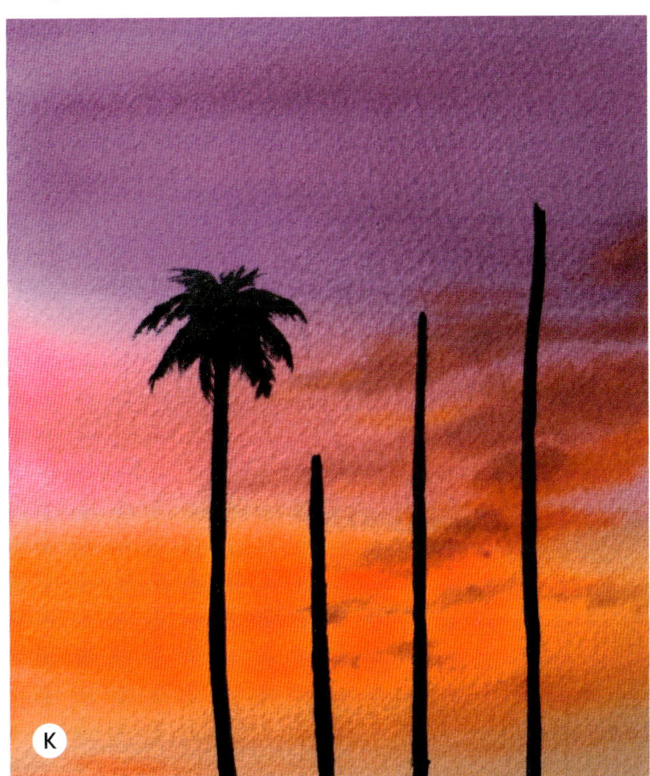

Add leaves to both sides of the fronds. (K)

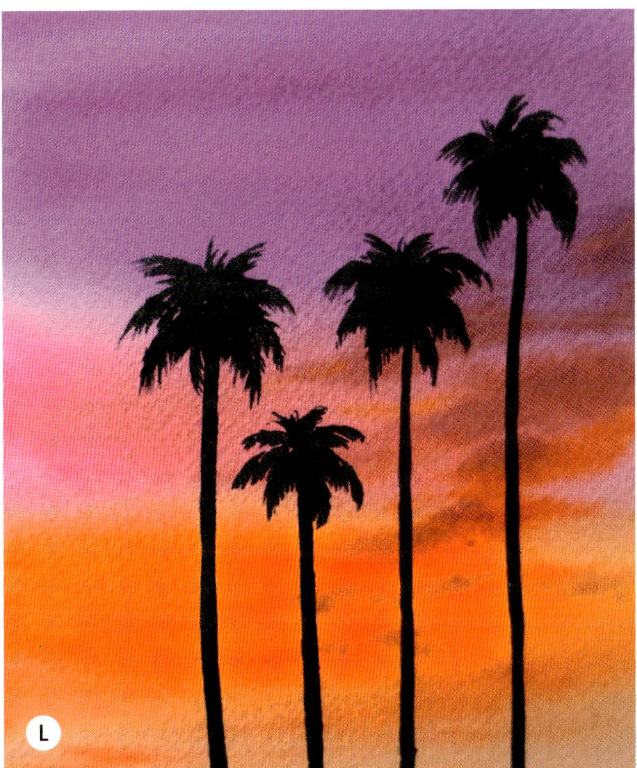

Add fronds to all of your palm trees to finish the painting. (L)

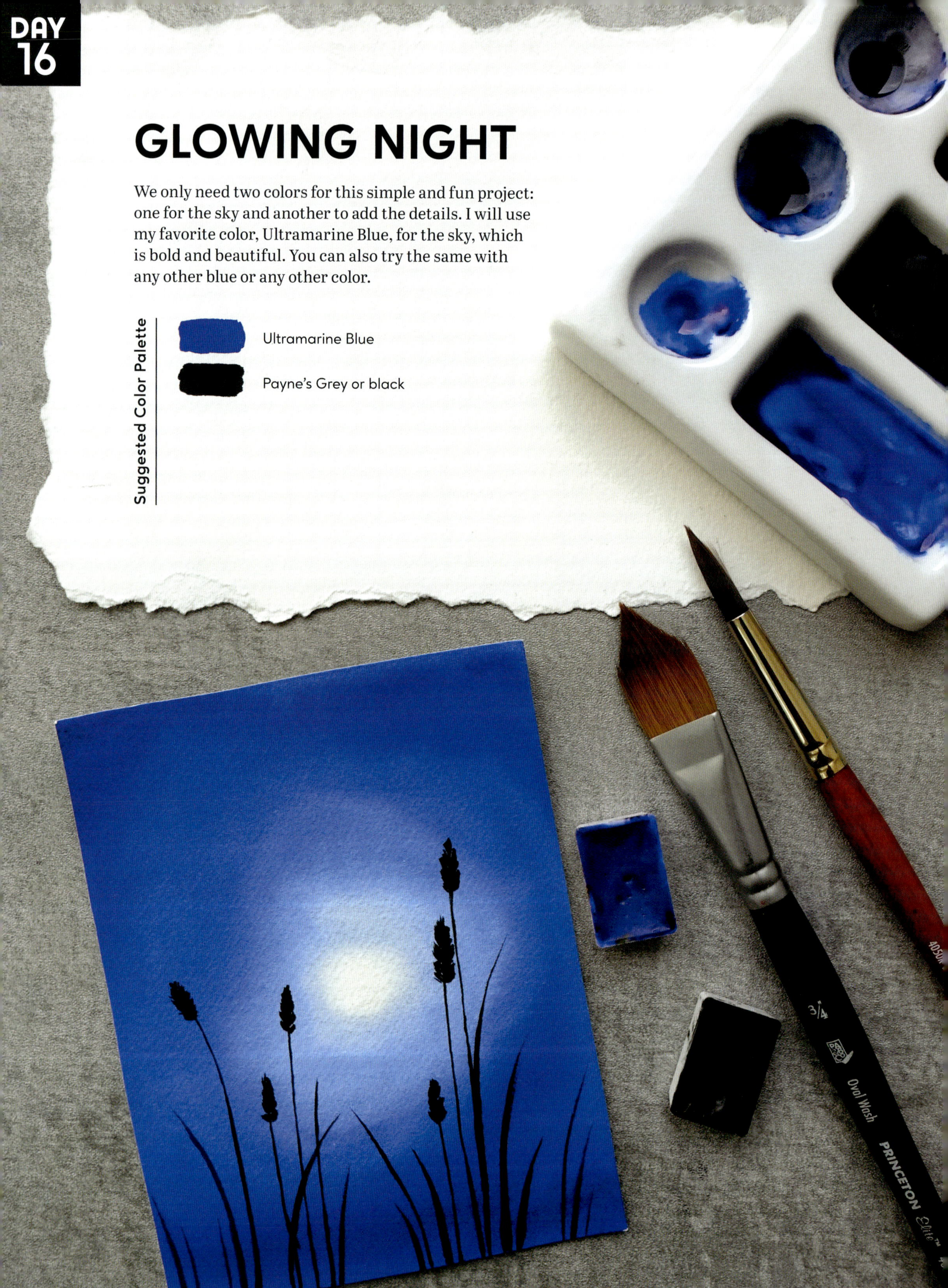

DAY 16

GLOWING NIGHT

We only need two colors for this simple and fun project: one for the sky and another to add the details. I will use my favorite color, Ultramarine Blue, for the sky, which is bold and beautiful. You can also try the same with any other blue or any other color.

Suggested Color Palette

- Ultramarine Blue
- Payne's Grey or black

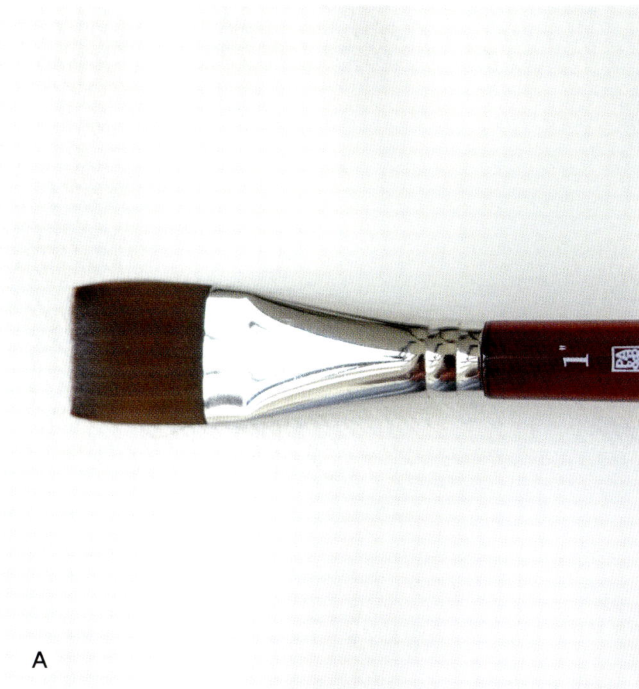

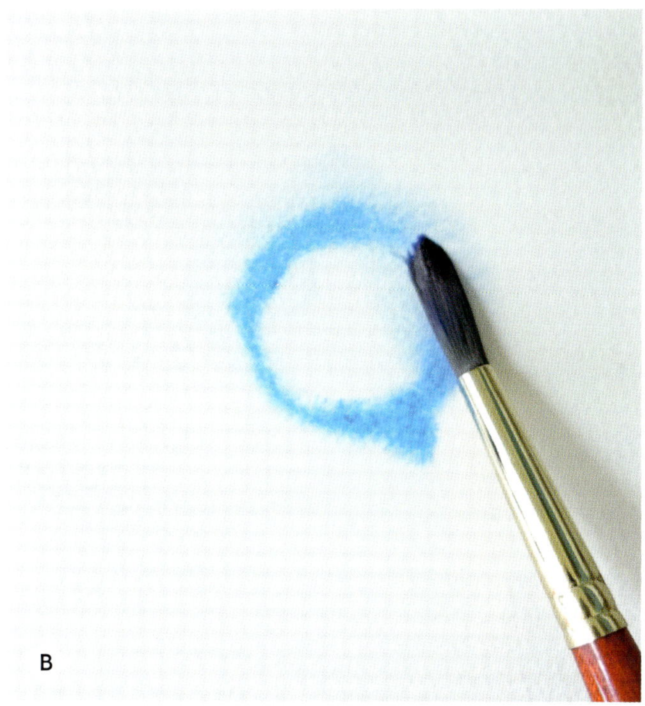

Step 1: Securing and Wetting the Paper. Secure your paper to a drawing board. Apply an even layer of clean water to the entire paper. (A)

Step 2: Background. Start with a lighter tone of blue or any of the colors you want to use. Add a circular shape for the moon using one of your medium round brushes. (B) Draw a slightly larger circle than you need because the colors in the background will spread out and the size of the circle will get smaller.

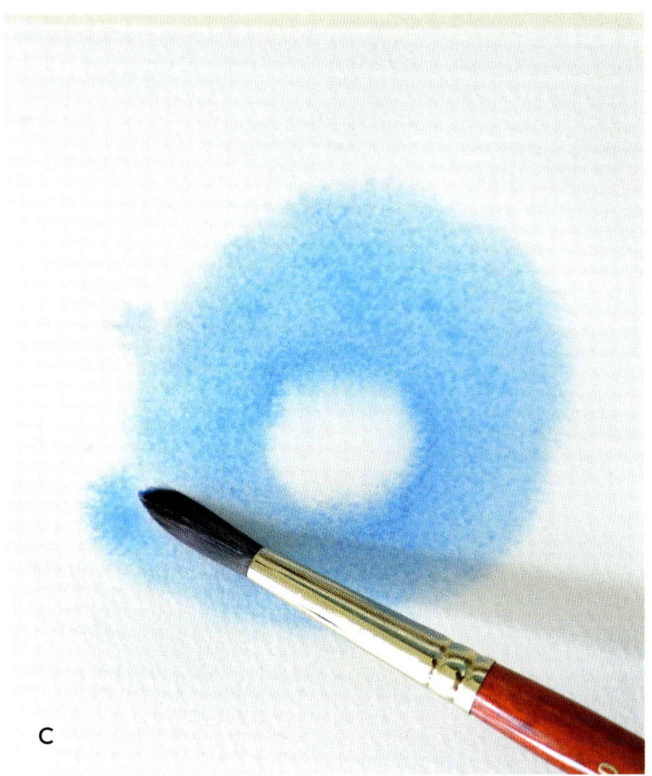

Use the same tonal value and add it around the moon. (C)

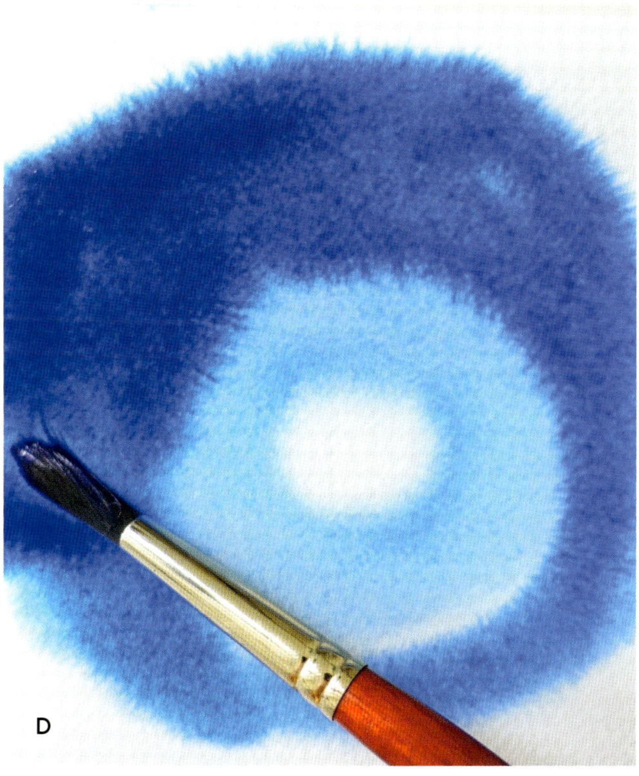

You want to make the color darker as you move away from the moon. Switch to a medium tone and add it around the moon. (D)

(continued)

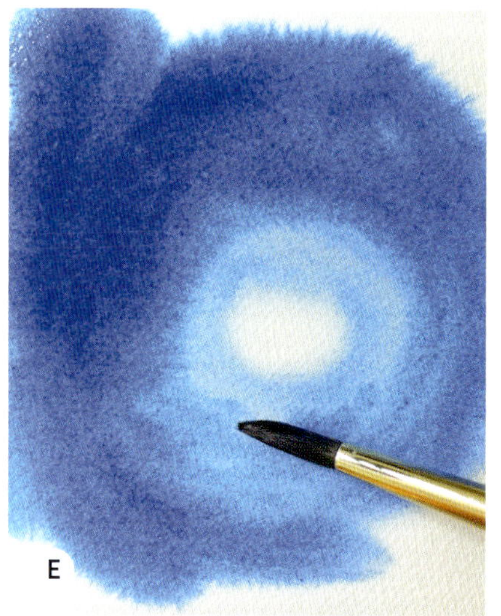

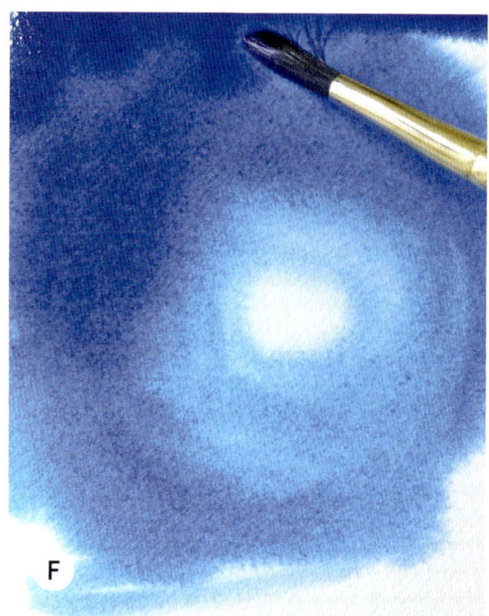

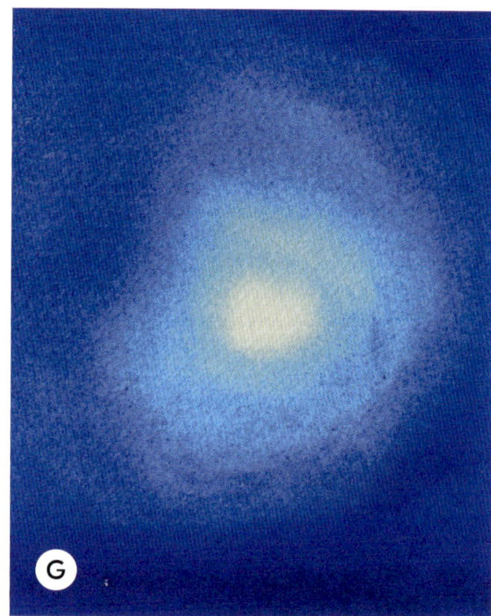

Switch to an even darker tone and fill in the remaining area. (E)

The area near the moon should be light and become bolder and stronger in tone moving toward the four corners of your paper. (F) Let dry completely. (G)

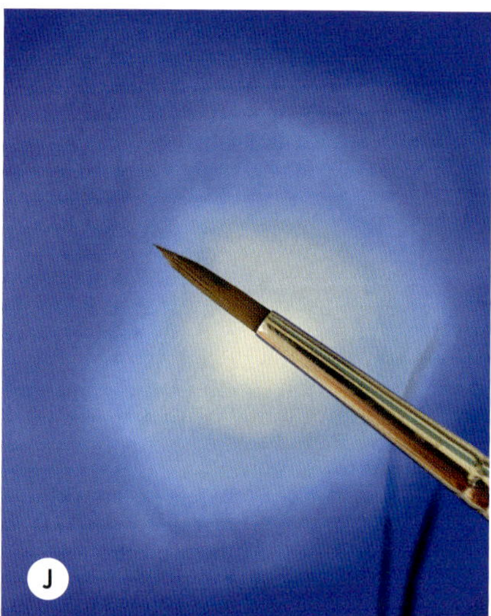

Step 3: Details. Add a grass silhouette (H) with a few thin and delicate lines (stems) and long, curved and pointed leaves using Payne's Grey or black. (I) To get these lines perfect, use a brush with a pointed tip or a detail brush. (J) You can add as many as you like.

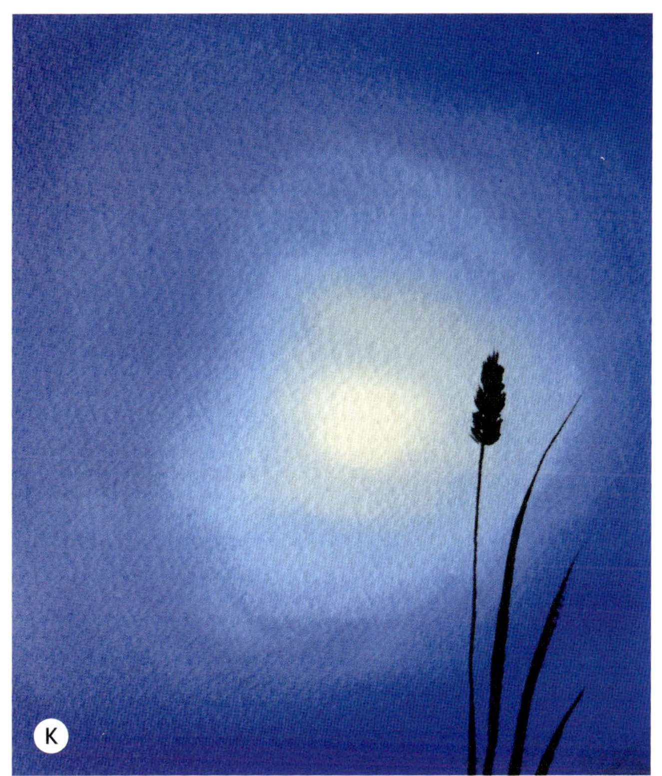

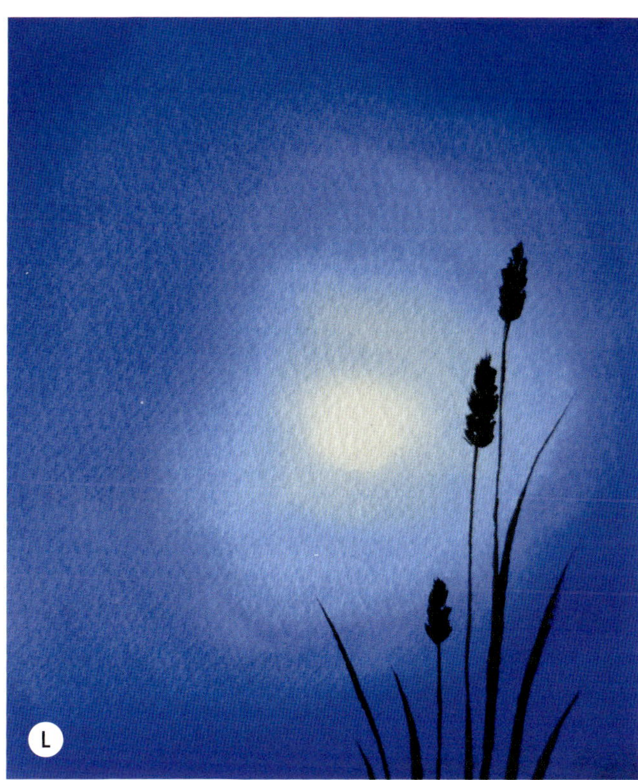

Add some feathery flowers on top of the stems at different heights. (K, L)

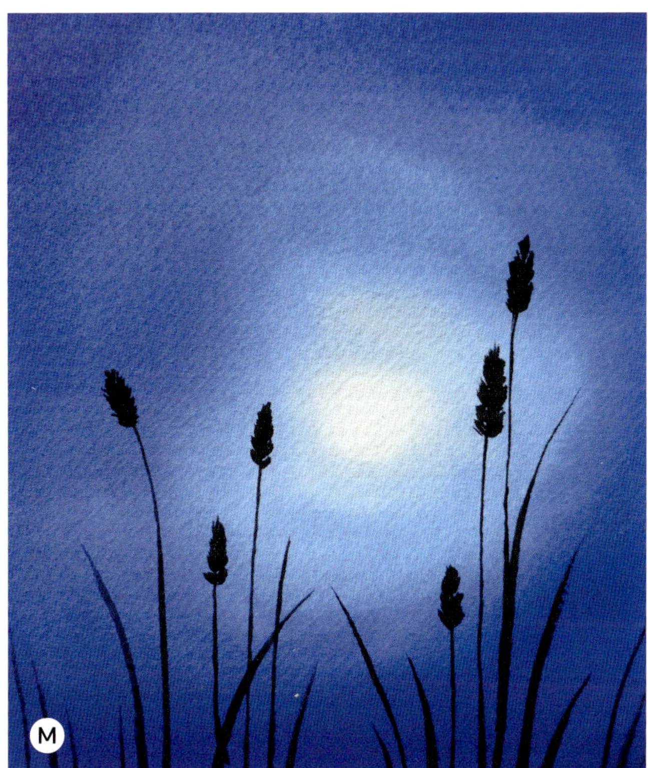

Add a grass silhouette on the left side for balance and to finish the painting. (M)

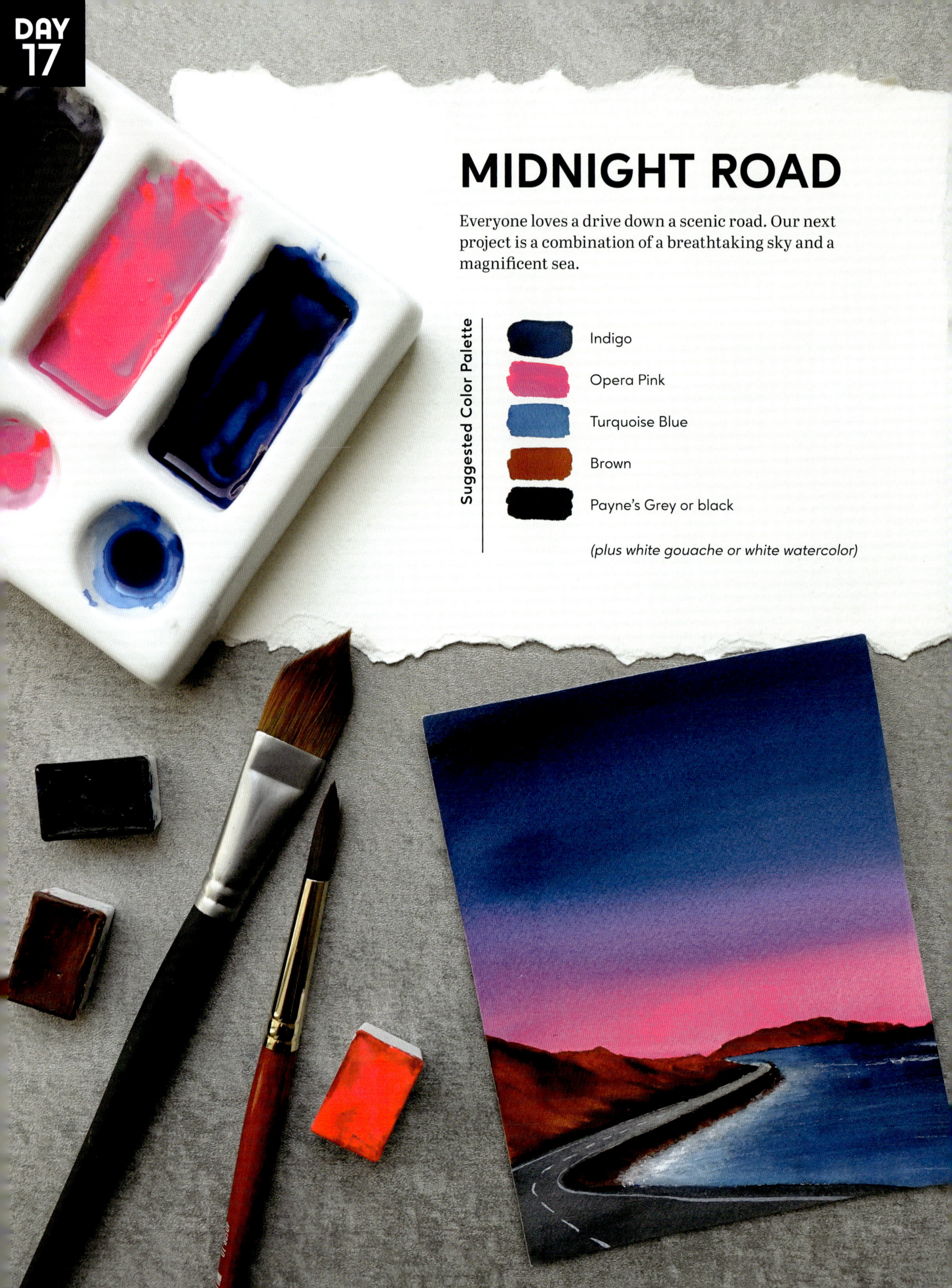

MIDNIGHT ROAD

Everyone loves a drive down a scenic road. Our next project is a combination of a breathtaking sky and a magnificent sea.

Suggested Color Palette

- Indigo
- Opera Pink
- Turquoise Blue
- Brown
- Payne's Grey or black

(plus white gouache or white watercolor)

Step 1: Adding the Sketch. Add a light pencil sketch of the mountains, the road, and the body of water. (A)

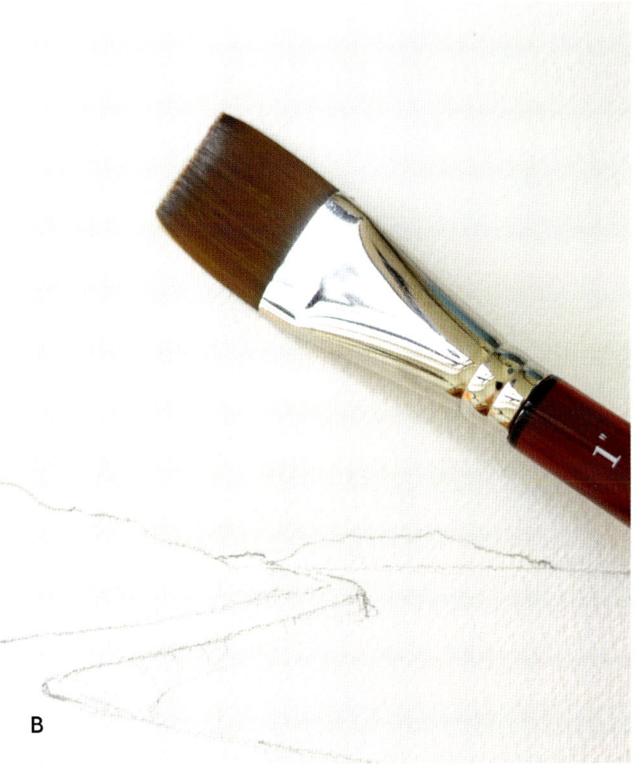

Step 2: Securing and Wetting the Paper. Secure your paper to a drawing board. Apply an even layer of clean water to the sky. (B)

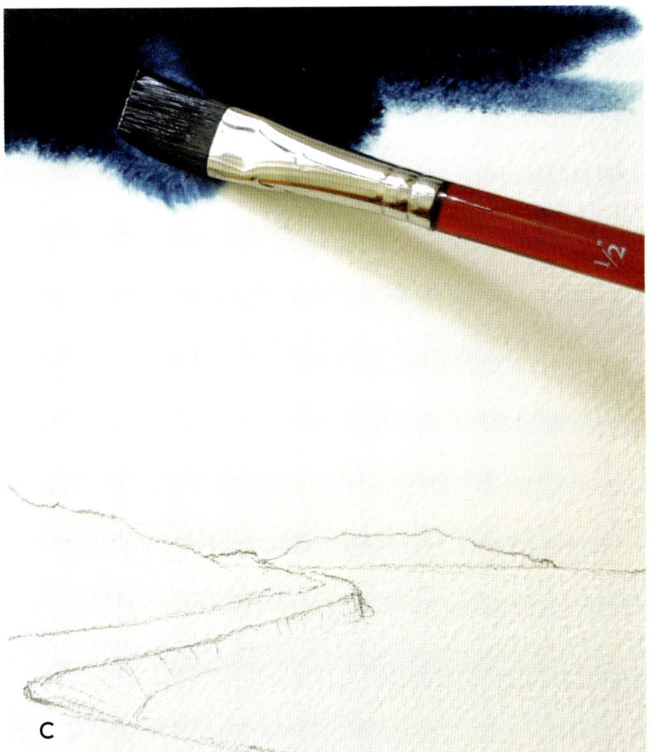

Step 3: Sky. Use a variegated mixture of two colors for the sky: Indigo and Opera Pink. You can choose any other colors you like. Apply Indigo to the upper part of the sky using a flat brush. (C) Switch to a stronger tone of Indigo and apply it to almost half of the sky. (D)

(continued)

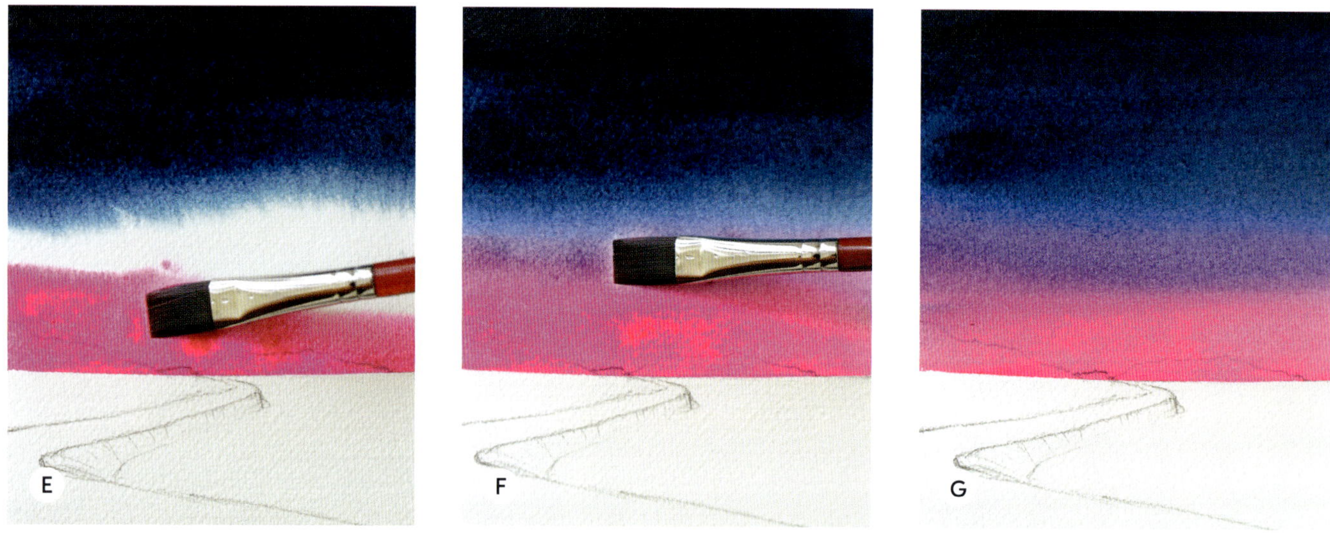

Clean your brush again and switch to Opera Pink. Apply it from the bottom up, (E) blending both colors together. (F, G) Let dry completely.

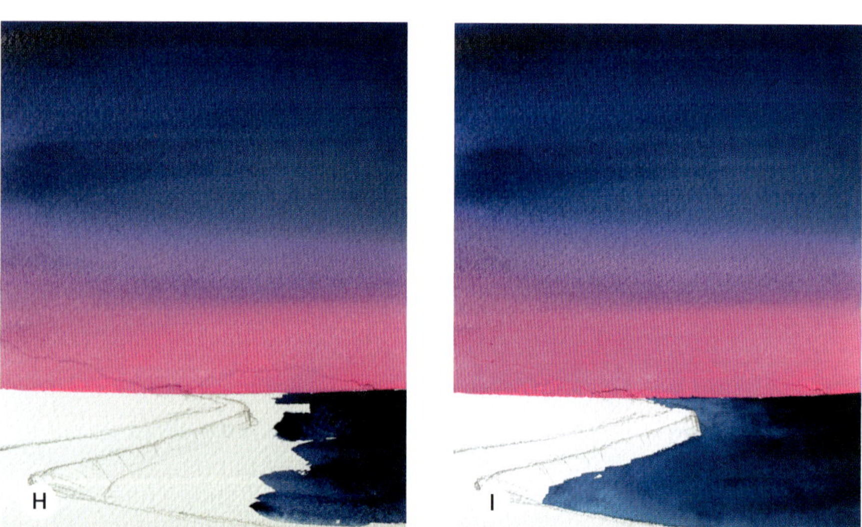

Step 4: Sea—Base Layer. For the base layer of the sea, start with Indigo, a similar tone as used for the sky. (H) Apply this color to almost half of the surface with a round brush. Quickly clean your brush and switch to Turquoise Blue. (I) Apply it to the rest of the area. Let dry completely.

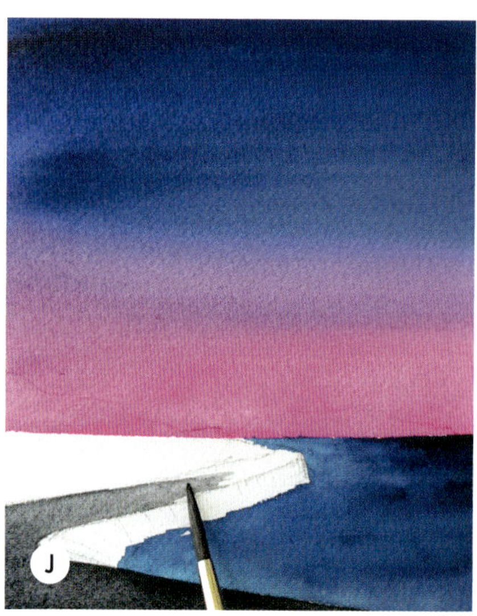

Step 5: Road. For the road, you can use either Payne's Grey or black. (J) Start with a darker tone in the wider area and make it lighter toward the narrow end.

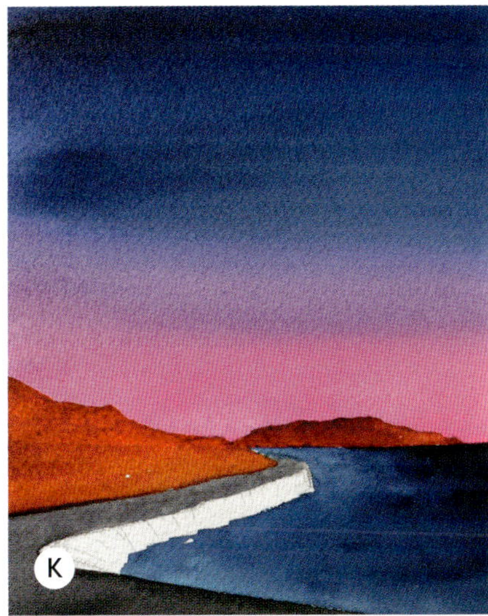

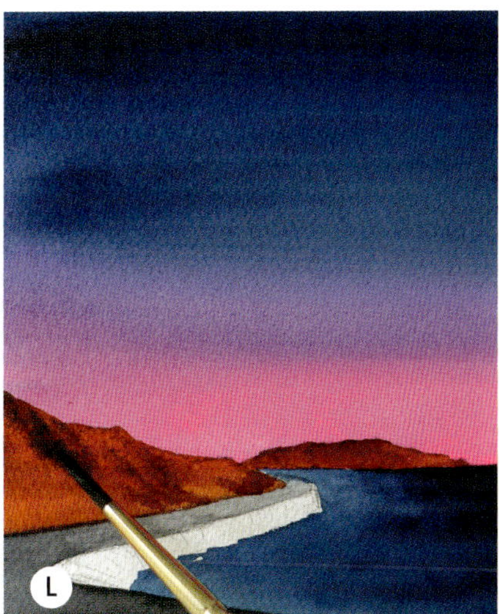

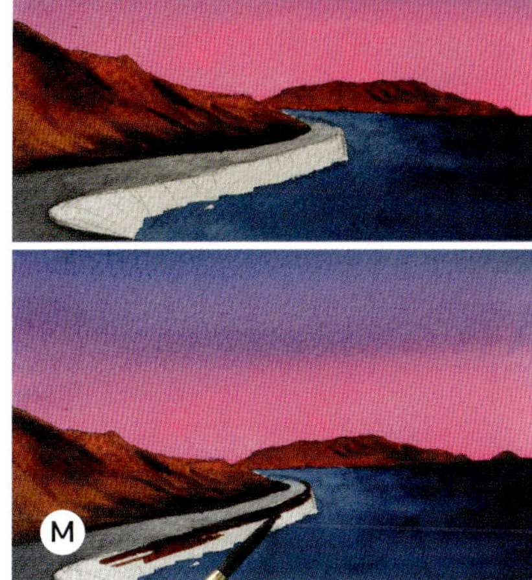

Step 6: Mountains. Apply a medium brown or Burnt Sienna to all the mountains, following the outlines. (K)

Add texture with a darker tone of brown (brown + Payne's Grey) while the background is still wet. Choose a smaller brush and add a few lines on the surface of the mountains diagonally from top to bottom. (L) Don't add too many. Use the same brush to paint the remaining area closer to the sea. Start with the darker brown and then switch to a medium tone of brown toward the bottom (M) and fill it in.

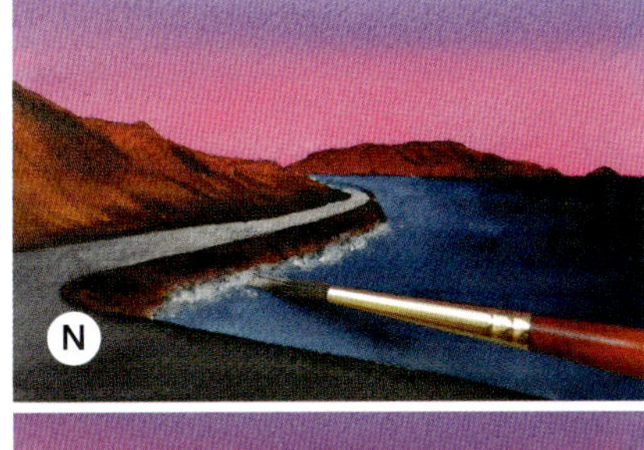

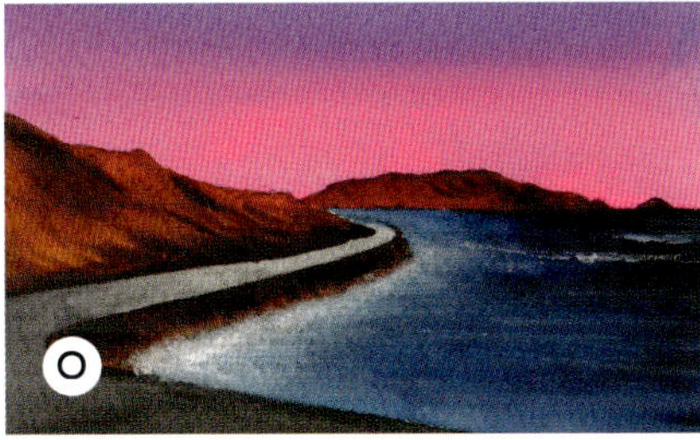

Step 7: Final Details. You need either white gouache or white watercolor for the final details. For the sea, load some dry white paint on the brush and dab it several times on a paper towel to remove excess water. Start adding dry white texture to represent the waves. (N) Once you add the dry patterns, just smudge them back into the sea to make it look natural. You can add more dry white patterns near the shore and one or two small waves in the distance. (O) Add the road markings to finish the painting: a solid line on both sides and a dashed line in the middle following the curve of the road. (P)

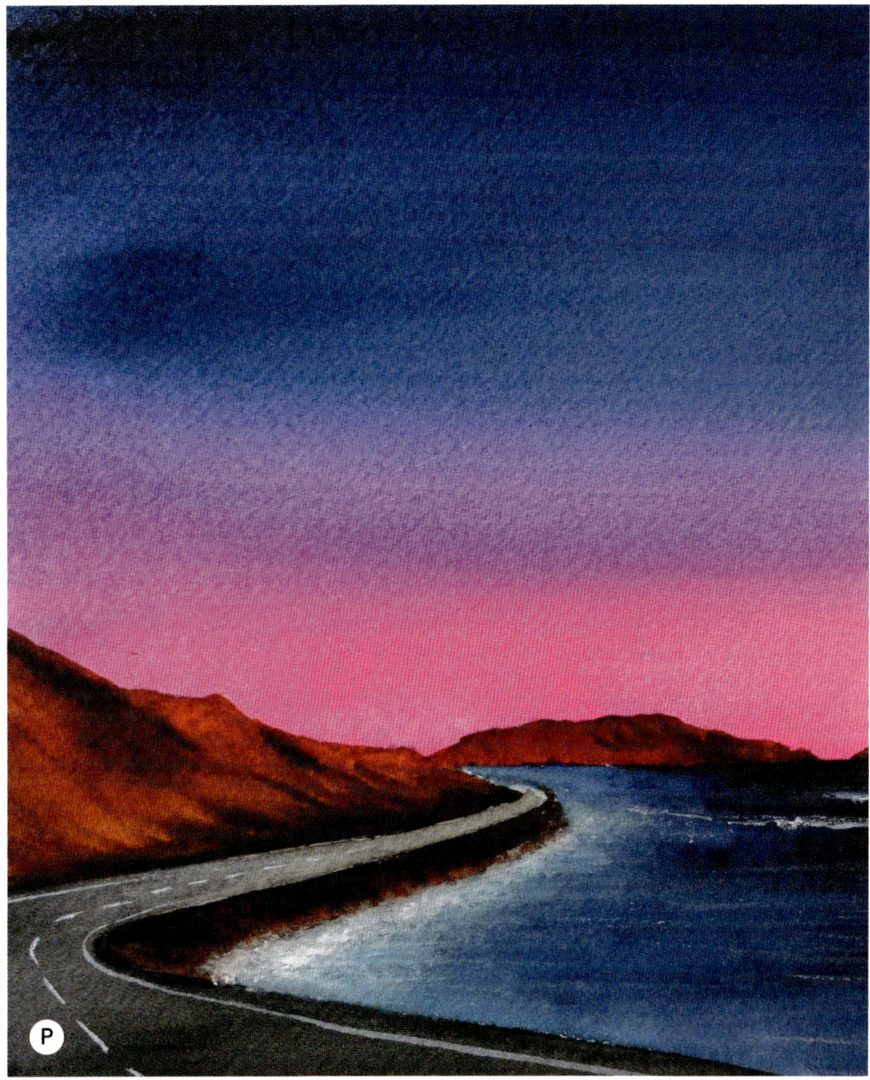

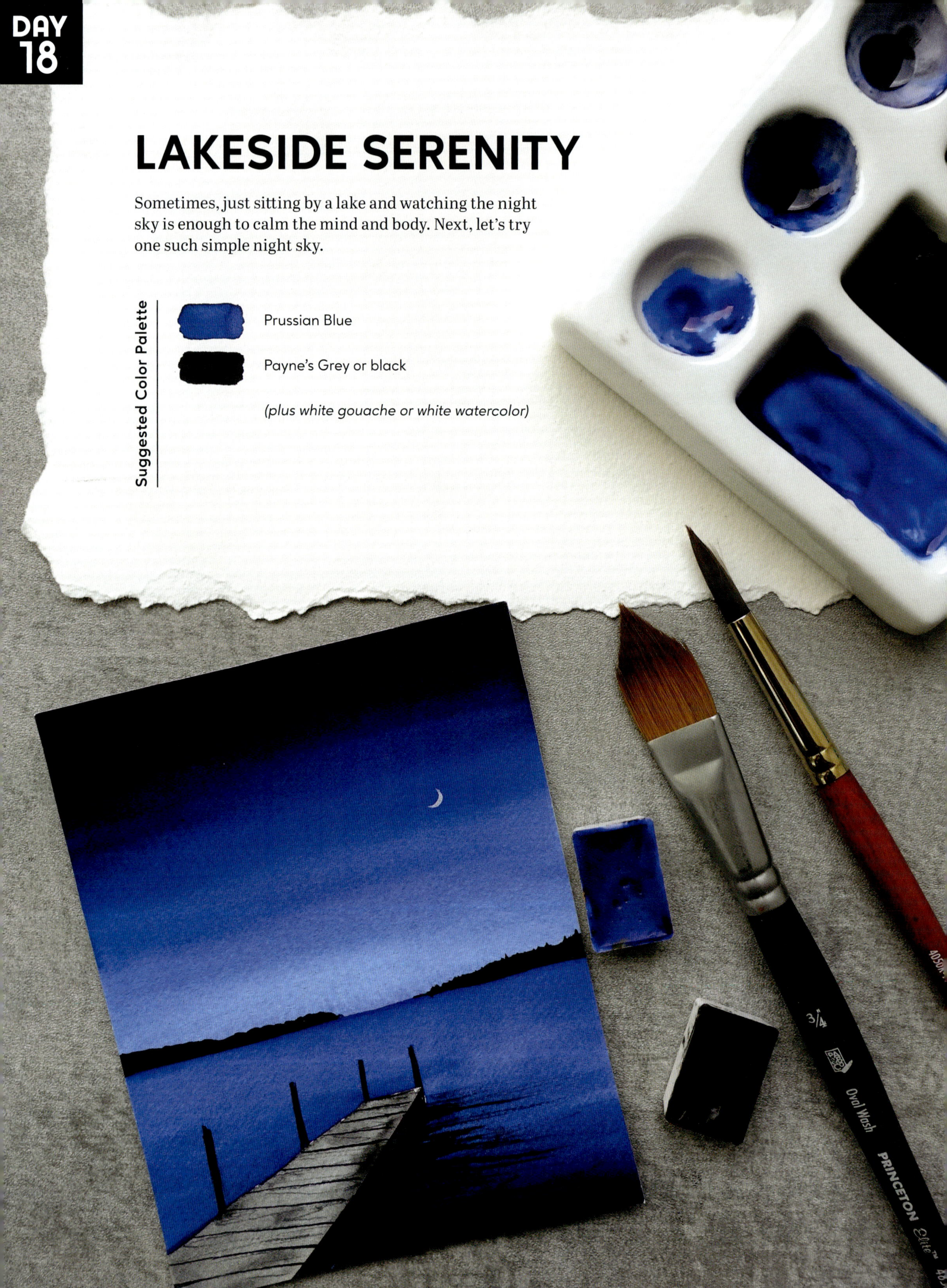

DAY 18

LAKESIDE SERENITY

Sometimes, just sitting by a lake and watching the night sky is enough to calm the mind and body. Next, let's try one such simple night sky.

Suggested Color Palette

- Prussian Blue
- Payne's Grey or black

(plus white gouache or white watercolor)

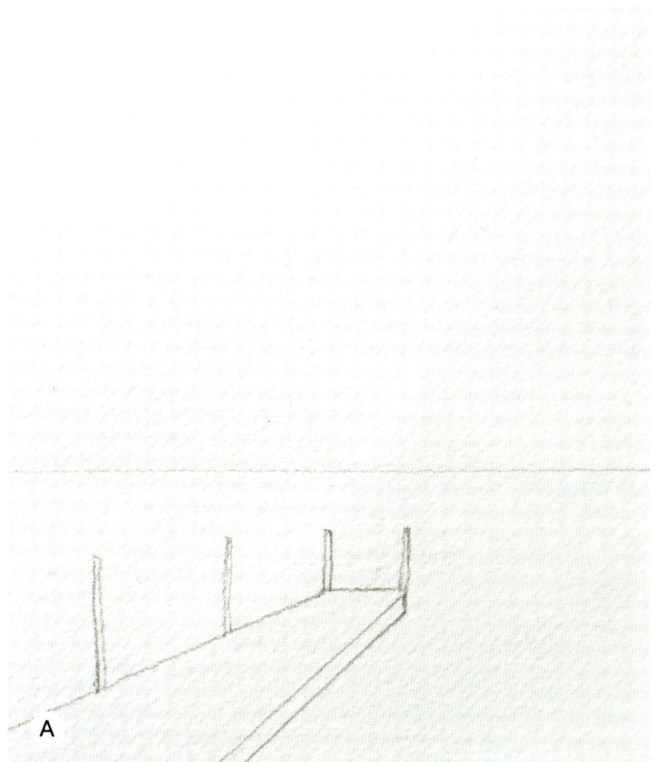

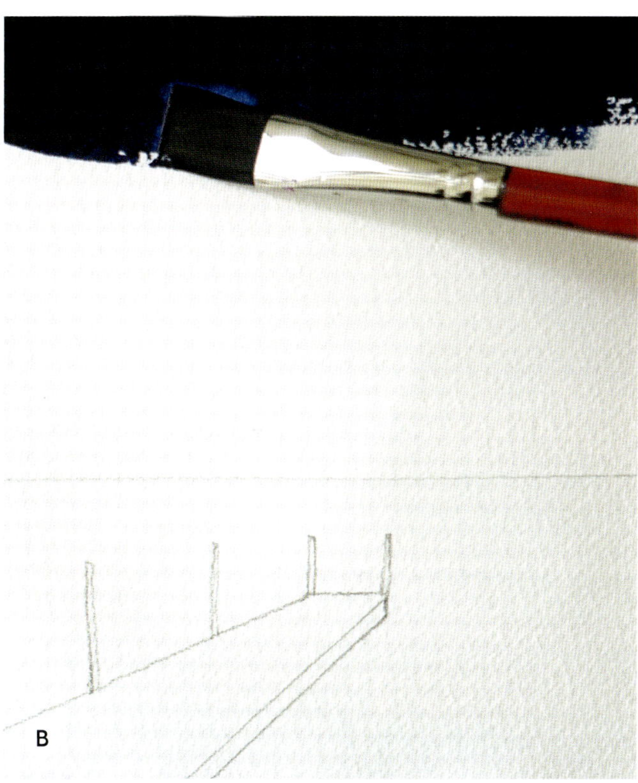

Step 1: Adding the Sketch. Add a light pencil sketch of the dock. Add a line for the horizon. (A)

Step 2: Sky. For the sky, I use the wet-on-dry technique, directly applying the wet paint to the dry paper. The sky is a simple color gradient with a darker value at the top and a lighter value closer to the horizon line. Apply a darker value of Prussian Blue to the sky with a flat brush. (B)

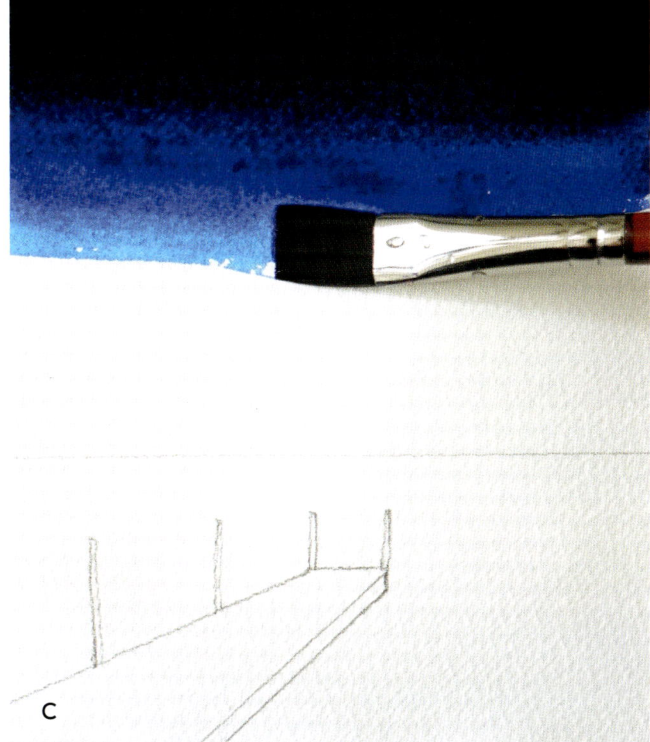

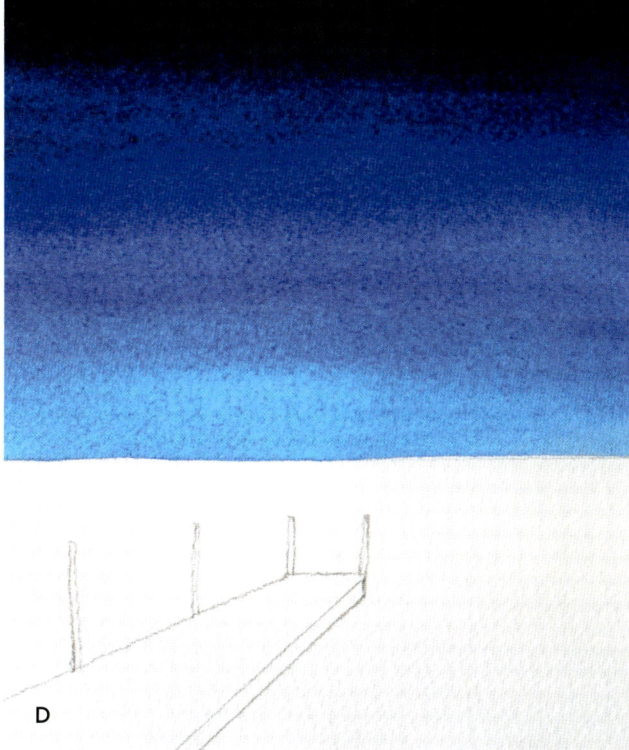

Quickly rinse your brush and continue with even, horizontal brushstrokes (C) until you reach the bottom, adding clean water as necessary to lighten the color. (D) Let dry completely.

(continued)

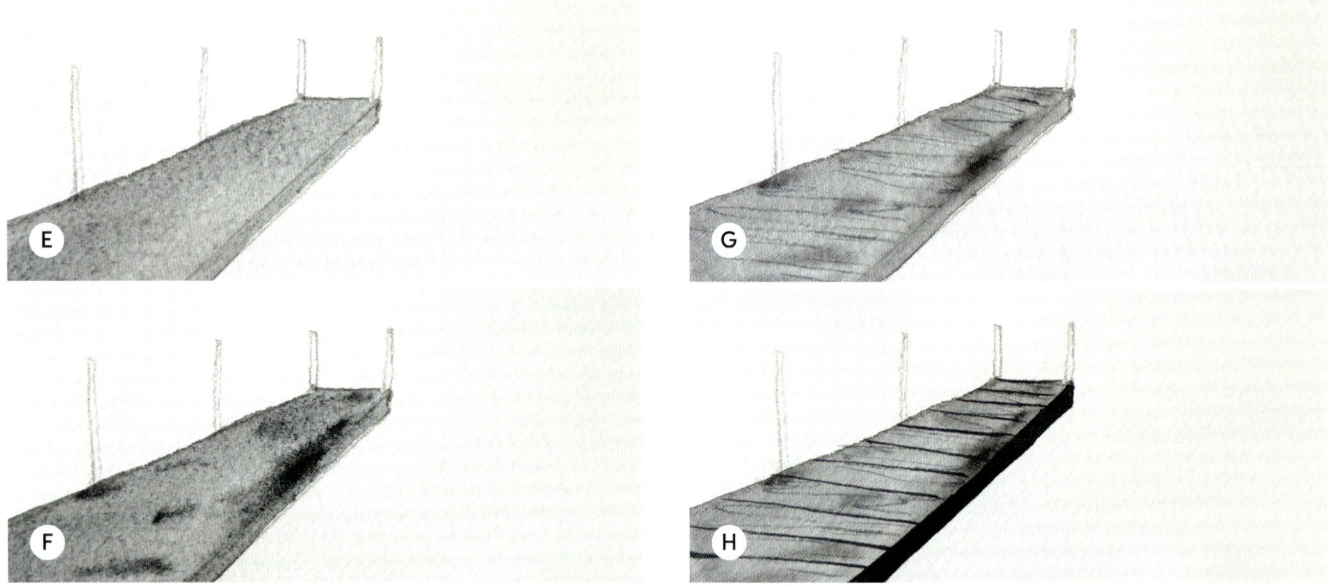

Step 3: Dock. We'll paint the dock in two steps: first painting a base layer, and then adding the textures and the final details. Choose a medium tone of Payne's Grey or black and apply it to the entire dock, carefully following the outlines. (E) For texture, add some random patterns to the background while it's still wet using a slightly darker tone of Payne's Grey. (F) Let dry completely. Take a smaller brush and add some random lines in the background: no particular shape and no particular length. (G) Add some thin lines at almost regular intervals and fill in the dock. Once you're done with that, paint the thickness of the deck with a darker tone. (H)

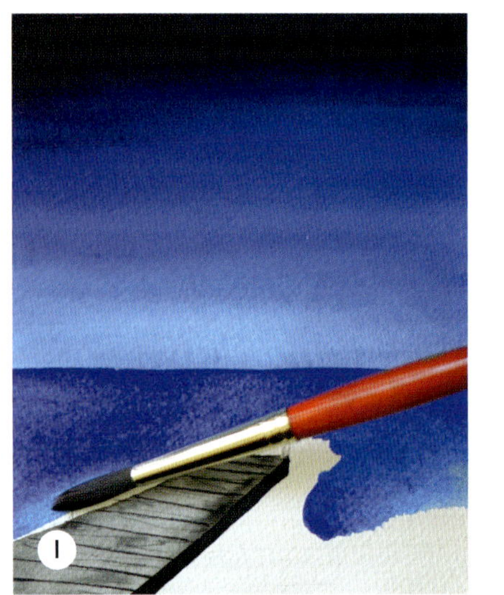

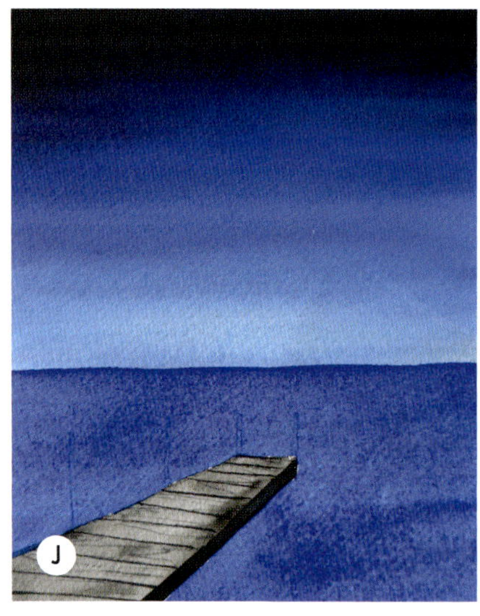

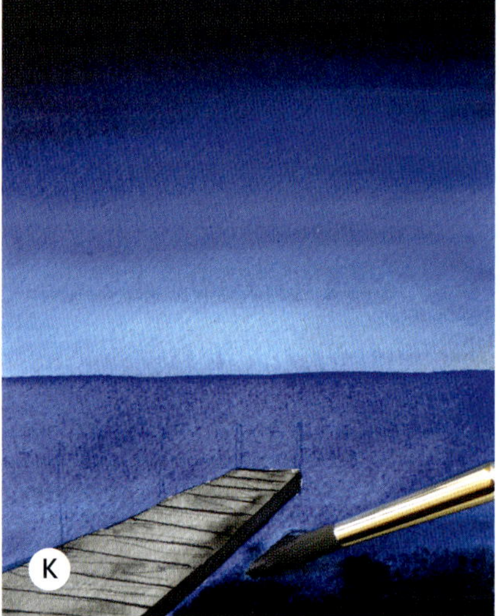

Step 4: Lake. Paint the entire lake a medium tone of blue. (I, J)

Clean your brush and switch to Payne's Grey. Add it to the lowest area and blend it in. (K)

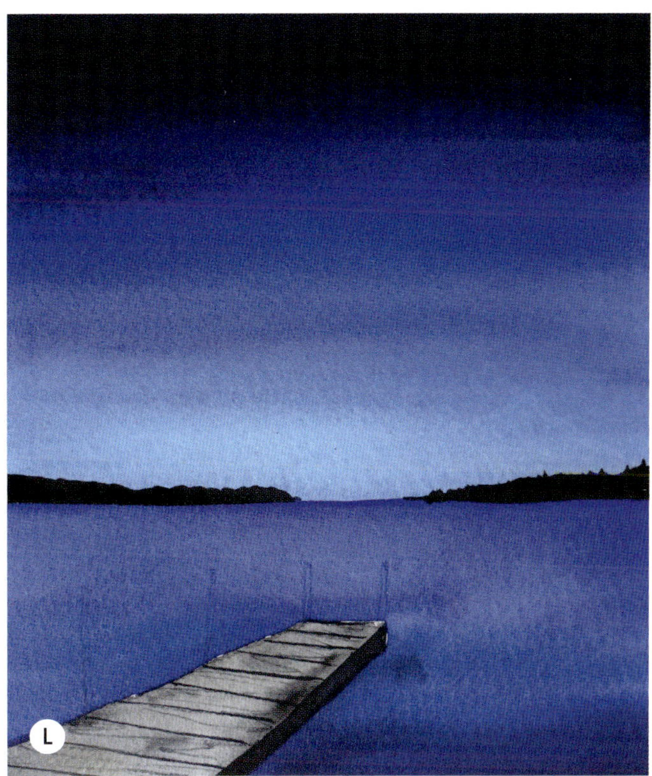

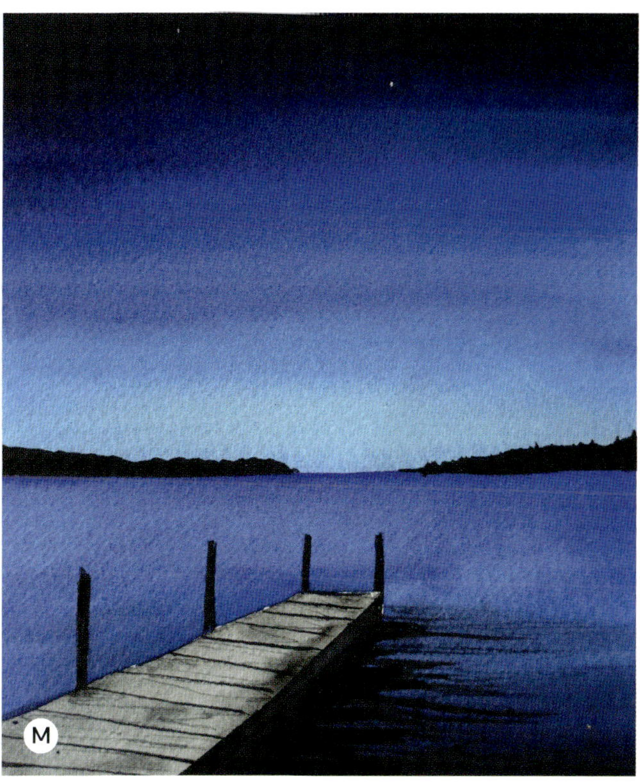

Step 5: Final Details. Add the details along the horizon line using a darker tone of Payne's Grey or black. Also add some tiny details along the horizon line to show the landscape in the distance. (L) Using the same tonal value, add the wooden posts along the dock. (M)

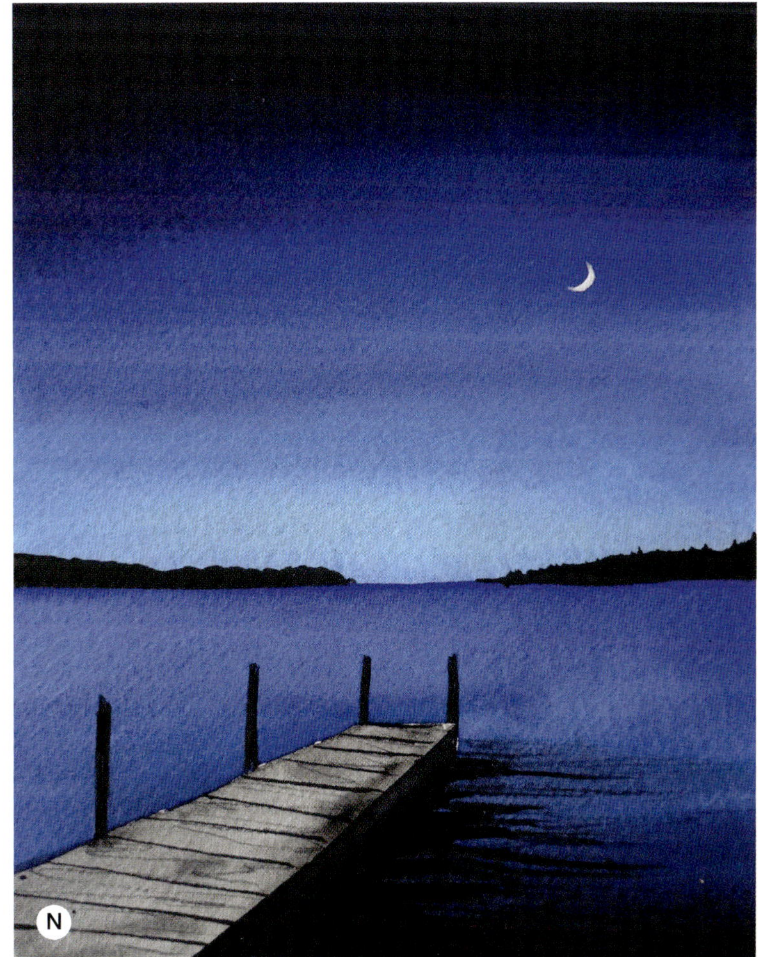

For the reflection, use a darker tone to add some curved lines under the dock at the bottom edge to show the movement in the water. Add a tiny little moon using white goauche or white watercolor to finish the painting. (N)

DAY 19

PASTEL EVENING

There's nothing more beautiful than a quiet evening. It's relaxing to watch the sky turn into a beautiful canvas. Our next project is a quiet and relaxing pastel evening. Pastel colors are already available on the market, but we'll create our own pastels by adding white to the colors.

Suggested Color Palette

- Permanent Rose
- Cadmium Orange
- Permanent Violet
- Payne's Grey or black

(plus white gouache or white watercolor)

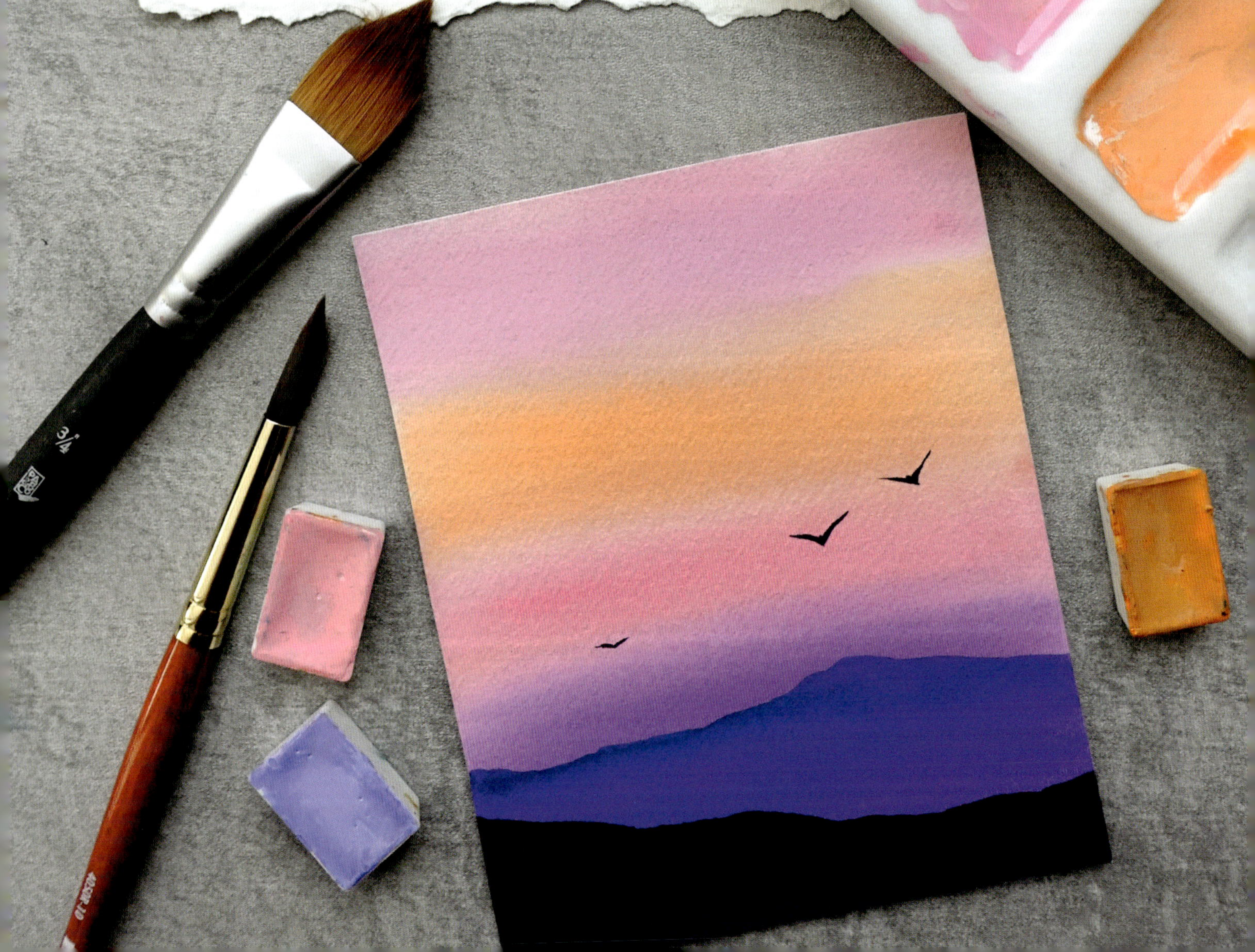

tips

- *To turn the palette colors into pastels, simply mix in a little white gouache or white watercolor. The more white you add, the lighter the colors will look, so vary the amount depending on the intensity you want.*
- *Premix your colors before you begin. We need a pastel pink, a pastel orange, and a pastel violet.*

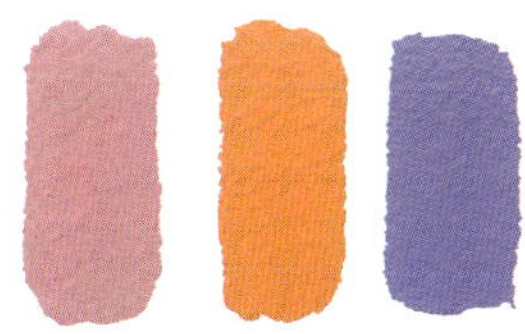

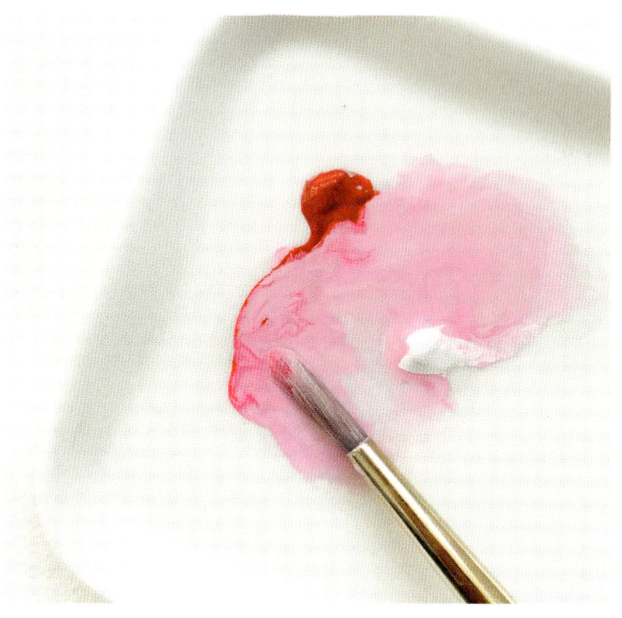

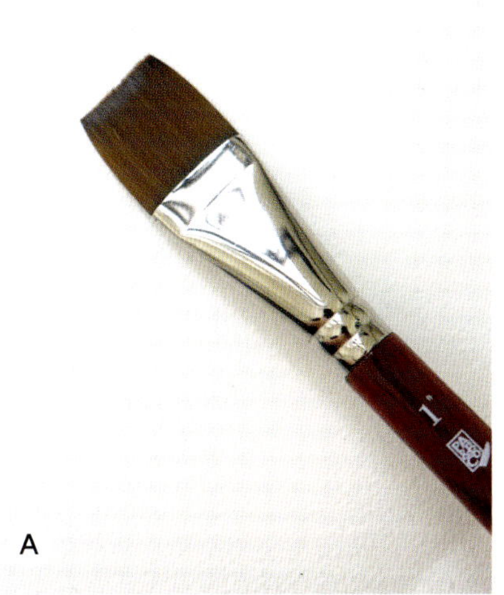

A

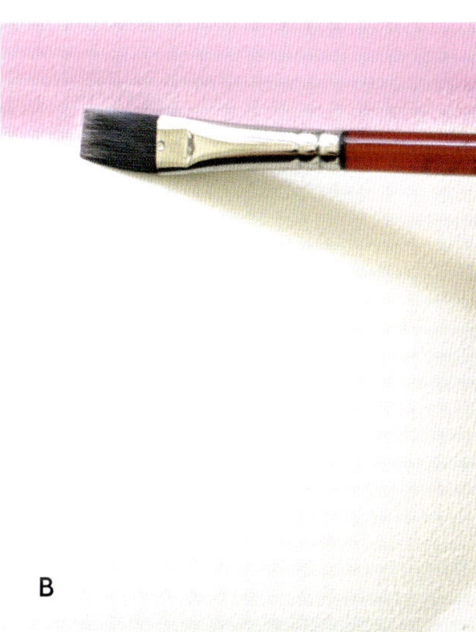

B

C

Step 1: Securing and Wetting the Paper. Secure your paper to a drawing board. Apply an even layer of clean water to the entire background. (A)

Step 2: Sky. Start with pastel pink (Permanent Rose + white) and apply it to the sky with a flat brush. (B, C)

(continued)

Clean your brush and switch to pastel orange (Cadmium Orange + white). Apply it to the wet background and blend with the pastel pink. (D)

Clean your brush again and switch back to the pastel pink. Apply it next to the pastel orange and blend the colors. (E)

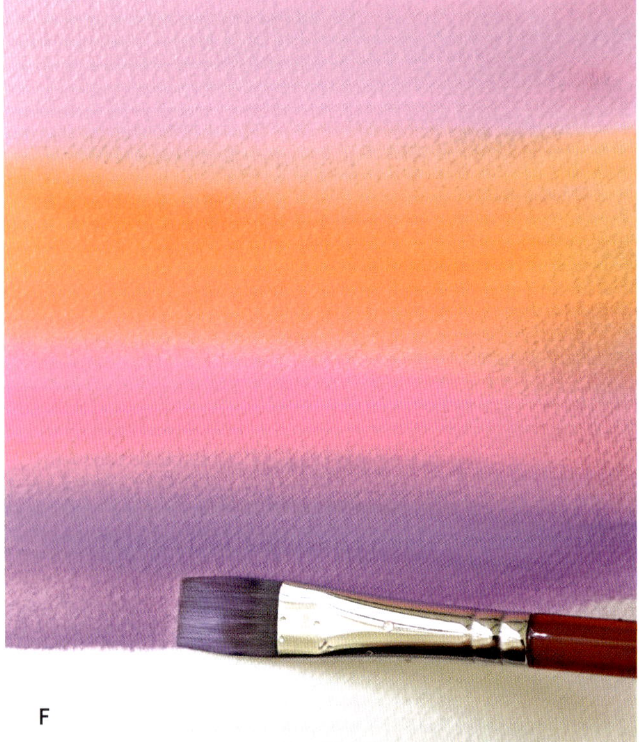

Use the pastel violet (Permanent Violet + white) and fill in the remaining area. Start with a lighter tone and gradually make the color a little more intense by reducing the amount of white gouache or white watercolor in the mix. (F) Let dry completely. (G)

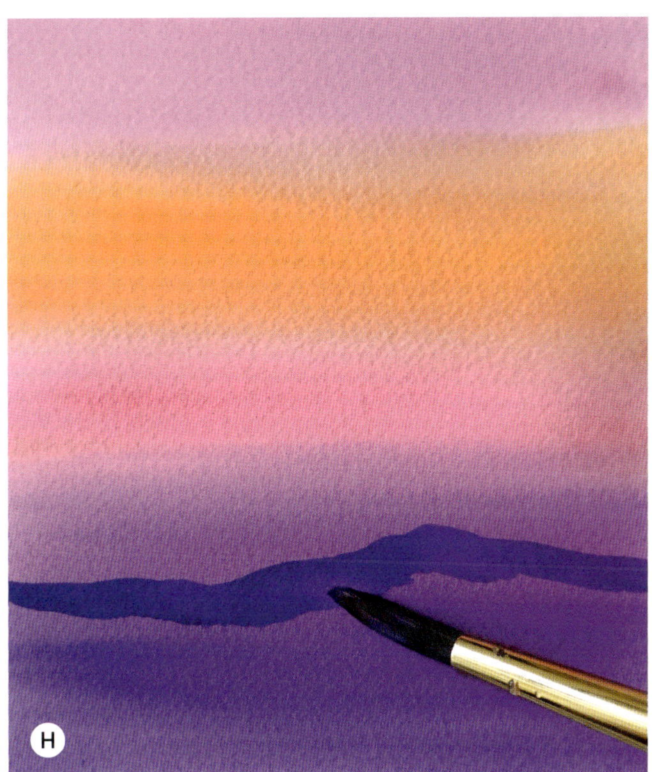

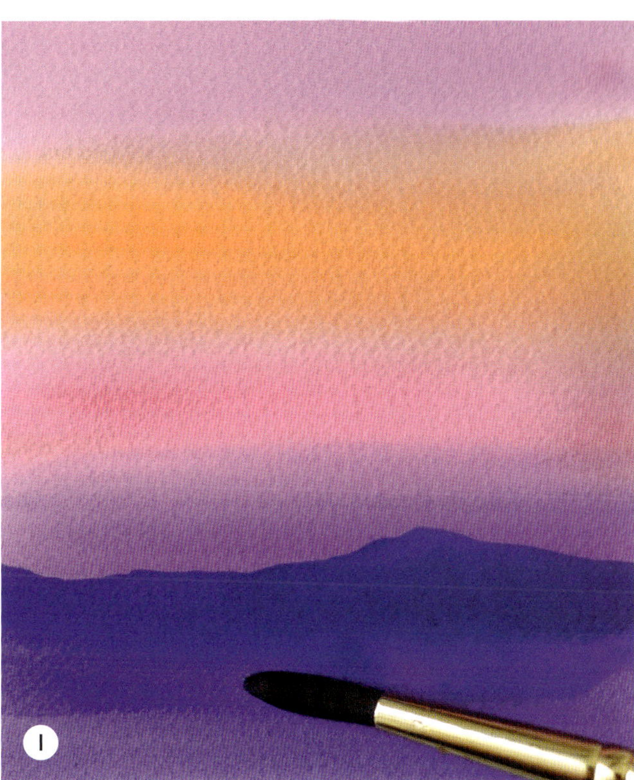

Step 3: Mountains. We'll add two mountains: one in the background and one in the foreground. Add the background mountain first. Choose a medium tone of Permanent Violet and add the shape of the mountain. You can keep the same tonal value almost halfway up the mountain. (H) Quickly rinse your brush and continue with even, horizontal brushstrokes until you reach the bottom, adding clean water as necessary to lighten the color. (I) Let dry completely.

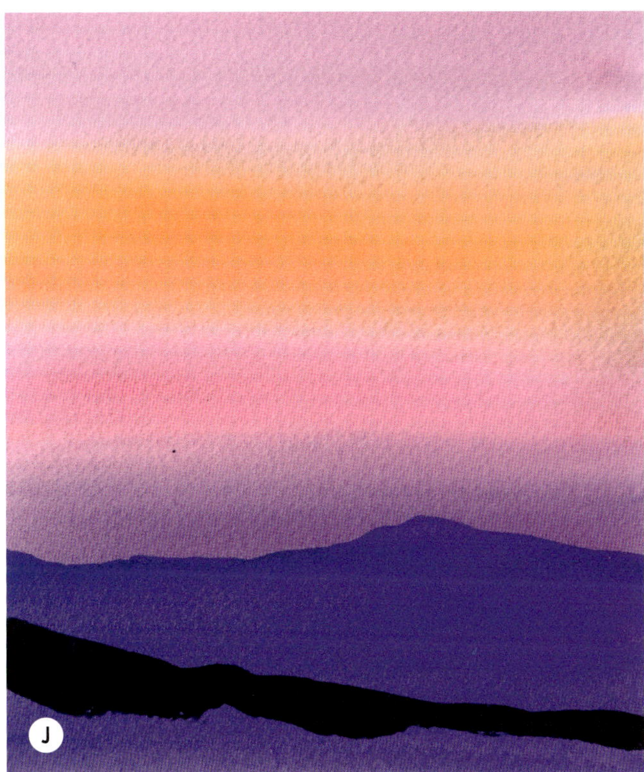

Add the mountain in the foreground using Payne's Grey or black. Once you've added the outline, fill in the mountain. (J)

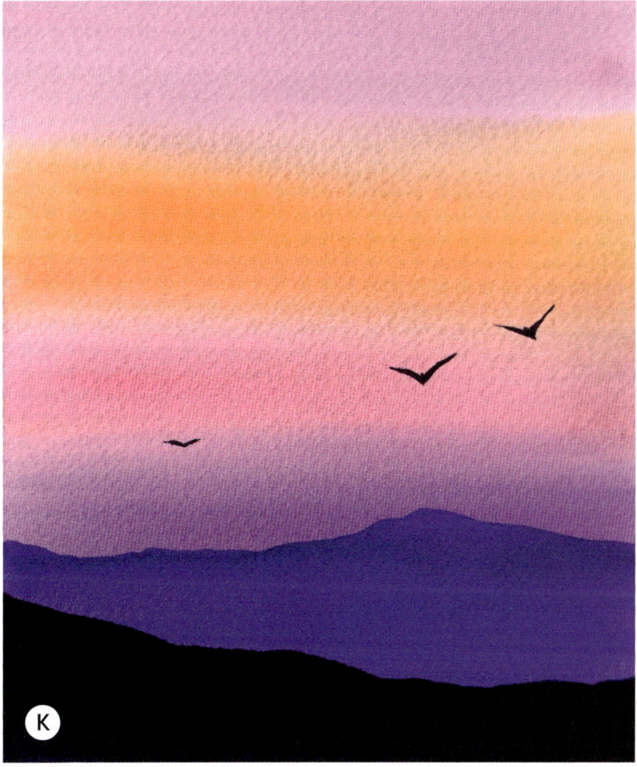

Step 4: Birds. Add some birds in the sky to finish the painting. (K)

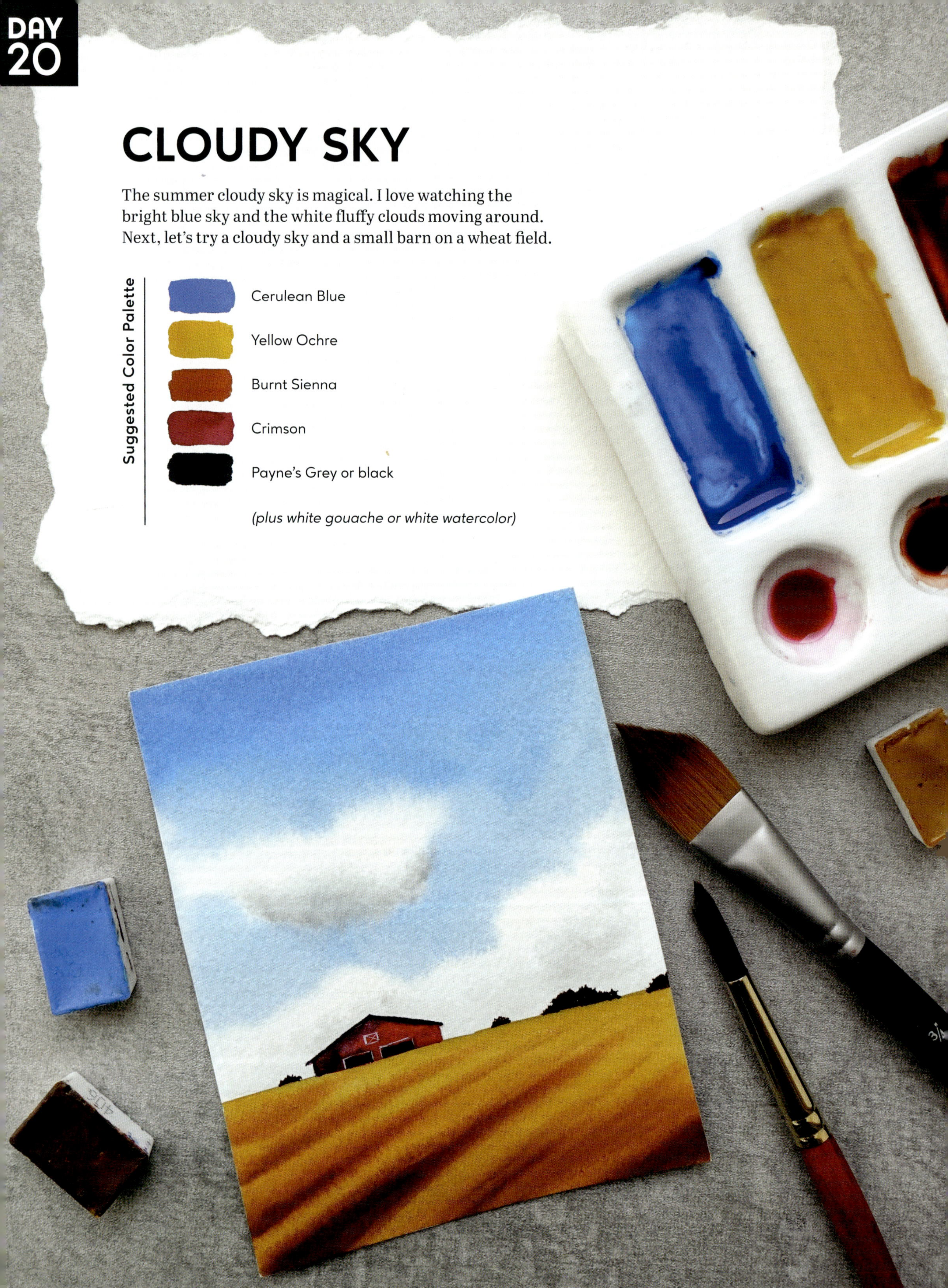

DAY 20

CLOUDY SKY

The summer cloudy sky is magical. I love watching the bright blue sky and the white fluffy clouds moving around. Next, let's try a cloudy sky and a small barn on a wheat field.

Suggested Color Palette

- Cerulean Blue
- Yellow Ochre
- Burnt Sienna
- Crimson
- Payne's Grey or black

(plus white gouache or white watercolor)

A

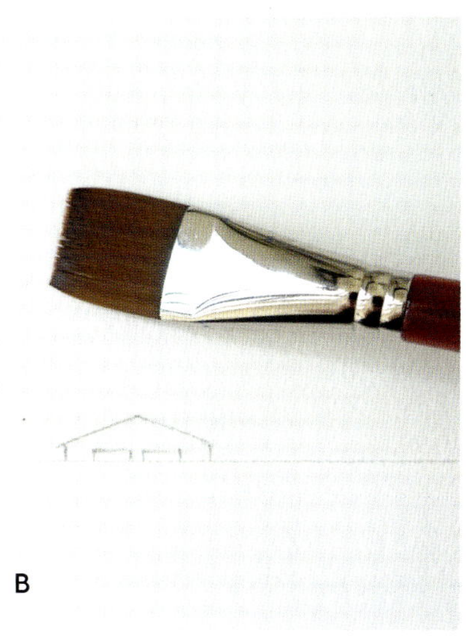
B

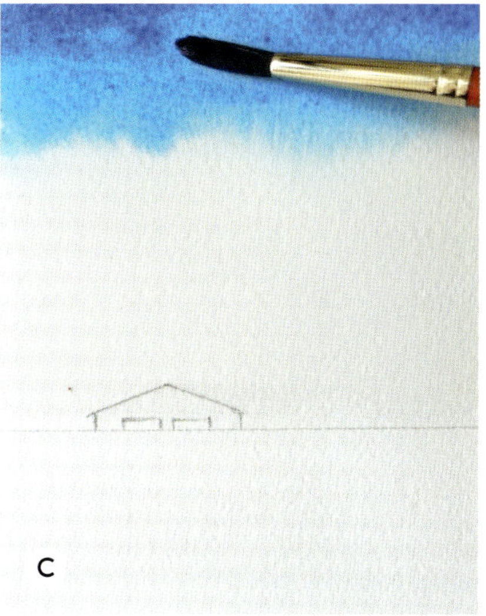
C

Step 1: Adding the Sketch. Add a light pencil sketch of the barn. Add a line for the ground. (A)

Step 2: Securing and Wetting the Paper. Secure your paper to a drawing board. Apply an even layer of clean water to the sky. (B)

Step 3: Sky. Choose a medium tone of blue. I'm using Cerulean Blue, but you can also use Prussian Blue or Cobalt Blue or any other blue you have. Take a medium round brush and start applying the paint to the upper part of the sky. (C)

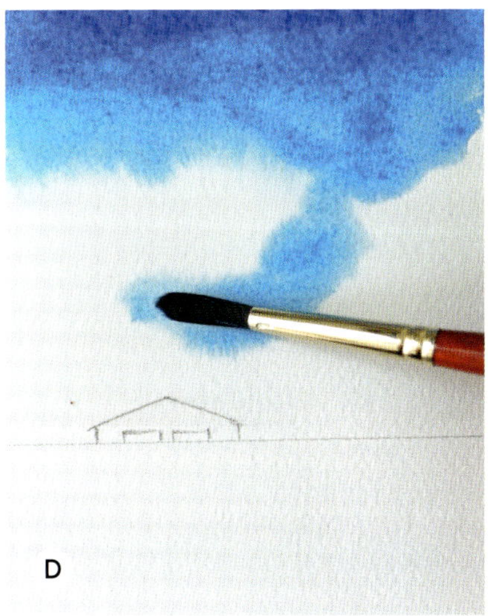
D

E

F

As you go downward, leave some random shapes in between for clouds. (D)

I'm positioning one cloud at the top and another larger one at the bottom. (E)

Clean your brush and switch to a lighter shade of blue. Add it along the horizon line. (F)

(continued)

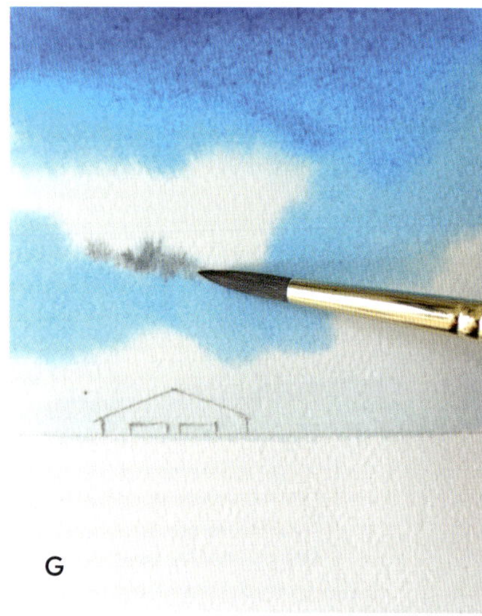

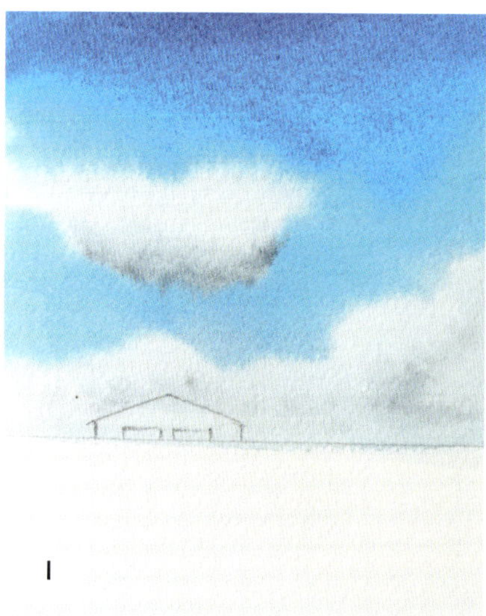

Before the background dries, add the shadow of the clouds to make them look more natural. For the shadows, choose a lighter shade of Payne's Grey and add it along the bottom shape of both clouds. (G, H)

Let dry completely. (I)

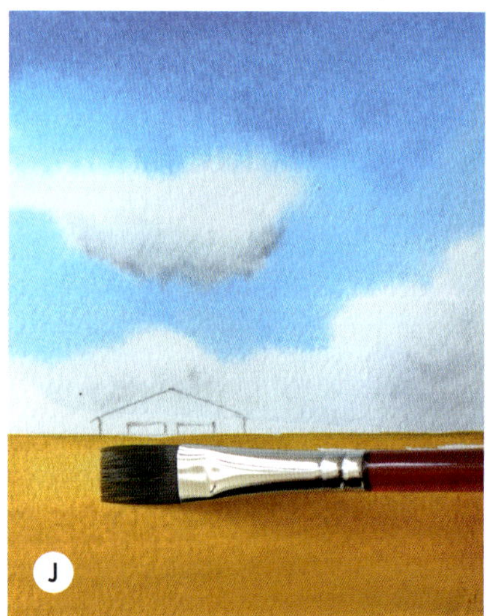

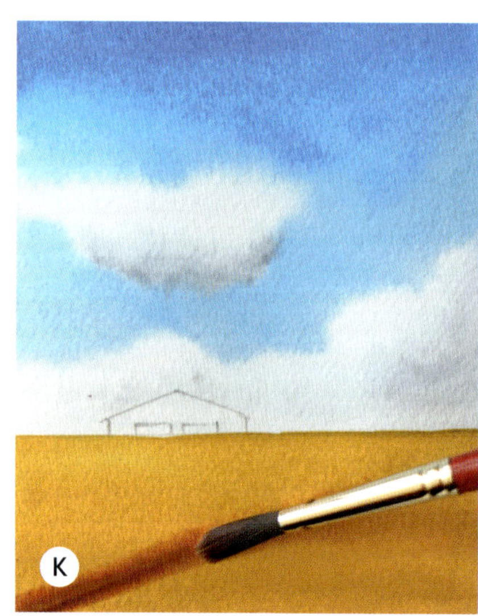

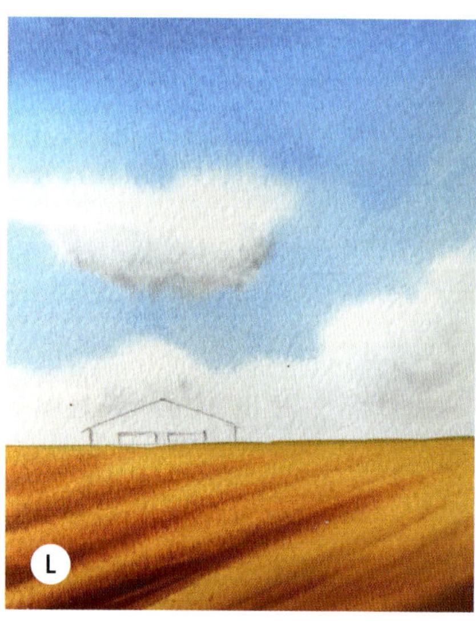

Step 4: Wheat Field. First, apply a solid layer of Yellow Ochre to the entire area for the wheat field. (J)

While this layer is still wet, add some diagonal lines on the background with Burnt Sienna. Use a small or medium round brush. Start at the bottom left and drag the brush diagonally, creating the subdivision of the wheat field. (K)

Keep adding similar diagonal lines throughout the wheat field. (L) Let dry completely.

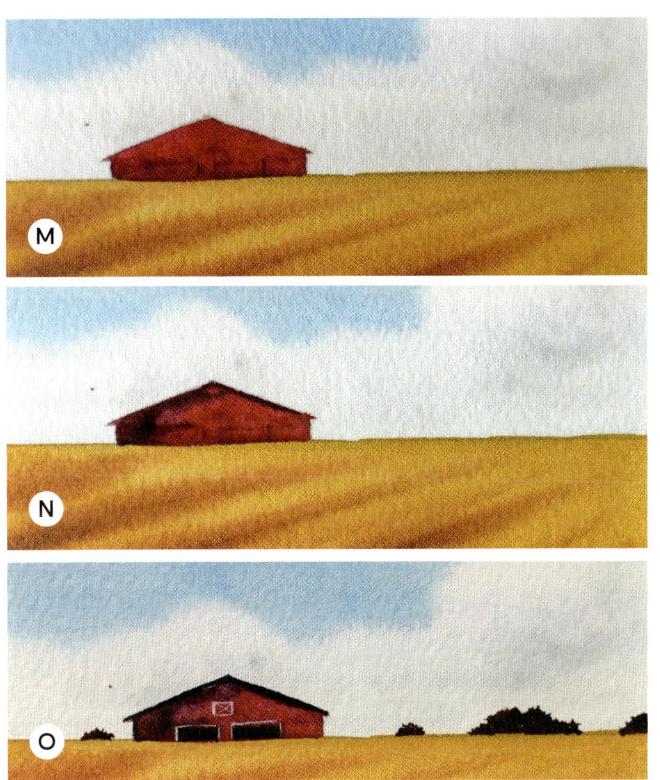

Step 5: Barn and Final Details. Choose a darker tone of Crimson, or any red, and fill in the entire barn. (M) Create a darker tone by adding a little Payne's Grey or black. While the background is still a little wet, add this shade with a smaller brush along the roofline and also on the left side to create shadows. (N) Let dry completely. In the meantime, you can add a landscape along the horizon line. This is far away, so it doesn't need to be very detailed. Just add some shapes as shown with darker brown. Add the rest of the details to the barn. Add the roofline and the doorway using Payne's Grey or black. Clean your brush and switch to white gouache or white watercolor and add an outline around the openings to finish the painting. (O, P)

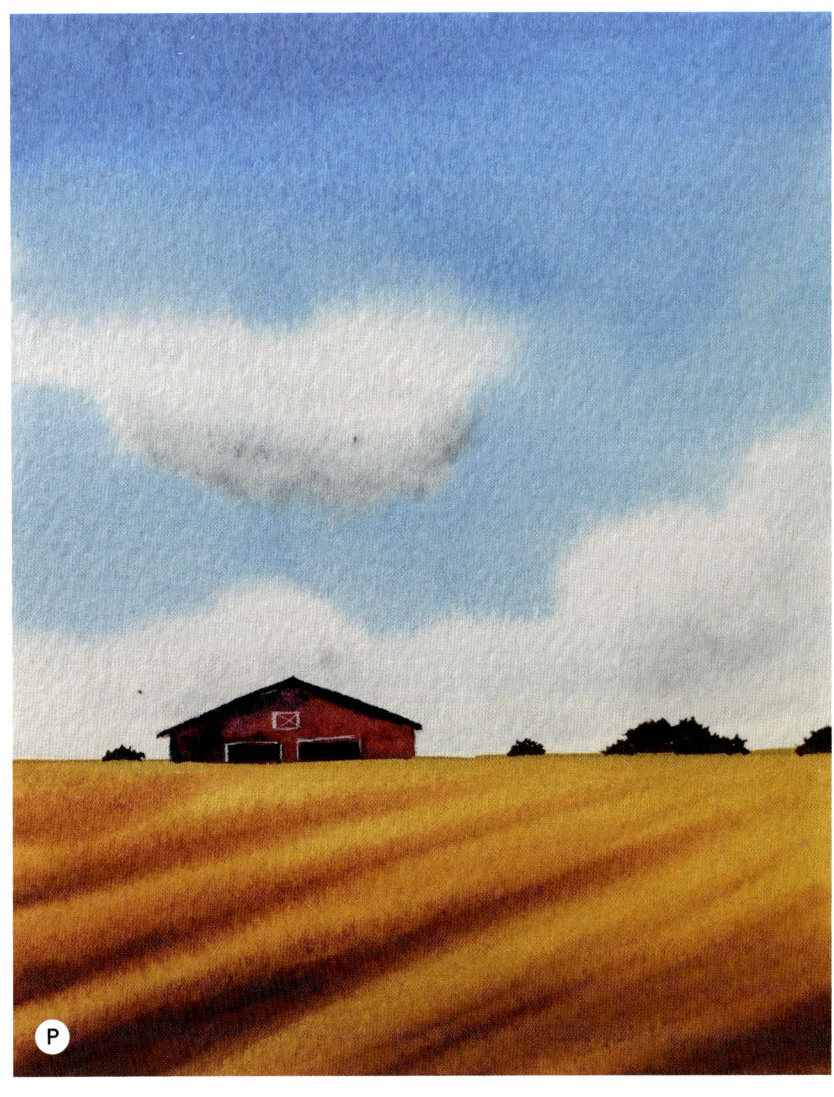

DAY 21

STORMY NIGHT

Our next project is a really dramatic dark and stormy night sky. Nature looks so gloomy and like it's from a science fiction movie when there's a thunderstorm, and that's what we're trying to achieve in our next project.

Suggested Color Palette

- Permanent Violet
- Indigo
- Payne's Grey or black

(plus white gouache or white watercolor)

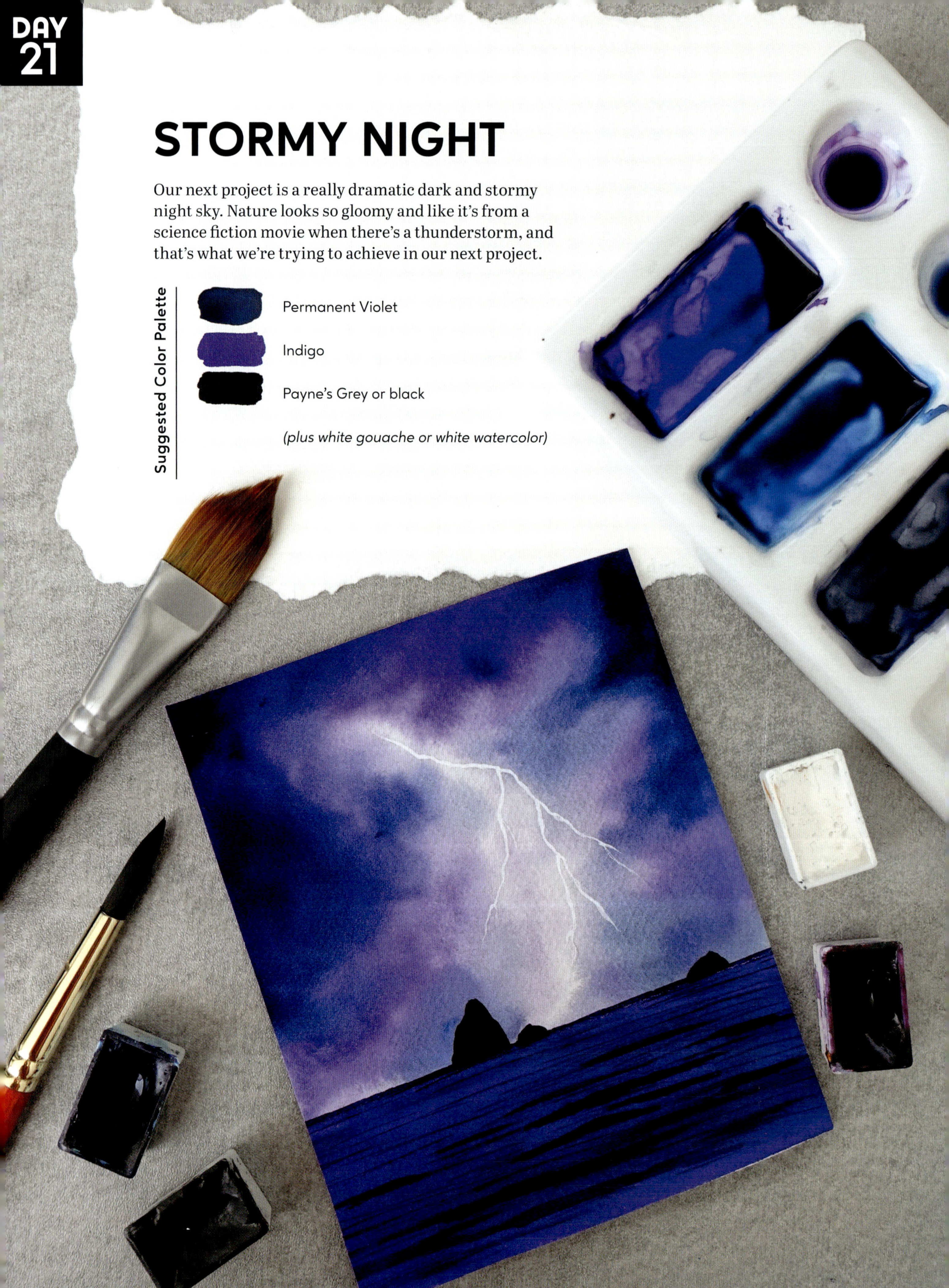

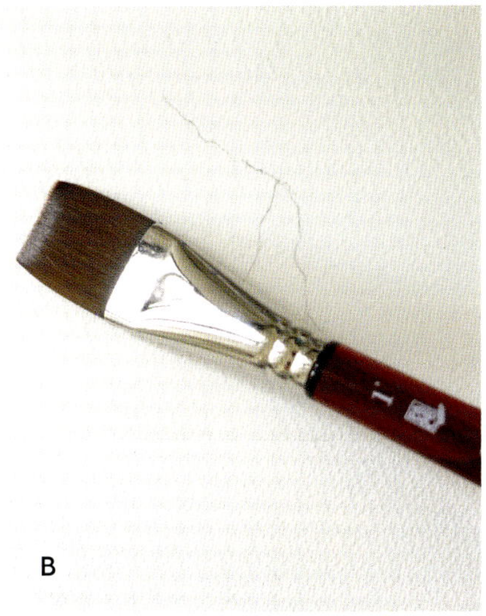

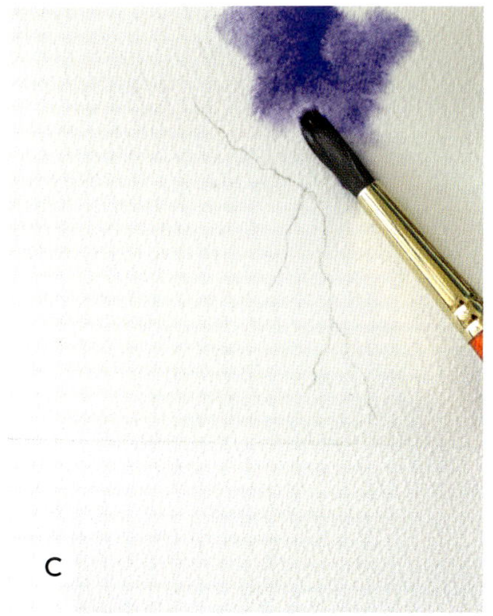

Step 1: Adding the Sketch. Add a light pencil sketch of a thunderstorm. (A)

Step 2: Securing and Wetting the Paper. Secure your paper to a drawing board. Apply an even layer of clean water to the sky. (B)

Step 3: Sky. Start with a lighter shade of Permanent Violet and apply it around the shape of the thunderstorm. (C)

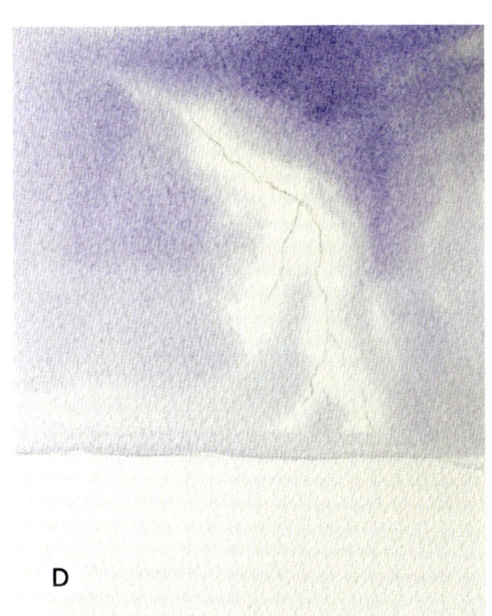

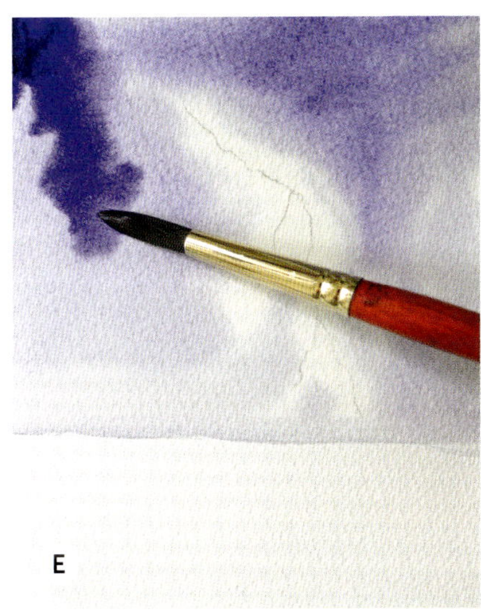

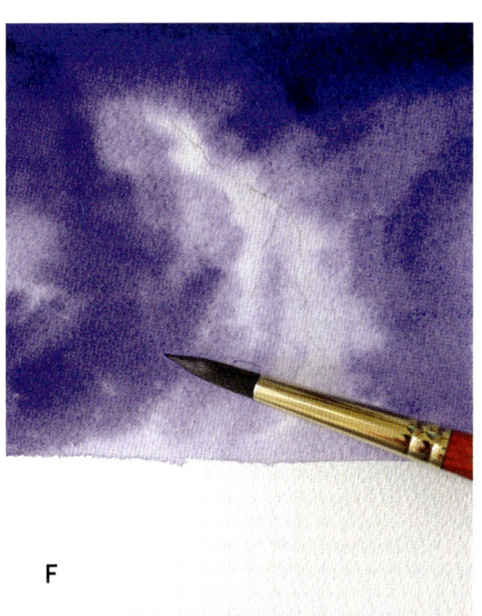

Gradually fill in the entire background in a lighter value of Permanent Violet. (D)

Switch to a medium shade of Permanent Violet and add it to the background. (E)

Keep the lighter values around the shape of the thunderstorm and add stronger darker tones of Permanent Violet in the outer areas and corners. (F)

(continued)

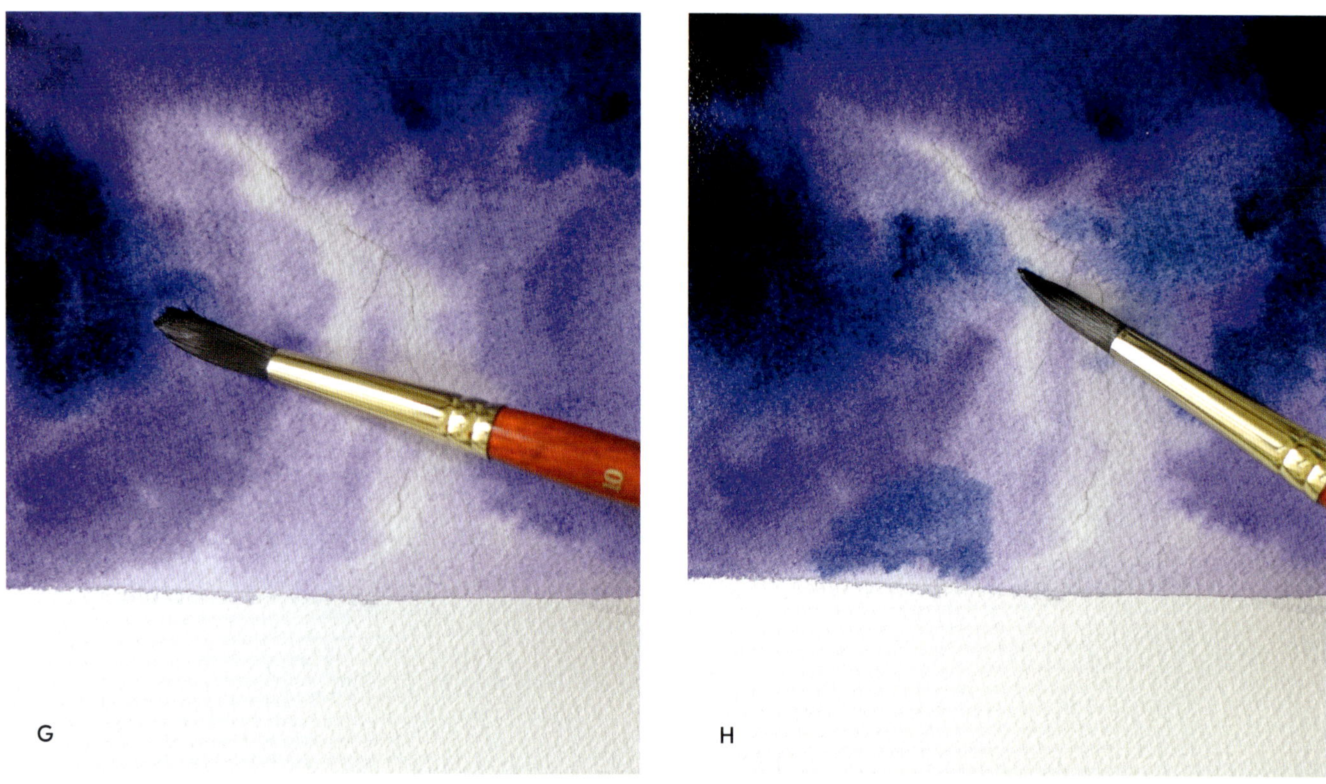

To make the sky interesting, you can also mix some Indigo in between. (G, H)

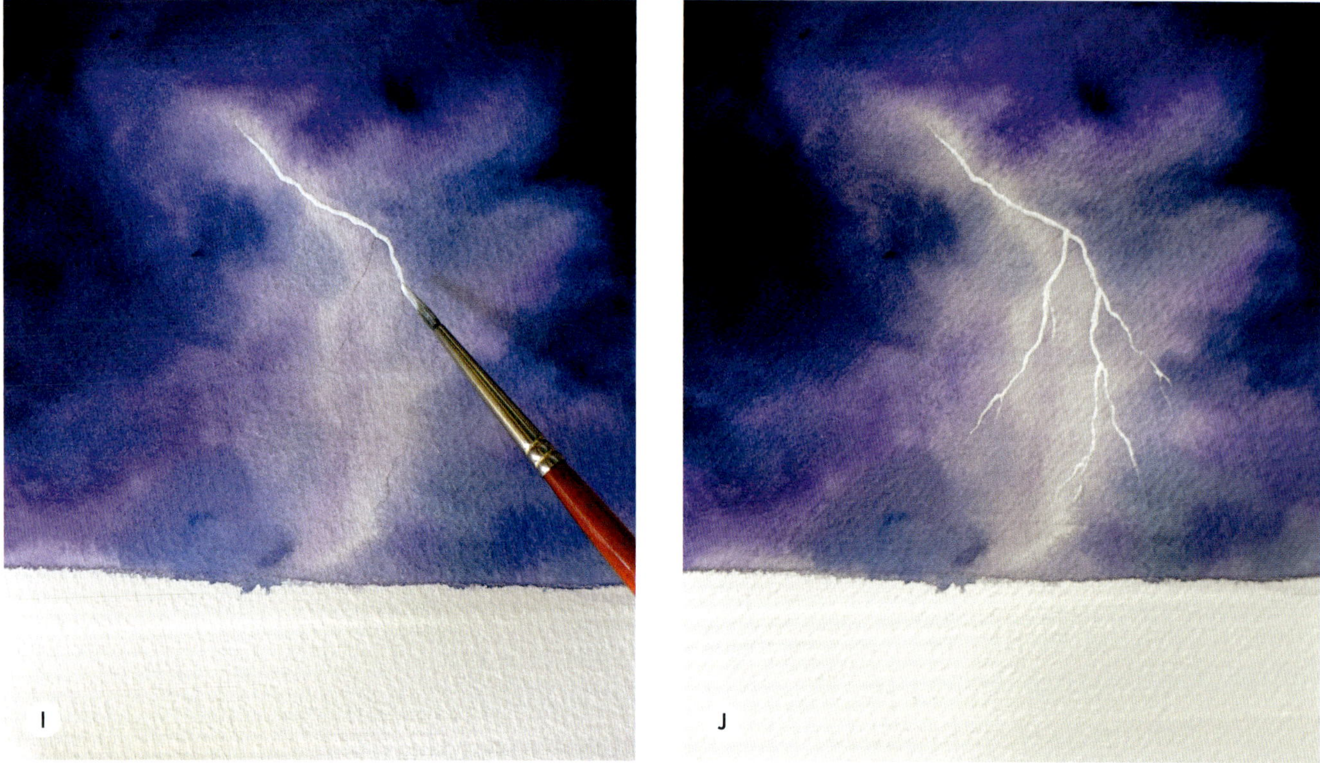

Step 4: Thunderstorm. Add the thunderstorm using white gouache or white watercolor on a brush with a pointed tip. You can modify the shape any way you want to. (I, J)

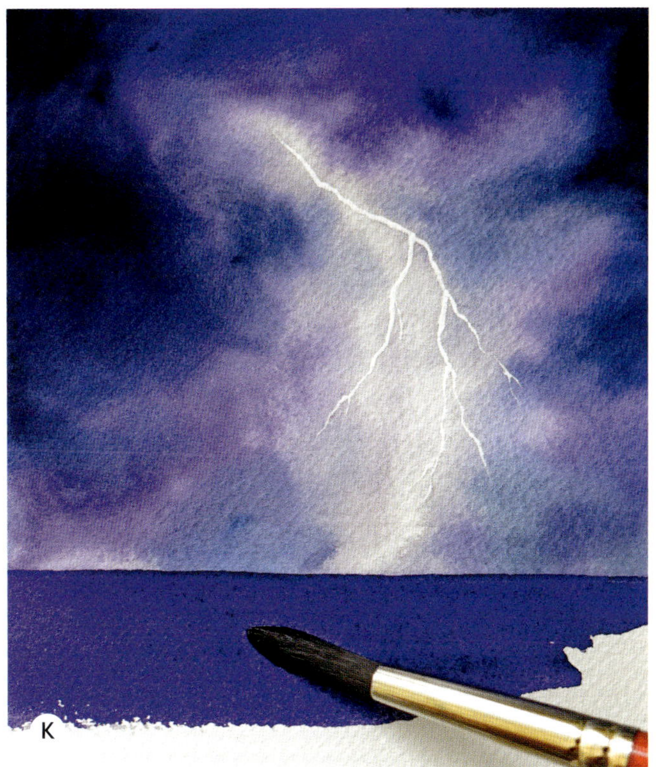

Step 5: Sea. First, apply a medium tone of Permanent Violet to the entire sea. (K)

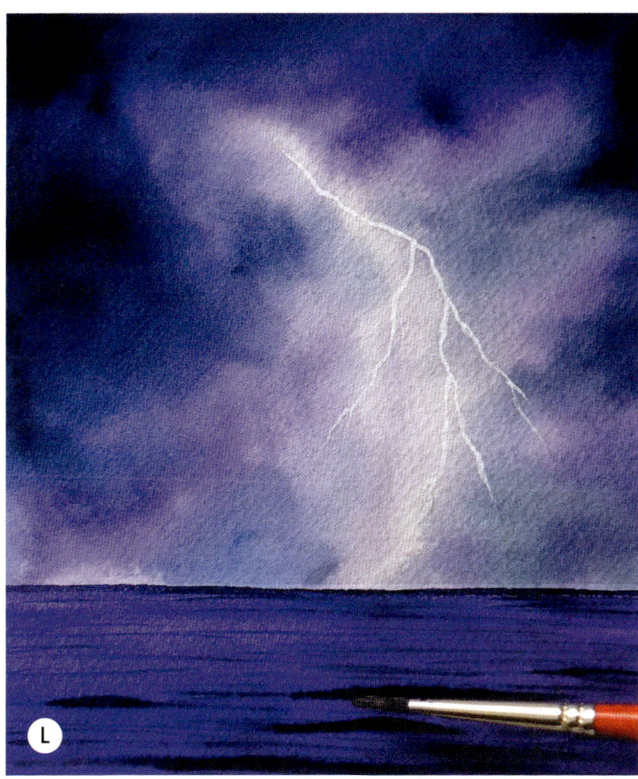

Add some lines on the background with a darker shade of Payne's Grey or black to show movement in the water. (L) You can add thinner lines closer to the horizon line and thicker lines on the bottom.

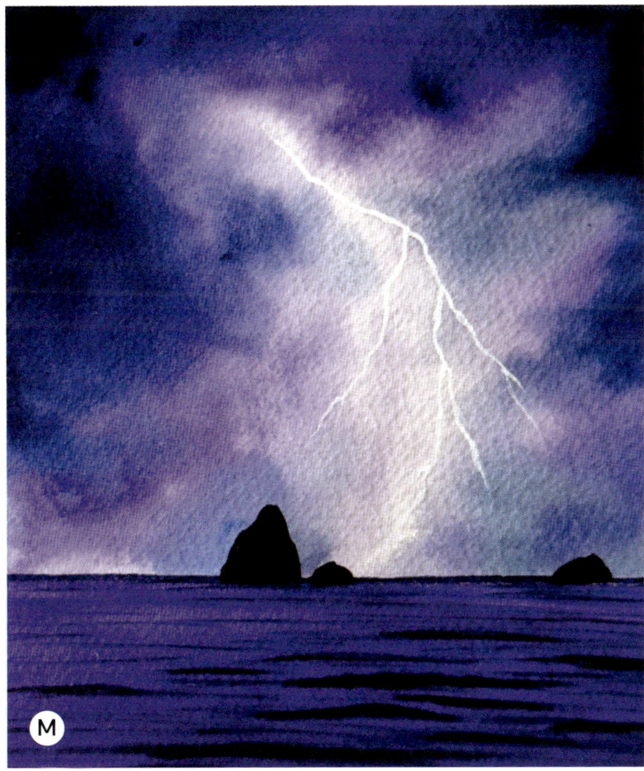

Add a few mountains in the distance along the horizon line to finish the painting. (M)

DAY 22

SUNSET LAKE

Everyone loves to watch the sunset and the changing colors of the sky. The color palette of the sky is the greatest inspiration for any artist. Our next project is a bold and beautiful sunset by the lake.

Suggested Color Palette

- Ultramarine Blue
- Permanent Rose
- Payne's Grey

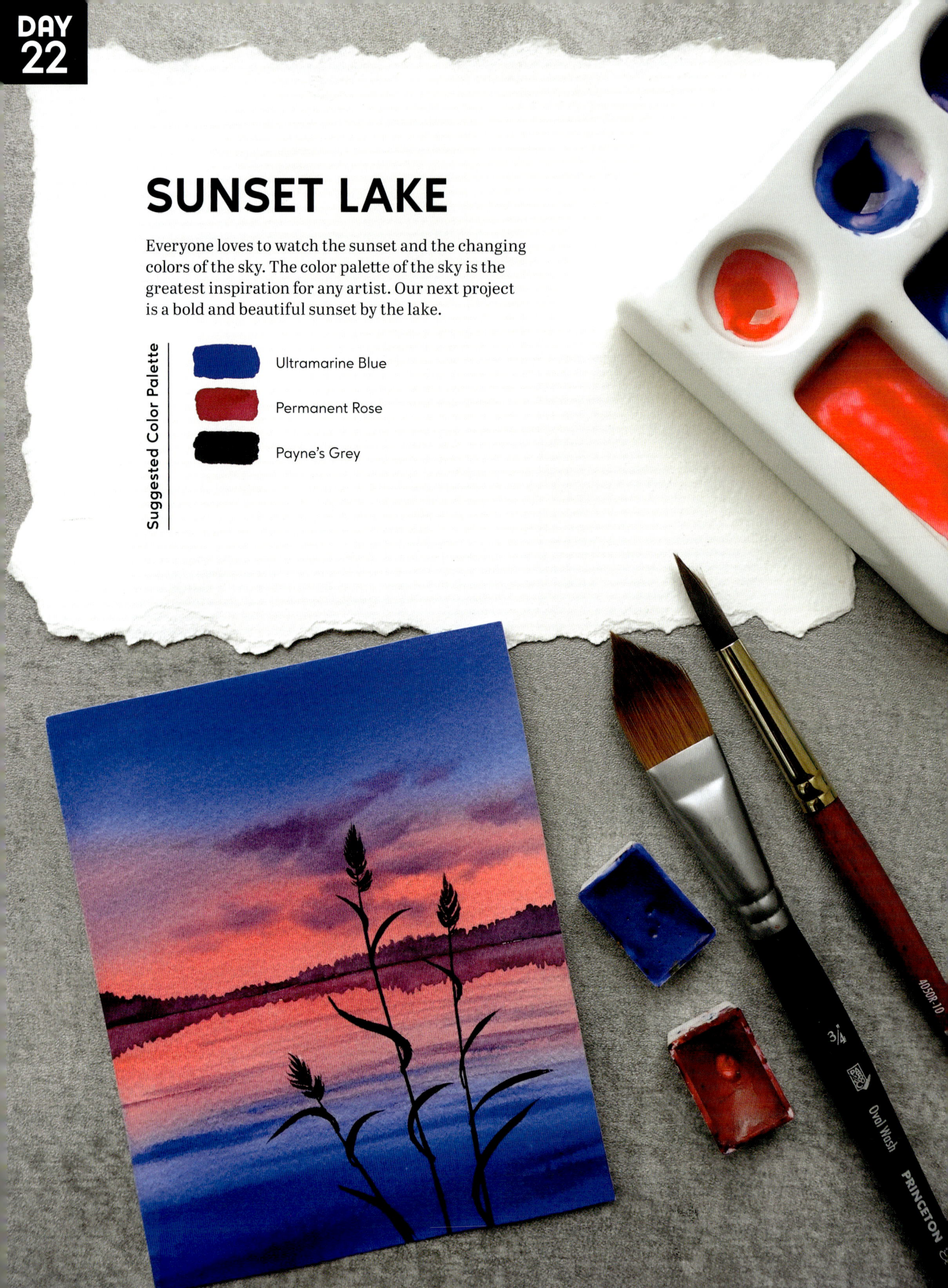

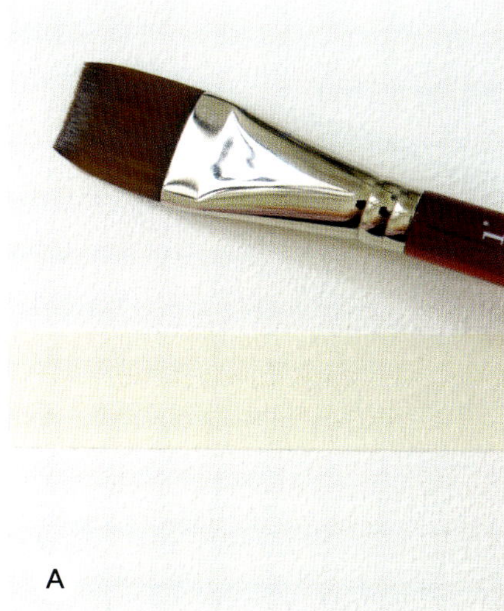

Step 1: Securing, Masking, and Wetting the Paper. Secure your paper to a drawing board. Place a piece of masking tape on the center of the paper to separate the sky and the lake. Apply an even layer of clean water to the sky. (A)

Step 2: Sky. The base layer is a variegated wash of Ultramarine Blue and Permanent Rose. Start with the Ultramarine Blue. (B) You can use any color of blue. Choose an intense tone and apply it to the upper half of the sky.

Clean your brush and switch to Permanent Rose. Start applying The Permanent Rose from the bottom upward and blend it with the Ultramarine Blue. (C)

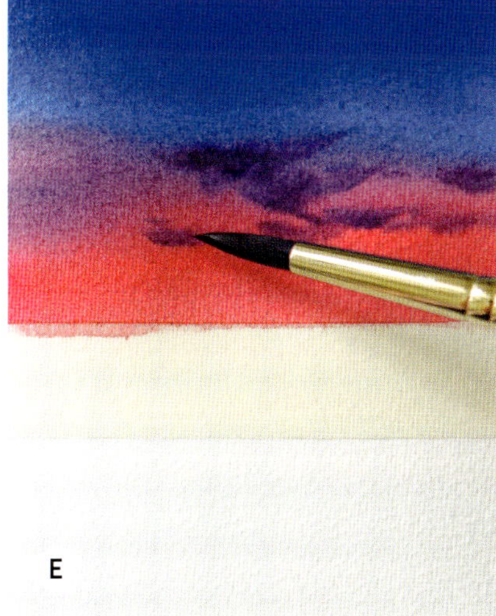

Add the clouds with a mixture of Ultramarine Blue and Permanent Rose while the background is still wet. Add more Permanent Rose than Ultramarine Blue to get a purple hue. Start adding the clouds in the middle of the sky (D) and then add more above and below. (E)

Let dry completely. (F)

(continued)

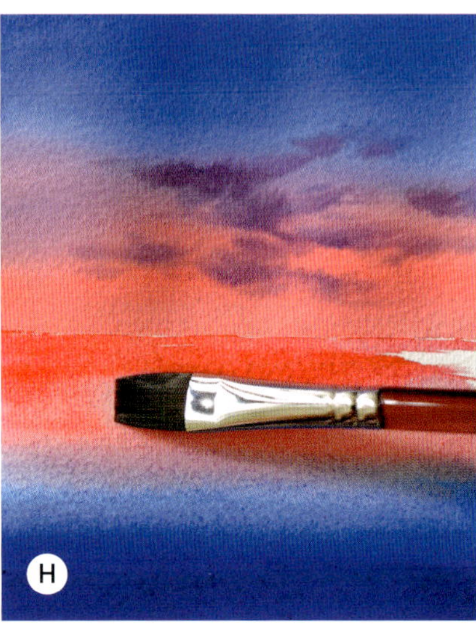

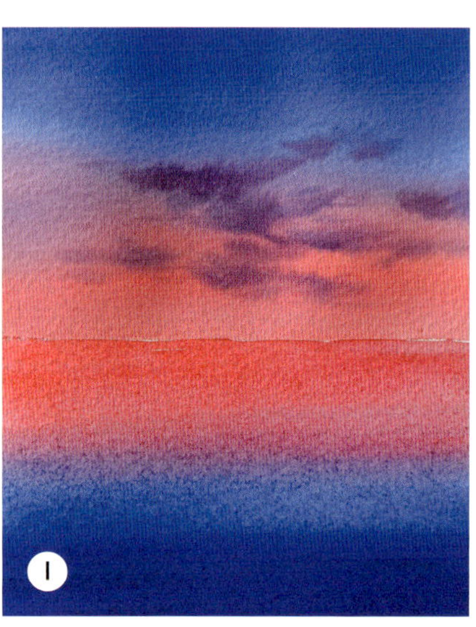

Step 3: Lake. Carefully peel off the masking tape. We'll paint the base layer of the lake similar to the sky. Start at the bottom and apply Ultramarine Blue to almost half of the surface. (G) You don't need to wet the background. You can just start applying blue from the bottom.

Once you reach halfway, clean your brush and switch to Permanent Rose, blending it with the Ultramarine Blue. (H, I)

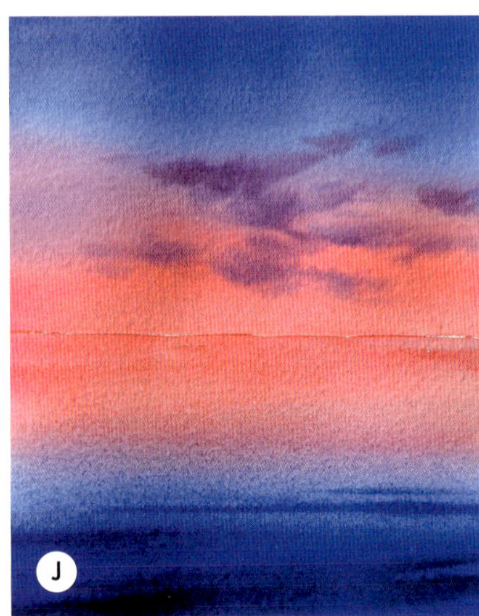

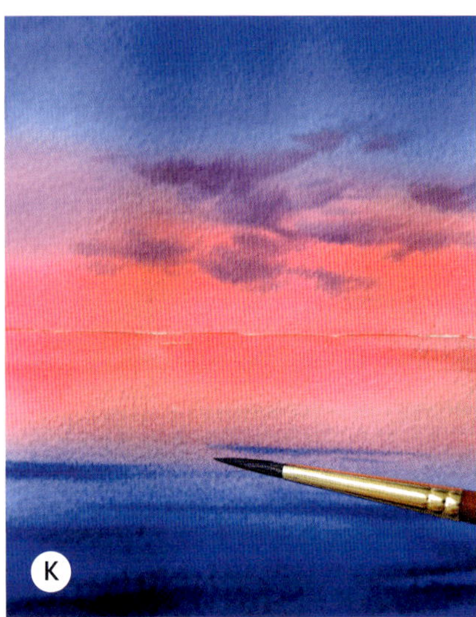

Add a few lines to the water to represent movement. (J) These lines are necessary to make your water look realistic. Add thicker lines on the bottom with an intense Ultramarine Blue tone and thinner ones near the horizon line with a medium tone of purple.

Switch to a smaller brush and continue adding lines in the background. (K)

Let dry completely. (L)

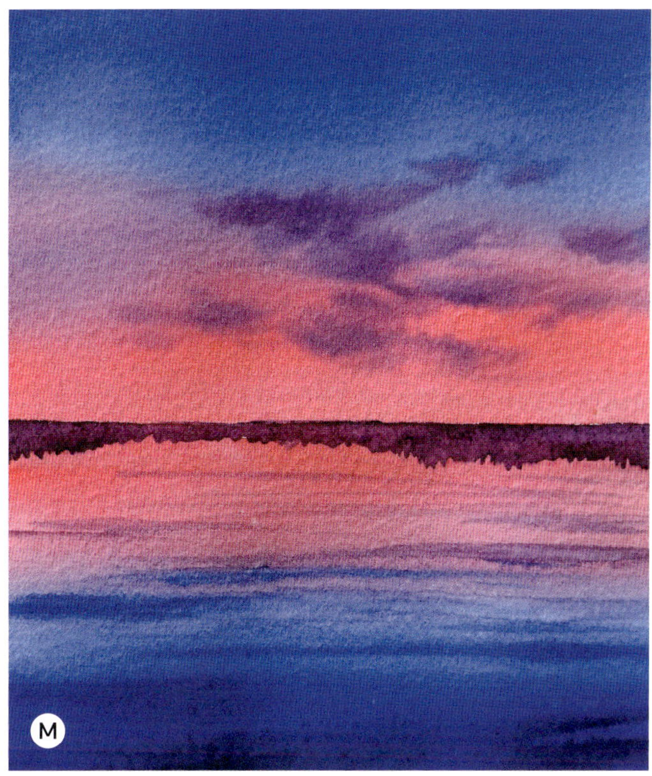

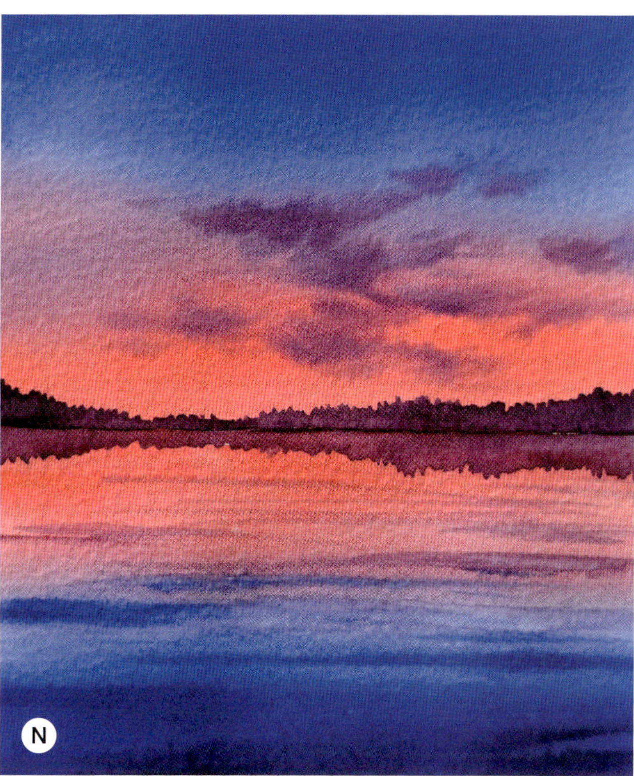

Step 4: Horizon Details. Use a medium shade of purple to add the reflection of the landscape, making it taller on either side and shorter toward the middle. (M)

Once that dries, add a similar detail above the horizon line with a slightly darker shade of purple to show the landscape in the distance. (N)

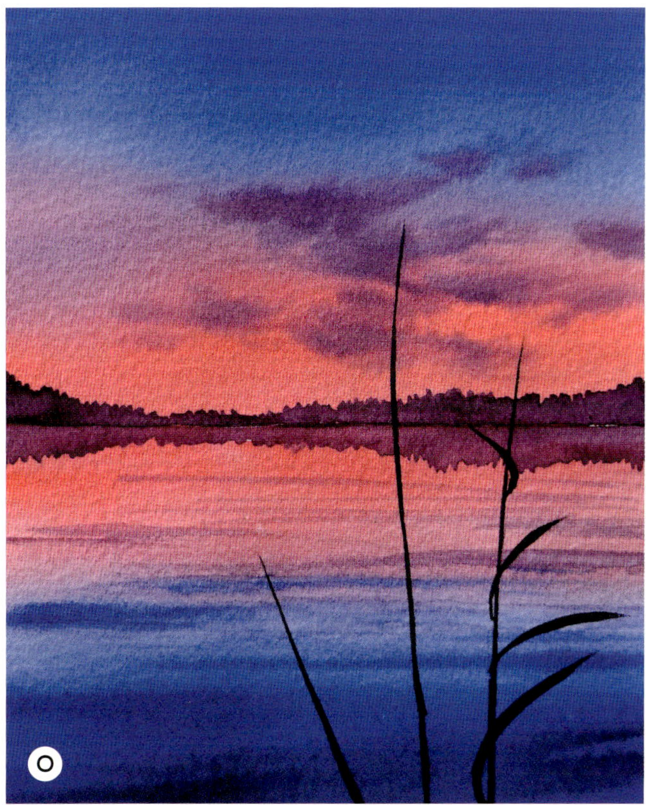

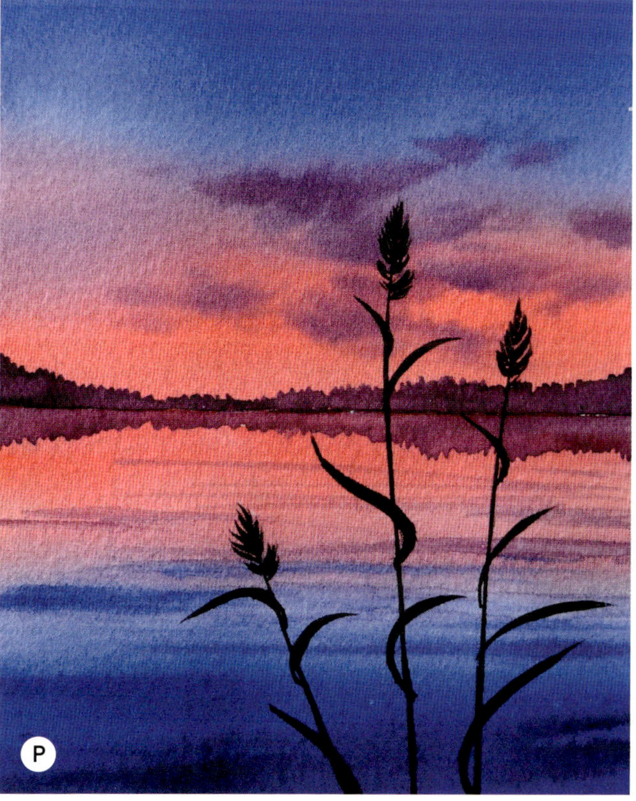

Step 5: Final Details. To add depth to the image, add some pampas grass in the foreground using Payne's Grey. First, add three or four lines that form the stem. Use a smaller brush or a detail brush with a pointed tip for this step. (O)

Once you've drawn the lines, add long, pointed leaves. Add them in diffeent directions, shapes, and sizes to make the image more interesting. Add the feathered flowers on top to finish the painting. (P)

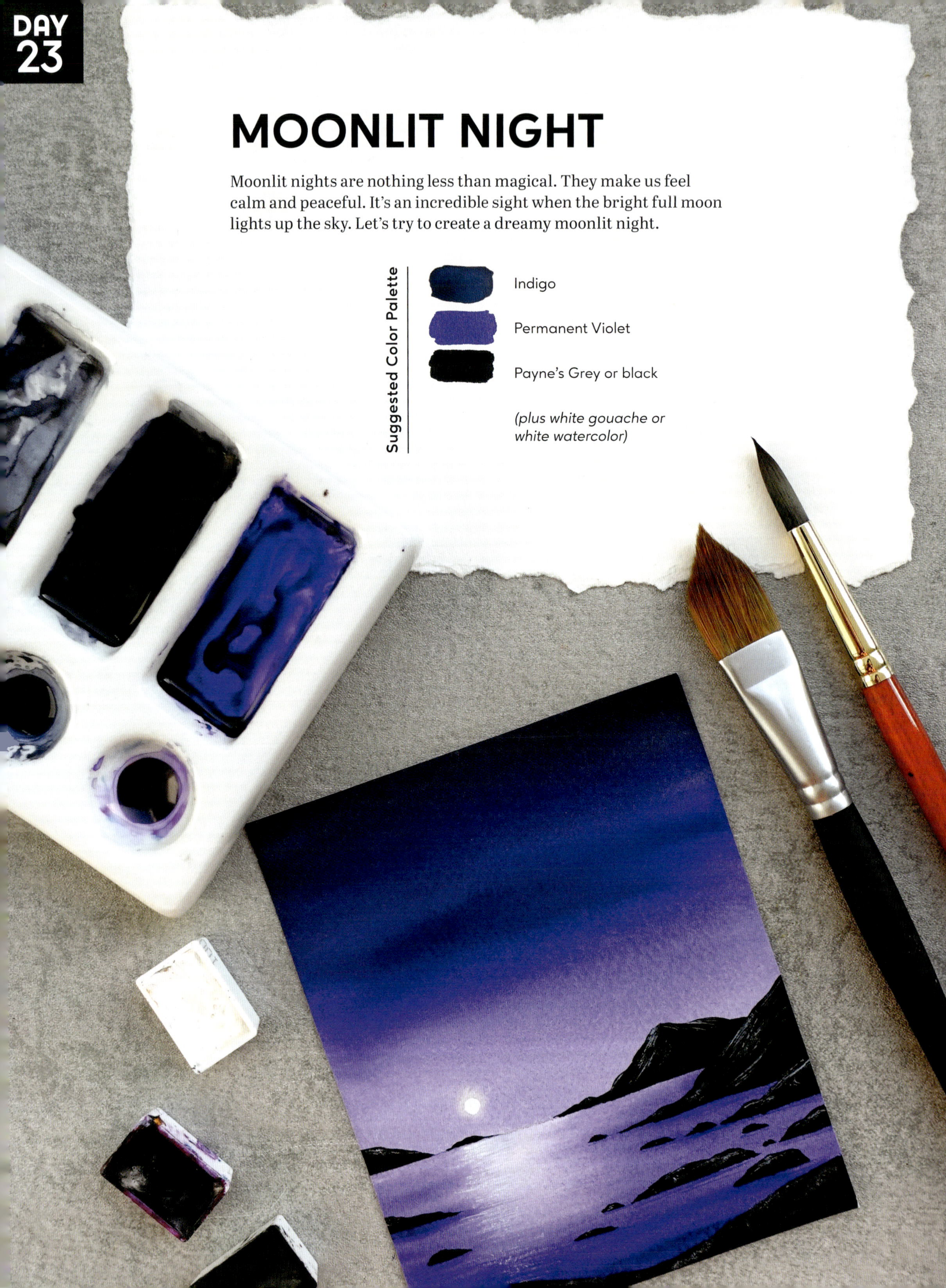

DAY 23

MOONLIT NIGHT

Moonlit nights are nothing less than magical. They make us feel calm and peaceful. It's an incredible sight when the bright full moon lights up the sky. Let's try to create a dreamy moonlit night.

Suggested Color Palette

- Indigo
- Permanent Violet
- Payne's Grey or black

(plus white gouache or white watercolor)

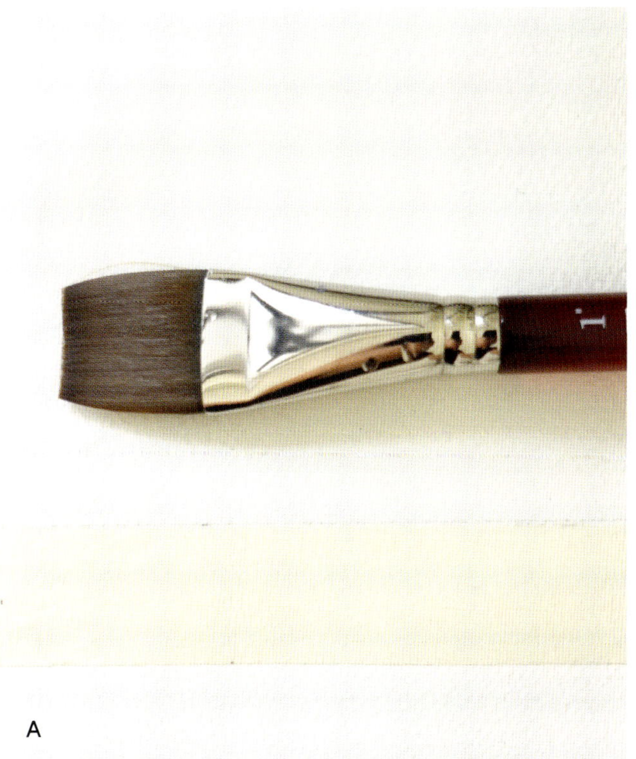

A

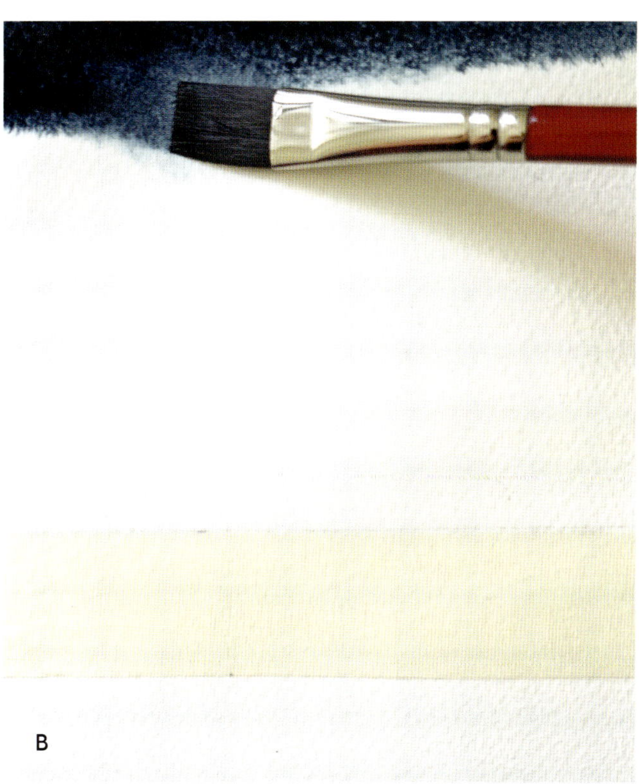

B

Step 1: Securing, Masking, and Wetting the Paper. Secure your paper to a drawing board. Place a piece of masking tape on the center of the paper to separate the sky and the lake. Apply an even layer of clean water to the entire sky. (A)

Step 2: Sky. Start with a darker shade of Indigo and apply it to the upper part of the sky. (B)

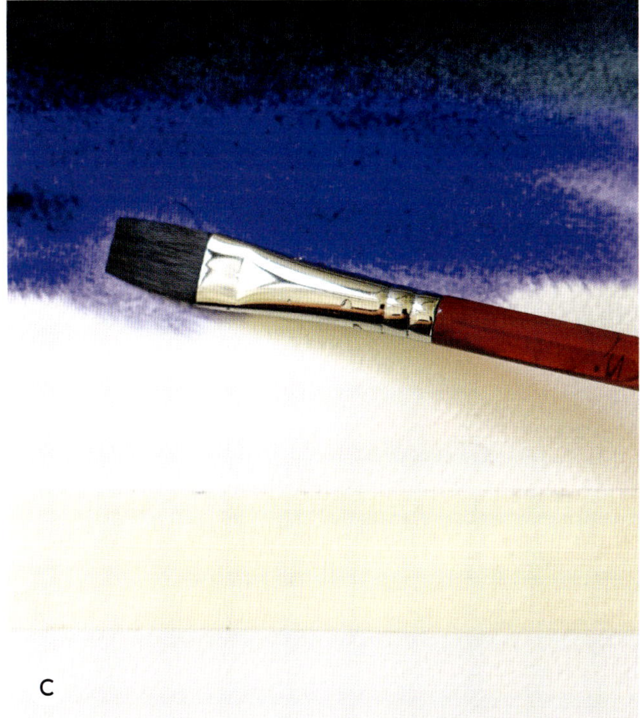

C

D

Clean your brush and switch to Permanent Violet. Apply it exactly where you left off with the Indigo and blend the colors well. (C)

Quickly rinse your brush and continue with even horizontal brushstrokes until you reach the horizon line, adding clean water as necessary to lighten the color. (D)

(continued)

Quickly switch to a clean, damp brush to take some paint off the background in a small circular shape. Just touch the brush gently to the wet background and lift off the color. (E) We only need a small circular area to add the moon. Once you're satisfied with the result, let it dry completely. Carefully peel off the masking tape. Add a tiny moon with white gouache or white watercolor. (F)

Step 3: Lake. Start with a lighter tone of Permanent Violet and apply it along the horizon line. Make the color stronger toward the bottom. (G)

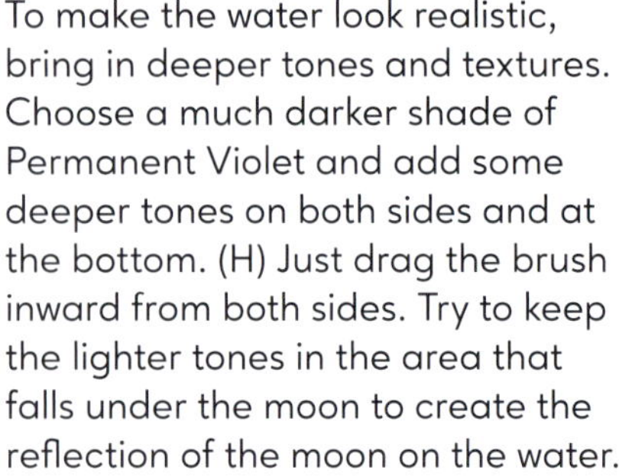

To make the water look realistic, bring in deeper tones and textures. Choose a much darker shade of Permanent Violet and add some deeper tones on both sides and at the bottom. (H) Just drag the brush inward from both sides. Try to keep the lighter tones in the area that falls under the moon to create the reflection of the moon on the water.

To make it more interesting, repeat the same step with the darker value of Indigo, keeping the lighter tone in the center. (I) Let dry completely.

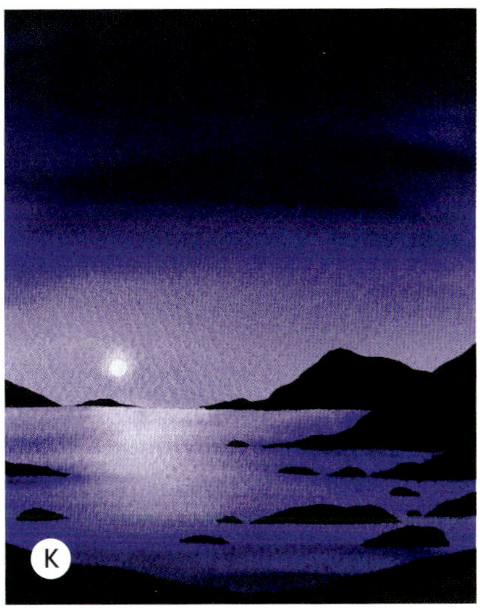

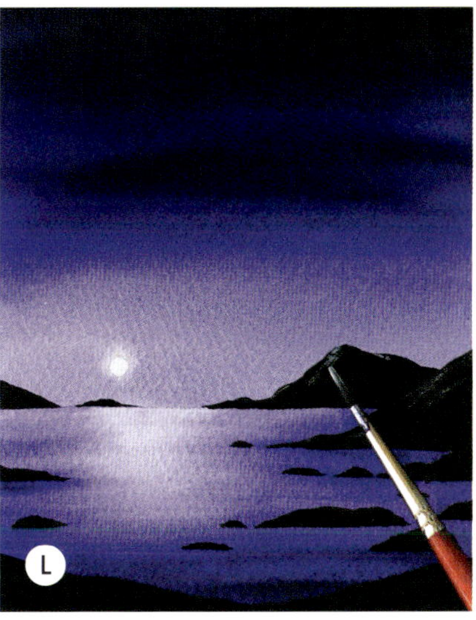

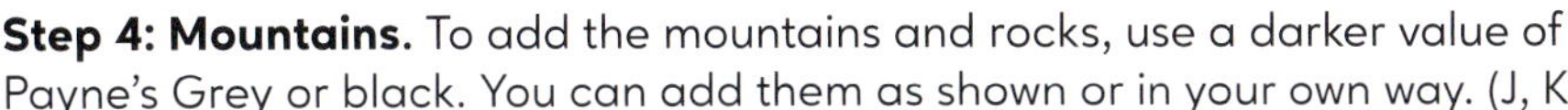

Step 4: Mountains. To add the mountains and rocks, use a darker value of Payne's Grey or black. You can add them as shown or in your own way. (J, K)

Add some textures to make the mountains stand out using dry white gouache or white watercolor. After loading the brush with paint, dab it several times on a paper towel to remove excess water. (L)

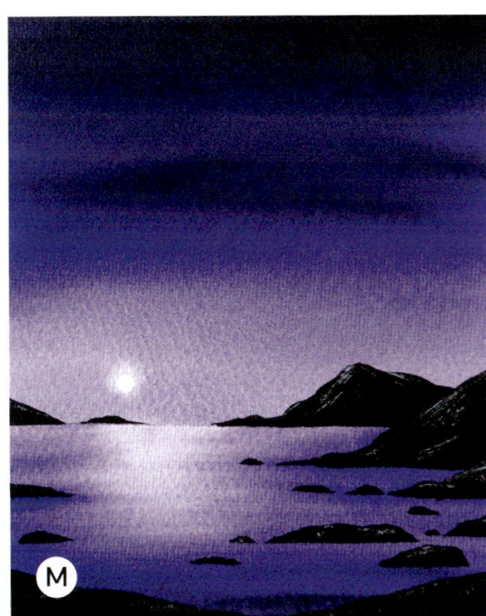

Add texture along the top of the mountain and also on the rocks. (M) Add some dry white lines below the moon to represent the reflection to finish the painting. (N)

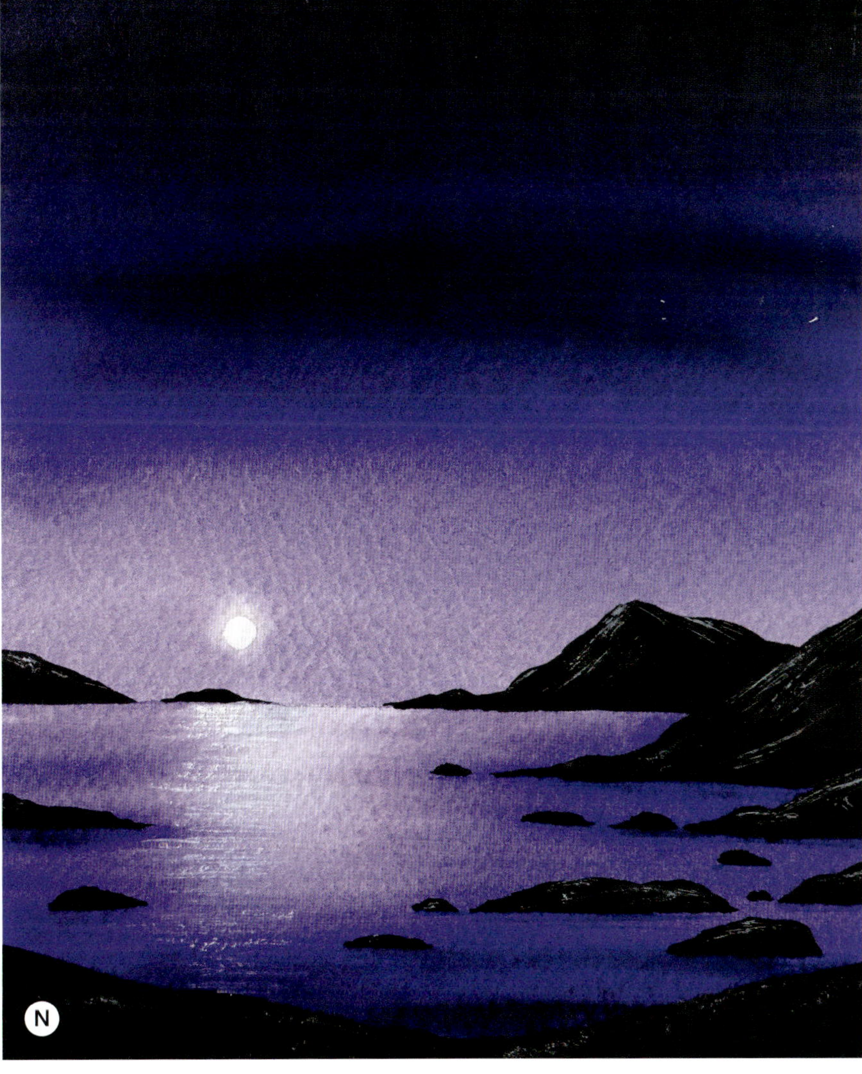

DAY 24

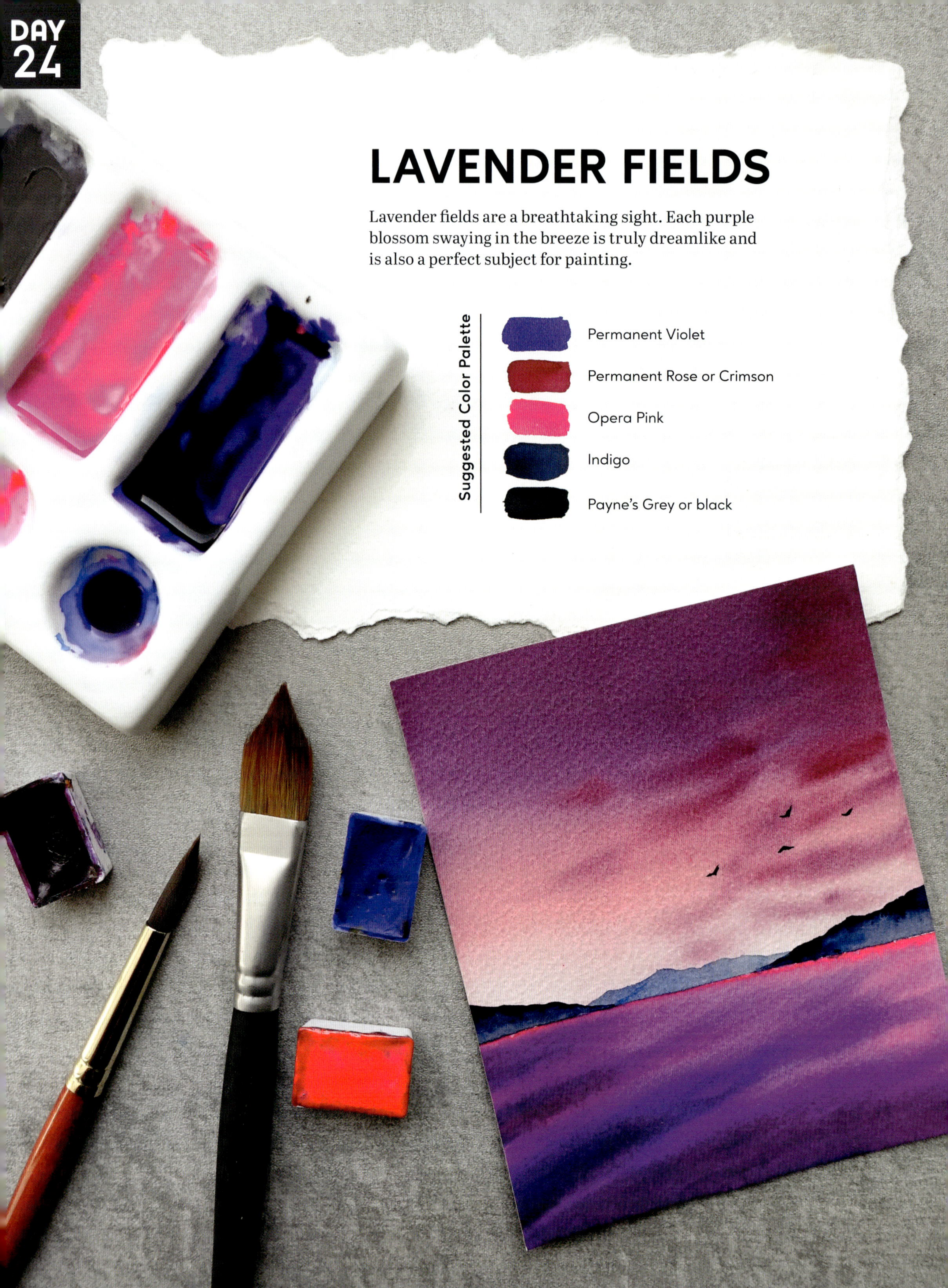

LAVENDER FIELDS

Lavender fields are a breathtaking sight. Each purple blossom swaying in the breeze is truly dreamlike and is also a perfect subject for painting.

Suggested Color Palette

- Permanent Violet
- Permanent Rose or Crimson
- Opera Pink
- Indigo
- Payne's Grey or black

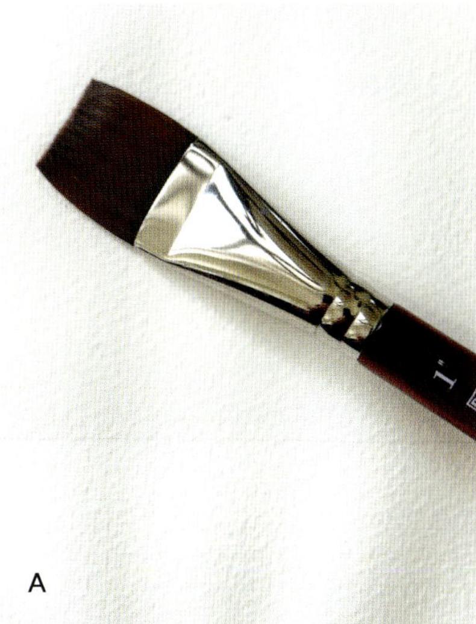

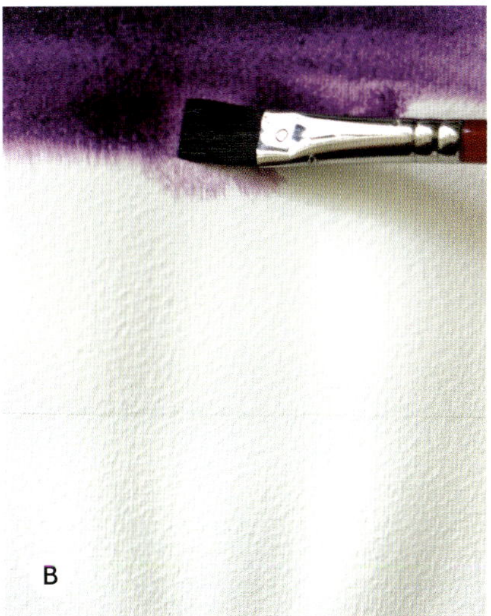

C

Step 1: Adding the Sketch; Securing and Wetting the Paper. Draw a horizon line slightly below the center of the paper. Secure your paper to a drawing board. Apply an even layer of clean water to the sky. (A)

Step 2: Sky. I'm using purple for the sky. You can either use Permanent Violet directly or you can mix a little of the Permanent Rose or Crimson to the Permanent Violet to create a beautiful purple. Apply to the top of the sky. (B, C)

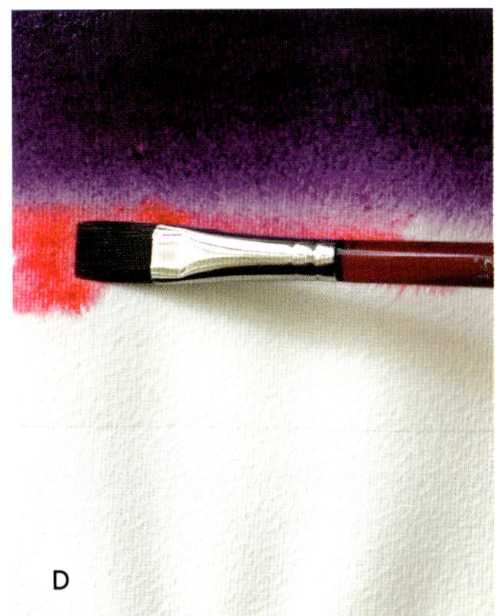

Clean your brush and switch to Permanent Rose. Apply it underneath the purple, (D) blending the two colors together. (E)

Quickly rinse your brush and continue with even horizontal brushstrokes until you reach the horizon line, adding clean water as necessary to lighten the color. (F)

(continued)

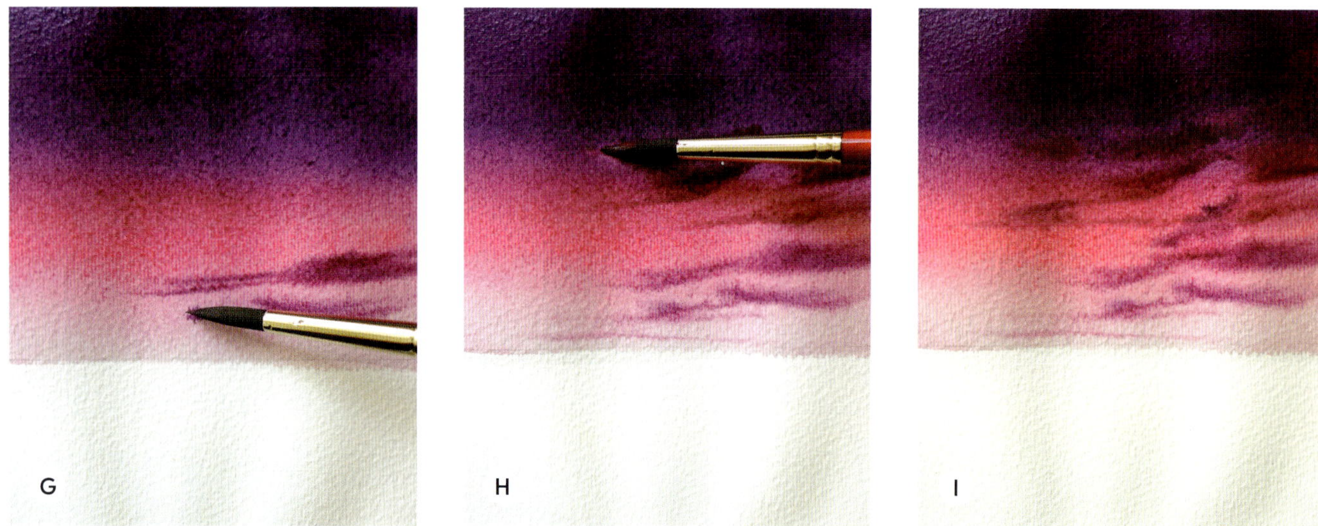

While the background is still wet, add the clouds a little above the horizon line. You can use the same purple we created earlier. (G, H, I) Let dry completely.

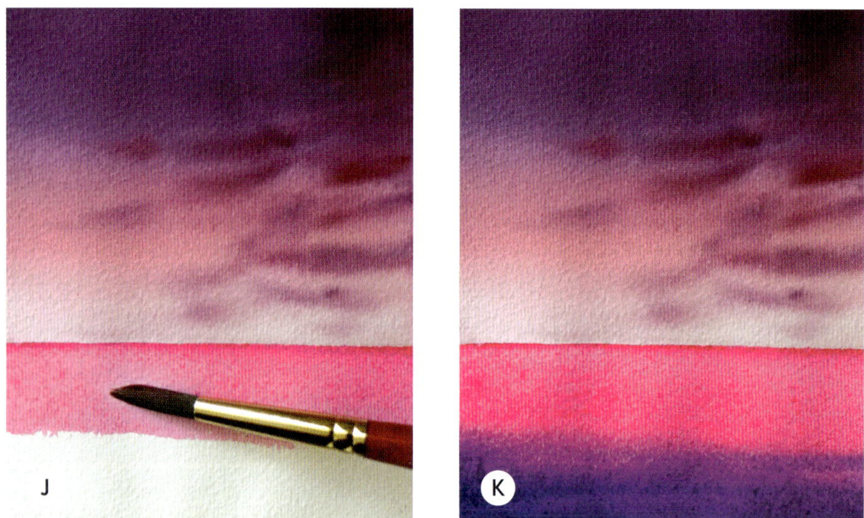

Step 3: Lavender Fields. Start with Opera Pink or Permanent Rose and apply this color to half of the field. (J) Clean your brush and switch to Permanent Violet. Apply it to the remaining area and blend the two colors together. (K)

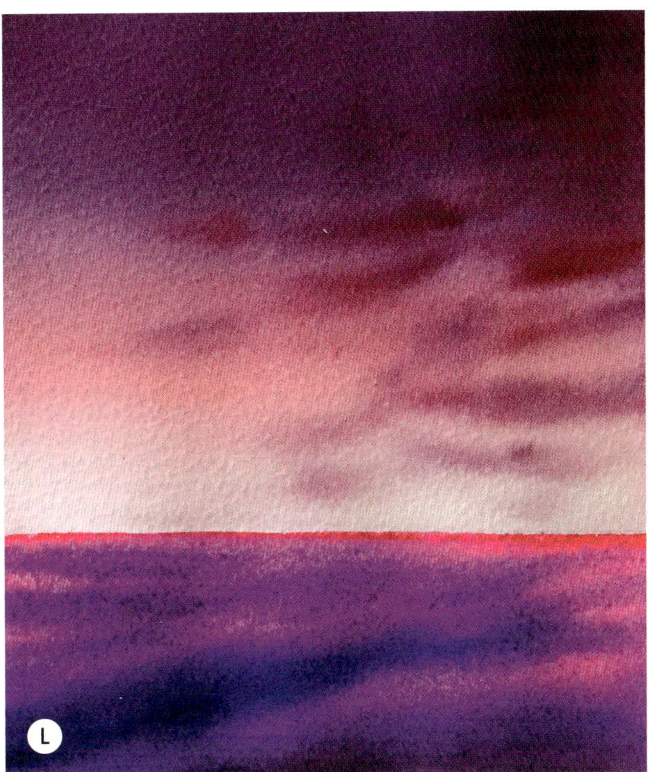

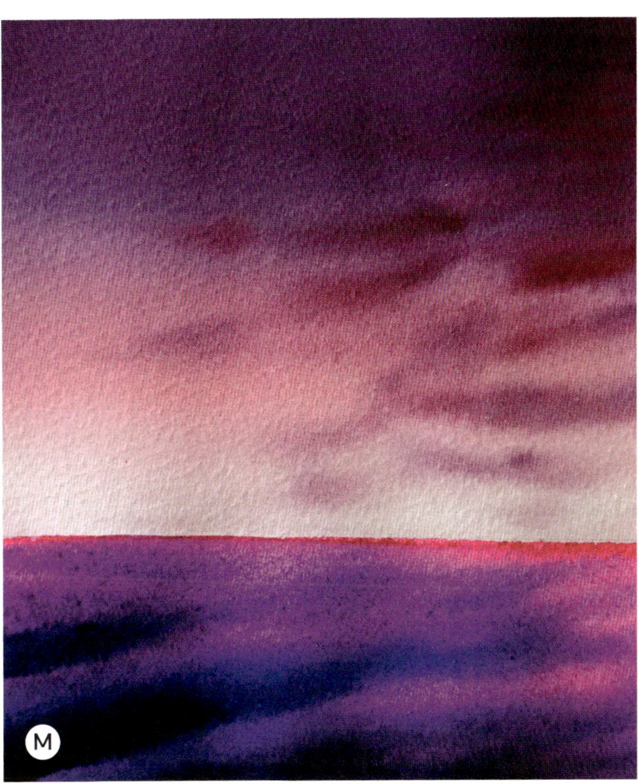

Use a darker value of Permanent Violet to add diagonal divisions to make it look like a lavender field. Start at the bottom left and drag the brush diagonally across the field. (L) Switch to a much darker value and make the lines stand out. (M) Let dry completely.

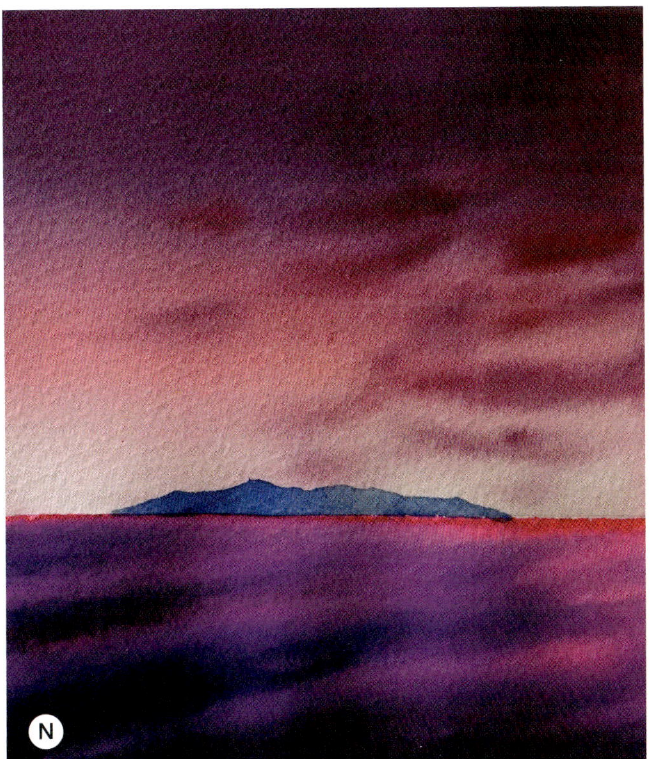

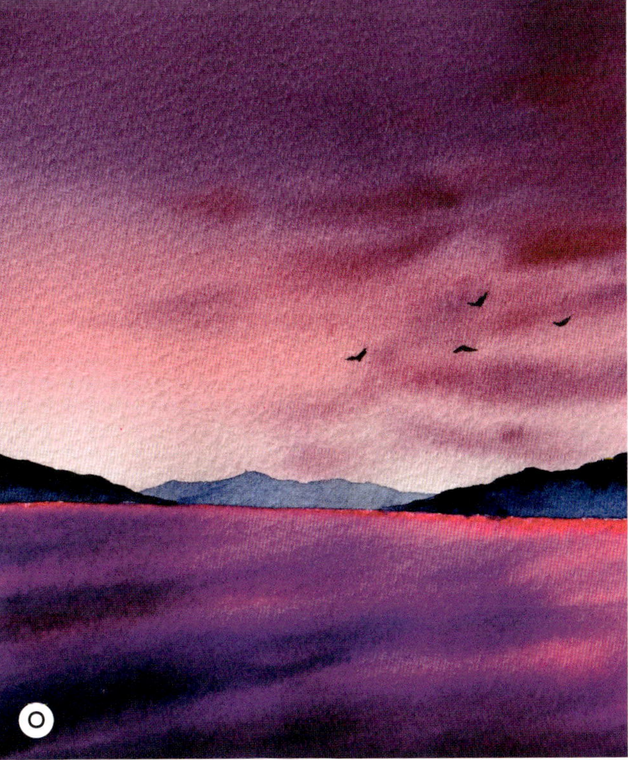

Step 4: Mountains. We'll add two layers of mountains: one in the background with a lighter value of Indigo and another in the foreground with a darker value of Indigo. (N) Choose a lighter value of Indigo and add the background mountain in the middle. Let dry completely. Use a darker value of Indigo to add the foreground layer. Add mountains on both sides. Add a few birds using Payne's Grey or black to finish the painting. (O)

DAY
25

BRIGHT BLUE SKY

Looking up at the blue sky on a bright sunny day can be a relaxing experience and a moment of your life to cherish. Each element of the atmosphere inspires in its own way. A bright blue sky and a fresh meadow are a pure joy to behold.

Suggested Color Palette

- Cerulean Blue
- Turquoise Blue
- Lemon Yellow
- Sap Green
- Indigo
- Burnt Sienna
- Payne's Grey or black

(plus white gouache or white watercolor)

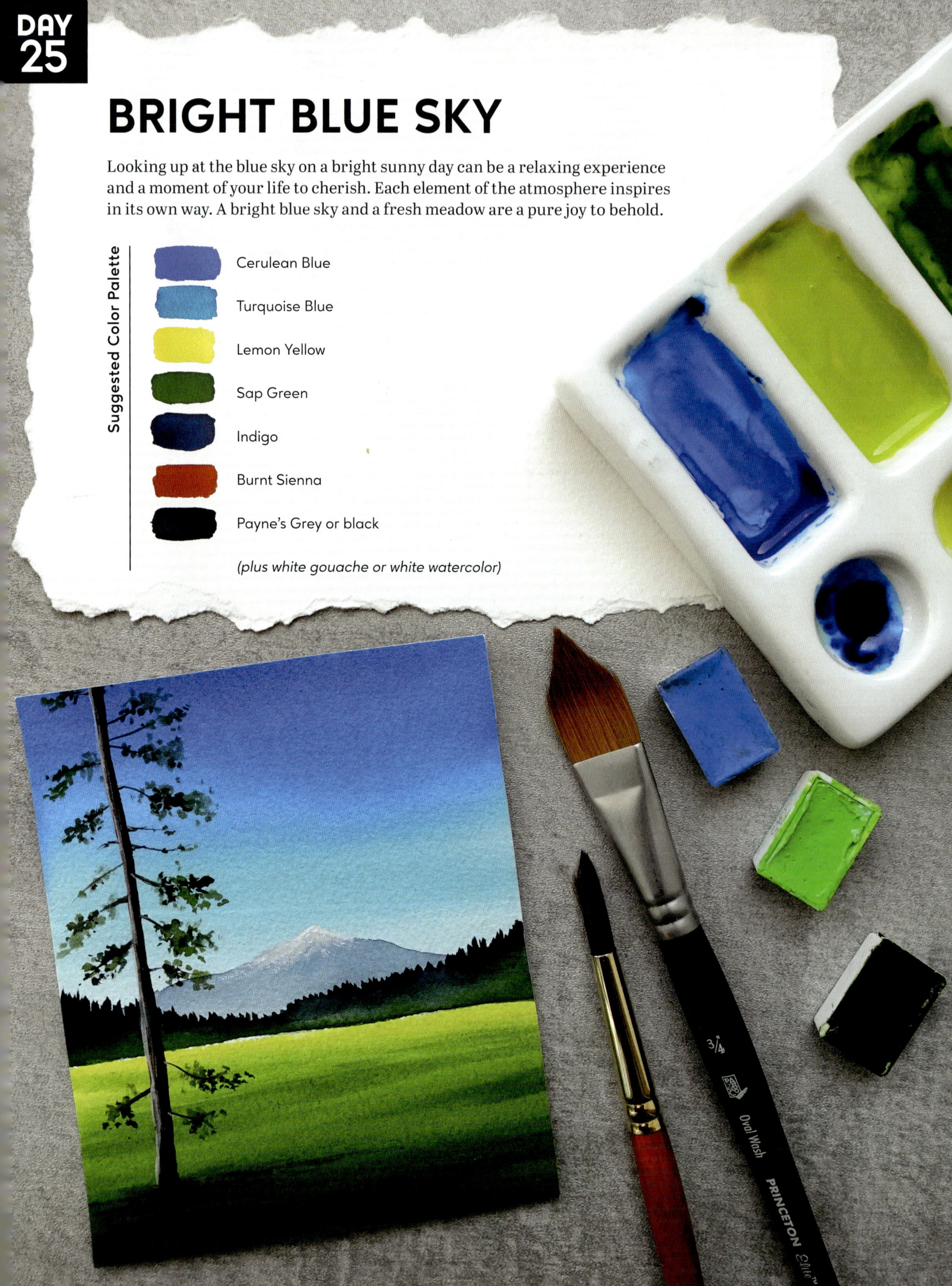

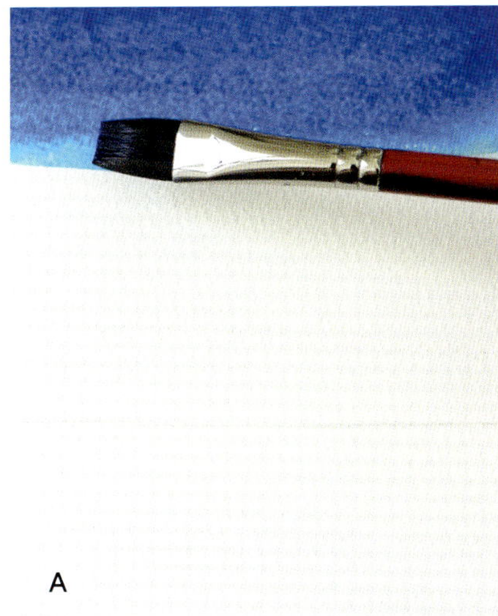

Step 1: Adding the Sketch; Securing and Wetting the Paper; Sky. Draw a horizon line slightly below the center of the paper. Secure your paper to a drawing board. Apply an even layer of clean water to the sky. For the sky, we'll use Cerulean Blue and Turquoise Blue. Start with a medium tone of Cerulean Blue and apply it to the top of the sky. (A)

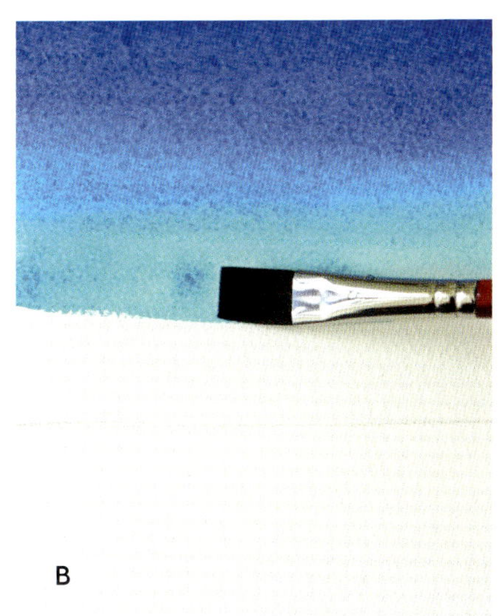

Quickly clean your brush and switch to a medium tone of Turquoise Blue, blending it with the Cerulean Blue. (B)

Quickly rinse your brush and continue with even horizontal brushstrokes until you reach the horizon line, adding clean water as necessary to lighten the color. (C) Let dry completely.

Add the mountain with a medium shade of Indigo and let it dry completely. (D)

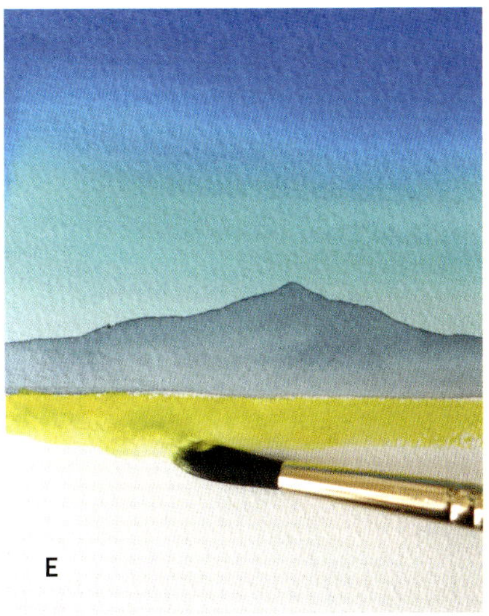

Step 2: Meadow. For the meadow, we'll start with a lighter green (Sap Green + Lemon Yellow) and apply it along the horizon line. Apply the lighter green almost halfway down the meadow. (E)

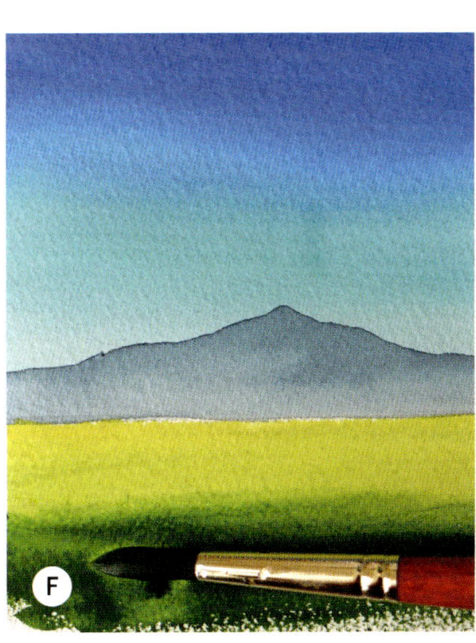

Clean your brush and switch to Sap Green. Fill in the remaining area. (F)

(continued)

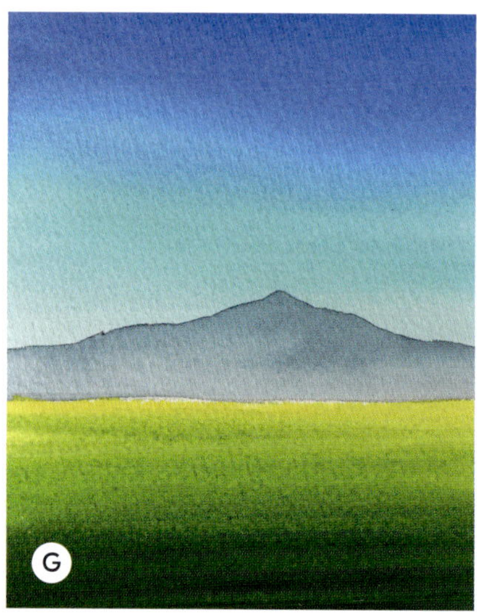

To bring in textures and shadows, add a few lines using Sap Green on the lighter area while the base layer is wet. (G)

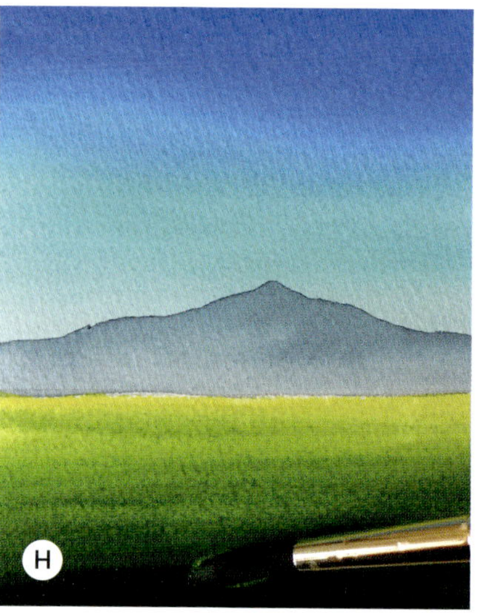

Create a darker green by mixing some Payne's Grey or black with Sap Green and add this darker tone to the lower area. (H)

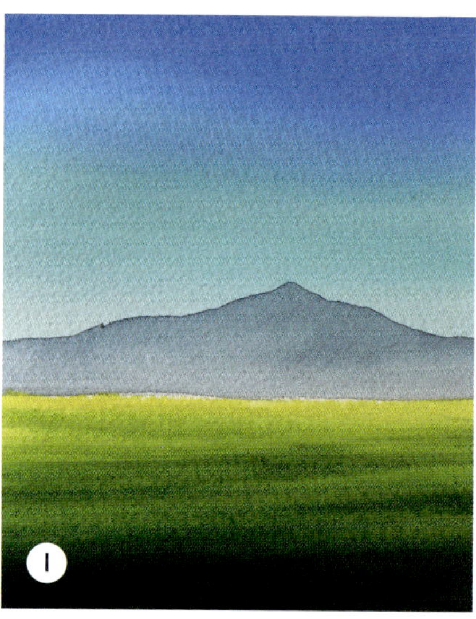

Add some lines with the same tone to create shadows and textures. (I) Let dry completely.

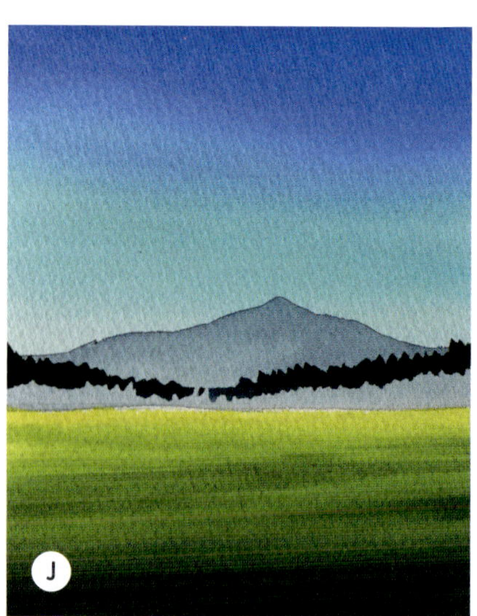

Step 3: Details. To bring more life to the painting, we need to add some more details. Start by adding the landscape in the distance. Use a darker shade of green for this. Add a rough shape, making it taller on both sides and shorter in the middle. (J)

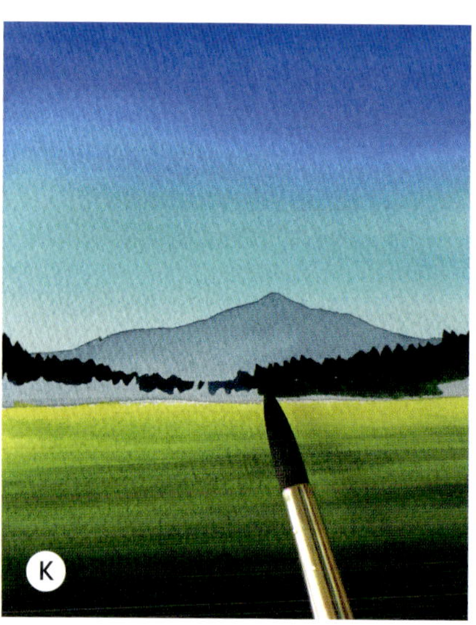

Fill in the rest with a medium tone. (K)

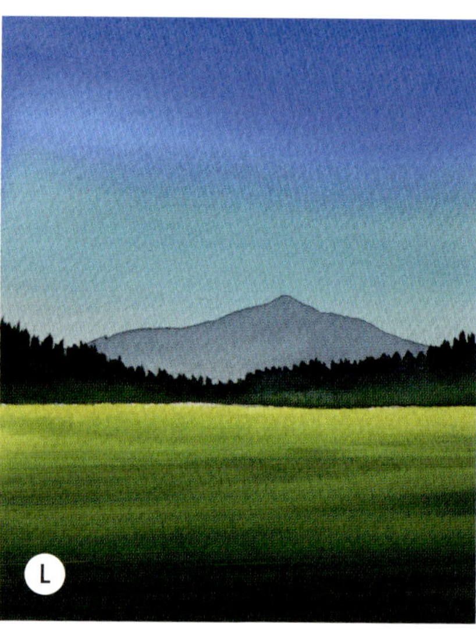

Let dry completely. (L)

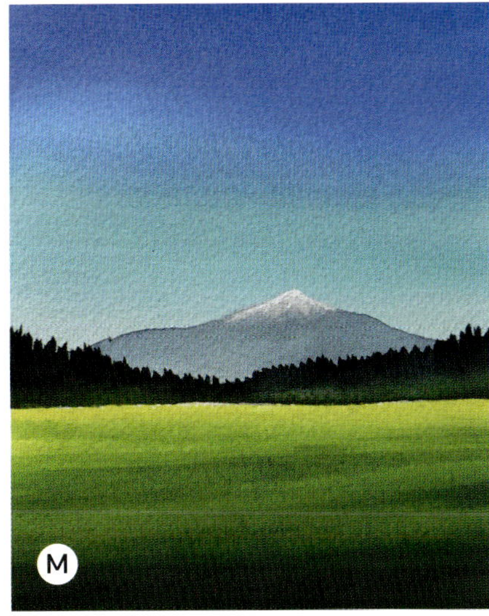

Use a dry white gouache or white watercolor to add snow on the mountain. After loading the brush with paint, dab it several times on a paper towel to remove the excess water. It's the same technique as the other paintings. Just add some dry white textures along the top of the mountain.

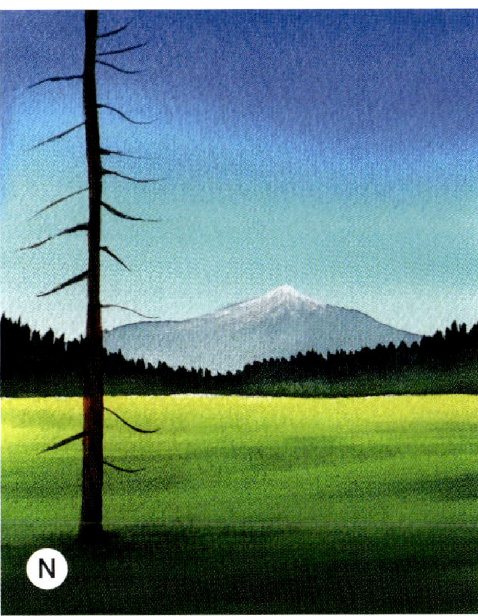

As a final detail, add a large pine tree. First, add the trunk of the tree with a darker brown (Burnt Sienna + Payne's Grey or black). Using the same color, add some branches on both sides of the tree. (N)

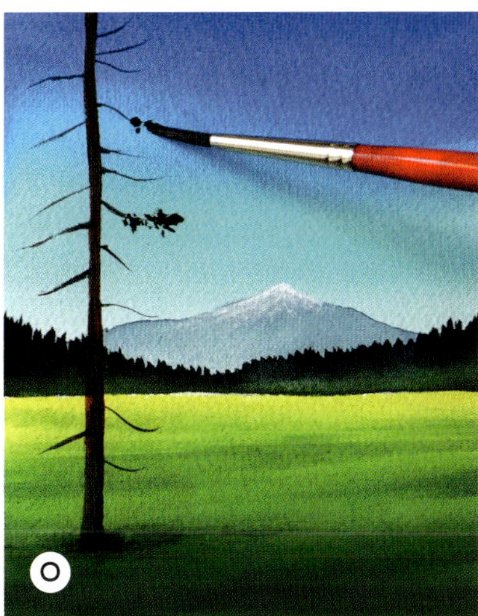

Add the foliage. Clean your brush and switch back to a darker green and keep adding tiny dots and small patterns with the brush tip. You don't have to put them on all the branches, just add them randomly to make it look more natural. (O)

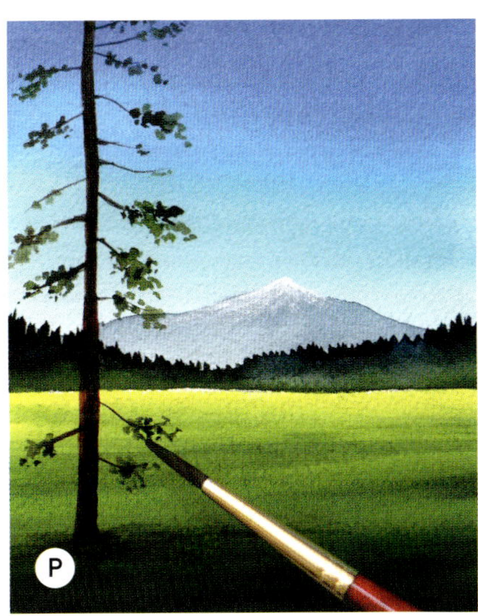

Switch to a medium shade of green and repeat the same step. This way, the foliage will have different shades of green and look more realistic. (P)

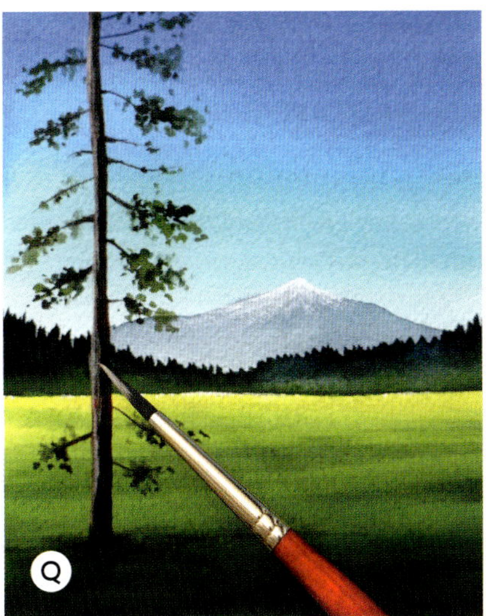

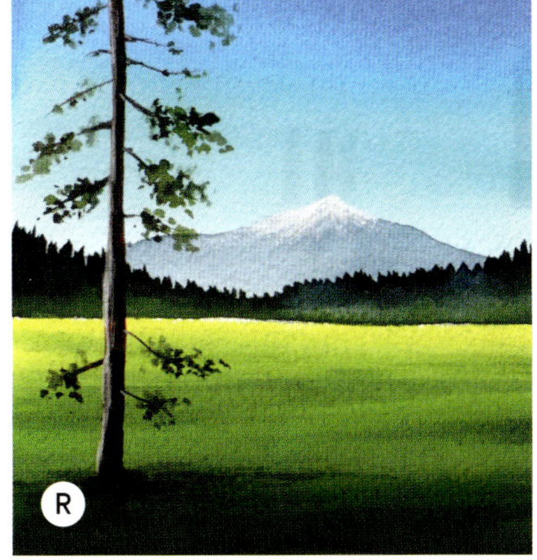

If you want to have a dense and thick foliage, you can keep adding more patterns. Add texture to the tree trunk using white gouache or white watercolor. (Q) Add a few lines on the left side of the tree trunk to finish the painting. (R)

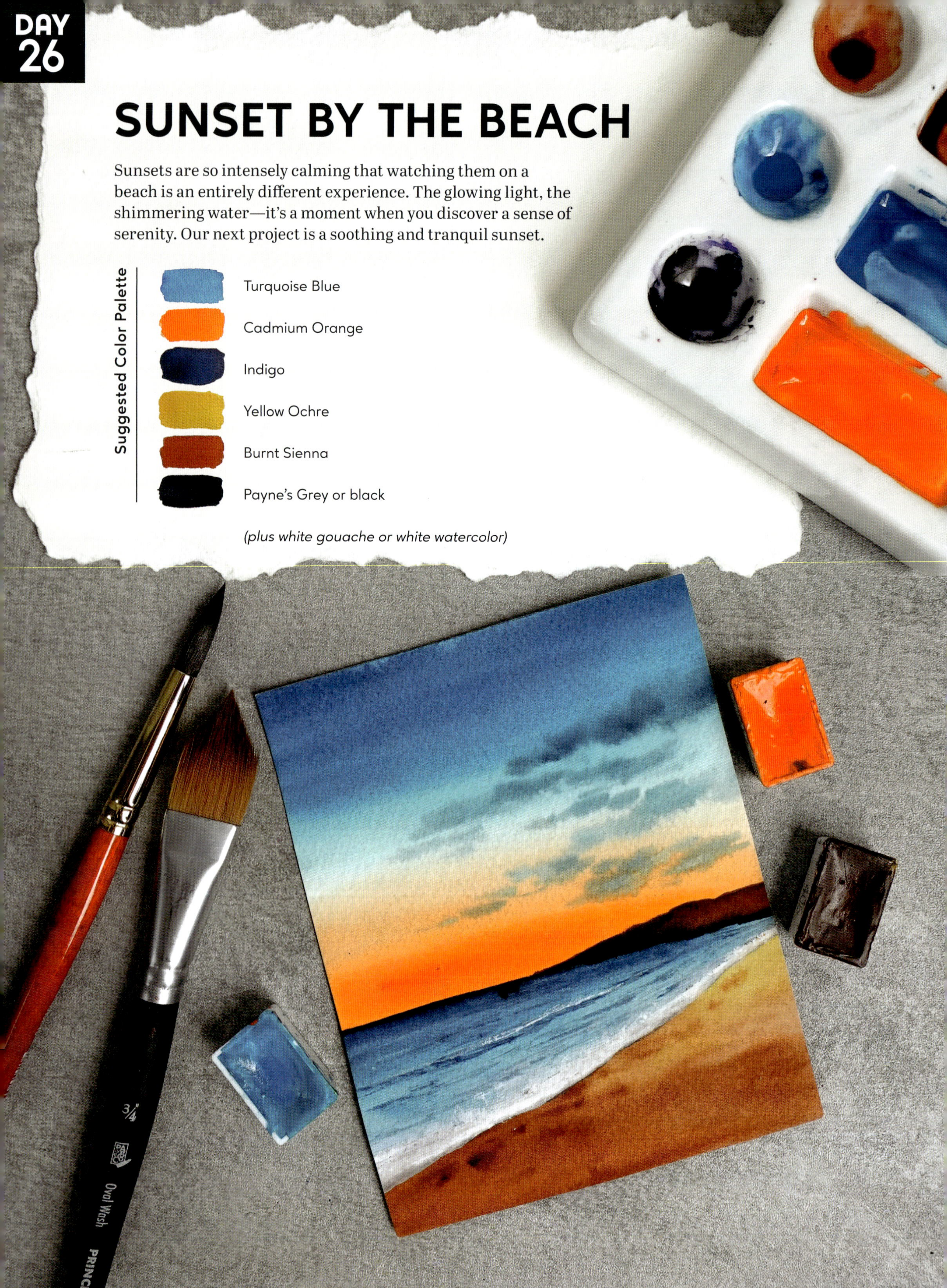

SUNSET BY THE BEACH

Sunsets are so intensely calming that watching them on a beach is an entirely different experience. The glowing light, the shimmering water—it's a moment when you discover a sense of serenity. Our next project is a soothing and tranquil sunset.

Suggested Color Palette

- Turquoise Blue
- Cadmium Orange
- Indigo
- Yellow Ochre
- Burnt Sienna
- Payne's Grey or black

(plus white gouache or white watercolor)

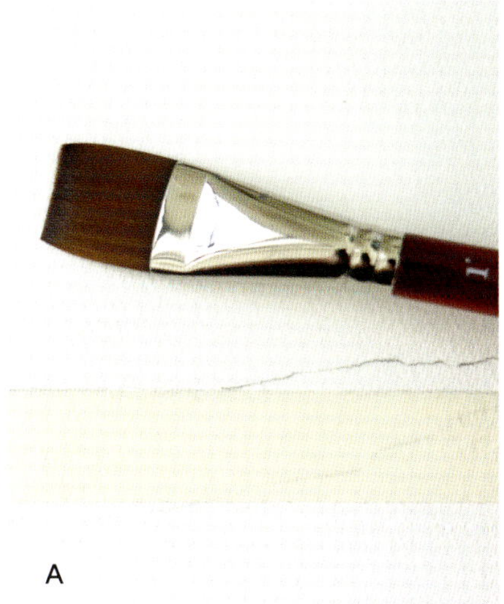

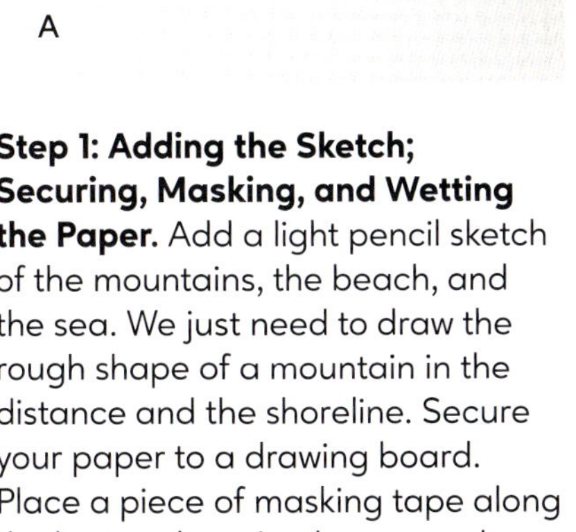

A

B

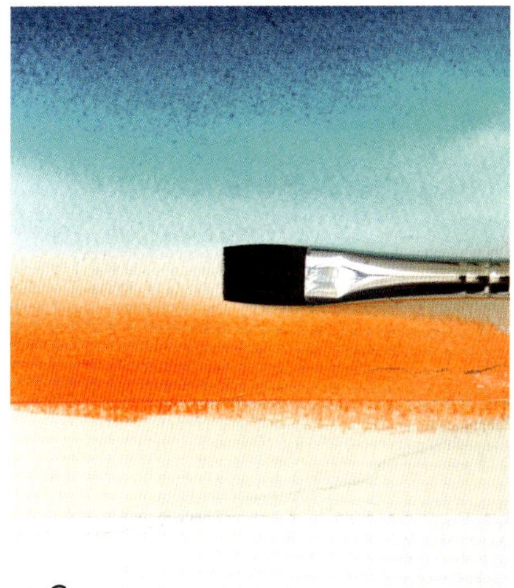

C

Step 1: Adding the Sketch; Securing, Masking, and Wetting the Paper. Add a light pencil sketch of the mountains, the beach, and the sea. We just need to draw the rough shape of a mountain in the distance and the shoreline. Secure your paper to a drawing board. Place a piece of masking tape along the horizon line. Apply an even layer of clean water to the sky. (A)

Step 2: Sky. Start with a medium tone of Turquoise Blue and apply it to the top of the sky. (B) When you're almost at the middle of the sky, quickly rinse your brush and continue with even horizontal brushstrokes until you reach the horizon line, adding clean water as necessary to lighten the color.

Quickly clean your brush and switch to Cadmium Orange. Start with a medium tone and apply it along the horizon line, making it lighter toward the top. (C) Try to achieve an even blend.

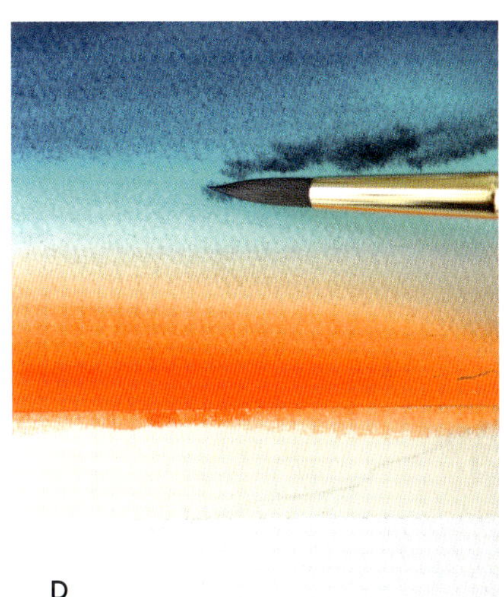

D

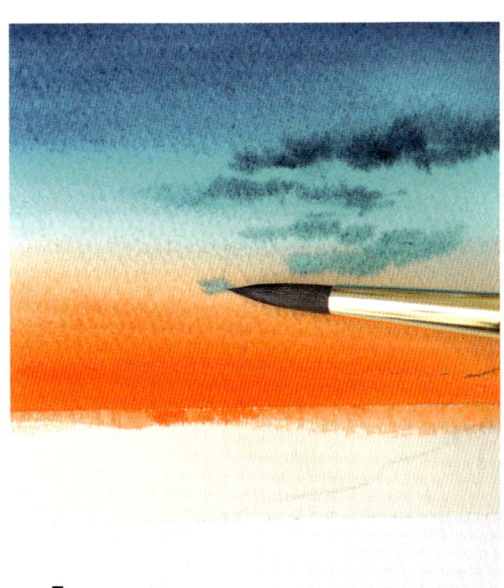

E

F

Use either a darker shade of Turquoise Blue or Indigo to add the clouds. (D) Be sure to add them before the base layer dries.

I'm using a medium shade of Indigo. I only want small clouds on the right side. You can add as many as you like. (E, F)

(continued)

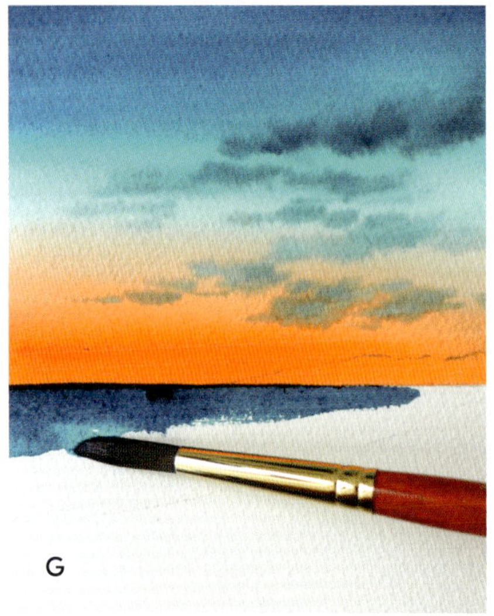

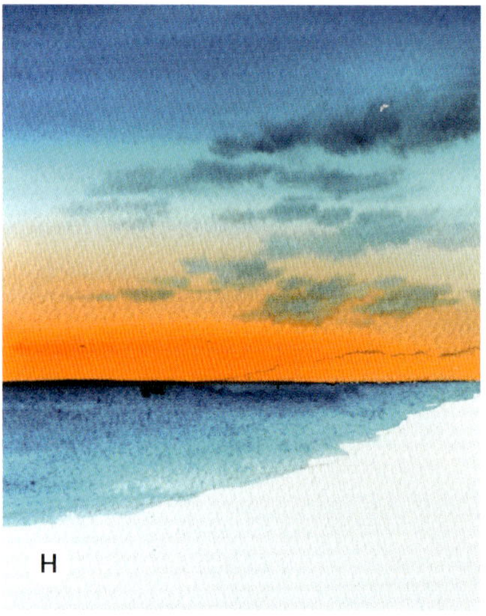

Step 3: Sea. Carefully peel off the masking tape. Start at the horizon with a darker shade of Turquoise Blue (G) and make it lighter as you get closer to the shoreline. (H) Let dry completely.

Step 4: Mountain. Create a darker shade of brown by mixing a little black or Payne's Grey with Burnt Sienna and paint the entire mountain. (I)

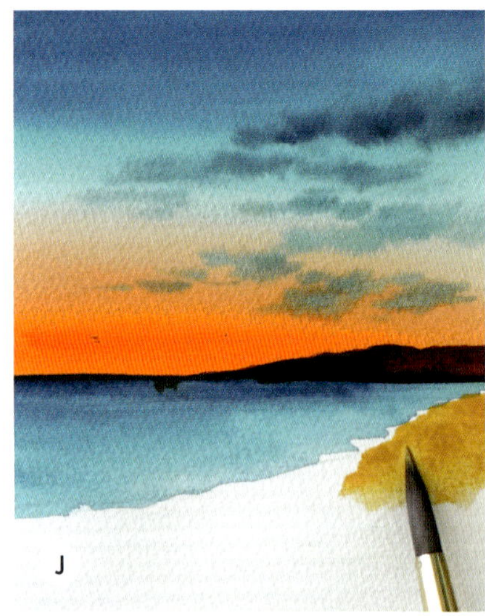

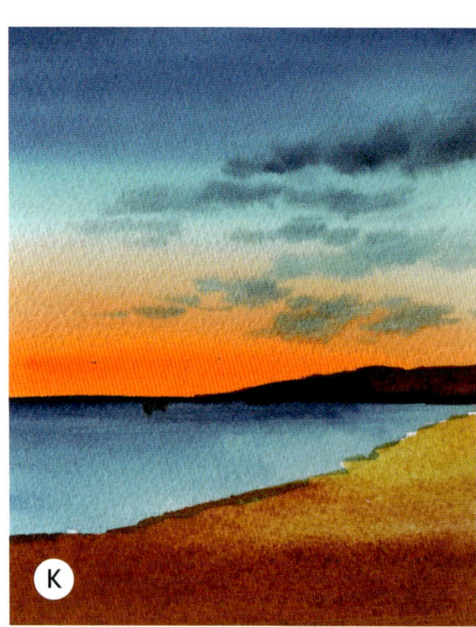

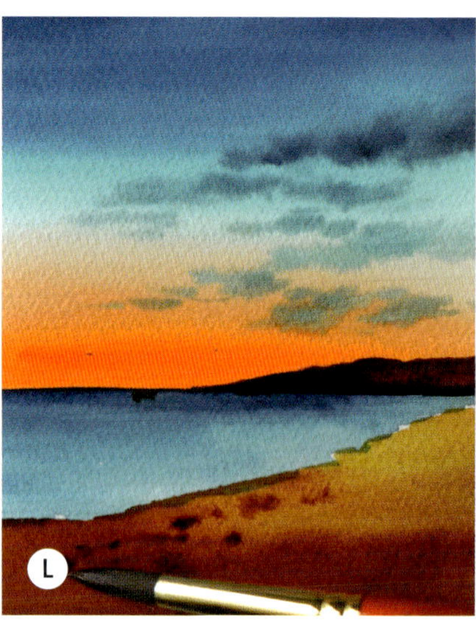

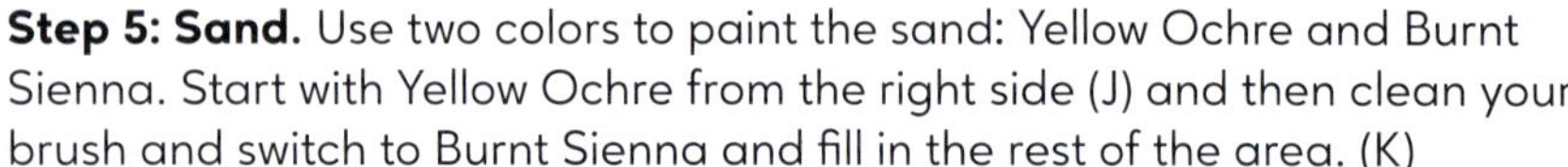

Step 5: Sand. Use two colors to paint the sand: Yellow Ochre and Burnt Sienna. Start with Yellow Ochre from the right side (J) and then clean your brush and switch to Burnt Sienna and fill in the rest of the area. (K)

Use a slightly darker shade of Burnt Sienna to add some texture. Simply add a few small random shapes on the wet background with the brush tip. (L) These patterns don't need to have a specific size or shape as we're just adding them for depth.

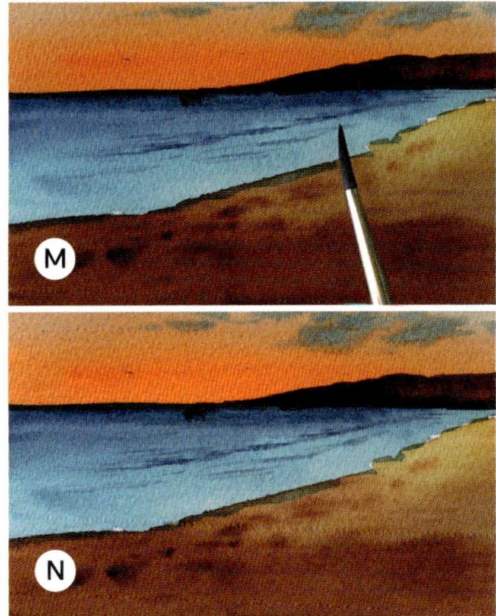

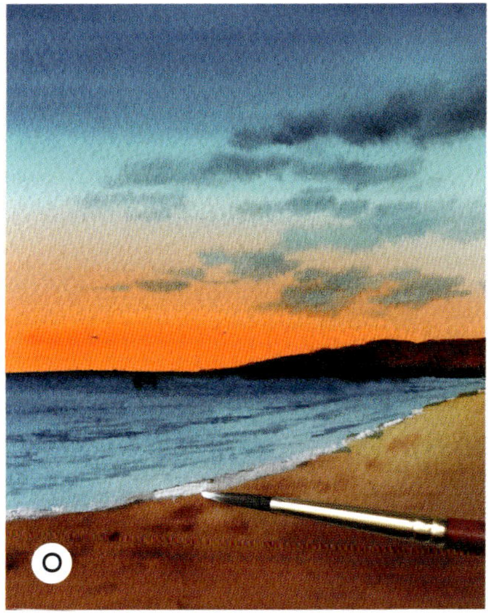

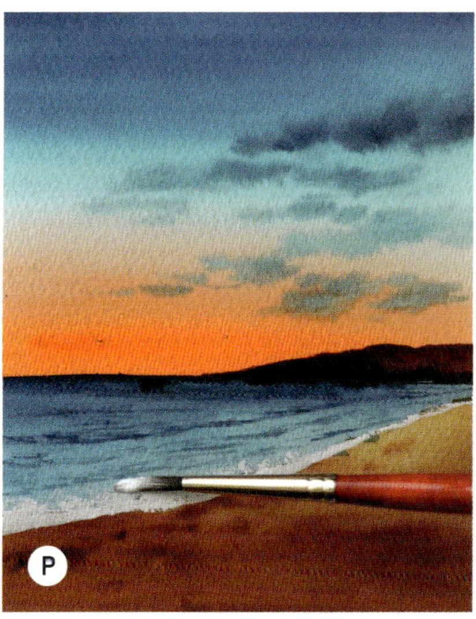

Step 6: Details. First, we need to add some lines and textures to the sea to represent the waves and the movement of the water. Use a smaller round brush and add many lines on the sea with a medium tone of Turquoise Blue to show the waves in the distance. (M, N)

Add a splashy wave at the shoreline. The wave must stand out clearly, so use an opaque white paint, either white gouache or white watercolor. Do not add too much water and choose a thicker consistency. Add the shape of the wave along the beach. (O)

Once you've defined the wave, use the same dry white paint and add dry texture along the top side of the wave. (P)

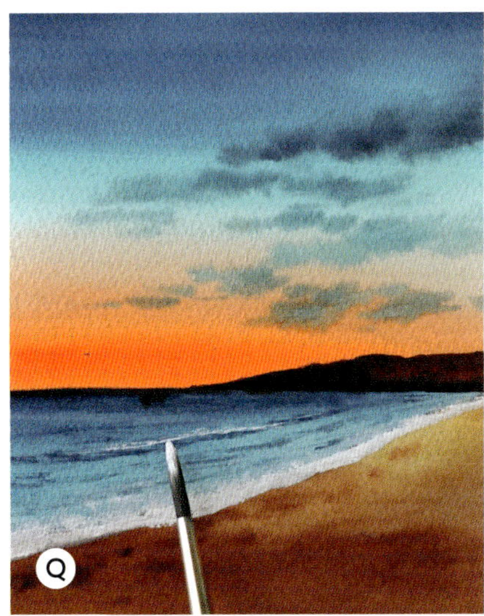

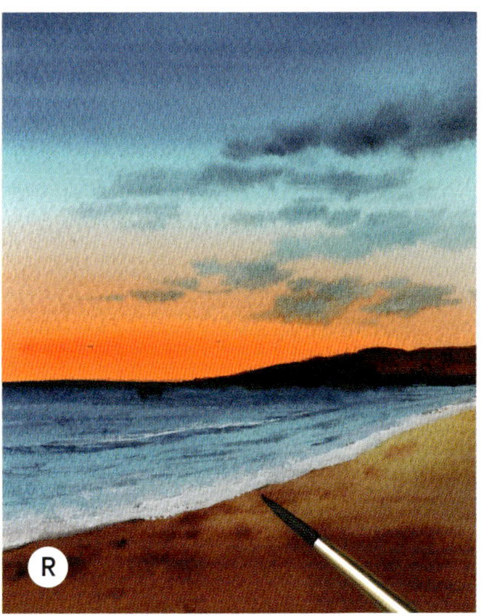

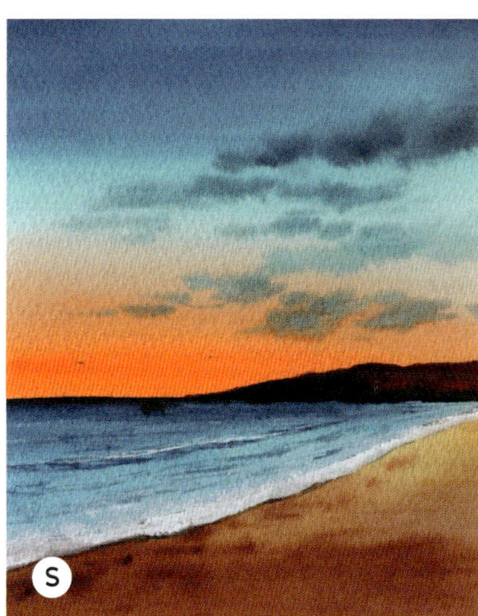

To make the sea a little more interesting, add another wave in the distance. (Q)

Using a darker shade of brown, add a delicate line of shadows along the shoreline to finish the painting. (R, S)

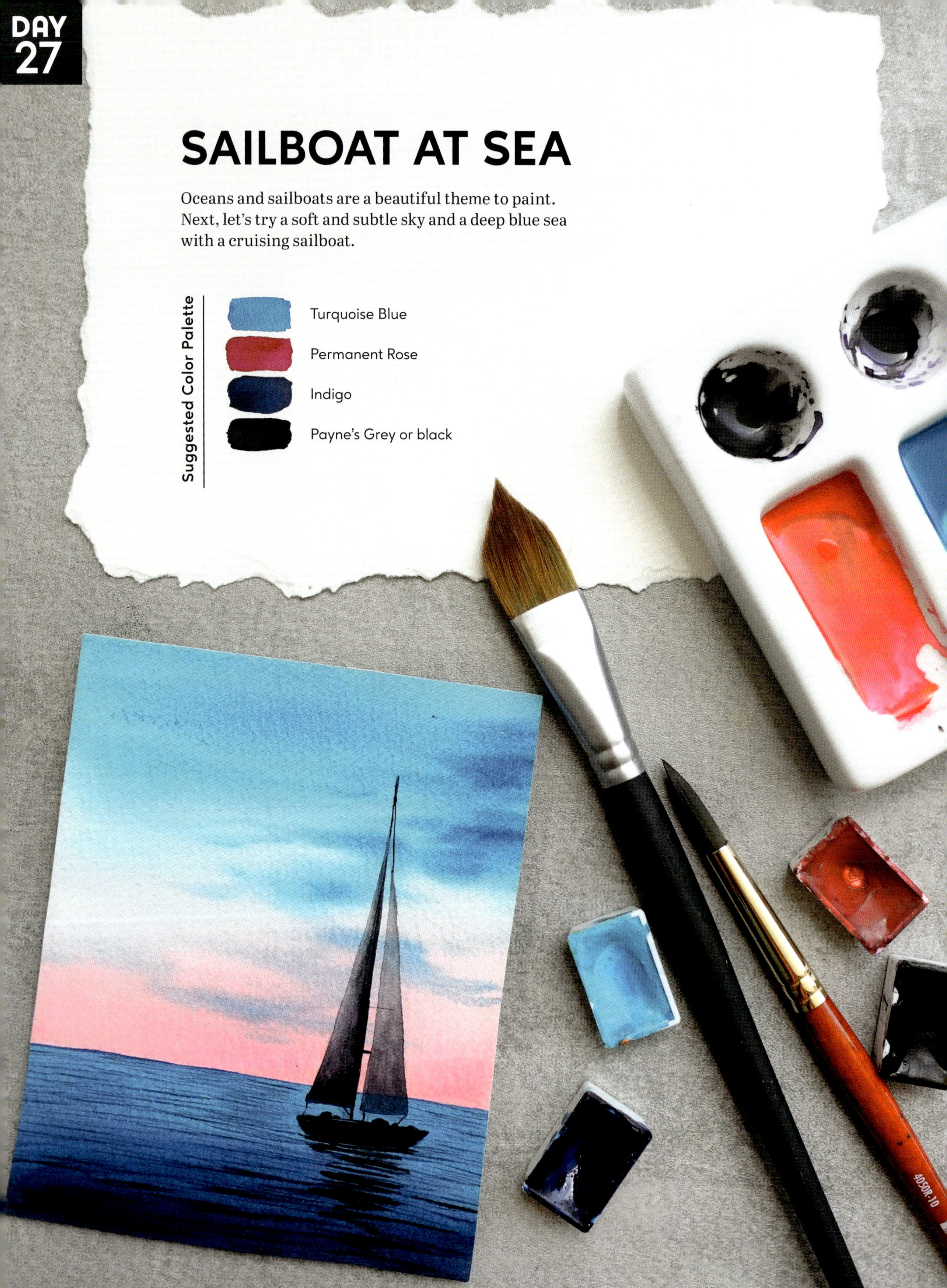

DAY 27

SAILBOAT AT SEA

Oceans and sailboats are a beautiful theme to paint. Next, let's try a soft and subtle sky and a deep blue sea with a cruising sailboat.

Suggested Color Palette

- Turquoise Blue
- Permanent Rose
- Indigo
- Payne's Grey or black

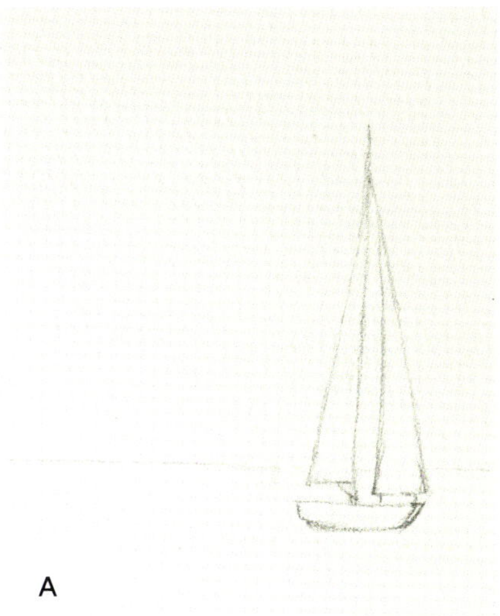

A

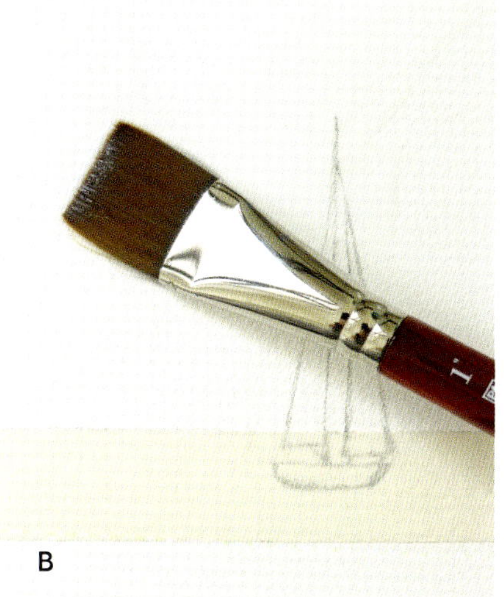

B

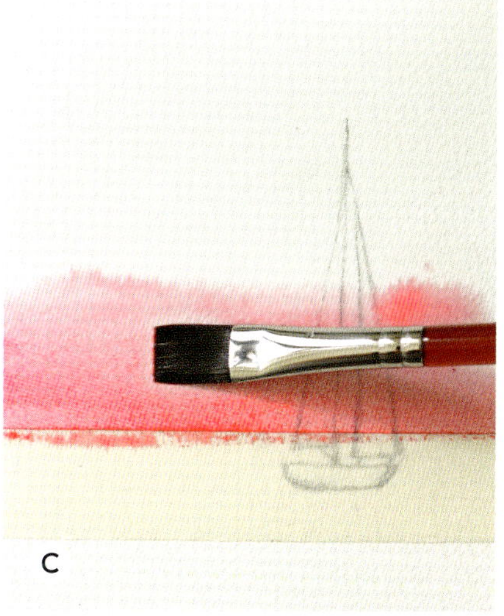

C

Step 1: Adding the Sketch. Begin by adding a light pencil sketch of the sailboat. Add a line for the horizon. (A)

Step 2: Securing, Masking, and Wetting the Paper. Secure your paper to a drawing board. Place a piece of masking tape three-quarters of the way down the paper for the horizon line. Add an even layer of clean water to the sky. (B)

Step 3: Sky. I'm starting with Permanent Rose along the horizon line and working up. (C) You can work either from top to bottom or bottom to top. It's your choice.

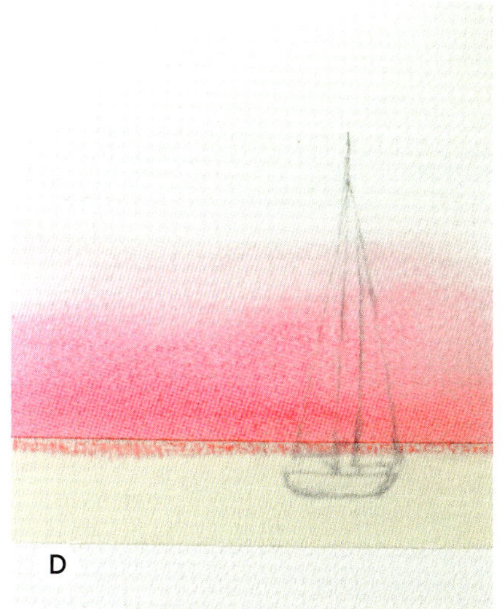

D

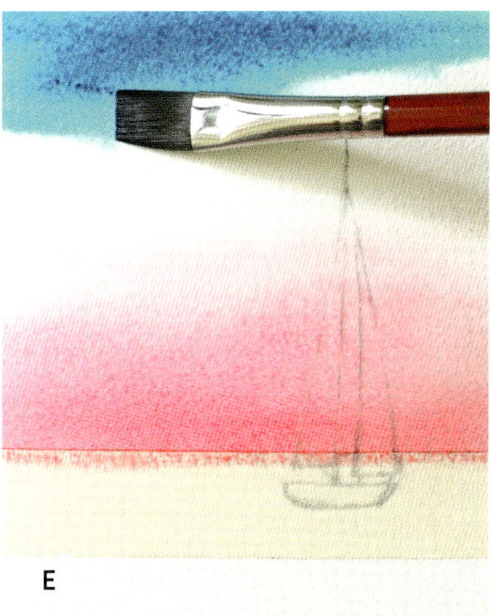

E

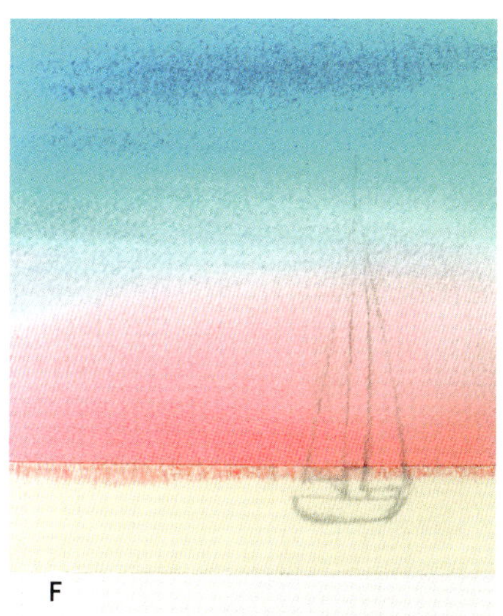

F

Use a medium shade along the horizon and lighten it up toward the top. (D)

Clean your brush and switch to Turquoise Blue. Apply it from top to bottom, (E) blending the colors. (F) This is the base layer. Add some clouds while the layer is wet.

(continued)

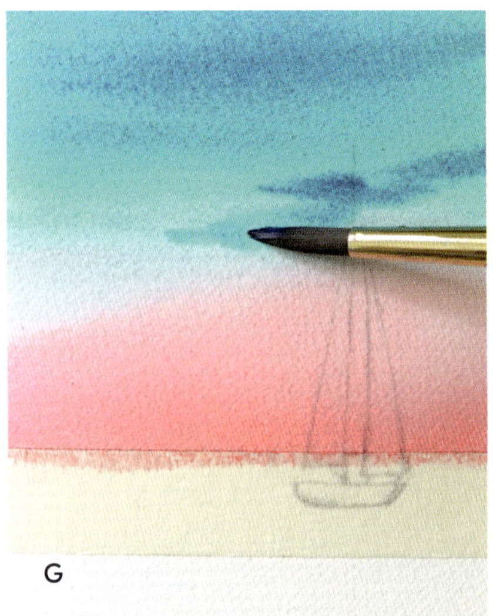

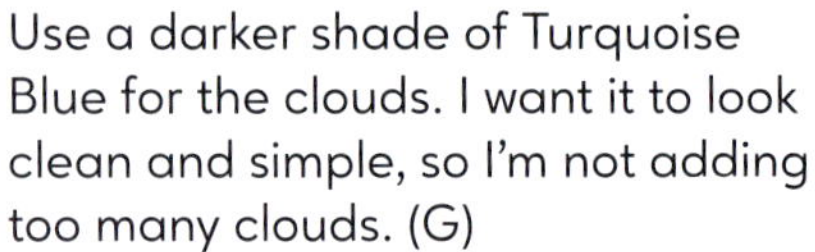

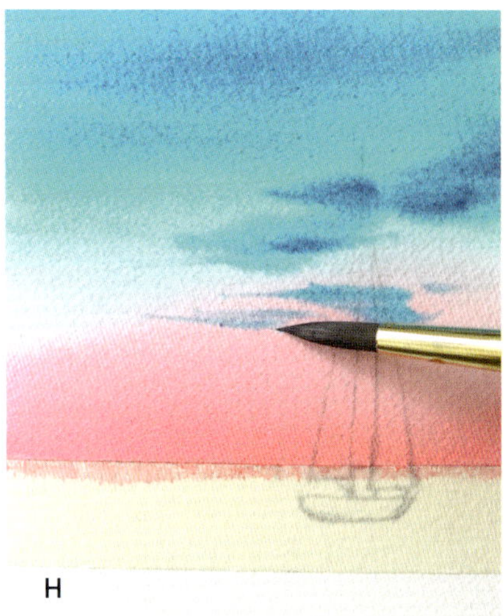

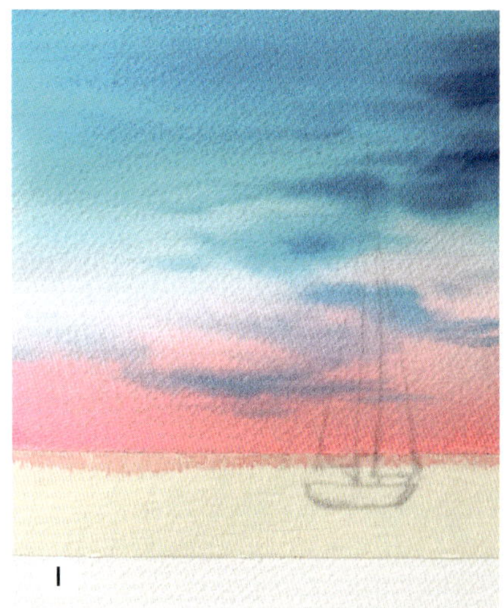

Use a darker shade of Turquoise Blue for the clouds. I want it to look clean and simple, so I'm not adding too many clouds. (G)

If you want to make the sky look dramatic, you can add more clouds. (H) Let dry completely. (I)

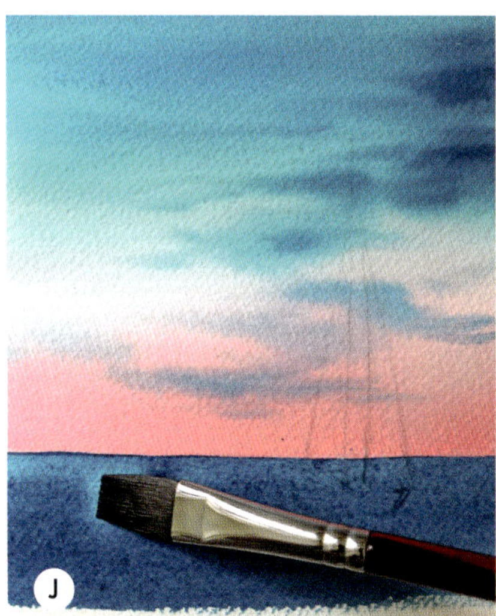

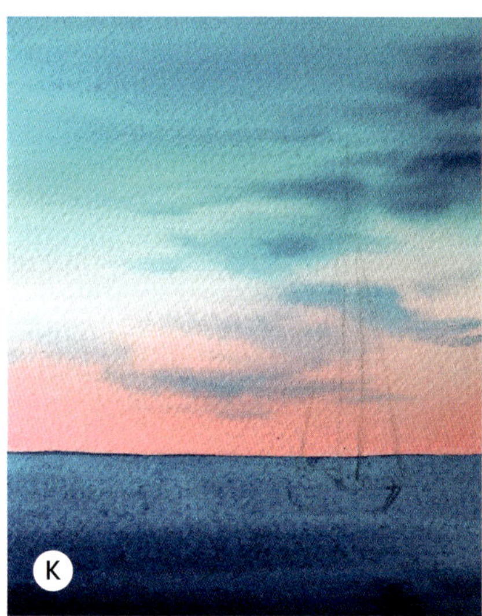

Step 4: Sea. Carefully peel off the masking tape. Start with a medium Turquoise Blue and add it along the horizon line. (J)

Clean your brush and switch to Indigo. Fill in the rest of the area, blending both colors. (K) Let dry completely.

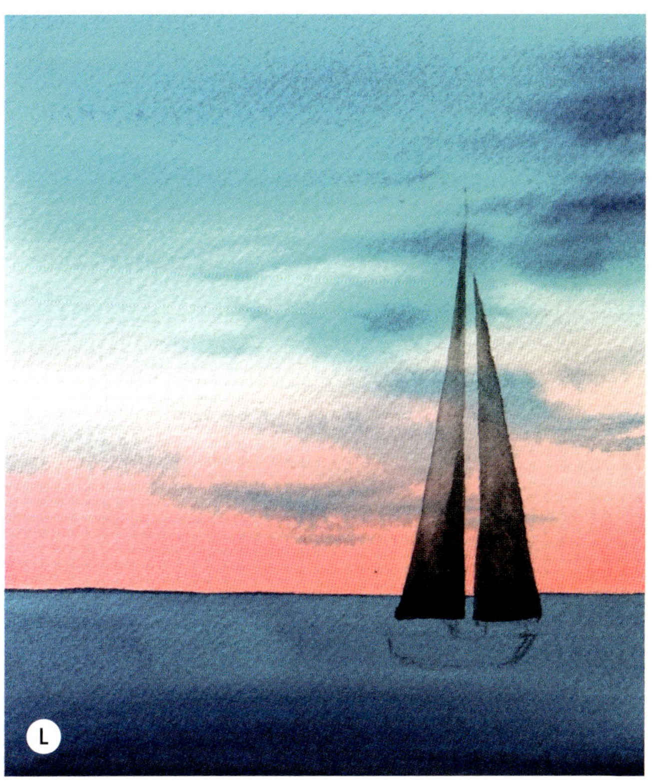

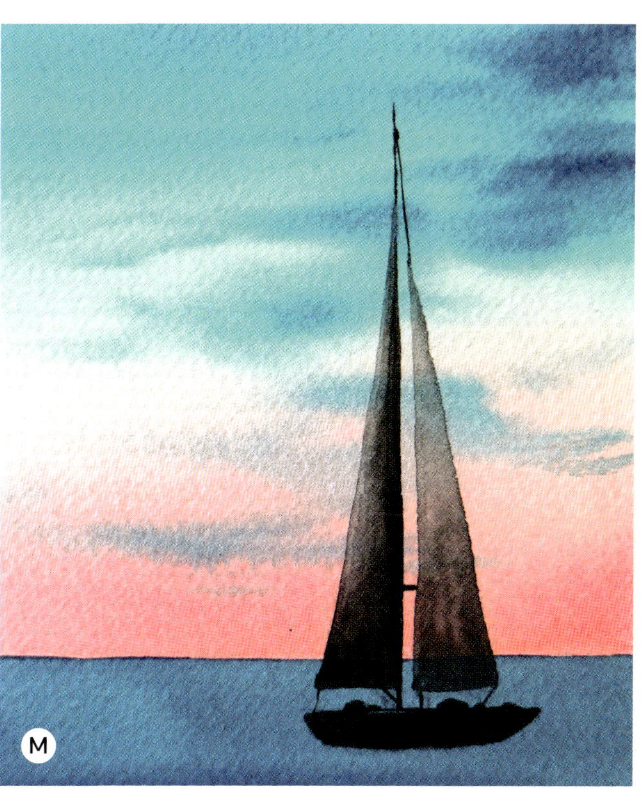

Step 5: Sailboat. Start with the sails. Paint both sails a medium tone of Payne's Grey. Quickly switch to a darker tone and add it to the bottom of the sails. (L)

Once the base coat is dry, add the rest of the details. (M)

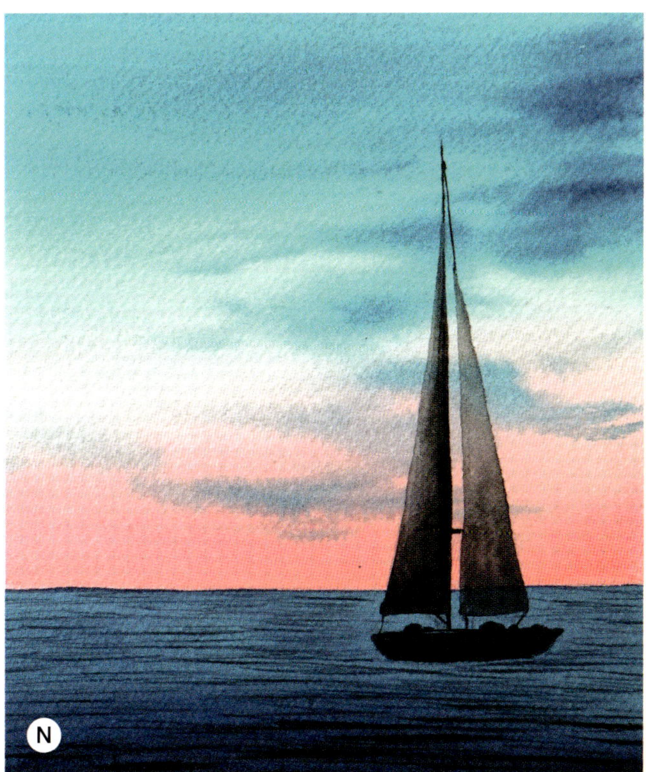

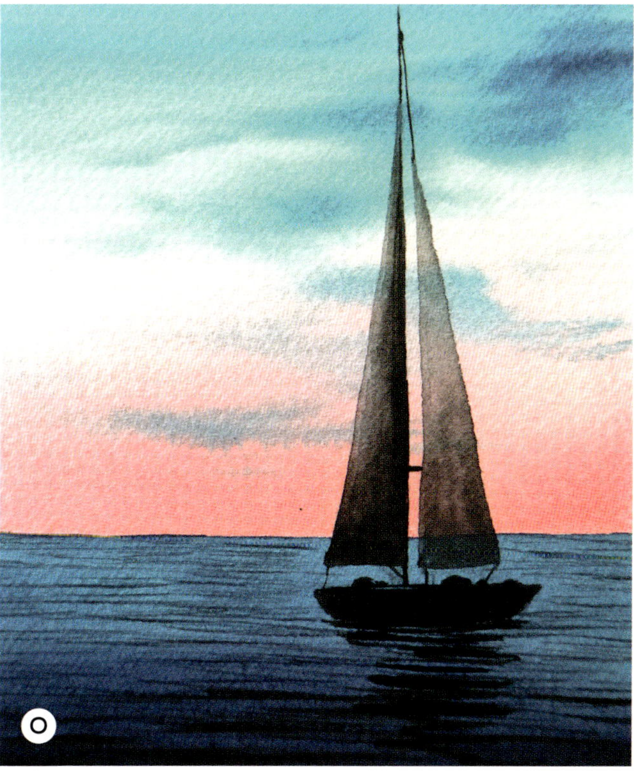

Add some texture on the sea. Start by adding small, fine lines all over. (N) Use a smaller brush or a brush with a pointed tip for this step.

Add the reflection of the boat. Use a darker shade of Payne's Grey or black and add some curved zigzag lines to finish the painting. (O)

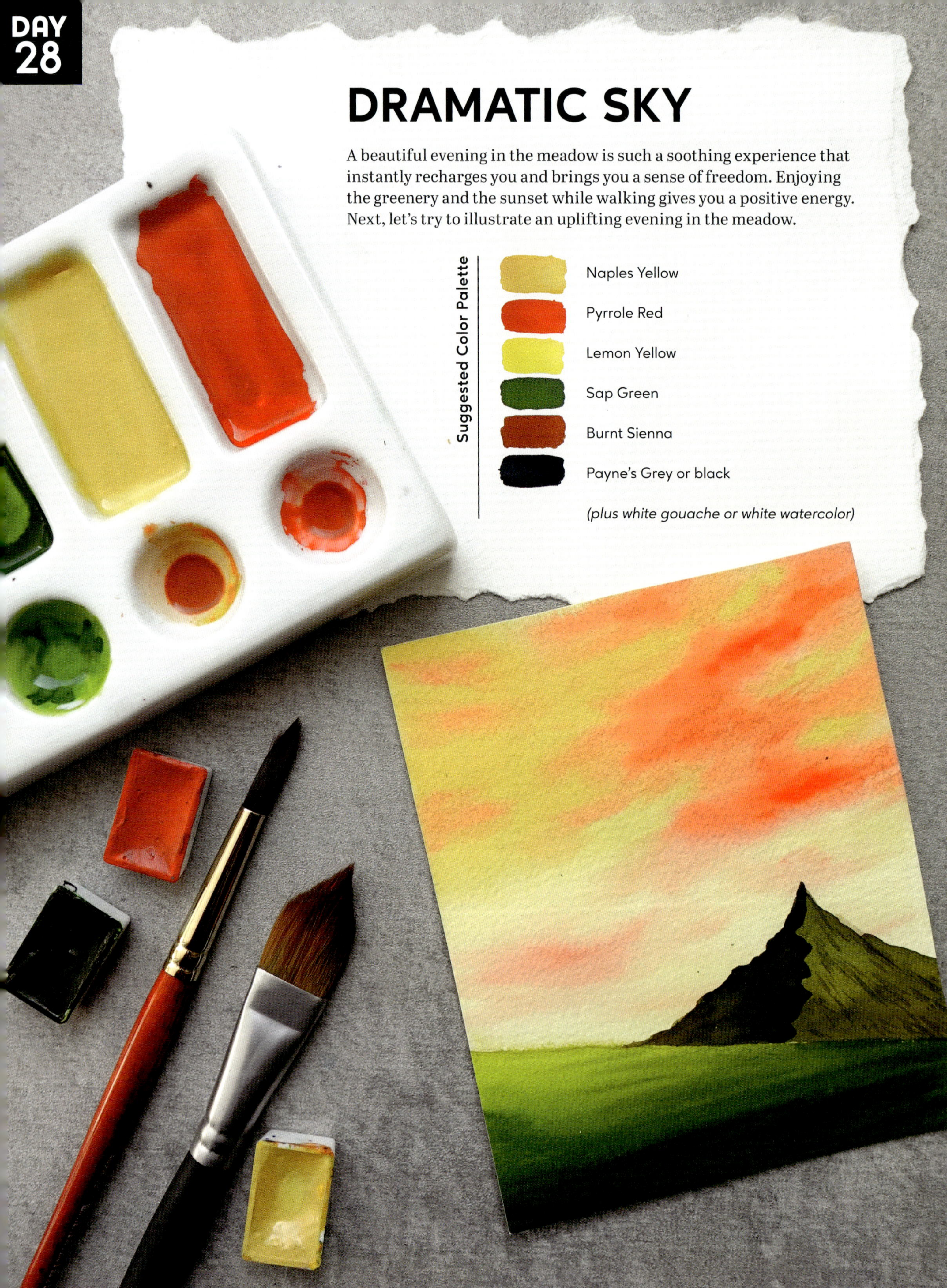

DAY 28

DRAMATIC SKY

A beautiful evening in the meadow is such a soothing experience that instantly recharges you and brings you a sense of freedom. Enjoying the greenery and the sunset while walking gives you a positive energy. Next, let's try to illustrate an uplifting evening in the meadow.

Suggested Color Palette

- Naples Yellow
- Pyrrole Red
- Lemon Yellow
- Sap Green
- Burnt Sienna
- Payne's Grey or black

(plus white gouache or white watercolor)

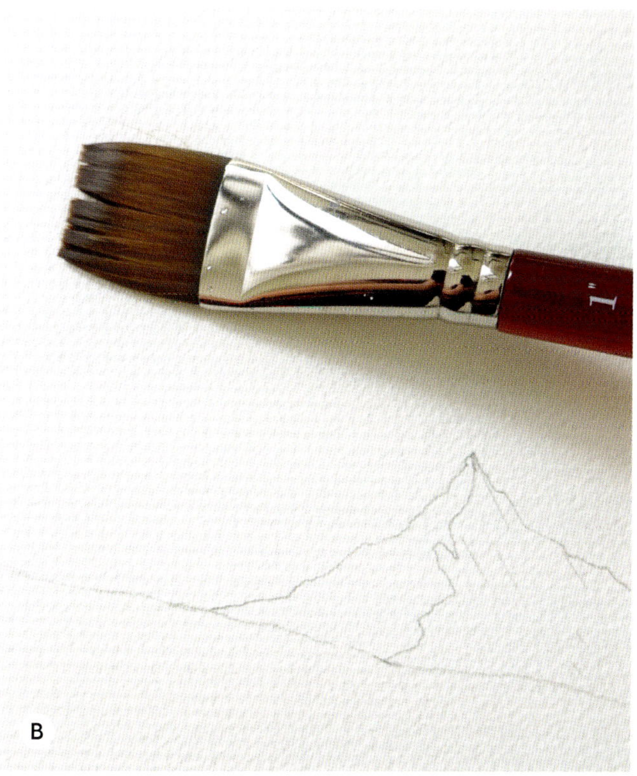

Step 1: Adding the Sketch. Add a light pencil sketch of the mountain and the meadow. (A)

Step 2: Securing and Wetting the Paper. Secure your paper to a drawing board. Apply an even layer of clean water to the sky. (B)

Step 3: Sky. Start by applying a layer of Naples Yellow to the entire sky. (C, D) Naples Yellow is a pastel yellow. You can create a similar color by adding some white gouache or white watercolor to whatever yellow you have.

(continued)

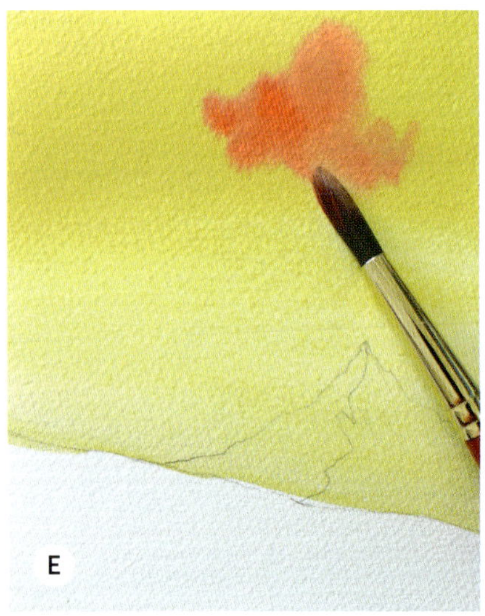

Once you've applied the yellow to the entire background, add the clouds with a medium tone of Pyrrole Red. (E)

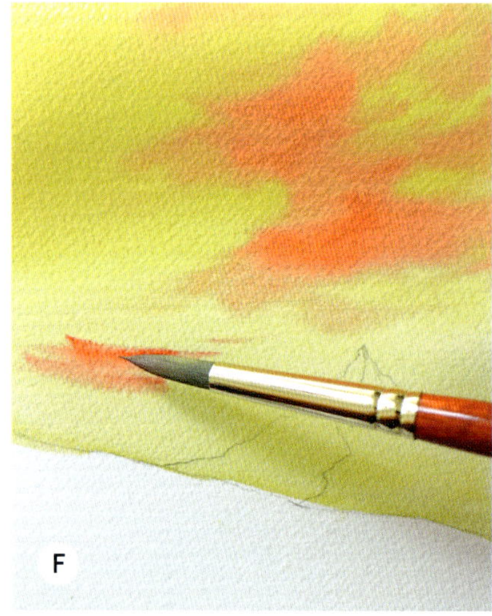

Because we used a pastel yellow for the background, the clouds you add in red will appear as a pastel orange red. These different tonal values of pastel colors will make your sky look more dramatic and intriguing. Add as many clouds as you like. (F)

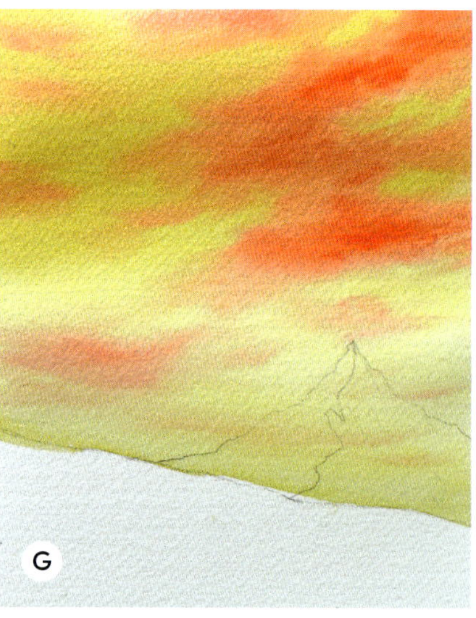

In between, also add some clouds in a stronger shade of Pyrrole Red to make the sky look even more intense. (G) Once you're satisfied with the result, let it dry completely.

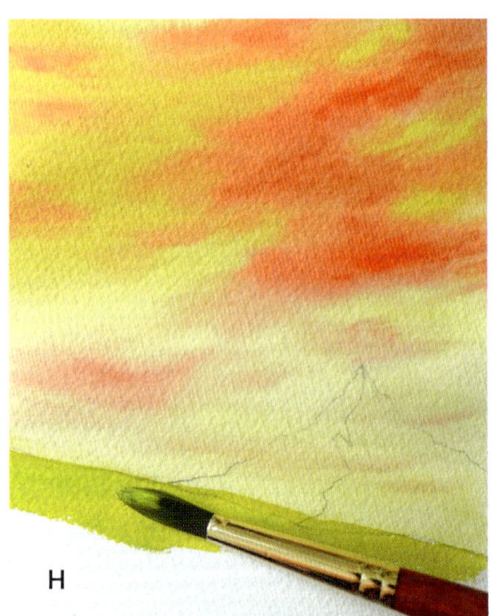

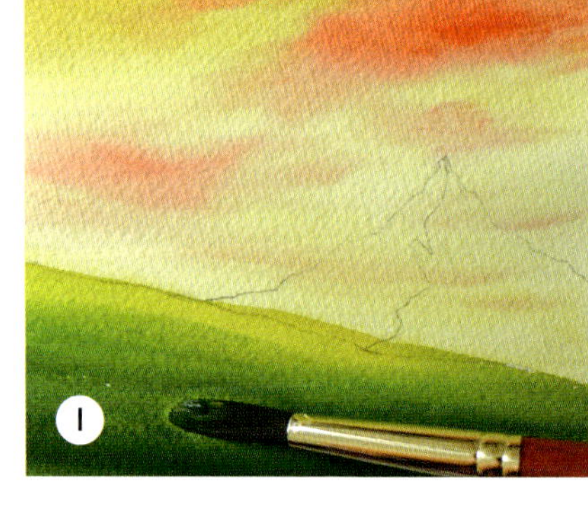

Step 4: Meadow. Mix a little Sap Green with Lemon Yellow to create a bright light green. Start with the upper part of the meadow (H) and once you reach halfway, clean your brush, switch to Sap Green, and fill in the rest of the area. (I)

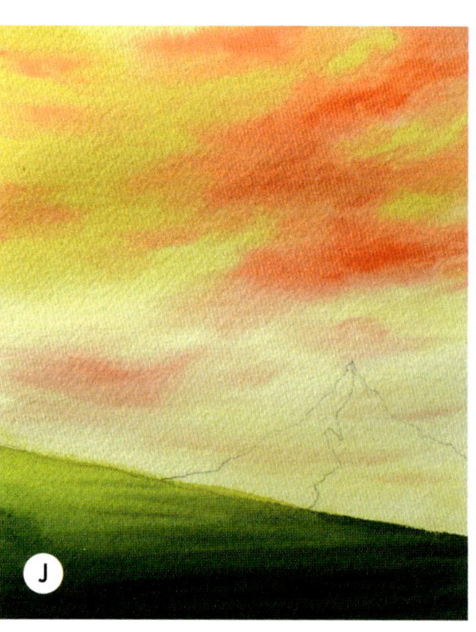

Create a darker green by mixing some Payne's Grey or black with Sap Green and add dark tones along the bottom area. (J) Using the same color, also add some lines diagonally from the top right to the bottom. Let dry completely.

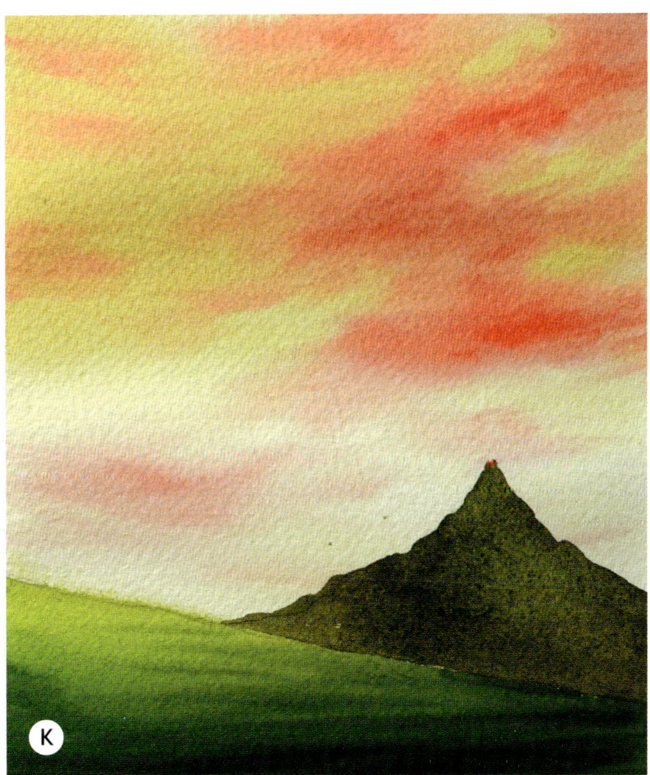

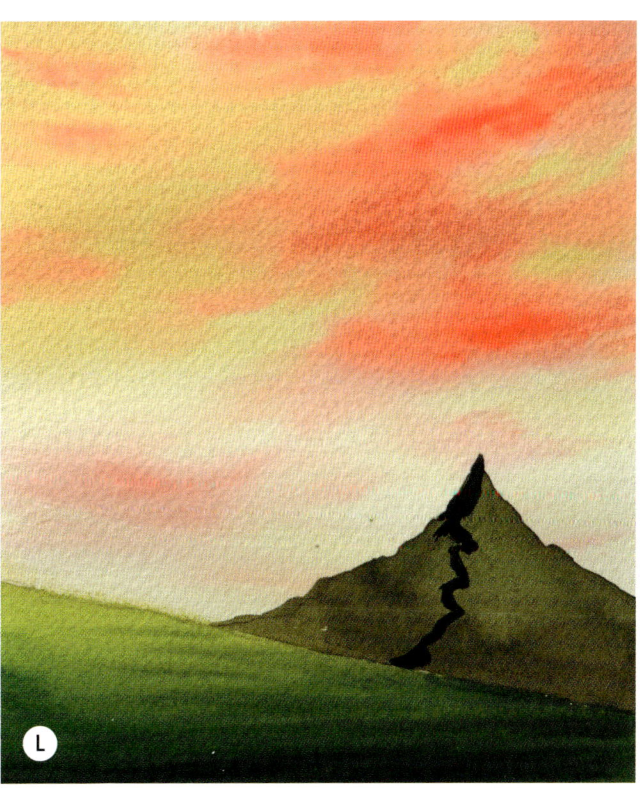

Step 5: Mountain. First, we need to paint the base layer. Add a little Burnt Sienna to Sap Green to get a brownish green. Add a little water to turn the color into a medium tone and apply this color to the entire mountain. (K) Let dry completely.

Use a darker tone of brownish green and define the irregular line along the center of the mountain. (L)

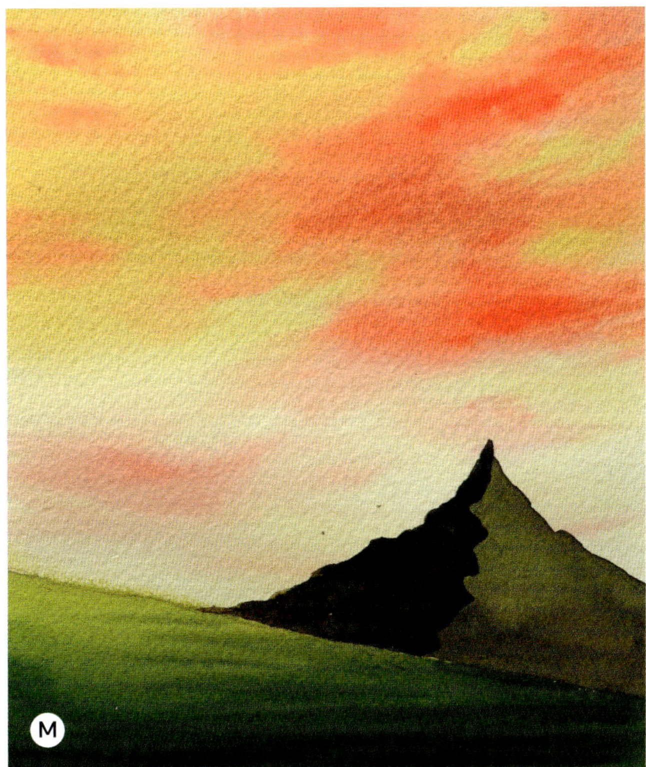

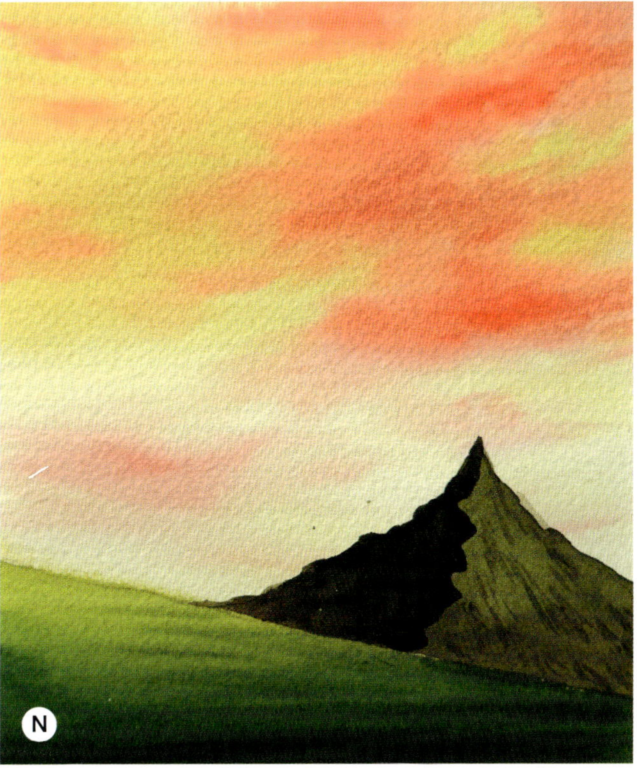

Fill in the left side of the mountain with the same color. (M)

We need to add some texture to the right side as well. Use a medium tone of brownish green and add a few random lines along the entire side to finish the painting. (N)

MILKY WAY NIGHT

Auroras and the Milky Way are the very first subjects I explored in watercolor, and they remain one of my favorites. I love painting bold and beautiful night skies and making them dramatic by adding the Milky Way, which is so easy and fun to paint with watercolors. Let's try it.

Suggested Color Palette

- Indigo
- Permanent Violet
- Permanent Rose
- Cadmium Orange
- Burnt Sienna
- Payne's Grey or black

(plus white gouache or white watercolor)

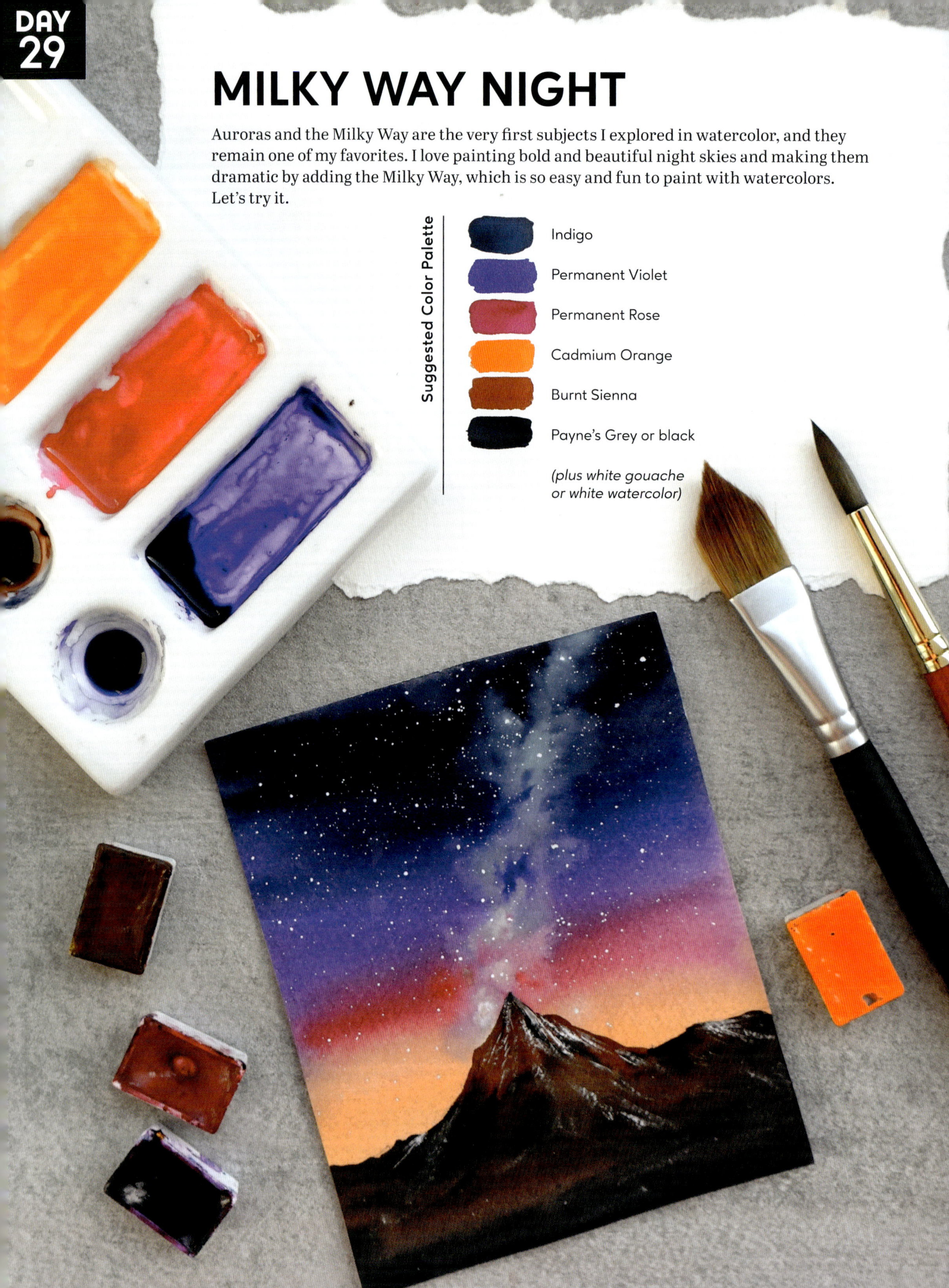

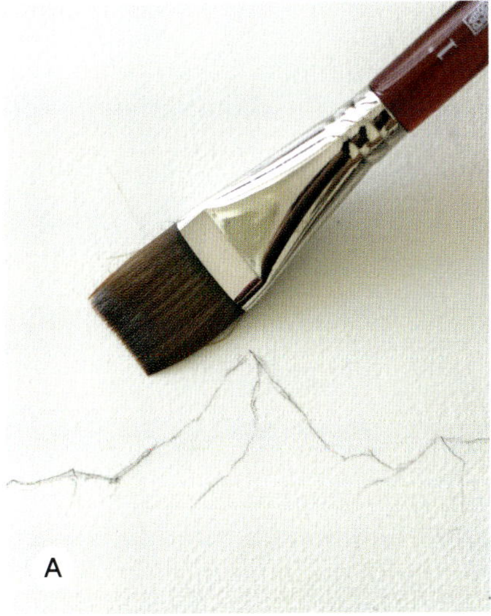

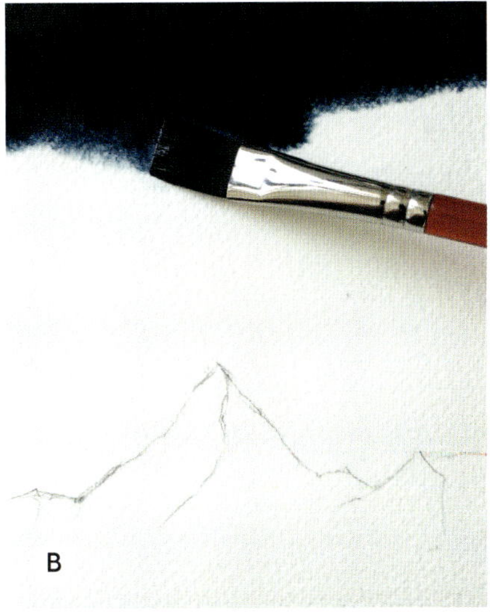

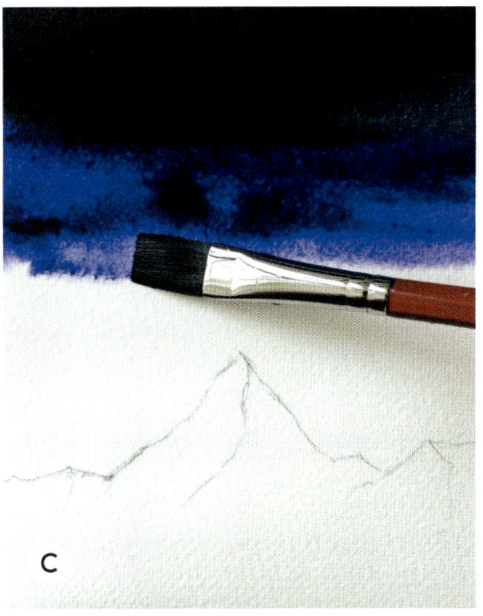

Step 1: Adding the Sketch; Securing and Wetting the Paper. Add a light pencil sketch of the mountain. Secure your paper to a drawing board. Apply an even layer of clean water to the sky. (A)

Step 2: Sky. Start painting the base layer. We'll use four colors for the sky. Choose a darker value of Indigo and apply it to the top of the sky. (B)

Clean your brush and switch to the Permanent Violet. Apply it exactly where you left off with the Indigo, (C) blending it together.

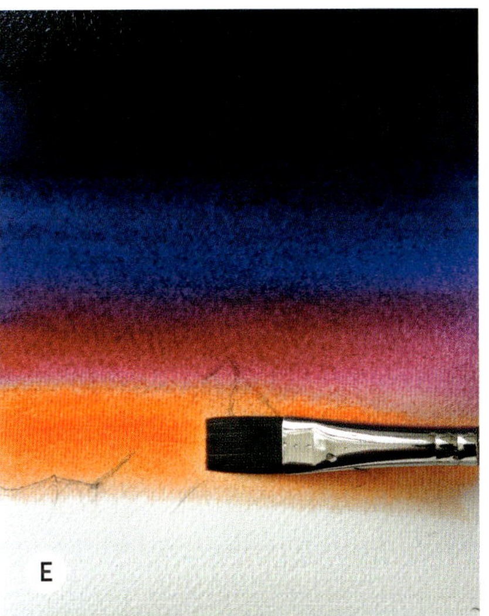

Clean your brush and switch to the Permanent Rose, (D) blending it with the Permanent Violet.

Clean your brush again and switch to the Cadmium Orange. (E) Blend it with the Permanent Rose. Quickly rinse your brush and continue with even horizontal brushstrokes until you reach the bottom, adding clean water as necessary to lighten the color. (F)

(continued)

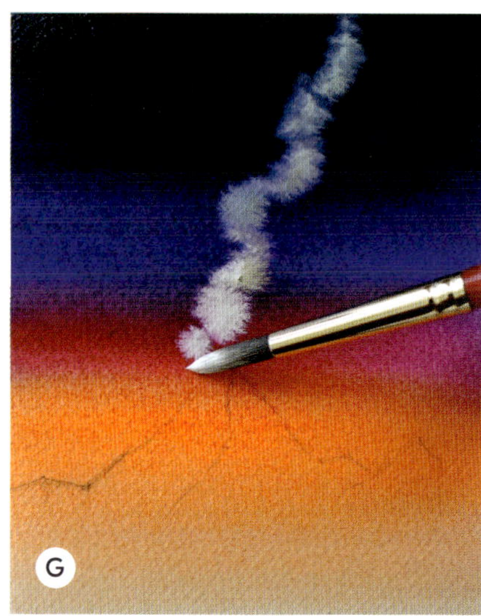

Switch to one of your round brushes and use white gouache or white watercolor to add the Milky Way. You need a thick consistency, so don't add a lot of water. Starting at the top, dab the brush to create a line of marks. (G)

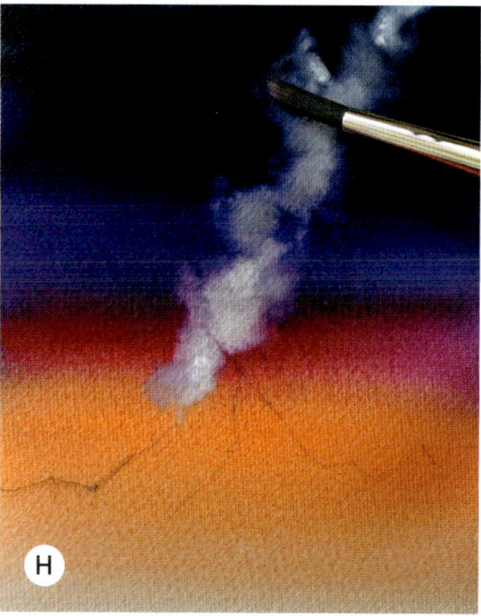

Quickly rinse your brush and smudge the white paint with the clean, damp brush to make it look softer. Gently dab the brush over the white marks without disturbing the base layer too much. (H)

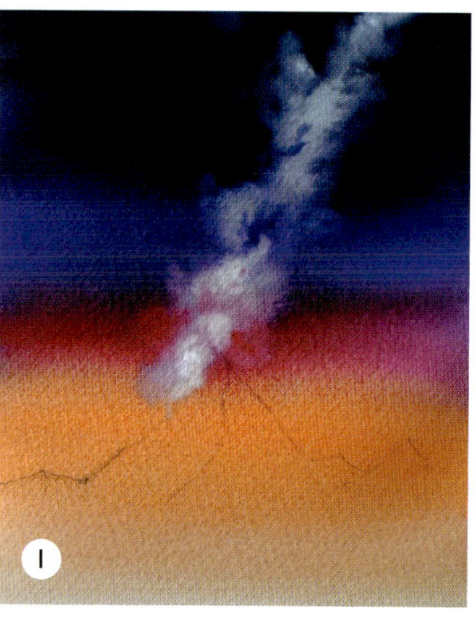

When you're satisfied with the result, let it dry completely. (I)

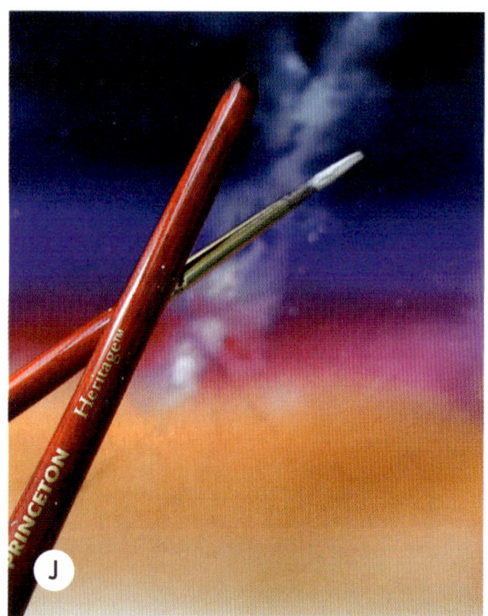

Splatter some stars on the sky. Load some white gouache or white watercolor on one of your smaller brushes and tap on it with another brush to splatter white paint on to your sky. (J)

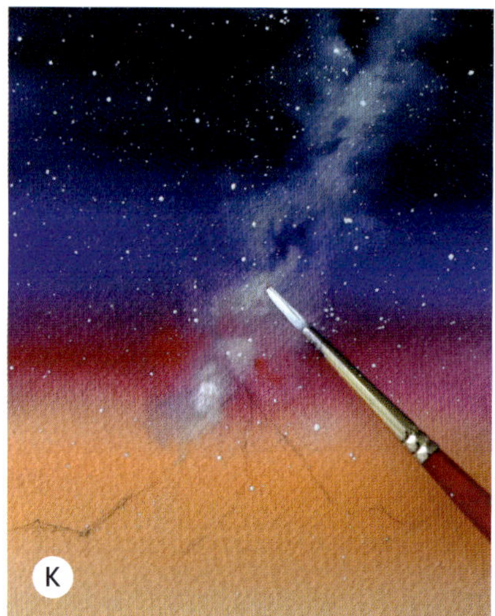

Repeat the previous step to create as many stars as you want. Add some larger dots with the same brush to show the prominent stars. (K) Let dry completely.

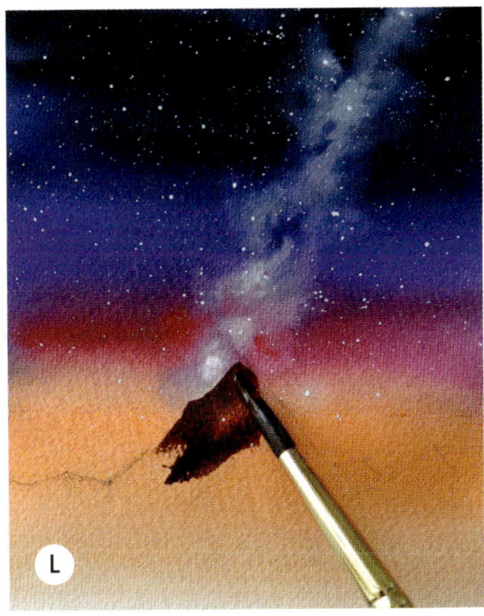

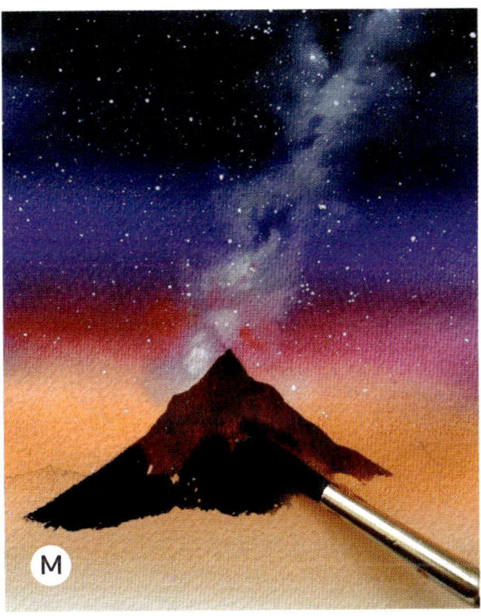

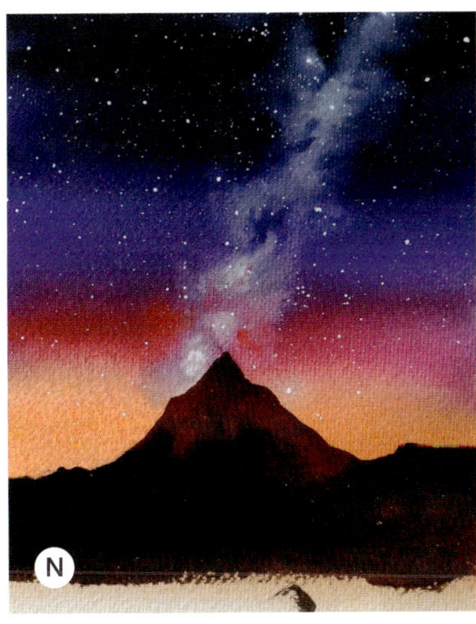

Step 3: Mountain. Start with a medium tone of Burnt Sienna and apply it to the top of the mountain. (L)

Use Payne's Grey or black for the rest of the mountain and fill it in. (M)

Let dry completely. (N)

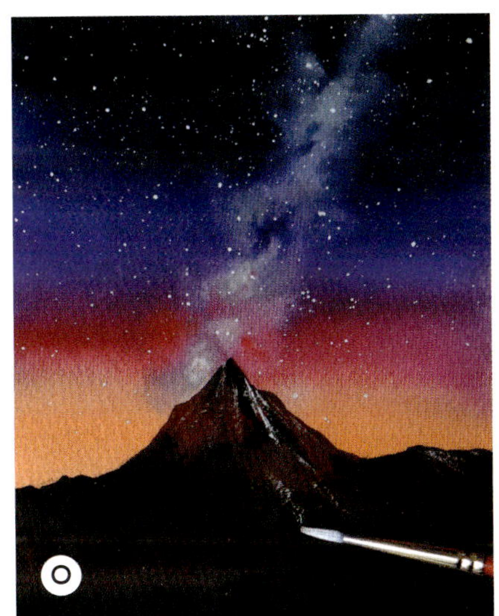

Optional: Add texture to the mountain using the dry white paint and any smaller round brush. After loading the brush with paint, dab it several times on a paper towel to remove the excess water. Add some dry patterns on the mountain to finish the painting. (O, P)

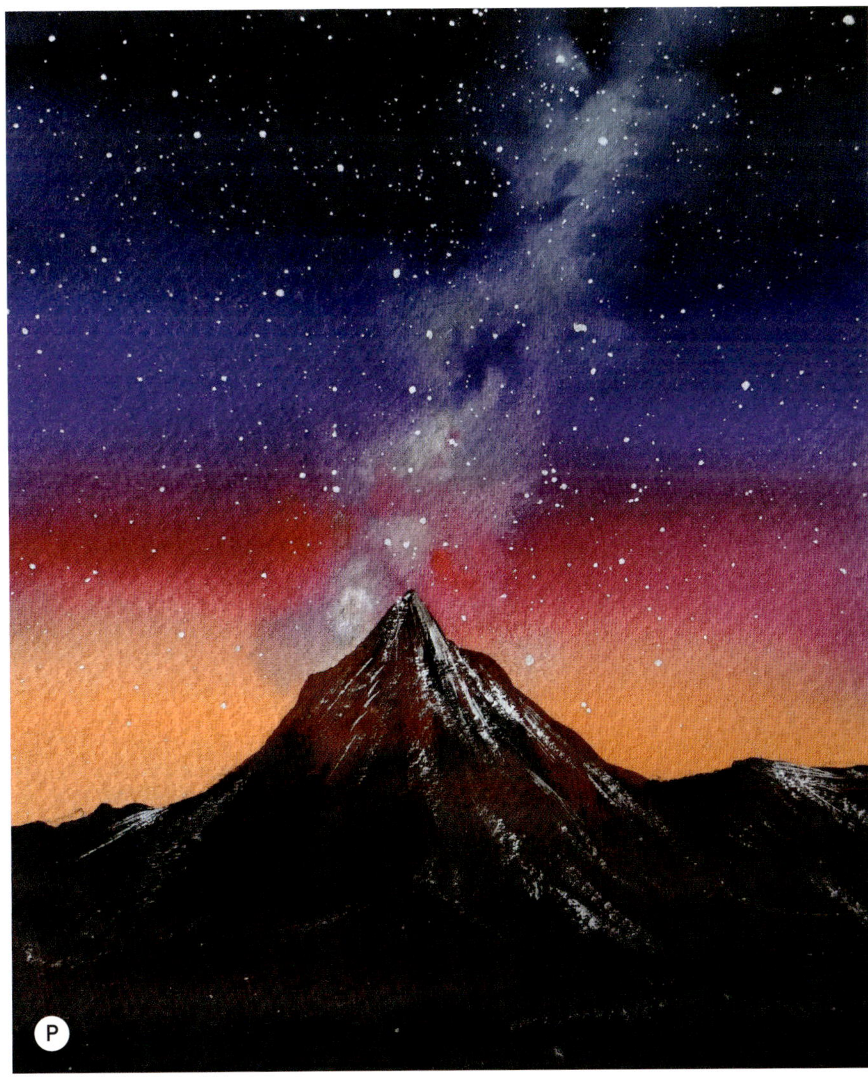

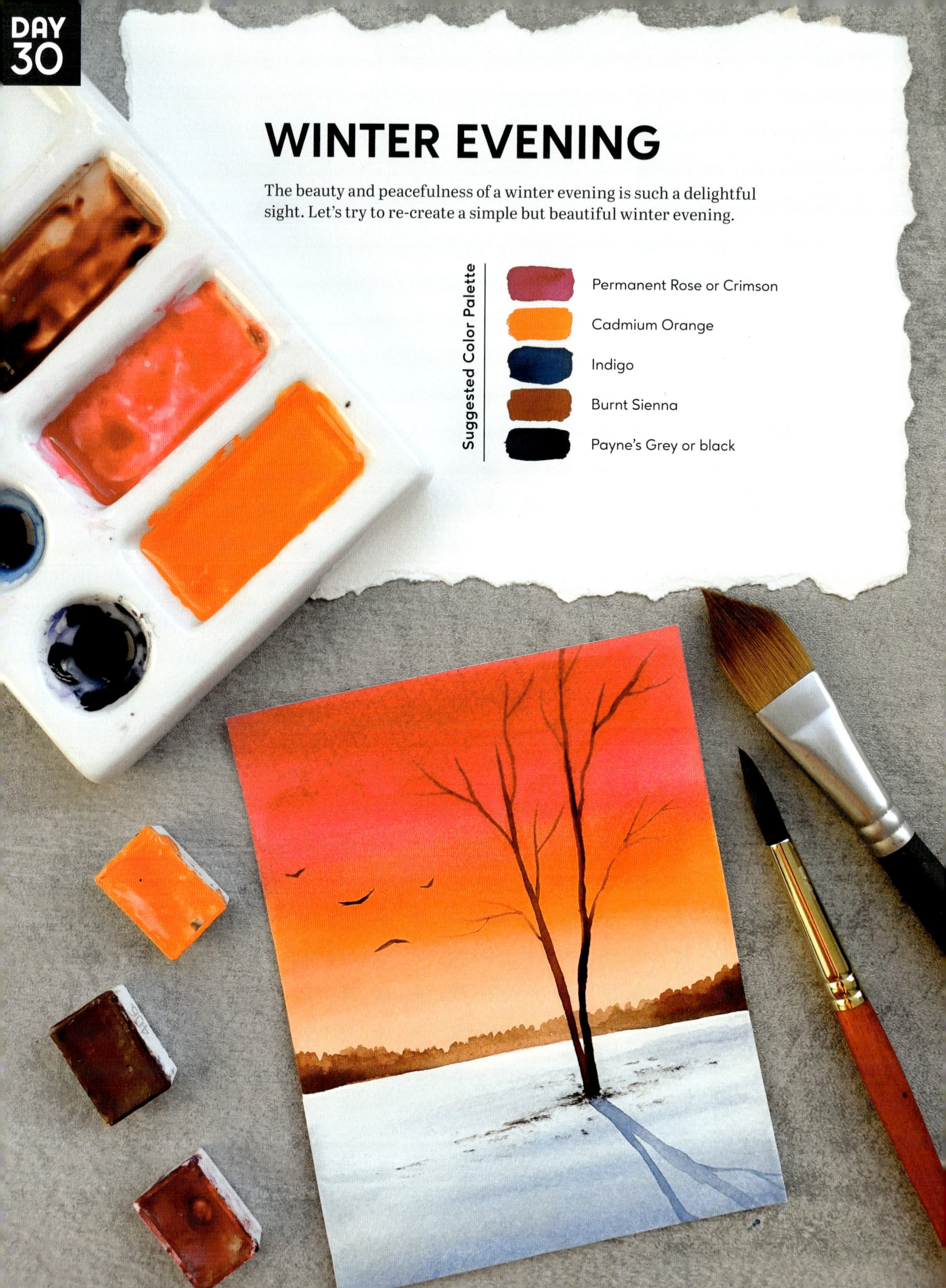

DAY 30

WINTER EVENING

The beauty and peacefulness of a winter evening is such a delightful sight. Let's try to re-create a simple but beautiful winter evening.

Suggested Color Palette

- Permanent Rose or Crimson
- Cadmium Orange
- Indigo
- Burnt Sienna
- Payne's Grey or black

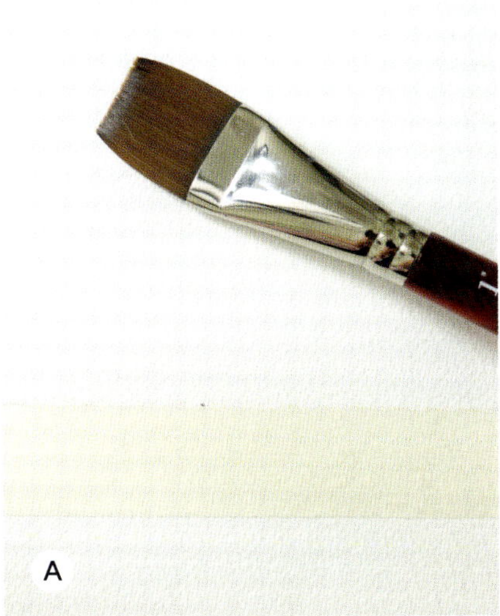

Step 1: Securing, Masking, and Wetting the Paper. Secure your paper to a drawing board. Place a piece of masking tape slightly below the center of the paper to separate the sky and the ground. Apply an even layer of clean water to the sky. (A)

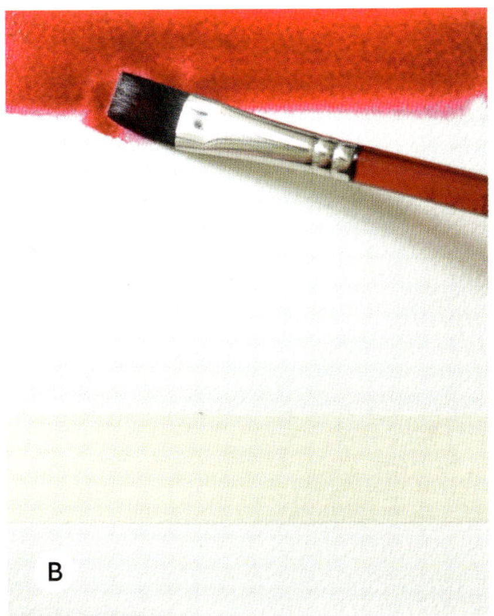

Step 2: Sky. We'll use two colors for the sky: Permanent Rose and Cadmium Orange. Start with a stronger tone of Permanent Rose or Crimson and apply it along the top of the sky. (B)

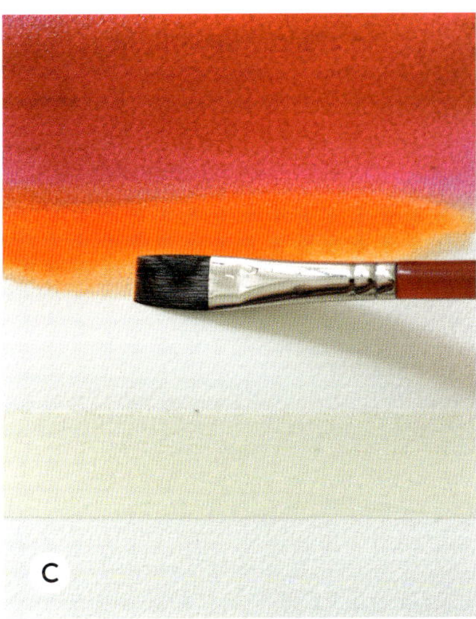

Once you're almost halfway through the sky, clean your brush and switch to Cadmium Orange, (C) blending the two colors together.

Quickly rinse your brush and continue with even horizontal brushstrokes until you reach the horizon line, adding clean water as necessary to lighten the color. (D) Let dry completely.

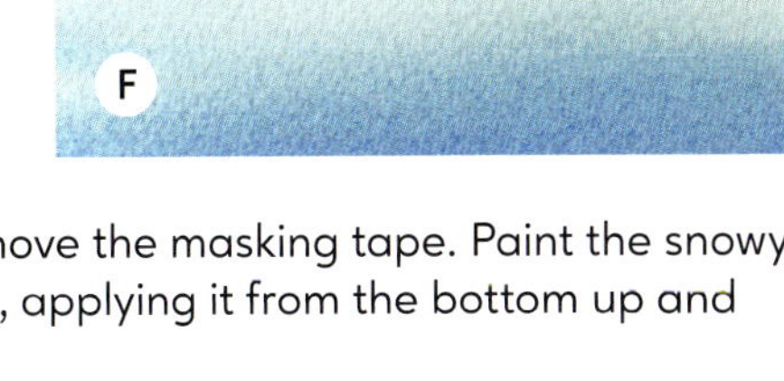

Step 3: Snowy Ground. Carefully remove the masking tape. Paint the snowy ground. Use a medium tone of Indigo, applying it from the bottom up and gradually lightening it. (E, F)

(continued)

Before the background dries, add a few lines in a medium tone with a round brush. (G)

Let dry completely. (H)

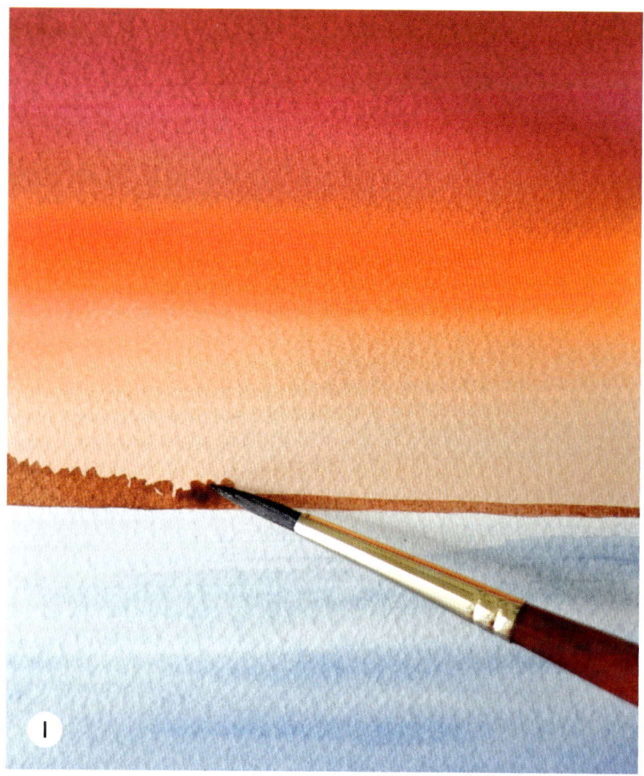

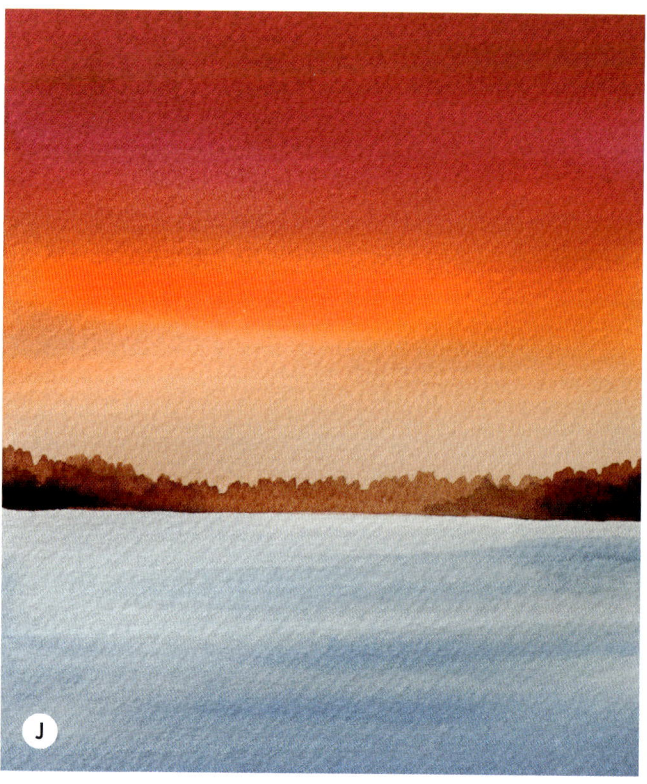

Step 4: Details. Add the landscape in the distance using a medium tone of Burnt Sienna. Add a rough shape along the horizon line as shown. (I)

Once you've added the shape with a medium tone, switch to a darker shade of brown and add deeper tones on both sides, keeping the medium tones in the center. (J) Let dry completely.

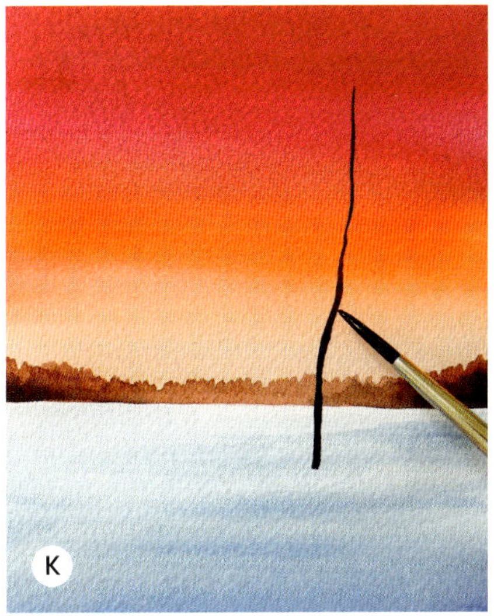

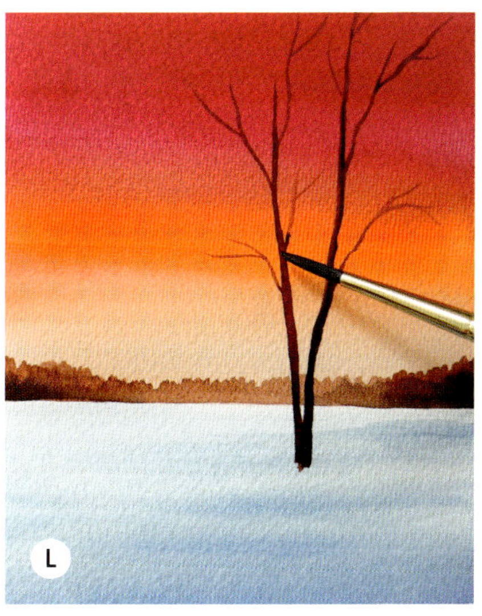

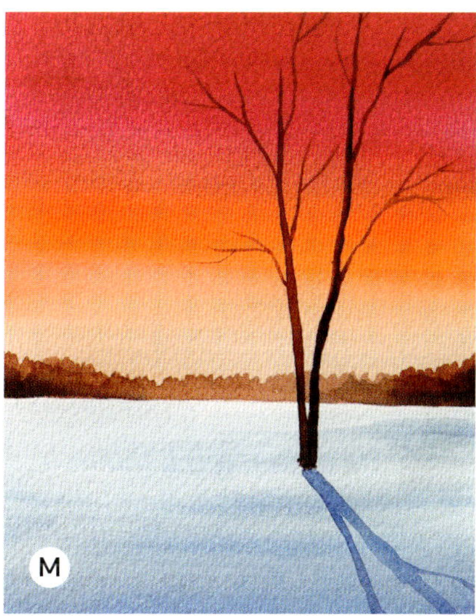

The next detail we'll add is a tree. Use a darker shade of brown and add a simple tree. (K) Use a smaller brush or a brush with a pointed tip and add the branches. (L) You can add as many branches as you like.

Add the shadow of the tree. Switch to a medium shade of Indigo and add the shadow, which should somewhat resemble the shape of the tree. (M) Let dry completely.

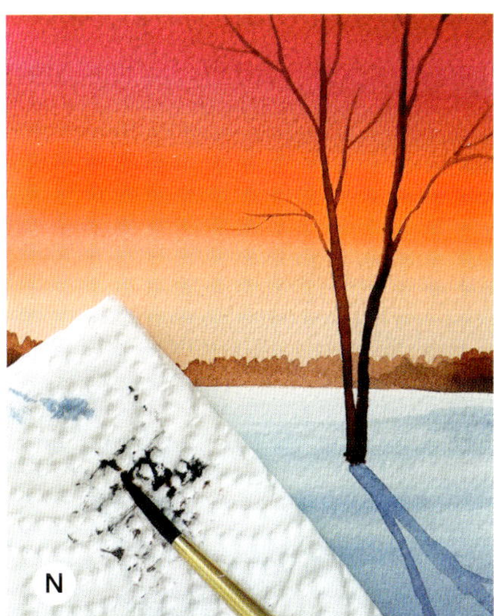

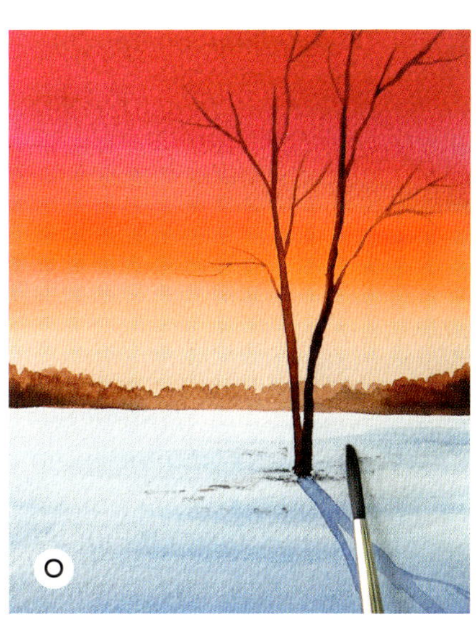

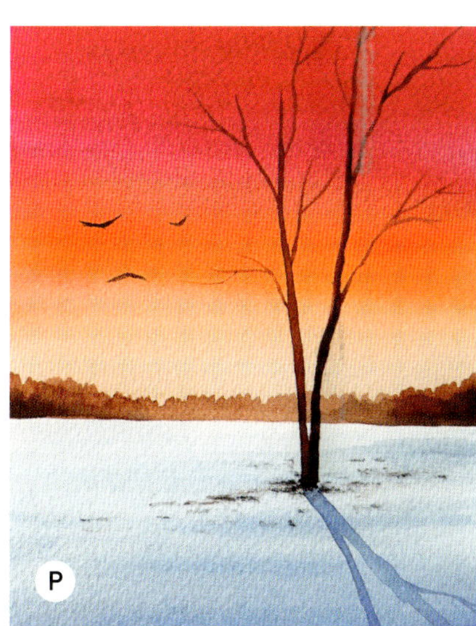

Add some dry brush patterns on the ground. Load some dark brown on a smaller brush and dab it several times on a paper towel to remove the excess water. Add some texture with the dry paint in the areas closer to the tree. (N, O)

You can also add a few birds using Payne's Grey or black to finish the painting. (P)

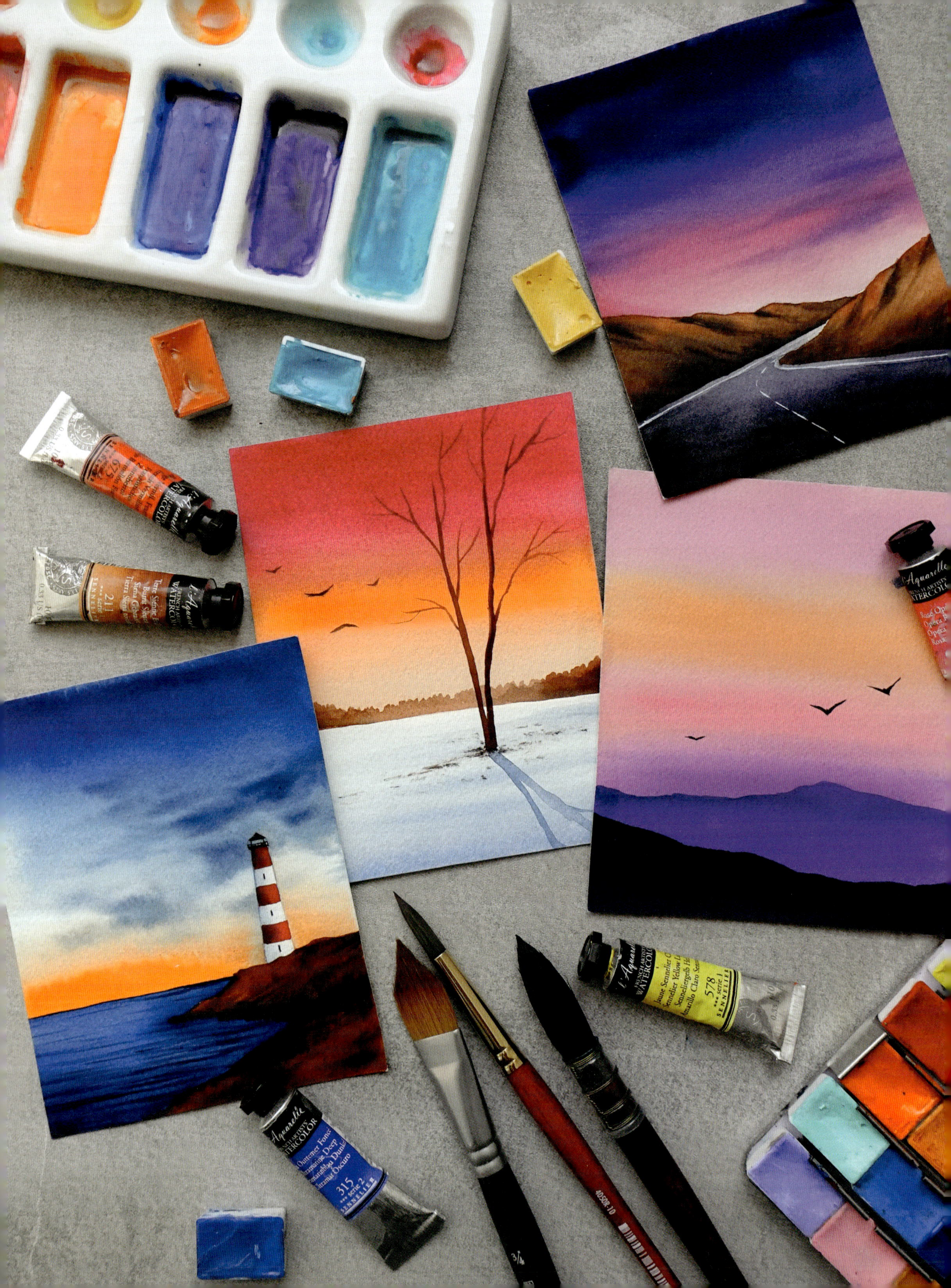
l'Aquarelle
FRENCH ARTISTS' WATERCOLOR
578
SENNELIER
Aquarelle
WATERCOLOR
Ultramarine Deep
Ultramar Oscuro
315
serie 2
SENNELIER
4050R-10
3/4

NEXT STEPS

We have explored a wide range of color combinations and learned to paint a variety of skies. Now it's time to take the skills you have learned to the next level and let your creativity run wild. Make up your own compositions, choose your own color combinations, and try painting a collection of skies in your own style. You can choose some of the projects we made and try them in a new color combination or you can look for reference images and turn them into stunning paintings.

Nature is a treasure and, if you look around, you will get a lot of inspiration and ideas. I always have a sketchbook with me. Whenever I feel inspired by a scene or place, I sketch it and later turn my idea into a painting.

As you continue to explore and experiment, you will become more confident in your skills and your art will become something special.

So, never stop painting, let creativity flow, and keep exploring and creating.

ACKNOWLEDGMENTS

I would like to thank everyone who helped me bring this book to life. First, I must thank my support system, my dear daughter Nuha, my mother, and my husband Nabeel, without whom this book would not have come into being. My mother recognized the artist in me and helped me believe that I can truly achieve my dreams if I just work hard enough.

Publishing a book has been one of my lifelong dreams and would not have been possible without my editor, Joy Aquilino, and the very kind Editorial Project Manager, Gabrielle Bethancourt-Hughes, who brought my paintings together in the most beautiful way. Many thanks to my very talented art director Hailey Toohey, designer Cindy Samargia Laun, editor Marilyn Kecyk, proofreader Karen Levy, and indexer Tim Griffin.

I will be forever grateful to the hardworking team at Quarto who helped me throughout the process and made this book truly bold and beautiful.

A special thank you for the support and constant motivation from my Instagram friends and complete strangers around the globe who have followed my little journey into the world of art. I am proud of the community I have created and this book is a result of the love and support you have shown me.

ABOUT THE AUTHOR

Zaneena Nabeel, aka Aurora by Z, is an architect by profession and an artist by vocation. She gave up her career as an architect to pursue her dream of art, finding healing and happiness through drawing, painting, and playing with color. This inspired her to start an Instagram page, where she shares her work. She began teaching art and enjoys helping beginners around the world gain confidence in their abilities. Since 2018, Zaneena has been teaching art professionally on various platforms. She is a top teacher on the online education platform Skillshare, where she has more than 50 watercolor and gouache classes and over 100,000 students have enrolled in her art courses. In addition to teaching online, she hosts art workshops and organizes exhibitions both locally and internationally. Originally from India, she is currently based in Dubai.

To see more of Zaneena's work, visit www.aurorabyz.com, @AurorabyZ on YouTube, and @aurorabyz on Instagram.

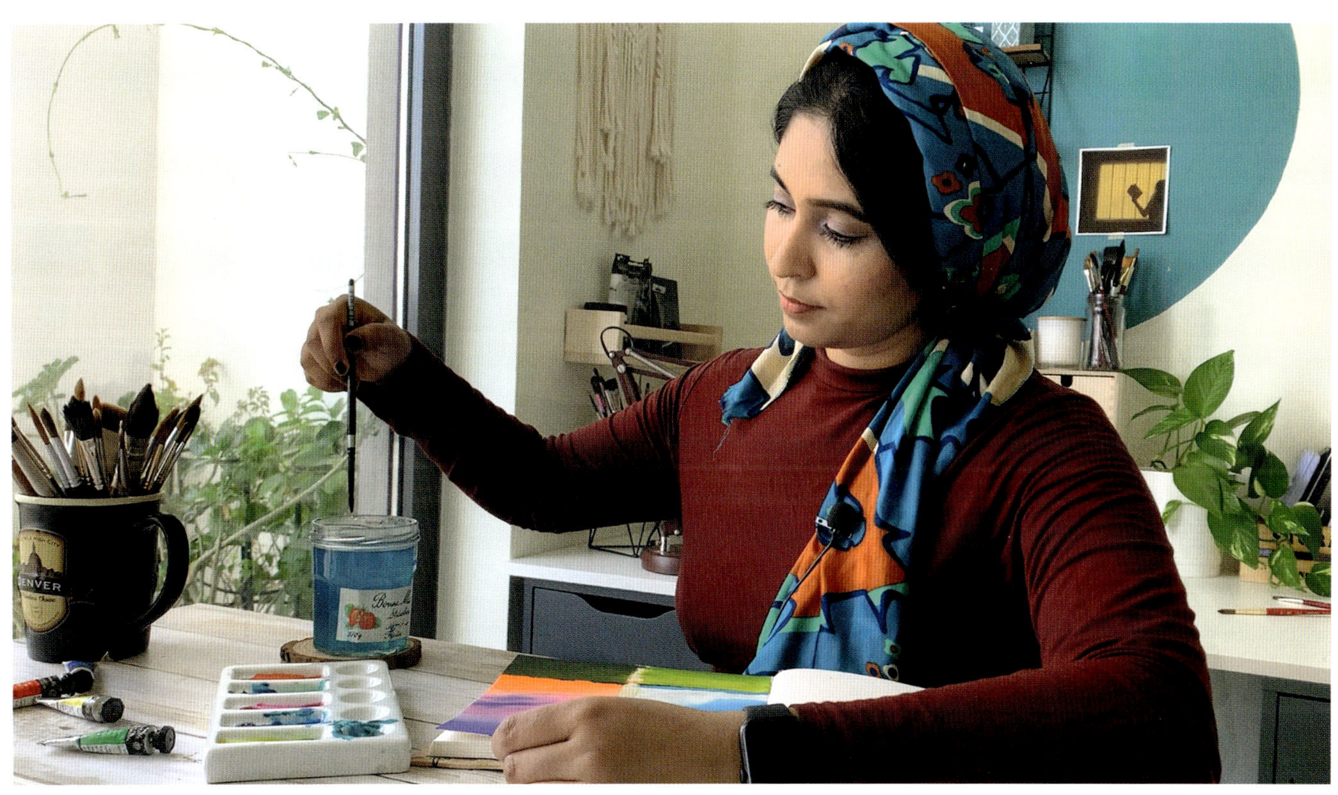

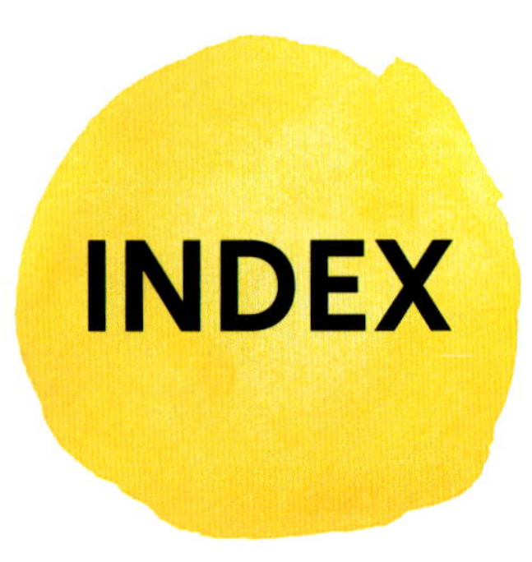

INDEX

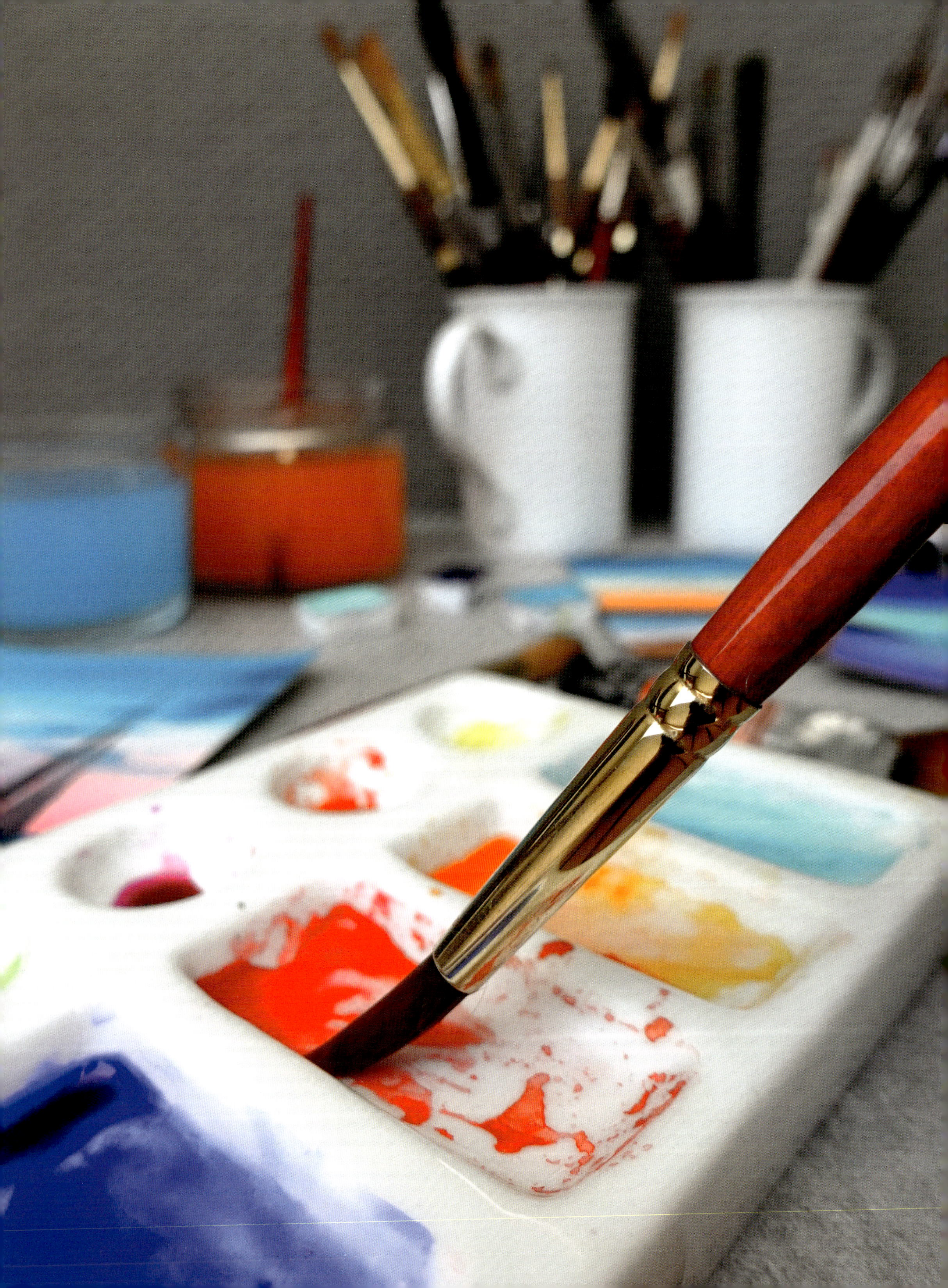